WELLINGTON AFTER WATERLOO

WELLINGTON
—AFTER—
WATERLOO

NEVILLE THOMPSON

ROUTLEDGE & KEGAN PAUL
LONDON AND NEW YORK

First published in 1986 by
Routledge & Kegan Paul Ltd
11 New Fetter Lane, London EC4P 4EE

Published in the USA by
Routledge & Kegan Paul Inc.
in association with Methuen Inc.
29 West 35th Street, New York, NY 10001

Set in 10 on 12 point Bembo
by Witwell Ltd, Liverpool
and printed in Great Britain
by T J Press (Padstow) Ltd
Padstow, Cornwall

Library of Congress Cataloging in Publication Data

Thompson Neville.
Wellington after Waterloo.

Bibliography: p.
Includes index.
1. Wellington, Arthur Wellesley, Duke of, 1769–1852.
2. Statesmen—Great Britain—Biography.   I. Title.
DA68.12.W4T4   1986   941.07′092′4 [B]   86–504

British Library CIP Data also available
ISBN 0–7102–0747–6

For my daughter
Elizabeth Anne Pidgeon
on her birthday

'Great men are the guide-posts and landmarks in the state.'
Edmund Burke, Speech on
American Taxation, 1774

CONTENTS

ILLUSTRATIONS

PREFACE AND
ACKNOWLEDGMENTS

I IS A pleasure to record my thanks to the many individuals and institutions whose assistance was essential to this book. My first thanks must be to my wife Gail, who endured with patience the long periods in which the events of the early nineteenth century seemed more immediate and pressing than those of the present, and bore with good humour my affliction not only with the Duke of Wellington's ailments but also his less appealing mannerisms. The writing of this preface coincided with the happy event commemorated in the dedication.

I am grateful to my colleague William Stockdale and my old friend Kenneth Lockridge of the University of Michigan who read the penultimate draft of the manuscript with close attention and friendly critical eyes. I am solely responsible for not accepting all their generous suggestions for improvement. In this as in much else Horatio Lovat Dickson, author, editor, publisher and man of letters, has been a source of inspiration and encouragement.

The archival research was made possible by grants from the Social Sciences and Humanities Research Council of Canada. Grants from McMaster University and the University of Western Ontario assisted in assembling published material. I was greatly helped by the librarians of both universities. The many drafts of the manuscript were typed by my former secretary Carmen Callon, my present secretary Christianne Speed, and by other secretaries of the History Department, particularly Jeanette Berry and Lori Morris.

Apart from the archival sources, this book is based on a steady stream of published material which began well before the end of the Duke of Wellington's life. Two recent books deserve special mention. The first is the magnificent volume of Wellington's political correspondence for 1833

and 1834 edited by John Brooke and Julia Gandy (1975) to the highest
unobtrusive standards of modern scholarship; everyone interested in the
Duke and early nineteenth century politics must hope that the remaining
volumes will not be long in appearing. The second is Elizabeth Longford's
biography of Wellington, the second volume of which (1972) was the first
to break the ground of the Duke's career after Waterloo. It will be
immediately obvious that my view of the man, of the events of the period
and the relation between them is not hers, but in the case of so towering a
figure as Wellington appreciation may take many forms.

By gracious permission of Her Majesty the Queen I was allowed to study
and quote material pertaining to the Duke of Wellington in the Royal
Archives at Windsor Castle. Sir Robert Mackworth-Young, the former
Librarian, and Miss Jane Langton, the Registrar, were most helpful in
assembling this material for me.

I am deeply grateful to the Duke of Wellington and his father, the
seventh Duke, who permitted me to use the Wellington Papers formerly at
Apsley House (now Crown copyright material, in the University of
Southampton Library, and reproduced by kind permission of the Public
Record Office). When I read them, the papers were at the Historical
Manuscripts Commission and I recall with much pleasure the facilities
made available to me and the unfailing help of the staff of the Commission
and the National Register of Archives.

I am grateful to the Earl Bathurst for permission to quote material from
the Bathurst Papers on loan to the British Library; and to the librarians and
archivists of the following institutions and other copyright holders for
their assistance and permission to reproduce unpublished material: the
British Library; the Public Record Office; the Surrey Record Office and
the Hon. James Leslie Hamilton; the Durham Record Office and the
Marquess of Londonderry; and the Sheffield City Libraries, the Director
of Libraries and Information Services and the Earl of Wharncliffe.

For permission to quote published material I am grateful to the
following copyright holders: Her Majesty's Stationery Office; Cambridge
University Press; David Higham Associates Ltd; Hodder and Stoughton
Ltd; Macmillan Publishers Ltd; John Murray (Publishers) Ltd; and the
Royal Historical Society.

Illustration 6 is reproduced by gracious permission of Her Majesty the
Queen; number 8 by kind permission of His Grace the Duke of Wellington
(photograph by David Carey); numbers 1 and 7 by kind permission of the
Trustees of the British Museum; numbers 2, 9, 10 and 12 by kind permission

of the Victoria and Albert Museum; numbers 3 and 4 by kind permission of the Courtauld Institute; number 5 by kind permission of the National Portrait Gallery; and number 11 by kind permission of the *Illustrated London News* Picture Library.

INTRODUCTION

T HE FIGURE of the Duke of Wellington stands like a colossus over
early nineteenth century Britain. Through all the rapidly changing
scenes of life in a period of unprecedented population growth,
industrialism, urbanization, social distress, protest and political challenge,
the hero of Waterloo remained the one permanent figure at the centre of
national life, the imperturbable, immutable symbol of stability and continuity amid the turbulence and uncertainties of the age. But in contrast to
his military career, on which there seems to be no end of the making of
books, his place in the life of the state for a third of a century has been
strangely neglected. This is particularly true of the twenty years following
the first Reform Act of 1832, the point at which the publication of his papers
stopped for a century.

The customary judgment of his venture into politics after Waterloo is
that it was an unfortunate postscript and detraction from his military fame.
In this very different sphere the qualities that had served him so well on
the battlefield have been accounted liabilities. No one then or later has
questioned the sincerity of his intentions as he applied himself to his duty as
he saw it, but he has usually been seen as out of step with the times, a
powerful obstacle to beneficial change and an embarrassing anachronism
to his more astute colleagues who saw the necessity of compromising with
the demand for reform.

There is much to this assessment. But the Duke was not alone in
perceiving great danger in tampering with the excellent order that had
stood the test of time, and most recently the ideological and military
challenge of the French Revolution and Napoleon. Nor was his long
involvement in politics an aberration from his military career. On the
contrary, it was a logical extension of it. Once the political and social

1

foundations of the country had been secured by force of arms, a place of power and influence in the councils of state offered the best means of ensuring that his achievement was preserved. Such a position also had the advantage of keeping him at the forefront of events where he could protect and even enhance his recently acquired personal reputation. Policy and personality combined to make the transition from the army to the cabinet in 1818 easy and natural. Once there he found himself engaged in many a strange adventure as circumstances and character drew him further into partisan politics than he thought he wanted or could at first have imagined. But although there were many opportunities to retire, it was no great sacrifice for the old soldier to reject the temptations of private ease for the demands of public service. To the end of his days he worked out his destiny in the public arena, playing a leading role in the events of his own day and casting a powerful shadow into the future.

In his political career Wellington was unable to avoid revealing far more of his closely guarded personality than he realized or had been required to do when protected by the authority and hierarchy of military command. But even here the revelations were so fragmentary that the pattern is clearer to later observers that it was to contemporaries, for whom he remained a forbiddingly simple, if mysterious figure. Interpretations of this evidence may vary but there is certainly far more on the hopes, fears, values and motivations of the private individual for the period after Waterloo than before, and an appreciation of it is essential for an understanding of the man or even the era.

Seen through the Duke's eyes, the familiar events of the early nineteenth century appear in unaccustomed perspective and tones. For him this was no age of progress and improvement, however painful and uneven, but one of fatal decline. More than most aristocrats, Wellington lived in a hermetic world, largely insulated from the forces that were transforming the country. His land was in the South; he owned no urban property or mines; and the annuity settled on him by Parliament was not affected by fluctuations in trade and the price of grain. From this detached eminence he could survey with extensive view the agitation for parliamentary reform, the abolition of the corn laws, Chartism and other demands for change as no more than the latest manifestations of the self-interested and misguided agitation that had always bedevilled politics and society. Such attacks might threaten the delicate balance between authority and freedom that had been worked out by the wisdom of generations since the last day of political creation, the Glorious Revolution of 1688, but these transitory eruptions could easily be defeated by a

2

resolute government and aristocracy. Not everyone shared this instinct for prompt and determined defence of every feature of the existing order and the Duke often found that concession by his allies had reduced his apparent choice to resistance that might provoke civil war and revolution or timely capitulation in order to preserve some elements of the traditional structure as the basis of future opposition. To the despair and anger of his more ardent but less reflective followers, in such circumstances the Duke reluctantly but invariably sounded the retreat.

Both reformers and adamant defenders of the old order were puzzled and aroused by the Duke's attitude and conduct towards reform. But few could long withhold respect from the formidable and transparently honest hero, and by 1852 the compromise between tradition and reform that had emerged in the state bore the mark of the powerful personality that had been impressed on it for a generation. To strive, to hold, but at the last when the price of absolute preservation was too high, to yield, was Wellington's great contribution to the adjustments of his own day and his great legacy to prosperity.

1 Lord Wellington, the Peninsula commander in 1812 – a sketch by Goya for the equestrian portrait (British Museum; reproduced by kind permission of the Trustees)

CHAPTER ONE

CHARACTER AND CIRCUMSTANCE

WHEN THE Duke of Wellington sailed for England at the end of 1818 he was standing at the very top of his shining hour. The conqueror of Napoleon, a duke in his own and three other countries, Prince of Waterloo in the Netherlands, field marshal or its equivalent in every major army and the holder of more than a score of knighthoods, he was the most renowned and glittering figure in Europe. As supreme commander of the allied army of occupation and British ambassador to France in the last three years he had added to his renown by the masterful and judicious manner in which he had superintended the imposition of peace terms on the country that had kept the continent in disarray for a generation. The crowned heads of state accepted him practically as an equal and his headquarters in Paris was the focus of attention for them and their ministers as they continued to seek the advice of the saviour and very symbol of their order.

Although he had no intimation of it, Wellington's departure from France marked one of the most important turning points in his life. He had fought his last battle and would never again command troops in the field; from now on his energies would be concentrated on the public affairs of his own country. The Duke never fully accepted this and, until his death, though not consistently, he continued to regard himself as a soldier only temporarily diverted to other matters. For over a quarter of a century after the allied army was disbanded he continued to believe that he would be recalled to lead it again. In the alarms and upheavals of the early nineteenth century this was not unreasonable. But general war was avoided in his lifetime and the summons never came. In the meantime he found an effective substitute for a military opponent in the threat to the political and social order at home. The domestic enemy was more devious, covert and plausible to the unthinking, but Wellington never doubted that he understood the challenge and knew how to deal with it. Unfortunately for the country as far as he was concerned, not everyone agreed and all too often his sound counsel was disregarded.

A long and close involvement in politics was far from the Duke's mind in 1818, but in the absence of a major war there were powerful forces pulling him in that direction. Lord Liverpool's government was in the usual precarious condition that had characterized it since its formation in 1812. Peace, accompanied by agricultural and industrial collapse, suffering and angry protests, had done nothing to lessen the difficulties of mediating between landed and urban interests. It had lost seats in the House of Commons in the bitter election in June and a poor harvest made it practically certain that there would be a revival of the agitation for parliamentary reform as a sovereign cure for all evils that some thought had brought the country to the brink of revolution in 1816 and 1817. In this sea of troubles the prestige of the Duke of Wellington was a mighty beacon of hope, and the Prime Minister lost no time in offering him a place in the cabinet when the army of occupation was breaking up.

Standing aloof of this critical juncture would have encouraged the disaffected to turn their efforts to enlisting the Duke in their cause. Wellington had no desire to add to the difficulties of ministers who had stood behind him in his campaigns; but the attraction of nominal office that would not require demeaning participation in partisan controversy went beyond mere loyalty to old colleagues.

Halfway through his fiftieth year, the Duke was enjoying his active life and position as the universal fount of wisdom. There may have been a shortage of worlds to conquer at the moment but he was not eager to exchange this happy lot for the tedious ease of a retired nobleman, fighting boredom by supervising his estates, riding, hunting and shooting; entertaining and visiting his fellow peers; going to London for Parliament and the social season; taking a proprietary but remote interest in the business of the House of Lords; and waiting like a hopeful Cincinnatus for the sound of the battle trumpet. The pleasures of aristocratic existence were enjoyable enough as relaxation from the serious business of life, but they were not sufficient for his restless but disciplined temperament. As he grumbled about the idleness of country house life fifteen years after he left the army: 'I, who have been engaged in business, commanding armies, *or something of that sort*, all my life, can scarcely conceive how people contrive to pass their time so totally without occupation.'[1]

His nature aside, Wellington was also keenly aware that his lofty position was really only the product of the last five years. He had worked his way up from the lowest reaches of the Irish peerage by a combination of talent and influence, but only recently had he emerged from the powerful shadow of his eldest brother, Richard, Marquess Wellesley, and managed to establish his own identity. Having realized his most ambitious dreams, cabinet office offered a continuing reaffirmation of his place at the centre of events. The amenable Lord Mulgrave stood aside, and was rewarded by being allowed to keep his place in the cabinet, and the Duke stepped into his place as Master General of the Ordnance.[2] The appointment was intended as a purely professional one, perhaps merely temporary if the great soldier were needed elsewhere, but within four years Wellington was drawn into the political maelstrom. And there, or not far outside it, he remained to the day of his death. From time to time he raged against the demands that he considered were imposed on him and threatened to abandon public life. But the many opportunities to leave with dignity always coincided with some fresh danger that forced him to put the interests of the country before personal convenience.

The focus of the Duke's activities after 1818 was Apsley House at Hyde Park Corner. He had purchased it from Lord Wellesley in 1817 and for the first decade of his occupancy it remained a modest red brick mansion. Between 1828 and 1830 he transformed it into a grand edifice appropriate to his rank and station. The original structure was altered and greatly enlarged and the whole building covered with Bath stone. It was a kind of monument in his own day, and since the Second World War has appropriately been the Wellington Museum in which the trophies and memorabilia, mostly from his military career, are displayed. Apart from the exhibit cases, the house is much as it was in his time. The furniture is still there; the decoration is little altered; and the portraits of his associates continue to share the walls with the magnificent paintings captured in the baggage train of Joseph Bonaparte after the battle of Vitoria. Even though they had been looted from Spain, the Spanish King in gratitude confirmed them as Wellington's property in 1816. The eleven foot marble nude statue of Napoleon by Canova, which still maintains its pride of place in the well of the great curving staircase, was presented in 1816 by the British government. On the floor above, in addition to reception rooms of appropriate grandeur, is the ninety foot long Waterloo Gallery in which the Duke held his annual banquet on the anniversary of the famous victory after 1830. Previously only the twenty generals who had been at the battle could be accommodated in the dining room of the original house, but the new wing provided a room that held over eighty. As death thinned the ranks, even those who had been junior officers on that memorable day were summoned to help their aged chief mark the occasion.

Apsley House was a fitting setting for the national hero. Behind the imposing dignified parts, in a section now reserved to the present Duke, was the efficient part. Here on the ground floor Wellington and his secretary had their rooms and a steady stream of visitors and correspondence bore testimony to his place in the life of the state. The letters were carefully preserved in the secretary's room, the incoming and outgoing bundles for each year being filed in separate compartments set into the panelling.

When the Duke stepped outside his house he could hardly avoid further evidence of his unequalled position. In 1822 the grateful women of England caused an eighteen foot nude bronze statue of Achilles with sword and buckler to be erected in his honour in Hyde Park immediately behind Apsley House. In 1844 an equestrian statue of him was unveiled outside the Royal Exchange. And after 1846 another equestrian statue of enormous proportions, atop a triumphal arch, cast its shadow over the front of his house. The walls of official buildings, clubs and private houses were adorned with iconic portraits and busts for which he was never loath to sit. Wherever he went in the capital at least, it was difficult to avoid evidence that he was the nation's household god.

With his life focused on London and having only a limited interest in the joys of rural life, Wellington was not much concerned about the usual aristocratic symbol, an impressive country seat. The house at Stratfield Saye, the estate purchased for him by Parliament after Waterloo, was not very remarkable. Some of his contemporaries thought it unworthy of his station while others found it distinctly ugly. But it suited the Duke well enough. He made a few alterations, including hot water heating and double windows in winter, redecorated it to his own taste and turned it into a comfortable house, and firmly rejected the proposal of replacing it with a monumental chilly pile like the Duke of Marlborough's Blenheim. Perhaps he was deterred by the ruinous expense of the latter, but one consideration must have been that Stratfield Saye was his wife's principal residence. During her lifetime he did not spend much time there and by the time she died in 1831 he had enjoyed the use of Walmer Castle for two years as Lord Warden of the Cinque Ports in succession to Lord Liverpool. He continued to use Stratfield Saye for sport and refreshment, but he much preferred the castle at Dover. The military atmosphere of that retreat, also redecorated, was as bracing as the sea air. And here he was not just the great national figure but also the local grandee, dispensing patronage and justice in his maritime court and wielding power and dominion without the challenge from aristocratic rivals that he had occasionally to suffer in Hampshire where he was Lord Lieutenant.

As well as enjoying a prescriptive place on public occasions, at social gatherings and in relation to the royal family, Wellington was a familiar figure in the streets of the capital. He rode and walked about like any private individual and was immediately recognizable by his distinctive lean five foot eight frame, his fresh colour and famous hooked nose and his almost unvarying dress: a blue tailcoat and round hat, blue trousers in winter and white in summer, a white waistcoat and a white stock fastened at the back by a silver buckle. The Duke and his generation wore military uniforms only on ceremonial occasions.

Physically he looked the part of an austere military hero and his formal, abrupt manner added to the effect. To those who greeted him he returned a salute by touching two fingers to the brim of his hat. By the time of his death he had become 'a fourth estate in the empire,' as the Conservative *Quarterly Review* called him,

> the best known man in London; everyone knew him by sight: like a
> city built on a hill, or his own colossal statue on the arch, he could not
> be hid. He was the observed of all observers, and the object of
> universal royal-like homage, which he neither courted nor shunned.

Half a century hence, the magazine predicted, his image would remain engraved on people's minds and they would still talk of 'his silvered head and his venerable form, bowed with the weight of years and honours, yet manfully stemming the crowded highways, struggling to the last against the advance of age, the conqueror of the conquerors.'[3] Because he was such a fixture in daily life people who did not know him thought that he must be less aloof and more receptive to their concerns than others who were set in authority over them. They wrote to him in great numbers, and in a confident manner that they would not have assumed towards other public figures. This never-ending flow of information, advice, opinion and solicitation must have made him one of the best informed men in the country, though there is no evidence that it altered his views.

Contrary to the impression conveyed by his manifest sociability, his unfailing presence on public occasions and his daily appearances when in London, Wellington was an intensely private person, obsessively concerned to protect his privacy and public reputation. When Col. John

2 The Duke of Wellington in 1814 by Sir Thomas Lawrence – victor in the Peninsula but not yet the hero of Waterloo (painting by Sir Thomas Lawrence, PRA, Wellington Museum; reproduced by kind permission of the Victoria and Albert Museum)

Gurwood, who had edited his despatches and parliamentary speeches, committed suicide at the end of 1845, he was furious to learn that the nervous literary drudge he had raised to the great height of Deputy Lieutenant of the Tower of London had been keeping a clandestine journal of his conversations in the expectation of profitable publication after his patron's death. The Irish famine and arguments over the repeal of the corn laws which were destroying the government he was doing his best to keep together did nothing to delay a rocket to Gurwood's widow demanding that the offending material be surrendered. The Duke insisted that there was no example in all history of such an unworthy act:

> It is anti-social; it puts an end to all the charms of society, to all familiar and private communication of thought between man and man; and, in fact, it places every individual in familiar society in the situation in which he puts himself in a publick assembly, with a gentleman of the press to report what he says.[4]

Gurwood had apparently burned the papers in his last unhappy days, but the strength of Wellington's reaction to his discovery is an indication of his anxiety not to disclose anything that would detract from the pure image of the calm, assured paragon of civic duty and private virtue. It is scarcely believable that the Duke, who was a considerable reader, should even in that heated moment have believed that people had not always been curious about great figures and recorded their sayings, habits, mannerisms, foibles and other details for the edification and instruction of themselves and posterity. It is even more surprising he did not at least suspect that some of his friends were doing the same in his case. Fortunately for historians they were; but if Wellington had known of it he would have insisted that the journals be destroyed, and probably have broken off the friendship as well. The Duke wanted no fine shades in his literary representation, and so far as he could he saw to it that this form was as impersonal and stylized as his portraits and statues.

He was able to achieve much by the close control he exercised over his own papers. There was in Wellington's view no need to elaborate and risk disturbing the gratifying general acclaim for the sterling qualities that had produced his military victories by publishing a memoir or authorizing a biography. Instead Gurwood was engaged to produce a selection of military despatches which began to be published in 1834. At a time of great abuse for his political activities, the praise with which successive volumes were greeted did much to raise Wellington's spirits and confirm him in the wisdom of persevering in his duty. When Lord Aberdeen in 1838 reported that Lord Brougham, the former Whig Chancellor and notorious egoist, had pronounced that the despatches would be remembered when even he and contemporaries were forgotten, the Duke did not allow inquiry into Brougham's motives to deter him from agreeing: 'It is very true: when I read them I was myself astonished, and I can't think how the devil I could have written them.'[5] He told Gurwood that he had presented the world with 'a work which must be usefull to Statesmen & Soldiers as containing the true details of important political & military operations of many years duration.' He professed astonishment that this should have resulted from material kept 'at first solely as memoranda & for reference & afterwards from idleness & the desire to avoid the trouble of working over the papers to see which might be destroyed.'[6]

The despatches certainly contain a great deal of valuable information on his campaigns; but much was omitted. This was partly for the laudable purpose of protecting others – 'When my papers are published, many statues will be taken down,' as he said – but also to ensure that the personality of their author, as far as it was revealed at all, conformed to the iconic image. There was little here to suggest that Wellington might occasionally succumb to such human failings as doubt, hesitation, anger, impulsiveness, suspicion or vindictiveness. All was calm, judicious, objective.

When the literary acolyte pressed on with his labours to produce a larger edition, the Duke's hesitations when asked to approve material for publication increased. Gurwood unburdened himself to his confidant, Lord Liverpool, about the strains of ensuring that Wellington was not exposed to any possibility of controversy. Even allowing for his paranoia there was undoubtedly much to his complaints that he was carefully attended by those devoted protectors of the Duke's reputation, Charles Arbuthnot and Lord Fitzroy Somerset, 'who are always on the lookout to catch me tripping.'[7] The delicacy of his occupation can have done nothing to lighten Gurwood's melancholy and nervous disposition. Not much was added to the original series in his lifetime and no successor was appointed after his suicide. The task languished for a decade until the second Duke altered the tone of the earlier publications by restoring many of the deletions and continued the work to 1832. After an interval of a century, the Historical Manuscripts Commission has now begun to extend the publication of political papers beyond that year.

Since his death a good proportion of Wellington's private as well as official correspondence has found its way into print. From this as well as material still in archives, it is clear that he was, even by the high standards of the day, an exceptionally assiduous writer. In contrast to his speeches in the House of Lords, in which he was frequently ill at ease, abrupt, repetitive and sometimes confused, the Duke suffered no disability when addressing paper. As a commander in the field he had had to spend more time with the pen than the sword, and the pace of his literary production neither faltered nor failed after he returned to England. Writing was not only a familiar outlet but also one better suited to his solitary and defensive nature than speaking in a debating chamber. He wrote letters as soon as he got up in the morning; late at night; and in between at the table in the House of Lords, in his office when he had one and in whatever house he was occupying or visiting. Other demands came to be resented as intrusions on this vital activity which occupied a major part of his daily routine. 'The fact is,' he groaned in the early 1830s,

> that my whole time is taken up from morning till night in receiving
> written suggestions for the public benefit from gentlemen with whom
> I have no connection or even acquaintance. Nobody is satisfied unless
> I write an answer. It is not surprising if these answers are at times not
> given at great length, and are not satisfactory to those to whom they
> are addressed.[8]

Wellington frequently protested against this burden, but apart from some lithographed forms devised in the 1840s to respond to applications for patronage, assistance or to view his houses, he never made any serious attempt to give it up, or even to delegate the bulk of it to someone else. Despite his complaints, the correspondence provided stimulus and a form of purposeful activity, a constant source of assurance about his place in the life of the state and a means of bolstering his public reputation. The older he became the more impertinence and dangerous opinions he detected in his correspondents. Instead of ignoring such letters, or sending a brief reply as he had when he first returned to England, he would be roused to an impassioned missive, sometimes adding a wrathful paragraph or two to the laconic lithographs, and frequently carrying on at great length on some small point. He was a master of the sarcastic phrase, but he sincerely believed that he was using his literary weapons in defence of that national institution, the Duke of Wellington, on which depended the whole eroding order of politics and society. In writing to those outside his immediate circle he invariably used the third person.

The Duke's compulsive letter writing became as legendary as his other characteristics and it was popularly believed that he responded to every letter in his own hand. In fact many of the final copies were written by

Algernon Greville, whose virtues as secretary included handwriting that was a legible version of Wellington's. But the Duke certainly read most of the incoming letters, docketed them, personally answered a good many and for the rest sketched out replies to be put into smooth sentences by Greville. Wellington's drafts were often cross hatched – written at right angles across the original script – or fitted into some blank space on the paper. As his handwriting shrank with age, so did the space required; and eventually a turned up corner sufficed to cram in a few words that probably could not be deciphered even with a microscope.

Thanks to the letters and the journals kept by his contemporaries, it can be seen that the stylized, carefully fostered representation of the Duke was not the reality, though it was a significant element in understanding him and was one eagerly accepted both then and later by those who wanted to believe in the ideal of classical heroism made flesh. Certainly those outside the very small group who customarily saw him at close quarters had no reason to believe that there was greater complexity behind the appearance. When they did catch a glimpse of his character, usually in a flash of anger, this could easily be fitted into the pattern firmly fixed in their minds.

Wellington did not reveal himself fully even to his friends, who were as puzzled and as admiring as anyone else. Mrs Arbuthnot, in whom he confided as much as anyone for over a decade, frequently complained that he did not tell her what he was going to do or his reasons. The person who understood the Duke best of all was her husband, who lived with him from her death in 1834 to his own in 1850. But Charles Arbuthnot, who spent thirty years smoothing his friend's path as his loyal go-between, apparently kept no diary and rarely allowed himself an indiscretion even in letters to his most trusted intimates. As Gurwood pointed out, he was one of Wellington's chief protectors.

If, as Wordsworth and modern psychiatry agree, the child is father of the man, the basis of the Duke's character must be sought in the experiences of his formative years. Unfortunately this is the period about which very little is known, and where the evidence is so sparse it is not very helpful to speculate or to read back into childhood what he became as an adult. But what is clear is that this fourth child of six was not highly regarded by his strong-willed mother or by his eldest brother, Richard, to whose charge the family was abruptly committed when he was twenty (and the future Wellington eleven) on the death of their father. The young Arthur was accounted plain if not ugly, devoid of intellectual gifts and so fond of playing the violin as to raise fears that he would follow the same feckless course as his father, who had almost ruined the family by devoting himself to music rather than the family estates. His record at Eton was unpromising and he was removed in order to concentrate the family's limited resources on keeping his seemingly more talented younger brothers, Gerald and Henry, thère. He received some tutoring at Brighton; spent a year with his mother in Brussels, where she was living to economize; and finally attended the French Royal Academy of Equitation at Angers. The last pointed to a standard career for an aristocratic younger son, and shortly before his eighteenth birthday his brother Richard secured him a commission in the 73rd Highland Regiment, then stationed in Ireland. Although he had shown no interest or aptitude for military life, it was soon evident that he had found a real vocation. Ample scope for its development was provided by the long wars against France. He shook off his idleness, which may simply have been boredom, burned his violin, and within a few years was well on the way to mastering his profession. By the time he entered the army he had also overcome his adolescent awkwardness and people were beginning to comment on his handsomeness and on the confident bearing and manner that were to be enduring hallmarks.

The Duke's spartan austerity, hard emotional shell, concern about his position, rigidity and desire to impose his will on every situation undoubtedly originated in the response of a sensitive nature to the neglect and humiliations of his youth. The indifference of his mother and the condescension of his eldest brother were particularly hard to bear, the latter all the more because his brother was vital to his advancement. In later life Wellington got along well enough with his younger brothers, the Rev. Gerald and Henry, Lord Cowley the diplomat, both of whom he could help and patronize. He also enjoyed fairly good relations with his second eldest brother, William, who changed his name to Wellesley-Pole on inheriting the estates of a relative, played a significant role first in Irish then in English politics, and was Master of the Mint when his brother returned in 1818. But the Duke had little to do with the third child, his sister Anne, an elegant, self-possessed woman who first married the son of the Earl of Southampton, and after his early death, Charles Culling Smith, the son of a rich nabob. And he treated his mother like a distant acquaintance. The Duke's coolness towards members of his family provoked comment even in those aristocratic circles not noted for warm family intimacy. In 1829 Charles Greville found evidence for his conviction that Wellington lacked emotions by pointing to the almost total neglect of his mother, then almost ninety, and his failure to visit his sister

3 The Marquess Wellesley, Wellington's eldest brother, as Governor General of Bengal and lord of all he surveyed (painting by Robert Horne, Apsley House; reproduced by kind permission of the Courtauld Institute of Art)

who was mourning the death of her only son, even though he passed her door every time he went to Stratfield Saye.[9] But well as Greville understood Wellington in many ways, he did not know the circumstances of his youth or grasp his concealed but continuing vulnerability.

Of all his relations, it was with his eldest brother that his dealings were most complex. This handsome, brilliant neurasthenic was born with a desire to shine in the great world and raged against the meagre inheritance and great responsibilities bequeathed to him by his father. In a characteristic dramatic gesture the new Lord Mornington left Oxford without taking a degree and applied himself to restoring the family fortunes by cultivating the prominent individuals in London he had already impressed as a classical scholar. As his efforts flourished he expanded the family name from plain Wesley to the older and more grandiose Latinate form of Wellesley. This did nothing to throw pious Victorian clergymen off tracing the remote genealogical connection between the founder of Methodism and the hero of Waterloo. After a succession of minor offices Mornington received something like what he considered his due when he was sent to India in 1797 as Governor General at the age of thirty-seven. Here at last he could give free rein to his natural talent for ruling in the imperial manner. Nor did he forget his family, least of all Arthur who had preceded him to the sub-continent and whose military victories greatly assisted his policy of expansion. But the East India Company was less interested in territory than in trade and the Marquess Wellesley returned home under a cloud in 1805.

Valuable as the connection with Wellesley was, it must have seemed to the young general that he would never manage to establish his independent reputation and have his achievements recognized in their own right or dissociate himself from the instability, deviousness and raffishness that were the dark side of Wellesley's great abilities. There were, not surprisingly, clashes between the two autocratic temperaments in India. When they returned to England it was Wellesley who was still for some years the dominating figure. His looming presence over the Portland ministry must have been a factor in discouraging any hesitation about giving his brother the command in the Peninsula in 1809. Wellesley continued to be a power to be reckoned with for a few more years, but after failing to become Prime Minister in 1812 his force was largely spent. He never found a place at the centre of English politics, though he twice served as Viceroy of Ireland. He lingered on to 1842, occasionally showing flashes of his old brilliance, but increasingly ineffective, impecunious, irrelevant and disregarded. This was mortification indeed for Narcissus, as his perceptive biographer Iris Butler has called him, and it did not help that for thirty years he was eclipsed by his younger brother.

The reversal of positions came very suddenly. Between the battles of Vitoria in 1813, the year after Wellesley was unable to form a ministry, and Waterloo in 1815, Wellington became the most prominent individual in Europe. Wellesley could not help resenting his brother's success while the Duke never completely got over thirty years of Wellesley's overbearing superiority. Neither could adjust to the change or develop a new association based on it. It was a point on one side in the continuing rivalry when Wellington bought Apsley House – at a generous price – from Wellesley who was as usual desperately in debt; it was a point on the other when Wellesley married one of the Duke's loves. They differed in politics, in which Wellesley was more liberal, particularly on Catholic emancipation and the government of Ireland, and in 1827 broke over a matter of family patronage. For a decade they treated each other with cold formality. But a few years before Wellesley's death, when his politics had become almost as conservative as his brother's and when the quarrels of recent years seemed more remote than the golden memories of distant youth, a friendly truce was established. Even during the years of estrangement Wellesley occasionally expressed admiration for the achievements of the brother whose career he had launched and superintended for so long, and Wellington never entirely lost his awe of 'the Governor.'

Similar as they were in appearance and temperament, the Duke had by 1818 managed to distinguish himself from his brother in every possible way. Where Wellesley was idle and negligent, he was industrious and punctilious in performing his real or imagined duty; where Wellesley was duplicitous and unreliable, he was scrupulously honest and hyper-sensitive to any implication to the contrary; where Wellesley was mercurial, he strove to be cool and controlled; where Wellesley was a notorious spendthrift who lost fortunes, he was frugal; where Wellesley loved pomp and ceremony, he preferred simplicity and, so long as it was duly rendered, affected indifference to the deference that was paid him; where Wellesley rejoiced in fine rhetoric, his language was plain, direct and even blunt; where Wellesley was the source of much low amusement for his womanizing, beginning with his first wife, an actress who bore him five children before they were married, Wellington was to all outward appearance honourable and considerate with women of his own rank. By reaction as well as direct effect, the Marquess Wellesley was a major force in shaping his brother by the time he became Duke of Wellington.

After Wellesley, it was with his wife that the Duke's relations were most awkward. His marriage was both symptomatic of his mature personality and a reinforcement of it. This was partly due to the fact that at thirty-seven he had developed a character that would have made it difficult to be really intimate with anyone; but at least as important was the connection between the marriage and the humiliations of his youth. When he had first courted Catherine (or Kitty as she was generally called) Pakenham in Dublin, he had been a mere captain of the light dragoons; despite being on the Viceroy's staff and a member of the Irish House of Commons he had no fortune or visible prospects beyond what could be provided by his brother's quick wits. She, on the other hand, was the sister of a substantial Irish peer, the Earl of Longford. The engagement was forbidden and the two parted with conventional expressions on his part that his feelings would never change and a vague understanding that he might renew the suit in the unlikely event that he managed to rise to an appropriate level in the world.

Twelve years passed during which they did not communicate; though intermediaries took it upon themselves to keep both parties informed about the other. When General Sir Arthur Wellesley, K B, returned to England in 1805 he was told that Kitty was still unmarried and pining for him. She was told much the same about him. This was far from the truth in both cases, but each had good reason for wanting to believe what was represented about the other. The soldier's passions may have been inflamed by a decade of isolation from Europeans in India and the romantic novels he read on the passage home, but more to the point he was now in a position to expunge the cavalier dismissal by Lord Longford. Even for a successful general who had accumulated a fortune and good political connections, the union with a leading family of the Anglo-Irish ascendency, the only aristocratic society he had known, would be advantageous in consolidating his position. It would certainly be an infinitely more impressive match than Wellesley's. For Kitty Pakenham, a markedly faded beauty of thirty-four in what since the union of Ireland with Britain was becoming a provincial backwater, the renewed offer from this dashing veteran who showed every indication of even greater achievement was a dream come true. She wasted no time in accepting and Wellesley hurried over to Dublin to claim his bride sight unseen. His brother Gerald accompanied him to perform the ceremony in the very drawing room in which he had been told that they could not marry.

Wellington had every reason to regard his marriage as a triumph and a vindication; but it was not long before he was bitterly regretting it. He

4 The Duchess of Wellington as Lady Wellington in 1811, aged 39 and 5 years after her marriage (pencil drawing with watercolour wash by J. Slater, Stratfield Saye; reproduced by kind permission of the Courtauld Institute)

expostulated to Mrs Arbuthnot in 1822: 'Is it not the most extraordinary thing you ever heard of! Would you have believed that anybody could have been such a *d–d* fool?' He claimed that he had not been the least in love, that he had married Kitty Pakenham only because 'they' expected it of him and because he had not understood himself: 'I thought I should never care for anybody again and that I shd. be with the army &, in short, I was a fool.'[10] There was much to what he said. Love probably did not have anything to do with the decision; he may have been somewhat disoriented when he returned from India; the matchmakers undoubtedly had much to answer for in encouraging him to think that it was his duty to prove his constancy no less than Kitty's; and it certainly never occurred to him that marriage would require any effort on his part.

But the real trouble with the marriage was that Wellington soon soared above the small world of Dublin, while Kitty never could. She made not the slightest effort to adapt to her position as the wife of a great hero, having neither inclination nor desire, and probably not the talent, to take a leading part in society. To the end of her days she remained a timid, retiring woman, baffled by the management of two large households, devoted to her children, uncritically admiring of her daunting husband who was practically a stranger, and the object of the amusement, condescension and contempt of his many woman friends. The Duke yearned for an appropriate consort: beautiful, charming, witty, well-informed, an easy household manager, effortlessly able to entertain his friends with the grace to which they were accustomed – a Mrs Arbuthnot or a Lady Salisbury. That at least was what he thought he wanted, but in the twenty years that he was a widower he carefully avoided matrimony. Perhaps this was a triumph of experience over hope. He may have feared that whomever he chose would fall short of his high ideal, or he may have recognized to some degree his solitary nature and fear of revealing himself to anyone. He was content with the bachelor life he had never really abandoned even during the years of marriage, and preferred to share it with women preferably safely married.

As long as she lived the Duchess was a source of endless vexation to her husband. She lived out of society, frittering her time away on good works, the minor arts and the concerns of her relatives, and serving as a constant reminder of the days when Wellington had been idle and foolish and forced to beg for favours in a manner that he now treated with contempt when used by others. There could be no thought of divorce or even real separation for one of his rigid code of honour and duty, but in practice they lived apart. The Duchess stayed mainly at Stratfield Saye while the

Duke travelled around the country from his base at Apsley House. Only after her death did he restrict his wanderings and have people mainly come to him.

Wellington received much sympathy for his unhappy marriage and unsuitable wife. But even Mrs Arbuthnot, who adored him and considered the Duchess 'the most abominably silly, stupid woman that ever was born,' felt obliged to tell him that he would get along much better with her if only he would be '*civil* to her but he is not. He never speaks to her & carefully avoids ever going near her.' He would not, and perhaps could not, make the effort to relax his rigidity and resentment in order to build at least an amicable relationship. When he countered Mrs Arbuthnot's criticisms and denied ever saying a harsh word to his wife, she could only conclude that he was oblivious to the fact that his manner was 'abrupt to the greatest degree to every body, particularly to her; and as she is frightened to death at him (a thing he detests) she always seems *consternée* when he comes near her.'[11]

Given his personality and the nature of his marriage, it is not surprising that the Duke never managed to establish satisfactory relations with his sons, Lord Douro and Lord Charles Wellesley. They were born in the first two years of his marriage and scarcely knew their father before he returned permanently to England in 1818. Wellington was always afraid that they would disgrace him by falling short of the high standards expected of his sons. He thought he saw in them too much of their mother, who did indulge them and shield them from their grim father, and perhaps too much of what he had been in his own youth, and feared that without the goad of poverty they would never develop his discipline but drift through life in an aimless and even dissolute manner. These fears were not entirely groundless. His sons could not remember when their father was not a great man and grew up accepting their place at the top of society as perfectly natural. The temptations, the least of which was idleness, were considerable; but despite Charles's rustication from Christ Church, Oxford for rowdiness, which led the Duke to remove both to Cambridge, and Douro's importunate womanizing, less discreet than his father's and more like Wellesley's, they were conventional enough sprigs of the aristocracy. Both followed unremarkable military and political careers and both in indirect ways provided their father with consolation in his old age. Douro's marriage to Lady Elizabeth Hay in 1839 was almost as bleak as Wellington's; but the beautiful Lady Douro was rescued from the fate of the late Duchess by her father-in-law who showered her with solicitude sharpened by reproach of her tongue-tied husband. Lord Charles got along better with his father but his chief contribution to the Duke's happiness was the provision of numerous grandchildren after his marriage to Sophia Pierrepont in 1844. As Douro had no children, two of these in succession became Dukes of Wellington.

Although he was guarded with everyone, the Duke was noticeably more relaxed away from his immediate family. He particularly enjoyed the company of women and children. On his campaigns he had shared the masculine amusements of his staff, but in peacetime he preferred female or mixed company. He saw enough of his male associates in the course of his official duties, in the House of Lords, on business at Apsley House and in the hunting field, so that although he graced a dozen clubs with his membership he never went to them. The leading hostesses naturally competed for him and until his last years he was relentlessly sociable. Surrounded by his devoted admirers he played to perfection the part of military hero taking his triumphant ease. His conversation sparkled and flowed as he fought all his battles over again and brought his great authority to bear on every topic that arose. Most of his pronouncements were deeply pessimistic but they were uttered with a laconic conviction worthy of Dr Johnson. Many were immediately written down, so that even if all the anecdotes and epigrams that cannot definitely be attributed to him are discounted, it is clear that he was one of the great conversationalists of all time.

In entertaining his women friends, of course, Wellington was also serving himself: articulating and refining his ideas, reinforcing his public image and basking in the comfortable glow of uncritical praise. But contrary to what many at the time thought, his political judgment was no more affected by this female court than by his male associates. Nor, despite rumour and innuendo, were any of these women his mistresses.

The person most usually assumed to be was Harriet Arbuthnot. In 1818 she was twenty-five, half the age of her husband, two years the Duke's senior, whom she had married as his second wife four years before. She had known Wellington since she was a child and when she and her husband went to visit him in Paris after Waterloo was much taken with the conquering hero, and he with her. But she was also devoted to her mild and kindly husband and to Lord Castlereagh, the Foreign Secretary. After Castlereagh's suicide in 1822 Mrs Arbuthnot became the Duke's closest friend. Lady Shelley, who knew them both well at this time and who had herself been suspected of being more than a friend of Wellington while he was still in Paris, wrote after his death that she was convinced that they had not been lovers: 'He admired her very much – for she had a manlike

5 'A sketch in the park' – a lithograph of the Duke and Mrs Arbuthnot with the Achilles statue in the background published just five days before Mrs Arbuthnot's death (lithography published by T. McLean, 27 July 1834; reproduced by kind permission of the National Portrait Gallery)

sense – but Mrs Arbuthnot was devoid of womanly passions, and was, above all, a loyal and truthful woman.'[12] This is not a very flattering assessment of Mrs Arbuthnot's charms, which went far beyond the courage to tell the Duke what others feared to say, and it is not necessarily conclusive. But there is no hint of physical intimacy in Mrs Arbuthnot's famous journal, which otherwise provides such a detailed record of their friendship. Indeed apart from within a few years of his return to England, there is no evidence of Wellington having an affair with anyone.

This is striking because in 1818 he had a well-earned reputation as a ladies' man. He had consorted with all sorts and conditions of women on his campaigns and during his previous residence in London, at the time of his marriage, he had patronized fashionable courtesans, including the celebrated Harriette Wilson. Turning to authorship for support in her declining years she sent out letters offering to exclude her former clients from her memoirs for a price; 'Publish and be damned!' was the Duke's alleged reply, and certainly he appeared in her account. During the occupation of France, too, he was romantically involved with several Englishwomen, including Lady Caroline Lamb who must have found the supreme commander a soothing relief from the tempestuous Lord Byron to whom she had been attached a few years before.

The key to the abrupt change in Wellington's conduct probably lies in the brief affair shortly after his return with Lady Charlotte Greville, the daughter of the Duke of Portland in whose administration he had served a decade earlier. Lady Charlotte was soon persuaded to renounce the romance by her shaken husband. Four years later, in 1824, her son Charles the diarist sought revenge by sending an anonymous letter to Mrs Arbuthnot (and one to Mrs Lane-Fox) accusing her of being the Duke's mistress. Mrs Arbuthnot was much upset and talked the matter over at great length with her husband and Wellington, who recognized Greville's handwriting. In order to avoid the risk of open scandal the Duke and Mrs Arbuthnot agreed that they should be more circumspect in future.[13]

Wellington remained a close friend of Lady Charlotte, enabling three of her family to make major contributions to his literary legacy. One son, Algernon, was his secretary; the journal of another, Charles, the Clerk of the Privy Council, provides the best continuous detached commentary on his last thirty years; and her son-in-law, Lord Francis Leveson-Gower, later Lord Ellesmere, kept another important record of his sayings and answers to his persistent questions. But this romantic interlude had threatened to wreck his idyllic relationship with Mrs Arbuthnot. If he wanted to continue in the same intimacy with her – circumspection was soon abandoned – and those he looked to a decade later after her death, he could not afford the breath of scandal. Dangerous liaisons would leave him open to blackmail, exposure and gossip and seriously compromise the exemplary reputation of the Duke of Wellington. If he did have affairs after 1820, he took good care to ensure that no trace of them would ever be discovered; but he was so well known and lived so much in the public eye that it is not easy to see how that could have been arranged. It is more likely that he recognized that his exalted position, his concern to be a model of probity and the warm friendship with the kind of women he craved, more than physical relations, made his past conduct impossible as the shades of nineteenth century morality closed around even members of the aristocracy who were concerned about conventional respectability. This was a considerable renunciation, but a tolerable bargain for a person who needed affection and admiration but who feared complete intimacy. Certainly this denial was consistent with the rest of his stern nature which manifested itself in indifference to food and wine, pride in not sleeping long and in unsparing dedication to work and duty.

Time no doubt reconciled him to this part of the price of being the Duke of Wellington. He found some outlet in sentimentality towards women and children, and perhaps also in musical performances to which he remained devoted even when deafness robbed him of much of their pleasure. When he did go further, as with the attractive young religious enthusiast Anna Marie Jenkins in the 1830s and apparently with Lady Georgiana Fane in his last years, it was with women well removed from his customary circle. The tension of denying his nature in order to play the part he considered expected of him may account for his fierce and unpredictable outbursts of temper. Wellington certainly did not lack passion, but like most inhibited people had difficulty in expressing it. His eruptions were fairly rare in the House of Lords and at social gatherings; more frequent in political discussions with his friends and in cabinet; and a permanent element in the climate of Apsley House. The most manageable outlet for his emotions as time went by was his correspondence, which he used like a journal to express his feelings to a disembodied audience that could not interrupt or immediately respond to them.

In 1818 the Duke was essentially what he would be for the rest of his life: passionate and high-strung but carefully controlled in most of his public appearances; unconcerned about form so long as others paid careful attention to it; happy fighting the good fight and out of spirits only when there was no apparent call for his services; and wise enough to recognize his need for a busy, disciplined routine to ensure a satisfactory existence that would reduce gloomy introspection to a minimum. Time would simply confirm and sharpen the outlines of his personality, but it would not make them any clearer to most people. To his death Wellington succeeded in remaining a figure of mystery and awe.

CHAPTER TWO

THE GOLDEN AGE

WHEN HE joined the cabinet ministers at the end of 1818 the Duke of Wellington neither entered a company of strangers nor came among them as a political neophyte. A decade before he had served as Chief Secretary for Ireland in the Duke of Portland's government, and many of his colleagues now had been his colleagues then. The present Prime Minister, Lord Liverpool, had been Home Secretary, and later as Secretary of State for War from 1809 to 1812 had been responsible for Wellington's operations in the Peninsula. Lord Castlereagh, the Foreign Secretary and Leader of the House of Commons, the chief pillar of Liverpool's ministry and the Duke's closest political friend, had been at the War Office in Portland's government. Lord Bathurst, the present Secretary of State for War with whom Wellington had been in practically daily correspondence since 1812, had sat with him in Portland's cabinet as President of the Board of Trade. In 1818 Lord Eldon still presided over the House of Lords, endeavouring to snare reform in the thickets of the law as Lord Chancellor as he had in Portland's day; the son of a Newcastle coal merchant, he had even less reason than the Duke to complain of the exclusiveness of the barriers to advancement. George Canning, who had been Foreign Secretary when Wellington went to the Peninsula, was at a low point in his erratic career in 1818, working his way back into favour by way of Indian affairs in the relatively lowly office of President of the Board of Control. Lord Sidmouth, the Home Secretary, was the only principal minister with whom the Duke had not served before; from 1801 to 1804 he had been Prime Minister as George III's Protestant saviour when Pitt had insisted on Catholic emancipation following the Act of Union with Ireland.

As well as his old associates, Wellington also joined the company of his brother, William Wellesley-Pole, the Master of the Mint, and Charles Arbuthnot, Joint Secretary of the Treasury (ministerial whip and patronage manager). If there were some ministers with whom he was not personally acquainted, there can have been few who were entirely unknown to him in the small world of Regency politics. The government at least for the moment consisted of congenial individuals whose outlook on domestic and international matters the Duke fully shared.

Wellington also had good reason to think that he was not without experience of politics, which had been a vital adjunct to his military career from the beginning. Just before his twenty-first birthday he had been elected to the Irish House of Commons for the family borough of Trim. He sat there from 1790 to 1795 in addition to his military duties and serving as aide-de-camp to the Lord Lieutenant. This was a modest enough apprenticeship, his chief duty being to vote at the government's call; but the issues of disloyalty and rebellion that occupied the Anglo-Irish ascendency as the French Revolution swept across Europe were real enough, and would dominate his outlook to the end of his days. The young MP loyally supported the legislation giving Catholics the franchise that was forced on the Irish landlords by the British cabinet, a vote he had long forgotten by the time he was outraging his own Protestant followers by enacting full Catholic emancipation in 1829. It was in the Irish Parliament, too, that he first knew Castlereagh, who was still in 1795 a Whig and an opponent of the administration.

When he returned to England in 1805, General Sir Arthur Wellesley took Castlereagh's advice and acquired a seat in the House of Commons to help defend his brother against charges of financial extravagance, abusing his powers and unnecessarily extending British involvement in India. The threat to Lord Wellesley passed but Sir Arthur continued as MP for three successive English boroughs and served as Irish Secretary for two years, even while on military expeditions. His position in the government was important in gaining him the command in the Peninsula, at which point he left politics once more.

But the fact that the Duke had served with many of his colleagues before did not mean that he slipped back into the old relationship with them when he returned in 1818. A decade earlier he had been an ordinary minister, though one with valuable military skills; now he was a great man whose views had to be attended to with respect and on whom it was worth spending much effort to get his agreement. He also came trailing clouds of impressive administrative experience in France. Even before that, in the Peninsula and in India, he had needed to be as much a diplomat and civil administrator as a field commander. For two decades he had carried on negotiations over troops, supplies, money, subsidies, transportation and military authority. No problem at home in peacetime could be beyond the talents of such a man. But for three years he scarcely needed to exert himself: the country was in the hands of sound and seasoned professionals like himself and there was no need for Wellington to stir himself to action.

In the general dislocation following the war, the first year of the Duke's return stood out then and later as a particularly dangerous time. But after his experience of the European civil war he never doubted that the one aristocratic system scarcely touched by the French Revolution could meet any challenges so long as it was resolute. At the time he was occasionally critical of his colleagues, but he later regarded the years before 1822, when the canker entered the bud, as a golden age of good administration from which standards all subsequent periods marked a sad decline.

The great disturbance of 1819 did not occur until the summer. In the meantime the new Master General of the Ordnance had ample time to become familiar with his new office. Whatever divided control of the land forces did to prevent military dictatorship, it did not do much for co-ordination or efficiency. The Ordnance controlled munitions, supplies, and the command of the artillery, engineers, artificers (builders) and drivers; the cavalry and infantry came under the Command in Chief; pay and finance were regulated by the Treasury and administered by the Secretary at War; and policy was the sphere of the Secretary of State for War and the Colonies. Superintending his particular province of this military empire at a time of retrenchment was no great strain on Wellington's abilities or energy. He had plenty of time to follow events on the continent, to share his wisdom with other ministers and to carry out his duties as the social lion of the day.

But the Ordnance never lacked that detailed attention for which the Master General was famous. When the construction and repair of public buildings were brought under his department, for example, he turned his thoughts to a simple expedient that would encourage others to live up to his high standards. He announced that henceforth a brass plaque would be attached to any building erected or repaired at a cost of over a thousand pounds, stating the estimated and actual costs, the dates of commencement and completion and the name of the responsible officer. A man would think twice, he concluded, before having his name go down to posterity as the builder of a tower or magazine rendered useless from damp as a result of using sea sand in the mortar, poor foundations or any other defect of construction.[1]

Such administrative diversions were rudely interrupted on 16 August by a serious challenge to the whole government when 50,000 people gathered in St Peter's Fields on the outskirts of Manchester to protest the town's lack of representation in Parliament. The crowd was dispersed only when the magistrates ordered a cavalry charge that left eleven dead and several hundred wounded. The outrage this provoked was magnified enormously when the half dozen cabinet ministers, including the Duke, who remained in London a month after Parliament had risen drew up a message for the Prince Regent congratulating the local authorities on their handling of the situation. Demonstrations broke out all over the North of England defending the legality of the meeting at Manchester, expressing sympathy with the victims, condemning the magistrates and calling for the dismissal of the ministry.

Wellington had no doubt that he and his colleagues had done the right thing: 'Unless the magistrates had been supported in this instance, other magistrates on future occasions would not act at all; and then what a state the country would be in!'[2] To the victor of Waterloo, 'Peterloo' was a mere scuffle. But as unrest spread through the towns of the mysterious industrial North, he and other ministers, reading the frantic appeals for help from local officials, detected in the disaffection a deep-seated movement to overthrow the whole political order. The Duke thought that the basic problem lay in the nature of the country's laws: 'every man who attends one of these meetings – whether for the purpose of deliberation of crime, or for that of secret conspiracy – thinks, and boasts, that he is performing a public duty; and it would be a sin to deprive the people of this gratification.'[3]

Military pensioners were called out to man the garrisons and free regular troops for active duty, and new yeomanry corps were formed, but Wellington still considered the number of soldiers inadequate for the general uprising he expected. He told the military commander in the North to expect that the conspirators would first test the troops by organizing a large meeting, after which they would 'proceed to business, which will be neither more nor less than the Radical plunder of the rich towns and houses which will fall in their way.' The forces must be kept together, away from the temptations and attempts at subversions of the towns and public houses, and precautions should be taken to ensure that they were not overpowered in any encounter:

It is much better that a town should be plundered, and even some lives lost, than that the whole country should be exposed to the danger which would result from the success of the mob against even a small detachment of the troops .... As long as no misfortune happens to them the mischief will be confined to plunder and a little *murder*, and will not be irretrievable; but it is impossible to foresee how far it will go if the mob should in any instance get the better of the troops.[4]

This was advice that he would repeat on numerous similar occasions over the next thirty years, but in 1819 it was not required. Peterloo was not a prelude to revolution; the protest meetings were orderly and unco-ordinated. But when the Clerk of the Ordnance, returning from the North a week after Wellington's letter to the commander there, told the Home Secretary that he had found the country 'very peaceable, and even civil, and very *anti-Radical*,' the fearful Sidmouth simply shook his head and pointed to the volumes of letters which painted a darker picture.[5] No doubt the Clerk got a sharper version of the same reproach if he dared to expose the deficiencies of his observation in his own department.

Alert to this danger, the ministry summoned Parliament at the end of November rather than waiting for the usual season in the new year to pass the Six Acts that have become collectively as notorious as Peterloo. Public meetings were restricted; military drilling by civilians outlawed; the search for arms authorized; taxes raised to restrict the cheap press; penalties for libel increased; and trials speeded up. Much pleased by these improvements to the law, the Duke pressed Sidmouth to demoralize the insurgents by a couple of columns of troops and cannon. The disaffected, he told the Home Secretary, 'are like conquerors; they must go forward; the moment they are stopped they are lost. Their adherents will lose all confidence, and by degrees every individual will relapse into his old habits of loyalty or indifference.'[6]

The calm that followed the Six Acts probably owed more to a lack of conspiracy and the revival of trade than to the legislation in which Wellington expressed such confidence. But there was ample scope for different interpretations of cause and effect. And even those sceptical of the government's measures were given pause when a real plot to murder the cabinet was uncovered early in the new year. These Cato Street conspirators, so named from the street where they met, planned to assassinate the ministers when they dined with Lord Harrowby on 23 February. They would then seize the Tower of London, the Bank of England and what artillery they could; set fire to the Mansion House, the military barracks and other public buildings; and proclaim a revolutionary government.

Two of the thirty plotters, either spies or carefully calculating the odds against this desperate enterprise, informed on their associates. The Duke, fearless as ever in the face of personal danger, wanted to meet the conspirators in hand-to-hand combat and proposed that policemen and braces of pistols for the ministers be smuggled into Harrowby's house before the dinner. But his colleagues declined this heroic course, which would have had no effect against grenades thrown in the windows. Police and troops were sent instead to arrest the desperadoes in their loft on the appointed evening; a dozen escaped in the confusion but were captured the next day. At the examination of prisoners there turned out to be no national organization, but it was revealed that one of the group had earlier tried to stab Wellington in Green Park and had been deterred only by his quarry meeting 'a gentleman with one arm,' presumably Lord Fitzroy Somerset, and walking with him to Apsley House.[7] When Lady Shelley wrote to express her relief at the Duke's happy escape from the Cato Street plot, he told her in high spirits: 'You may rely upon it, there is no danger and that we shall hang as many of the miscreants as we please.'[8] Five were publicly hanged and decapitated without protest from the crowd.

Three weeks before this conspiracy the government had been threatened in a different way by the death of George III on 29 January. Old, blind, mad and almost forgotten in the seclusion of Windsor Castle, he was widely revered. Having endured two of his sons as monarchs and two others as perennial political nuisances, Wellington fifteen years later pronounced him 'the best *King* England ever had ... [who] understood *Kingcraft* the most thoroughly; a far superior man in real ability to [George IV], tho' he had not the same quickness and talent.'[9] In many ways the formal accession of George IV made little practical difference as he had been Prince Regent since 1810; but it did give new importance to the status of his wife. As Prince of Wales he had married Caroline of Brunswick in 1795 principally to increase his parliamentary allowance and had left her almost immediately. In 1814 he had banned her from his court and she had since wandered around the continent with a motley crew of retainers. Their only child, Princess Charlotte, had died in 1817 and the Prince increased the pressure for a divorce. But ministers had no interest in proceedings that would endanger the institution of monarchy by bringing to light details of the Prince's own far from spotless life. When he came to the throne the cabinet unanimously resolved that it would not move on a divorce. After the usual peevish tantrums and threats to retire to Hanover, the King finally relented on condition that Caroline's name be omitted from the prayers for the royal family in the liturgy of the Church of England.

The government tried to rid itself of this embarrassment by offering the Queen an allowance of £50,000 a year in return for surrendering her title and most other rights and staying out of the country. The Duke urbanely proposed sending the handsome young diplomat Sir Frederick Lamb to charm Caroline and her raffish followers into accepting this settlement: 'He should have told them: you are going to lose your golden eggs – you are going to kill your goose! Once in England, and you will not be able to live with her on your present footing and retain your present allowances.'[10] The other ministers ignored this advice and decided instead to deal with the Queen's Attorney General, the brilliant but mercurial Whig barrister Henry Brougham. But he turned out not to have the influence of which he boasted and was unable to prevent the Queen from coming in triumph to England as the darling of the Radicals and self-appointed champion of the people.

So popular was the Queen when she arrived in London after rapturous receptions in towns along the way, that the government feared losing control of the metropolis. There was even a mutiny in the Guards. The complaints were the usual ones of overcrowding, excessive duty and low pay, but the timing linked this insubordination to other grievances gathering wider support by association with the cause of the Queen. When the offending battalion was marched out of town at four in the morning Wellington went to watch and was shaken that the soldiers did not show their customary pleasure at seeing him. He told the Prime Minister that they had left shouting 'the cry of disaffection of the day,' and he was alarmed to think that there was reason to doubt 'the only security we have, not only against revolution but for the property and life of every individual in this country who has anything to lose.' The Duke thought that the fundamental trouble was that the 3,000 Guards were 'all of the class of the people, and even of the lowest of that class.' Perhaps nothing could be done to improve the social composition of the army, but something should be done about a command which permitted the King, the Secretary of State for War, the Commander in Chief, the Field Officer in Waiting, the Gold Stick and the Silver Stick each to send separate and even contradictory orders to the bewildered officers. In any disturbance lasting more than a few days 'nobody knows who is on or off duty, all the troops are harrassed, and the duty is ill done after all.' Wellington considered that a police or special military force would be a far more satisfactory means of keeping order in the capital.[11] But it took Robert Peel, who pursued the issue, nine years to prevail against those who feared that a paramilitary force like those on the continent would mean the end of English liberties, in order to create the Metropolitan Police Force in 1829 when the Duke was Prime Minister.

The Queen, safe in the affections of the citizens of London who continued demonstrating for her and against the ministry, at length graciously indicated that she might consider a settlement. The cabinet despatched Wellington and Castlereagh, correctly turned out in formal dress, to meet her representatives who appeared in equally symbolic plain clothes. But neither side could yield on the liturgy and the talks collapsed after five days. An address from the House of Commons begging the Queen to waive her claims on the prayers had no more effect. This obstinacy allowed her husband to have his way at last, and the reluctant ministers drafted a Bill of Pains and Penalties depriving Caroline of her titles and privileges and dissolving the marriage on grounds of adultery. On 5 July the Bill was introduced in the House of Lords, which as a judicial body had established procedures for hearings. There was also likely to be less controversy there than in the Commons. The 'trial' with counsel and witnesses heard at the bar on second reading was set for 17 August. The interval provided time for the foreign witnesses to arrive and ample opportunity for further expressions of support for the Queen. The Duke continued uneasy about the state of the Guards, though he doubted that the disaffection amounted to more than 'the loose conversation of some in Public Houses,' and considered that 'all will do their Duty under any circumstances when called upon.' Additional troops were nevertheless brought in from the provinces. Wellington was also affected by the misgivings of foreign diplomats about the dubious proceedings touching the monarchy. And he warned the Prime Minister that Lord Eldon, who would preside as Lord Chancellor, was going about declaring that '"There was no Peer who should go down to the House of Lords the first day who could be certain of returning;" which you will agree is not likely to improve the Publick Confidence.'[12]

The examination of witnesses and the arguments of the opposing counsel dragged on for two and a half months. Revelations about the home life of the dear Queen provided much low amusement but did nothing to impair her popularity or reduce the criticism of the King. In this charged situation the government prudently hesitated to apply the restrictions on the press and meetings enacted after Peterloo.

Diverting as the testimony relating to adultery was, the House of Lords did not find it conclusive. On third reading the majority was only nine. If this was all that could be achieved in the Lords there was practically no chance that the bill would survive the House of Commons. The Prime Minister's announcement that it was being withdrawn brought fresh outbursts from the crowds and the palace. The Duke found himself unpopular in the streets and when Parliament reassembled in January he was attacked in the House of Lords by a Whig peer for refusing as Lord Lieutenant of Hampshire to call a meeting to endorse a petition supporting the Queen. With little recent experience of such debating tactics, Wellington gratified the opposition by leaping to his feet and retorting that as he had already presented an address to the King bearing nine thousand loyal signatures, opinion had been sufficiently expressed without 'the farce of a county meeting.' His anger had delivered him into the hands of his adversaries and the phrase was not soon forgotten. When he was immediately accused of contempt for the rights of subjects the Duke tried in vain to repair the damage by insisting that he was willing to admit that 'county meetings, if properly regulated, were a fair constitutional mode of taking the sense of the county; but this could not happen when they were attended by a mob for the express purpose of supporting one side.'[13]

The ministry staggered on despite George IV's threats of dismissal. But in George Canning it lost one of its most able defenders in the House of Commons. He told his colleagues that as an old friend of the Queen he could not be one of her accusers, and offered to resign on the eve of the trial. He was persuaded to stay but went out of the country for most of the hearing. When the bill was dropped in December he announced that he could not remain any longer. Wellington was sent to dissuade him, but Canning recounted that he had been with Caroline when she had received the letter from the King giving her her freedom and taking back his own, and that 'they took advantage of it on the spot.' Having set her on the path that had marked her life ever since, Canning did not think that he could take the position that she was unfit to be Queen.[14] If this was the real reason it did him great credit, but there were many who suspected that Canning was cleverly seizing the opportunity to abandon an apparently sinking ship.

By a combination of luck and good management, the government's fortunes improved in 1821. The Queen lost most of her popularity when she finally agreed to a house and an allowance. Her claim to be crowned with the King in July was rejected by the Privy Council. When she went to Westminster Abbey on the day of the coronation and was told that she would be admitted only as a guest she lost her courage and slunk away to the jeers of her fickle supporters. Her death three weeks later temporarily revived her popularity but the procession through London taking her body back to Brunswick was the last occasion that she could serve as a focus for discontent.

The ministry added to its strength by gaining the tiny band of Grenvillites, essentially Pitt the Younger's family connection, who had stood apart from the Whigs since the end of the war by calling for more repression even than the government. Perhaps because Lord Wellesley was part of this group, the Duke was one of the principal negotiators. On every matter except Catholic emancipation, the Grenvillites moved immediately to the wing of the ministerialists most opposed to change. They were well rewarded for putting the responsibilities of government above the delights of opposition. The Marquess of Buckingham, the titular head of the clan, was promoted duke and others were ensconced in untaxing but sufficiently rewarding posts. Wellesley, who badly needed the income, went to Ireland as Viceroy. At first it had been thought to send his younger brother, but Wellington warned his colleagues: 'Take care that you don't let off your great gun against a sparrow!' In retrospect, however, he regretted the appointment of a supporter of Catholic claims: 'So they sent Lord Wellesley,' he reflected after coming to grief on Ireland himself, 'and after him Lord Anglesey; and the affairs of Ireland, as you see, have gone from bad to worse to my government.'[15]

At the end of 1821, in a move unrelated to the entry of the Grenvillites, Robert Peel became Home Secretary in succession to Sidmouth. Liverpool wanted Canning for the office and was willing to stake his administration on the King's acceptance but the Duke advised that the matter was far too important to turn on George IV's prejudices about Caroline's lovers. Present ministers had to consider their duty: 'Whether we shall bear all that we have to endure, or give up the government to the Whigs and Radicals, or, in other words, the country and its relations to irretrievable ruin?'[16]

After three tempestuous years since his return, it must finally have seemed to Wellington that the government and the country were on an even keel at the beginning of 1822. But the events of that year made those since his return to England pale into insignificance. He lost his closest ally in the cabinet; the ministry changed in an alarming direction, for which he had to bear some responsibility; the threat from outside that could be met by united determination was replaced by internal divisions and subversion; the Duke was dragged into political controversy; and even his health underwent a permanent deterioration.

By the end of the parliamentary session in August, Lord Castlereagh (or Londonderry as he had become in the previous year on succeeding to his father's Irish peerage but remaining in the House of Commons) was so exhausted that he could not get out of bed until mid-afternoon when he had to go back to Parliament. For the first time in his life, Mrs Arbuthnot wrote, he seemed tired of office and anxious to be free of it.[17] The strain of leading the Commons and conducting foreign affairs on the sensitive nature that lay behind a courtliness that impressed even those who saw him as the very symbol of repression had lately been increased by threats of blackmail. On the way home from the Commons three years earlier, he had been enticed into a brothel by what turned out to be a young man in woman's clothes. Those who had organized and burst in on this encounter thereafter waited outside his house to taunt him at his going out and coming in.

Wellington knew of the blackmail attempts and did not try to relieve his old friend's distress when Castlereagh called him into his house in St James's Square as he was riding by. He agreed with the Foreign Secretary that his mind was not in its usual state and urged him to consult Dr Bankhead, the aristocracy's favourite physician. He even offered to put off his annual inspection of the fortresses in the Netherlands, but Castlereagh insisted that he go for fear of the rumours that would be provoked by the delay. From Calais the Duke wrote to Mrs Arbuthnot, to whom with her husband and Dr Bankhead he had entrusted the care of their friend: 'To see a Man with such a sober mind, who one would think could not be influenced by any Illusion in a state bordering upon Insanity is not calculated to raise one's opinion of the strength of the Human mind. Poor Human Nature! How little we are after all!'[18] Just a few days later he was recalled to England by the news that Castlereagh had committed suicide by cutting his throat with a penknife he had secreted in the pocket of his dressing gown when his other sharp instruments were taken away.

At first it seemed that the Duke might be the new Foreign Secretary. He shared Castlereagh's outlook on foreign policy and was even better known and acceptable to the continental rulers. Countess Lieven, the wife of the Russian ambassador, Metternich's mistress (perforce largely by correspondence) and one of Wellington's intimate circle, quizzed him on this as they travelled back from the funeral. 'No,' he told her, 'I don't want to be; that would mean deviating from my position and my career. I should be compelled to adopt the opinions of my party and my individual opinions would no longer be free.' He would take the job if necessary, but he did not think that it would come to that. He had lived outside England for so long that he had lost the habit of speaking in Parliament. But he believed the country's foreign policy was so firmly established that it made practically no difference who actually administered it: 'Listen – I have such confidence in the system that I believe that, if Lord Grey [the Whig leader] were to become Minister today, he would maintain it just as we do.' This faith was amply illustrated when he added that the cabinet had decided on Canning. 'In Heaven's name, don't have him,' Countess Lieven burst out; 'that man will cheat you.'[19]

The reaction of some other ministers was much the same. But Liverpool and most of his colleagues were persuaded that Canning, who was about to leave for India as Governor General in order to find consolation for his political disappointments in accumulating the usual fortune, was essential for the Foreign Office and even more for the House of Commons where the backbenchers were insisting on a strong Leader. Wellington accepted these imperatives and from his high standing in royal favour was in a good position to convince the King to accept the man he despised. By the time George IV returned from a state visit to Scotland, however, the Duke was unable to see him. A month earlier he had stood too far forward at a howitzer demonstration and after suffering pains in his ears ever since he had finally consulted an aurist. The doctor had treated the left ear with a solution of lunar caustic. The tough military veteran could not admit physical discomfort during the operation, even though the acid increased his agony. On the way home he almost fell off his horse while passing a cart loaded with iron bars. After struggling to keep on his feet for a few days he was forced to surrender. 'I never was so unwell,' he told Mrs Arbuthnot,

> as I do not remember before in my life having passed a day in bed. All my efforts to bully & bluster failed for the first time; and strange to say! I was near fainting in the effort to dress myself, & was obliged to give it up. We are sad Creatures after all![20]

When the excruciating pain finally did subside, he discovered that he was permanently deaf in his left ear which, he told Lord Wellesley, 'has deranged my power of hearing very much indeed; and I cannot tell from whence a sound comes.'[21]

Learning that his soundest minister was ill, the King promptly declared that he could not act without his advice, no doubt expecting him to be as opposed to Canning as those staunch Protestant defenders of the old order, Lord Eldon and Lord Sidmouth. But in the midst of his suffering the Duke managed to write a letter in place of an interview. He told Mrs

Arbuthnot: 'I have not been idle; and I think I have been of some use in driving the Nail which we are at present hammering at.'[22] Emphasizing the 'ease and comfort' that the monarch would derive from a minister who would serve with 'ability, zeal and fidelity,' Wellington assured the King that Canning's principles were 'in all the main points of your Majesty's policy, domestic as well as foreign, the same as those of your other servants.' He pointed out that the House of Commons needed a strong Leader; dismissed Eldon's complaints of insult as no more than the common usage of politics; and countered Sidmouth's Protestant fears by pronouncing that there was no reason to think that Canning would use his position unfairly to promote the Catholic cause. Turning to the fundamental objection, Canning's relationship with Caroline, the Duke judiciously observed that the fault lay entirely on Canning's side but assured the gracious sovereign that his honour would be perfectly safe in extending forgiveness to this errant subject in the interests of good government.[23]

On the basis of this impressive testimonial, every word of which Wellington soon bitterly regretted, George IV accepted Canning and praised the Duke as his best, most loyal and most devoted servant for pointing the way out of a difficult situation. Canning was not delighted at the imputation that he had committed some great sin for which royal forgiveness was necessary, but neither did he risk the glittering prize by standing on his dignity.

The appointment of a new Foreign Secretary was simply the most notable of a series of changes between 1821 and 1823 that altered the nature of the ministry. After Canning, Frederick Robinson became Chancellor of the Exchequer and was succeeded as President of the Board by William Huskisson. In the minor adjustments thus entailed, Charles Arbuthnot became First Commissioner of Land Revenue and William Wellesley-Pole, now Lord Maryborough, was removed from the government and 'went to the dogs' as Master of the Royal Buckhounds.

The new ministers, supported by Lord Liverpool, turned their efforts to reform, particularly ones that would stimulate trade. Huskisson, a free trader, tackled tariff barriers while Robinson worked to rationalize taxes and eliminate the chronic budget deficit. Canning, the leader of the group, ostentatiously turned his back on the legitimist regimes of Europe and declared himself the friend of liberty and constitutionalism abroad; states proclaiming these ideals in a far from enthusiastic world were happy to associate with Britain in diplomacy, finance and goods. Peel, whose dedication to the established Protestant order detached him somewhat from these colleagues, was with them in spirit in turning his energies to consolidating and humanizing the law and pressing for a police force for London.

The change from obsession with revolution to piecemeal redress of abuses and anomalies seems modest enough, but it was sufficient to split the ministry into two hostile factions, both of which could appeal to the example of their patron political saint, Pitt the Younger. The Liberal Tories, as historians have called them, trying to make adjustments to promote the interests of an expanding industrial and commercial society, had a fearless and articulate champion in Canning. The Ultra Tories, as they were called even at the time, wanting to preserve things as they were and continuing to fear social and political upheaval, naturally looked to the Duke who had so confidently guaranteed Canning's behaviour. Wellington could not decline the part for which he had blithely volunteered, and from which there proved to be no early or easy retreat.

Whoever had succeeded Castlereagh would have had an awkward relationship with the Duke unless he had been willing to put himself completely under his direction. Wellington was accustomed to being consulted on foreign affairs as a matter of course and was completely unprepared for contradiction. In domestic matters he may have been less sure, but he had no difficulty in detecting any deviation from the principles and their application that he considered had preserved the country from disaster. In every way except for Catholic emancipation, he saw himself as the guardian of Castlereagh's legacy, and, like many in such a position, he was more rigid than the person whose memory he was preserving. In the activities of Canning and his allies he saw the forces of revolution and the destruction of the present excellent order. He was not alone in this nor in the strength of his devotion to the attitude that had dominated the government when he returned to England. But apart from a guilty recognition of his responsibility for Canning's appointment, the violence of his opposition to the reformers undoubtedly owed a good deal to the illnesses that coincided with the change in the ministry.

The operation that left him deaf in his left ear certainly had more serious and lasting complications than Wellington was prepared to admit, and perhaps even realized. While he was still confined to bed Countess Lieven wrote to Metternich that his doctor had told her that he had been in the gravest danger. The inflammation had gone to his head and he had been cupped in order to relieve the congestion.[24] But within a few weeks he was able to make a late start for the Congress of Verona. The long journey, by

41

way of Vienna where the meeting had originally assembled, was a great ordeal and he arrived in Italy exhausted and suffering from a cold. Bravely he told Mrs Arbuthnot that all was well: 'I am going on as usual. Sometimes I do not feel very secure in my Ballance. Yet I am as strong & stout as ever in other respects.'[25] Those who had not seen him for a few years, however, saw a great decline. The strain of the conference did nothing to speed his recovery and in England Lord Liverpool pointedly told Charles Arbuthnot that they must ensure that the Duke took care of himself when he returned:

> He has had a strong warning which comes upon every man a little sooner or later when he approaches or is past fifty, and he will feel himself compel'd to alter his mode of life. It is most unlucky that he should not find in domestick comforts a proportion at least of that repose he now so much wants.[26]

The following January, perhaps owing to his lack of balance, he was struck on the side and knocked down by a gig. Mrs Arbuthnot thought it pure luck that he was not killed. A few weeks later he finally admitted that he had suffered inflammatory attacks ever since the operation and had to be careful of himself and what he ate. At the same time he railed against the restrictions that Dr Hume tried to impose on him. When the doctor wanted to bleed him, he replied that he would have to wait twelve hours, 'because I had matters to attend to, which would take me till that Hour; as if I can sit at home with my hands before me, doing nothing or asleep in my chair!!!' When Hume wanted to prevent him from dining out, he countered: 'if one neither eats nor drinks it cannot much signify where one sits during dinner time; and it cannot hurt me to go in my Carriage from my own House to that in which I dine & to return.'

When Hume appealed to Mrs Arbuthnot for help in restraining his patient, Wellington's anger knew no bounds. 'All Doctors are more or less *Quacks!*' he burst out,

> and there is nothing more comical than that Dr. Hume should have made you believe that I am an *Idiot!* rather than the truth, that he as well as others of the Medical Profession is a bit of a *Charlatan!* ... I know what is good for me as well [as] Dr. Hume or any Doctor of the Profession.

Seizing on the advice to relax in the country, he claimed that it was no worse for him to dine quietly with a dozen people in London than with sixteen at Stratfield Saye, 'every Man, Woman & Child of whom expects

that the Duke of W. will amuse them all day and all night long, & who,
will not be amused otherwise; for this is always the case *chez moi!*' Going
sixty miles in a carriage was no worse than twenty-five in a cabriolet and
then another thirty on horseback following the hounds. As for more rest,
nothing did him more harm than lying in bed:

> I am never unwell but at night; and I get well from the moment I rise
> in the morning, & better till I go to bed again. The whole Medical
> profession cannot tell the reason any more than they can tell now
> whether I am deaf or not, or whether I shall ever hear again; or what
> I am to do to hear.[27]

Given the state of the medical arts at the time, the Duke may have been
wise in sticking to his own prescription. But this did not restore him to
perfect health. In May he was ill for several days with a stomach ailment
and just before Christmas 1823, a member of the government wrote that
he had had another attack, 'similar to that which he experienced last
winter, and previous to his journey to the Congress. It was very alarming
while it lasted, but by copious bleeding he was relieved.' He added that
Wellington was anxious to keep this illness secret and professed himself
quite well, 'but you may reply upon it he is quite otherwise, and when I
last saw him nothing could look more wretched or broken.' In the spring
of 1824 the same minister reported that the Duke had again been
alarmingly ill and was still in danger, though once more the whole matter
was being kept secret: 'On Wednesday or Thursday, I don't know which,
he was seized with a violent bowel attack, which was with difficulty
removed by calomel (*I believe*). On Thursday he was better, but yesterday
had a relapse, and the fear was that it was cholera morbus.'[28]

It is hard to know what to make of this scanty evidence on the nature,
severity, duration and frequency of the Duke's ailments. The various
illnesses may have been linked by common symptoms or they may have
been separate afflictions. Some of them may have been continuing
complications from the operation on his ear, particularly if the arteries to
the brain had been damaged. It is also possible that he had recurring bouts
of malaria from India, where he first suffered fevers, or had infections of
the digestive organs, as suggested by cholera morbus. Wellington had to
endure the bloodletting, purges and medicines inflicted on him by his
physicians, but he knew that he could get the better of his illnesses and the
arthritis and rheumatism that were gaining on him and wring the most out
of his physical frame by an austere lifestyle, eating and drinking little,
keeping warm and dry, not spending much time in bed, and adhering to a

busy, ordered routine.

The Duke was clearly quite ill for a couple of years after Canning's appointment, and never again did he enjoy the robust health of his first fifty years, despite the impression he continued to convey and even believed himself most of the time. The state of his health reinforced his natural pessimism and affected the tone and style of his struggle with the Foreign Secretary and his allies, which was simply one of a series that lasted to the end of his life. Others adapted to new circumstances, but, largely immune from the pressures that affected even most of the aristocracy, Wellington endeavoured to cleave to the simple, ancient verities preserved from the period before Castlereagh's death. To himself at least, the vigour and consistency with which he continued to proclaim them were proof that age and debility were still being held at bay.

From a detached point of view the differences between the Duke and Canning were more ones of emphasis and style than substance, but the clashes were real enough. A year after the Foreign Secretary's appointment Wellington conceded that Countess Lieven had been right in her warning, clutching his head and telling her: 'How foolish, how stupid, how blind I was to put that man into the Cabinet!'[29] Every question was studied in advance by Canning and Liverpool and only the parts that they chose were brought to the other ministers, who felt that they were treading on a mine. 'In short,' he told Mrs Arbuthnot who mourned with him how much better business had been ordered under their dear departed friend, 'things were no longer managed in the fair, honest, open way which he had been accustomed to, & . . . he was completely disgusted with the state of affairs.'[30] Cabinet meetings frequently degenerated into shouting matches between Wellington and Canning. The Prime Minister was also a prime target for having abandoned the principles on which his government had been based. Arriving at a dinner hot from the House of Lords in the summer of 1823, the Duke roared at the astonished company: *'My Lord Liverpool is neither more nor less than a common prostitute.'* Only when he noticed that there were women present did he mumble a few words of apology, while the others tried to cover their embarrassment with laughter.[31]

By the time of this outburst the Duke of York and other Ultras were pressing their champion to prepare to put himself forward as Prime Minister if Liverpool resigned. Wellington did not believe that Canning would ever be offered the post – 'No, no, no! Impossible! Out of the question! He would be thrown out twenty times before one of us budged'

– but he did agree to be a candidate if necessary to prevent it. When Countess Lieven reminded him of his talk about lacking parliamentary experience, he showed none of the hesitation he had at the time of Castlereagh's death: 'To begin with, I can learn: if I want it, it will come back to me. And even if I can't, the Duke of Portland had no more idea of speaking than I have; and yet he was at the head of the administration.'[32]

The truth of the matter, whatever he thought, was that the Duke did not understand the country's complex worldwide diplomatic and commercial interests as well as either Canning or Castlereagh. He was above all sympathetic to the legitimist rulers of Europe and fearful of anything that altered the post-war settlement which, with pride of authorship, he considered a bulwark against revolution and renewed hostilities. Charles Arbuthnot told Lord Bathurst that he believed 'our Adherence to the Quintuple Alliance & the Preservation of the Peace of the World to be so blended together that he for one never wd agree to anything wch was to separate us from the Continental Powers'.[33] Even Castlereagh had been working to disentangle the country from continental powers' obligations and had refused any automatic commitment to oppose change in countries which traded with England. Canning did not go much further, but his boastful manner, dramatic pronouncements and arrogant disregard for the views of his colleagues created the impression that he was embarking on a new course. Wellington was soon convinced that he knew 'no more of foreign politics than a child & had neither temper nor address to deal with foreigners; that he so managed as to be completely in the dark about what was going on. None of the Foreign ministers confided in him.' He told Mrs Arbuthnot that he would cut his hand off before recommending Canning again as he had after Castlereagh's death.[34]

The Duke, the King and the Ultras would have accepted Canning's foreign policy without question from the circumspect Castlereagh in whom they reposed their trust. This was in effect what Wellington did when he went to the Congress of Verona. He told the other great powers that Britain would not support a French invasion of Spain to free Ferdinand VII from the revolutionaries who were forcing him to submit to the constitution and national assembly he had accepted at the time of his restoration in 1814 but shortly thereafter suspended. This was certainly what Canning wanted, but the instructions had been drafted by Castlereagh. The Duke tried to use his standing as the liberator as well as grandee and landowner in Spain to persuade the government to avoid war by giving the King more power. His efforts came to nothing, but his conciliatory efforts were in the spirit of both past and present Foreign Secretaries.

When France, despite Britain's refusal of support, invaded Spain in the spring of 1823, matters went beyond what Castlereagh had foreseen. Canning was determined that the occupation should be only temporary and that Portugal should not be attacked. But above all the liberated colonies in South America should not be conquered by France in the name of Spain. British merchants were looking for an expansion of their already prosperous trade in those states, to which Castlereagh had given *de facto* recognition a few months before his death. With the French army in Spain, Canning increased the resistance by appointing consuls to the ports and pressing for full recognition to prevent them from falling into the orbit of the United States, which recognized them in 1822 and at the end of 1823 proclaimed the Monroe Doctrine against European intervention in the Western Hemisphere. Castlereagh would probably have done much the same, but Wellington was thoroughly alarmed that Canning should be supporting rebels against legitimate authority at the very moment that the same danger was looming in Ireland, a prospect hailed by 'the bad with hope, the good with apprehension and dread.' He warned the Foreign Secretary not to be induced 'by clamour, by self-interested views, by stock-jobbing, or by faction, to give the sanction of our approbation to what are called the governments of these insurgent provinces.'[35] He confided to Mrs Arbuthnot his fears that the Prime Minister, now 'the slave of Mr Canning,' was working to break away from the other European powers in order to join 'the revolutionary rascals and blackguards of Europe and America.'[36]

This was exactly the view of George IV. He and the Duke drew close together and found much mutual comfort in abusing Canning's policy towards South America. But Wellington refused to go further and act as the monarch's henchman in getting rid of Liverpool. He sternly warned the King that 'in these times no publick Man could be borne, or could serve the King or himself, who should allow himself to be made the Instrument of an Intrigue against another.'[37] Wellington's close ties nevertheless led him to be regarded as the royal spokesman in the cabinet. He in turn complained that everyone avoided him 'from fear of any appearance of intrigue, & ... those who thought with him still constantly sided against him from this feeling.' He felt so isolated that he said he would resign immediately if the King expressed any intention of appointing him as Liverpool's successor. Charles Arbuthnot became so alarmed at the danger of the Duke's departure that he appealed to that kindred spirit, Lord Bathurst, not to remain silent but to voice his support when their friend spoke in cabinet.[38]

At the end of 1824 Wellington tried to stop the recognition of the South American states by threatening his resignation. He grudgingly conceded that a form of recognition at some time would be necessary, but recommended that this be delayed as long as possible. He warned the Prime Minister that Britain's influence would end at the moment of recognition, but the risk of war with Spain, 'a Power whose only strength is its nakedness,' would increase. He reminded Liverpool that he had come into his government 'to support yourself and the principles on which you had been acting, and for which we had struggled in the field,' and made it clear that he was willing to leave whenever the Prime Minister wanted. But Liverpool would not budge. He told the Duke that he had not formed his judgment hastily and considered that refusing recognition would be fatal to British interests and perhaps safety. Without taking issue with Wellington's views directly, he dismissed the King's as the product of ignorance and observed that 'the opinions which he sometimes avows upon the subject of legitimacy would carry him to the full length of the principles of the Emperor of Russia and Prince Metternich.'[39]

This sharp and uncompromising riposte might have settled the matter if the Duke really had been prepared to go, thereby weakening if not destroying the ministry. But, unwilling to take that step, he made one last bid by trying to enlist the support of Peel, the colleague in the House of Commons most likely to be sympathetic to his stand. He told the Home Secretary that Christmas Day at the Royal Lodge had been enlivened by the monarch's brilliant analysis of the government's inconsistency in prosecuting the Irish leader Daniel O'Connell, who was appealing to the example of Bolivar (with whom he had sent his son to fight), while at the same time preparing to recognize Bolivar as ruler of Colombia. Such reasoning, Wellington observed with satisfaction, could be answered only by splitting hairs, 'which, for a great country like this, and in great questions, is the worst of all systems.' Unfortunately Peel was unimpressed by this logic and briskly replied that O'Connell would be charged with sedition for his activities, no matter whom he appealed to for legitimacy, Bolivar, Washington or even Wellington himself. At this sad news the Duke knew he was beaten. In resigned but unconvincing tones he told Peel: 'I shall be satisfied with what you may determine to do.'[40] Liverpool and Canning were already converting the other sceptics in the cabinet by threats of resignation and early in 1825 the King with scant grace accepted the recognition of Mexico, Buenos Aires, Colombia, and later in the year the monarchical empire of Brazil.

As the Duke indicated to Peel, the diplomatic issue was closely related to the problem of Ireland that was urgently forcing itself on the ministry's attention in the early 1820s. The end of the war had produced not only a general collapse of agricultural prices but also bad harvests of potatoes on which most of the population of Ireland lived. Famine, illness and econmic suffering resulted on a scale that was eclipsed only by the greater tragedy a quarter of a century later. In 1822 there was a further small famine. Pondering the condition of the land of his birth in that year, Wellington thought that the country was 'fated from her peculiar circumstances to be always at war against the laws.' Some remedy would be afforded by the landlords' residing on their estates, taking their part as magistrates and gaining the goodwill of the peasants by the seasonable exercise of paternalism; but as this could not be enforced by legislation, the government had no alternative but to appoint special commissions to hang and banish as many of the lawbreakers as they could catch. The landlords must expect their property to suffer.[41] Two years later the Duke thought that residence could be encouraged by imposing a heavy tax on absentees. The clergy of the Church of Ireland should be compelled to live in their parishes and pluralism forbidden. The practice of providing labourers with plots of land should also be prohibited; agricultural workers should instead be paid money wages, which would force them to buy their food in the market, stimulate their desire for material goods and encourage men to postpone marriage until they could afford to support a family. Unless this change were made, he predicted with gloomy prescience, 'all Ireland will be a nest of paupers dependent upon England for food.'[42]

Desirable as a comprehensive reconstruction of the Irish economy and system of land tenure might be, law and order were more pressing. The drunken joviality of the monarch on his visit in 1821 had increased his personal popularity but did nothing to reduce political discontent. Nor did the appointment of a supporter of Catholic emancipation as Viceroy the following year. Wellesley was unpopular with the Dublin tradesmen because he could not afford to live in the style expected of the Lord Lieutenant, and no less so with the Protestants for his open partiality towards Catholics. The opposite antipathy was aroused by the Chief Secretary, Henry Goulburn, a Protestant so strong that the Catholics believed he was an Orangeman. In 1823 Daniel O'Connell, an eloquent barrister and tireless opponent of the union with Britain, formed the Catholic Association which quickly became a national movement for full political rights. Speakers from Dublin addressed eager gatherings all over the country; priests collected the 'Catholic rent' to pay for the

Association's activities; and in the capital debates were held on political issues. By the end of 1824 the Catholic Association was becoming a state within the state and expanding its activities to the Irish population in the North of England.

Wellington took the gravest view of these activities, telling Peel that the disaffected were better organized than they had been in 1798, the year of rebellion. The Association would be able to buy good arms if it raised enough money, and he urged the Home Secretary to look to the military resources of the country. The army would no doubt triumph in a civil war, but it was far better to suppress the new Association as soon as possible; even after a military success, 'We should find the same enemies blasting the prosperity of the country, and ready to take advantage of the weakness of this country at any moment to do us all the harm in their power.'[43] Hard on the Duke's heels was the King, who warned the Prime Minister that if the lawlessness continued he would not allow Catholic emancipation to remain an open question in the government.[44] Wellington did not disagree with the King's Protestant sentiments, but pointed out that a mixed administration was a surer defence than a purely Protestant one that would probably be defeated in the House of Commons.[45]

The success of the Catholic Association and the failure to secure a charge of sedition against O'Connell resulted in a measure banning all political associations in Ireland; this proved ineffective against the Association, which reconstituted itself to evade the terms of the act, but it had occasionally to be invoked against the Orangemen. The excitement also emboldened those favouring emancipation to find a solution acceptable to Parliament. A relief bill was introduced in the Commons, accompanied by two supplementary measures, 'the wings,' raising the property qualification for the franchise and providing for state payment, and thereby some control of the Catholic clergy. These easily passed the Commons and Protestant ministers quailed lest the House of Lords also be seduced by the securities.

To all outward appearance the Duke of Wellington was unwavering in his defence of the Protestant constitution. He called for a large increase of troops in Ireland and told his colleagues: 'We must get the better of this rebellion immediately, or we shall have the whole world in arms against us; whether secretly or otherwise will not much signify.' But he also repeated that force alone could not solve the problem: 'Let the Roman Catholic Association be put down to-morrow, the organization will still exist in the hands of Mr. O'Connell and his associates.'[46] The Emancipation Bill must be fought 'tooth & nail' owing to 'the mode of executing the measure & not from any illiberal bigotry,' but once it had been defeated those dedicated to the Protestant interest must find a permanent solution and persuade the King to yield. For himself he declared that he would support anything that would protect the landlords and control the Catholic church.[47]

The Duke elaborated these startling views in a long paper. He pointed out that despite both harshness and concession throughout the eighteenth century, the Catholic party was as strong as ever and was only kept down in the last resort by English arms. There was not a Protestant landlord in Ireland who did not fear a sudden and general uprising. The majority in favour of emancipation in the Commons was bound to increase and even in the Lords the Protestant cause was safe only as long as Liverpool and Eldon retained their places. The present ministers had an obligation to tackle the matter in a way that would control the change and preserve as much as possible of the existing order while they still enjoyed the safeguards of the House of Lords, forced tranquillity in Ireland and universal respect for the government. They could not shirk their obligations and abandon the King and their Protestant supporters by resignation. Some agreement with the Pope was essential, difficult as negotiations might be, because it alone would make it safe to repeal the discriminatory legislation.[48] Wellington could not make a public statement of this advice, and apart from Peel, Liverpool, the Arbuthnots and a few others, there was no reason for anyone to think that his attitude was distinguishable from Lord Eldon's.

The immediate danger passed when the Emancipation Bill was decisively rejected by the Lords in a vote of 178 to 130. The debate featured a ringing declaration from the Duke of York, the heir presumptive whose splendid physique seemed to ensure him a long succession to his decayed brother, that he would uphold the priciples to the end of his life. Wellington complained that this gave 'all the low, shabby people in Parliament a sort of standard to which they may rally, which would prevent them from supporting anything of which the object might be a settlement.'[49] But his advice to the Prime Minister to seize the opportunity presented by this Protestant enthusiasm to increase the administration's strength in the House of Commons did nothing to convince anyone that he had budged an inch on Catholic emancipation. Liverpool instead accepted Canning's plea to postpone dissolution until 1826 in return for a promise that the Catholic question would not be raised until the new Parliament met.

In the midst of these strong feelings about Catholics and Ireland, Marianne

Paterson told the Duke that she was going to Dublin to marry his brother. This was a triple blow indeed. Mrs Paterson and her then unmarried sisters, Louisa (successively Lady Harvey and Duchess of Leeds) and Elizabeth (later Lady Stafford), the 'three Graces' from Baltimore, had been leading lights among Wellington's admirers in France after Waterloo. He developed a strong attachment to her, though the friendship diminished when she returned to the United States. When her husband died in 1822 Mrs Paterson hastened to England in the hope of emulating the good fortune of her sisters. At Stratfield Saye she met Lord Wellesley, as fatally attractive to women as ever. No doubt seeing a chance to restore his vanished fortunes by marrying the reputedly rich widow as well as the satisfaction of taking her away from his overweening brother, Wellesley decided on a union with a woman whose sister-in-law, Betsy Paterson, had for a time been married to Napoleon's brother Jerome. As a supporter of Catholic rights he had no objection to that being her religion.

When Wellington heard of the proposed marriage he was dumbfounded. He wrote immediately to Mrs Paterson, warning that his brother was totally ruined and when he left Ireland would not even have a house to take her to or money to keep a carriage: 'he had not a shilling in the world &, moreover, was of a jealous disposition, a violent temper & . . . he had entirely worn out his constitution by the profligate habits of his life.'[50] Mrs Paterson discovered the truth of all this soon enough, but she was not to be put off what seemed an advantageous match by the impotent ravings of a frustrated lover. When it was clear that she would not be deterred, Wellington salvaged something of the friendship by congratulating his brother, telling him that 'in disposition temper sense acquirements and manners she is the equal if not the superior to any Woman of any Country with whom I have ever been in Society.' He hoped the marriage would make Wellesley happy and 'afford me additional opportunities of Intercourse and Society with you.'[51]

By the time of the wedding, however, the Duke had lost his benign equanimity. It was bad enough that an official who by law had to be a member of the Established Church was marrying a Catholic, but when he flaunted his sympathies by having the Anglican ceremony followed by a Catholic one at which the Archbishop of Dublin officiated in his vestments, Wellington was not alone in angry astonishment. The King fulminated at this desecration of his Irish palace while the Duke asked Peel if it was not illegal for the Archbishop to appear robed. The Home Secretary certainly agreed that it was unwise in the state of Protestant feeling, but in Ireland, unlike England, it was not illegal.[52] Other ministers hoped that the Viceroy's wife, Catholic or not, would do something to curb the excesses of his conduct. But Wellesley's roving eye had only momentarily fixed on one object and the new Marchioness quickly found herself in the midst of the sordid quarrels that were a feature of her husband's home life. The Duke was full of bitterness and concern, but three months after the wedding, at the beginning of February 1826, he was able to manage a civil letter in response to Wellesley's inquiry about the state of his health as he prepared to leave for Russia. Wellington wrote that he was delighted to hear of his brother's 'domestick Happiness' and assured him that he was equal to the arduous journey. 'It is impossible to say whether I shall succeed in maintaining the peace of the World,' he told Wellesley. 'But I will do the very best thing I can.'[53]

The Duke did not exaggerate his mission, which was to try to prevent war between Russia and the Ottoman Empire over Greece. The occasion was the death of Alexander I in December 1825 and, after a revolt in favour of another brother, the succession of his brother as Nicholas I. Wellington was the obvious person to send with British condolences and congratulations. Although he was just recovering from an illness, he assured the Foreign Secretary that he was well enough to go. Canning was nothing loath to lose his antagonist to the Russian winter for a while, and rightly observed that 'the selection of *another* person would have done his health more prejudice than all the frosts and thaws of the hyperborean regions can do it.'[54] As the funeral was not to be held until April, there was ample time to consider the Duke's instructions. Canning, despite his nationalist sympathies, had no intention of going to war for 'Aristides or St. Paul' against the Ottoman empire, which was the chief barrier to Russian expansion into the Mediterranean. He decided that the least dangerous course was a joint demand with Russia that Constantinople recognize the Greek claims. This was endorsed by the Russian ambassador, Count Lieven, and his wife who now saw virtues in the man they had previously despised. They also pressed for Wellington as emissary.

This was not the most welcome mission the Duke had ever undertaken, but he could not refuse and undoubtedly felt that he could handle the delicate negotiations better than anyone else. It took him a month, travelling fourteen to sixteen hours a day over thawing roads, to reach St Petersburg at the beginning of March. The new emperor received him like a member of the family. Three weeks later the 'terrible ceremony' he had been sent to attend was finally held. Wellington found the Orthodox liturgy moving, but he was astounded at the lamentations of the mourners:

'it might really have been believed that the Deceased had been carried off only the preceding Week, instead of nearly four Months ago; and that nothing had occurred to divert the attention of His family, attendants, friends and Subjects from their Grief for his Loss.' He was also relieved that the decaying corpse was to be buried at last.[55]

In the diplomatic negotiations the Duke and the emperor were in amicable agreement in their low view of the Greeks as rebels. The Russian ruler nevertheless had reasons for wanting to support them against the Turks. The soundness of this exceptionally autocratic Tsar's outlook and the presence of Count Lieven induced Wellington to go further in agreeing with him than Canning would have liked. They decided that Greece should remain nominally subject to the Ottoman empire and continue paying tribute, but it would be governed by its own authorities and enjoy freedom of religion and trade. This did not eliminate the possibility of war and much depended, as the Duke wrote from Russia, 'upon the Prudence of the Turks, upon the Advice to be given to them, & the degree of Energy in giving that advice, & not upon the measures adopted here.'[56] The pact between Britain and Russia was extended to include France; a provision, to which Wellington objected, was added to support the arrangement by force if necessary; and the three countries despatched a fleet to the eastern Mediterranean for this purpose. The Turks did not desist from their repression, in October 1827 their fleet was destroyed at Navarino by the allied squadron, and war began between the Russian and Ottoman empires. By that time Canning, who might have forbidden the use of arms, was dead and Wellington was no longer in the government. But both his condemnation of the bombardment in support of the heroes of liberal Europe and the negotiations which had laid the groundwork for the attack proved easy targets at a vulnerable moment.

On his return the Duke discovered that the situation in the cabinet had not improved in the last three months. Canning, who would have been glad to have him remain in Russia for the coronation, had used his time to advantage with the King and Wellington discovered that he was not as welcome as before at the Royal Lodge. He also detected a plot to abolish the corn laws under the pretext of relieving the distress caused by the economic collapse of 1825. The 1815 law had already been modified in 1822, but the price necessary to bring the new scale into effect had never been reached. With an election pending, the divided government struggled to find a compromise that would satisfy both the agricultural and urban interests. Canning and Huskisson kept the issue out of Parliament by promising the opposition that they would have something to propose after the election. In the meantime the duties were temporarily suspended to meet the immediate suffering.

The corn laws were bound to be an issue for the candidates. When Huskisson told his electors at Liverpool that he favoured complete free trade in grain, the Duke angrily protested to the Prime Minister:

> We shall by-and-by be told that opinions have been given upon this subject, and that the measures which the government might advise cannot be adopted, because certain individuals have given such opinions. The discretion of the Cabinet is thus tied up by those individuals, and the discussion comes to be one of the existence or non-existence [of the ministry], instead of one upon the merits of the particular question.

Liverpool tried to soothe Wellington's fears by claiming that Huskisson's speech had probably been exaggerated in the press, though he added that '*some alteration* in the law is absolutely necessary; but I consider myself as wholly uncommitted even to the *principle* upon which that alteration is to be made.'[57] Everything pointed to bitter division in 1827 when the corn laws would be discussed at the very time that the Catholic question would be raised once more.

Shortly after the election Wellington's relations with the Prime Minister were strained almost to breaking point over a matter of family patronage. In August Lord Wellesley wrote to Liverpool proposing his brother Gerald for an Irish bishopric. Ten years before, to the great annoyance of Wellesley and the Duke, the Prime Minister had refused an appointment to the English episcopate on the grounds that Gerald was living apart from his wife. Although he refused to seek a divorce out of consideration for his children, his restraint cast unfavourable implications on his own conduct. The Viceroy now expressed the hope that the passage of time, Gerald's irreproachable conduct and the approbation of the Bishop of London and the Archbishop of Canterbury had altered the case. At the same time he professed himself unwilling to recommend anything contrary to the high principles he claimed to share with Liverpool and expressed himself content to accept whatever he decided.[58] On the same day, however, he wrote to Wellington urging him to press Liverpool strongly on the appointment.[59] When the Prime Minister refused on the grounds that it would cause a scandal in the most criticized established church in all Europe and because the Lord Lieutenant would be accused of doing for a brother what he would not do for anyone else, Wellesley languidly expressed compliance. But once more he exhorted the Duke not to abandon their brother and assured him that there were ample grounds for disputing the decision.[60]

Wellington did not hesitate to take up the cudgels for family honour. In a long letter to Liverpool he protested that the Prime Minister had persistently refused to do anything for Gerald. He pointed out that his interference in this appointment was not strictly called for, and told him that he should at least have made careful inquiries about Gerald's conduct before forbidding his elevation. He claimed that the King was anxious to see Gerald well provided for. And he observed that even the objectionable Dean of Christ Church (who had rusticated the Duke's son Charles the year before) had been appointed Dean of Durham, while all the government had ever done for Gerald was to offer him a living in Yorkshire that was not worth his trouble to accept. No one, Wellington went on, had served the Prime Minister more faithfully than he. All he asked in return was 'justice, forbearance from prejudice and passion, and fair, candid, and deliberate inquiry previous to decision; and I am willing to abide by the result.' Liverpool confined himself to a soft answer that he hoped might turn away further wrath, but a week later he recited to Charles Arbuthnot all that he had done for the Duke's family during his years in office: pensions for his mother and sister, a good office for his brother-in-law, and cabinet office and later a peerage for Wellesley-Pole. 'I have, in fact,' he pointed out, 'done much more for them than I have for my own.'[61] The Prime Minister knew that he could rely on Arbuthnot to disobey his instructions not to mention this to Wellington, and a week later he reinforced this by requesting Arbuthnot to show the letters from Wellesley to the Duke.[62] The revelation produced an immediate coolness between Wellington and his brother. It may not have distressed Wellesley much at the moment, but when he returned from Ireland in financial need, the Duke did not lift a finger to help him. Gerald came out of it well enough. When two bishops died early in 1827, Liverpool provided him with a rich living in the North and arranged for him to exchange his stall in St Paul's for one in Durham Cathedral.[63]

Before this reasonably happy resolution, the handling of Gerald's claims for promotion simply provided more material for Wellington's disgust with politics and the low esteem in which he held those who controlled real power. Charles Arbuthnot warned the Prime Minister that the Duke had been dissatisfied with foreign policy ever since the death of

Castlereagh. If Canning failed to avert the war that seemed imminent between Spain and Portugal, he would certainly resign; and if domestic matters were discussed in Parliament before being settled in cabinet, he would feel free to oppose them.[64] Fortunately for all parties, war in the Peninsula was forestalled by Canning's despatch of troops to 'the well-known heights of Lisbon' to defend the constitutional government of that country against the restored absolutism in Spain. In the House of Lords the most famous veteran of the last intervention reluctantly supported Canning's daring act in the hope that it would bring the King of Spain to 'that sense of what was due to himself and his own dignity, which would prevent him from allowing any aggression on the territories of his neighbour, our near ally.'[65] For the moment at least Wellington abandoned his talk of resignation.

At the beginning of 1827 the Duke of York succumbed to the dropsy that had overtaken his formerly strong frame. The Duke of Wellington was the obvious person to succeed him as Commander in Chief. But despite the King's virtual promise in the happy days when they had been political soulmates, he now muttered about giving the post to the Duke of Cambridge or even taking it himself. The Duke left the capital to avoid any appearance of intrigue for the appointment, morosely regarding George IV's promise, 'like so many others, as so many empty and unmeaning words and phrases.' But if the monarch announced any intention of taking the command himself, he would protest 'in the most formal manner, and with all the earnestness in my power, for the sake of the army, for that of the government, and, above all, for the sake of the public.'[66] The Prime Minister, keeping a better sense of proportion, dismissed the King's notion as 'so preposterous that if I hear of it, which I do not think likely, I shall have no difficulty in resisting it.'[67] His recommendation of Wellington as Commander in Chief was accepted without a murmur.

The Duke could well have decided at this point that one office was sufficient and have retired from the ministry. Even if he wanted to remain in the cabinet, the united command of the army provided him with ample reason to concentrate on military affairs and to withdraw from the day-to-day concerns with general political issues into which he had been drawn in the last four years. But he was scarcely installed in his new office when Liverpool collapsed from a stroke. The whole political world was plunged into uncertainty from which Wellington could not possibly remain detached.

CHAPTER THREE

CHAOS AND ORDER

IT WAS six weeks before Lord Liverpool recovered to the point of being able to reply to his wife's comforting assurances that he would soon be well enough to resume his duties, 'No, no, not I – too weak, too weak.'[1] In the interval there was much speculation about his replacement, but it was in everyone's interests to postpone a decision. The King refused to discuss the matter, telling Canning that 'it would be a great satisfaction to us all, when Lord Liverpool came to himself sufficiently to learn what had passed, that there had been no step taken, or even mooted, for the disposal of his succession.'[2]

The Duke of Wellington, as Commander in Chief, seemed out of the running; and those who had rejoiced at his appointment only a few days ago were now regretting it. When J.W. Croker, Secretary of the Admiralty and Tory polemicist, tried to draw him out on his intentions the day after Liverpool's collapse, the Duke told him: 'I am in my proper place, in the place to which I was destined by my trade. I am a soldier, and am in my place at the head of the army, as the Chancellor, who is a lawyer, is in his place on the woolsack.' His sole desire was to keep the present government together, for 'after them *comes chaos.*'[3] The best way to ensure continuity was to find some Protestant peer under whom all Liverpool's ministers would serve: 'it wd be a *pis aller*, but better than having the Whigs.'[4] When the Ultras proposed a representation to the King to make Wellington Prime Minister as well as Commander in Chief, to preserve what was blandly described as 'a balanced government without Mr Canning's assistance,' he prevented them from 'a thousand follies' by telling them that this would be a highly indecorous encroachment on the royal prerogative.[5]

Canning was nevertheless the person to stop. He would probably not serve under anyone else and in opposition he would be fatal. The King was now pleased with the foreign policy that had raised the prestige of the country and thereby his own. Canning took pains to amuse him and was solicitous in the use of patronage to royal advantage. He was committed to Catholic emancipation but he also had the skill to prevent it from succeeding. In Lady Conyngham, the King's mistress, and Sir William Knighton, formerly the royal physician and now confidential adviser as Keeper of the Privy Purse, he had powerful advocates. And during Liverpool's incapacity Canning demonstrated his parliamentary ability by undertaking successfully to persuade the House of Commons to accept a sliding scale of duties on corn from 20s. a quarter when the domestic price was 60s to 1s. at 70s. and above. He supported a Radical motion to remove Catholic disabilities, but its failure in a House slightly more Protestant than the one before the election did his ambitions no harm.

The main task of Canning's partisans was to secure the support of the Duke, who would be followed by most of the Ultras and the uncommitted. Wellington carefully avoided the King to prevent any charge of intrigue before a decision was made. Knighton took advantage of this to tell him and Arbuthnot that the King was going to appoint Canning. He added that Eldon would have to go because he neglected his judicial business, but the Duke would have to stay 'because he was the person that forced Canning upon the King.' Wellington did not deign to reply to this transparent attempt to get him to commit himself; but Arbuthnot was so badly rattled that the next day he hurried to Knighton to impress on him Canning's unsuitability, the necessity of a Protestant Prime Minister to keep the Catholic question quiet, and to praise the qualifications of the Duke of Wellington. When the Duke heard of this he was furious. He said nothing to Arbuthnot but told his wife that he had 'never in his life asked for any thing or put himself forward in any way for political aggrandisement that, please God!, he never will, and that he would rather serve under Mr Canning than be supposed to quit from anything like personal pique.' He would not embarrass the King by putting himself at the head of any faction. And he told Knighton, to the latter's great satisfaction, that he was out of the question as Prime Minister.

Shortly afterwards the King made a brief appearance in London to present Wellington with what Mrs Arbuthnot called a 'foolish collar' of enamelled gold marking his victories, in the hope that it would keep him in good humour. The next day they had a talk at Windsor and agreed that the Duke's position in the army made it impossible for him to be considered as Prime Minister. Wellington was relieved that the monarch apparently also ruled out Canning on the grounds of his Catholic principles, and hoped that things might go on as they were under Lord Bathurst or Lord Bexley.[6]

Once it was clear that Liverpool would not recover, the bidding became more intense. Knighton produced a letter for the King from a whip in the Commons stating that the best way to ensure a continuation of Liverpool's policies was to have Canning form a ministry on precisely the same basis, 'retaining with him all those who will give him their cordial support and co-operation, leaving to him the selection of new persons in the place of those who decline.' The whip deplored the efforts of the Ultras to jeopardize the 'unrivalled fame of his Grace, shining with higher lustre than ever in the great duties of Commander in Chief' by promoting him as the head of an exclusively Tory government.[7]

Two days later George IV tried out this proposal on the Duke, conveying the impression that he was reluctant to appoint Canning but feared to lose him. When Wellington raised the Catholic issue, the King to his amazement told him that he had assurances from Canning that the Whigs were anxious to keep the matter quiet. His suspicions about the Foreign Secretary's intrigues with the opposition, fuelled by the recent appointment of Whig relatives to office, now suddenly confirmed, the Duke could not contain himself: 'And now, Sir, can Yr Majesty be surprised that the Tory Party detest Mr Canning? Can you be surprised that they cabal against him as a measure of defence against a man who is himself engaged in such a cabal as this?' The King angrily retorted with similar charges against the Ultra peers, but Wellington insisted that there had been no plot and that he had himself kept them in check.[8]

Realizing that the opposition to Canning was far stronger than he had been led to believe, George IV tried to find some arrangement that would keep Canning at his post under someone else as Prime Minister. When he instructed Canning to find a basis on which the present government could continue, the Foreign Secretary discussed the matter for three hours with the Duke. Perhaps to flush out Wellington's intentions, Canning argued that it would be possible to form a purely Protestant ministry; but the Duke insisted that this was as impractical as a purely Catholic one: only a mixed government would do.[9] The King then sent Peel to sound out Canning on the possibility of serving under Wellington; but Canning would not accept this, and he and Peel could not agree on anyone else. After this failure, the King decided to grasp the nettle and charged Canning with forming a ministry on the same basis as Liverpool's, no doubt trusting that the Duke's insistence on a mixed administration and his famous sense of duty would keep him and his associates in their places. But leaving the way open for retreat and compromise if necessary, he did not actually name Canning Prime Minister.

Canning wrote immediately to solicit Wellington's assistance. A visit or a request for an interview would have been a better way to approach such a crucial and brittle individual; but the Foreign Secretary probably hoped that a letter would spare him acrimonious and even compromising discussion. The Duke, probably knowing that Canning had not been appointed Prime Minister, cautiously replied, 'before I can give an answer to your obliging proposition, I should wish to know who the person is whom you intend to propose to his Majesty as the head of the government.' Canning in turn used this letter to get the King to state that he intended him to be Prime Minister. Armed with this assurance he loftily informed Wellington that it was 'so generally understood that the King usually entrusts the formation of an administration to the individual whom it is his Majesty's gracious intention to place at the head of it' that it had not occurred to him to mention that the usual custom would be followed. The Duke later insisted that the 'temper and tone' of this letter were insulting and reminded the House of Lords that when Lord Liverpool was trying to form a ministry in 1812, Canning's first question had been: 'Who is to be the First Lord of the Treasury?' But that was three weeks later, when he was trying to justify unsuccessful actions. There was something to what Wellington said about Canning's letter, but even he tolerated less considerate language when it suited him.

The King's decision on Canning produced the reaction the Duke had resolved on some years before. He did not want to be Prime Minister himself, but he was determined that Canning should not be. In his reply to Canning's second letter he made no reference to language but observed that as he believed that the principles of Liverpool's administration would ultimately be abandoned, the ministry's proposals in the meantime 'viewed with suspicion by the usual supporters of the government,' and he himself at last forced to leave at a more inconvenient moment than the present, it was better for him to go now.[10] His example was immediately followed by Eldon, Peel, Bathurst, Arbuthnot, Melville (the pro-catholic First Lord of the Admiralty), and others to a total of about twenty. Writing to the King the next day to resign both his cabinet office and the command of the army, Wellington was at pains to reconcile his refusal to serve under the individual whose talents he had claimed were essential to the government five years ago. Recommending him as Foreign Secretary was one thing, though even there the Duke insisted that special circumstances had given unusual weight to his advice, but having him as head of the ministry was quite another.

George IV must have remembered all too well their discussions in the days when he too had disliked Canning and undoubtedly knew exactly what Wellington was doing. But after the conversations of the last few weeks he may sincerely have felt betrayed. Tersely accepting the resignation he added: 'The King abstains from any further expression of his feelings.'[11] The next day, however, he poured out his resentment to Lord Londonderry, Castlereagh's half-brother, who came to resign as Lord of the Bedchamber. 'To those persons who pressed Mr Canning upon me against my will,' he raged, '– to those who now leave me in the lurch – may all the mischief and perplexity which I feel be ascribed.' He was willing to forgive Eldon and Peel on account of their strong Protestant principles, but he attributed the Duke's resignation entirely to disappointment at not becoming Prime Minister. How could the King have expected that he would leave the Horse Guards for that? 'If ever there was a man to whom I have paid every honour and devotion, it is him' he told Londonderry; 'I have bestowed on him every gift of my crown; not that he does not deserve it, but I have done as much on my part as he has done for me.'[12]

Canning used the King's anger to persuade him that the desertion of the Ultras was an attack on his royal prerogative and the monarch formally named him Prime Minister. Convinced that Canning's efforts would come to grief on George IV's insistence on Protestant guarantees, Wellington withdrew to Stratfield Saye until the logic of events demanded his return. He told Mrs Arbuthnot that staying away from the mischief of the Ultras was in the best interests of 'our Party' – 'the Bishops & Clergy, the Great Aristocracy, the landed Interest, the Magistracy of the Country, the great Merchants and Bankers, in short the *parti conservateur* of the Country.' It could never suit such people to enter into factious opposition to the government, which had now fallen into the hands of 'an unworthy Individual, the tendency of whose Politics & views & personal Interests would lead him to unite with Whigs.' The Duke and those of a like mind should do nothing to hasten such a union but should try to provide the King with time to reflect on the dangers of such a course.[13] In the meantime Canning's friends put it about that Mrs Arbuthnot, who was at her house in Northamptonshire, was expressing Wellington's views of the King in loud and angry language, even wishing him '*a fit of gout for his pains.*'[14]

As the Duke had predicted, Canning opened negotiations with the Whigs. A few were appointed to minor office without objection from the King and most of the rest undertook to support his administration. The fiction of mixed government was preserved by the continuation in office of the Protestant Lord Bexley and the elevation to the woolsack as Lord Lyndhurst of that ambitious Protestant lawyer Sir John Copley, whom Canning had only lately been publicly abusing. Some of the posts were filled by *'warming pans'*[15] until the fate and direction of the ministry became clear. But with the support of the Whigs it was secure in the Commons.

While these arrangements were being worked out, Wellington continued to transact business at the Horse Guards until his successor was appointed. When the King met the new cabinet at the end of April he raised this matter, inquired when the Duke intended to leave and questioned the legality of his acts in the three weeks since his resignation. This may simply have been a request for information, or perhaps he was hoping that Wellington could be persuaded to stay, but as soon as the news reached the Duke he packed his papers and departed immediately.[16]

The next day he explained the reasons for resigning to a sympathetic House of Lords. He told his follow peers that he would have been 'worse than mad' to aspire to be Prime Minister, 'a situation for which I am sensible that I am not qualified; and to which, moreover neither His Majesty, nor [Canning], nor any, wished to see me called.' He insisted that he had not been involved in any plot and that no one knew what he intended until he resigned. Turning to his decision to resign the army as well as his seat in the cabinet, he admitted that he had never believed that political differences should count any more at the Horse Guards than in the field, but Canning's letter made it impossible for him to remain at a post that required close relations with the Prime Minister: 'How was it possible for me to consider that I was likely to possess the Right Honourable gentleman's confidence on any of these points, after receiving from him in his Majesty's name, such a rebuke as was contained in his letter to me of the 11th.?'[17] This was hardly a compelling defence, but concentrating on his own sincere lack of ambition to become Prime Minister did avoid the issue of attempting to stop Canning and provided a plausible explanation of his action consistent with his sense of honour and duty.

Having failed to prevent Canning, Wellington immediately regretted that he had also given up the army. No great gift was necessary to perceive this and efforts were soon made to strengthen the new Prime Minister by enticing him back. Even before he actually left the office Sir William

Knighton was telling Mrs Arbuthnot that there was no reason for his resignation: 'he had done it in pique & anger . . . the King loved him as a brother . . . he had no feeling but that of deep sorrow at his loss.' When Mrs Arbuthnot questioned this representation of the King's attitude, Knighton attributed the coolness of the last year to the enormous quantities of laudanum he had been taking. Now that he was down to thirty drops a day his old affection was restored: 'if his heart could be looked into, the Duke of Wellington's name wd be found written there.' But the real point of the visit was to see if the Duke would go to Ireland with Arbuthnot as Chief Secretary. The appointment would be made directly by the King; Wellington would be given powers as Captain General second only to the monarch; and he would serve as 'a *barrier against the Whigs* & an earnest of the King's feeling about the Protestant question.' The Duke had already heard of Canning's scheme to enlist his prestige while removing him to a safe distance and dismissed it with a laugh.[18]

A week later, when the Prime Minister admitted more Whigs to bolster his administration, a more vigorous attempt was made to get Wellington back. The command was still vacant and Sir Henry Taylor, the Military Secretary at the Horse Guards, tried the ground by writing to express the hope that the differences between his former chief and Canning did not close the door to reconciliation and return. The Duke promptly replied that he had left only because he had received a rebuke in the King's name. If his interpretation was wrong and if confidence in him still existed, it was open to the monarch and his advisers to decide that he should resume his post.[19] Elated by Wellington's seeming eagerness to return, Canning got the King to write an effusive letter to his 'dear friend,' expressing his warm regard and telling him: 'if you choose to recall that resignation, which it grieved me so much to receive, you have my *sincere* permission to do so.' But the Duke would not return without a humiliating apology from Canning. Replying stiffly through the Prime Minister, he observed that he had not been aware that his communications with Taylor were known to the monarch, entreated the King to recollect his reason for leaving and pointed out that if he simply took back his resignation, 'I should by that act admit that I had not been justified in retiring; and I should disable myself from rendering that useful service to your Majesty which it would be, as it ever had been, the pride of my life to render.'[20]

This unrelenting hostility towards the Prime Minister appeared to find expression in an attempt to destroy the government in the House of Lords ten days later. In the debate on the Corn Bill Wellington moved that no imported corn be taken out of bonded warehouses until the price reached

66s. a quarter. This seemed the cry to rally the agricultural interest against the ministry, even though he had told Lady Shelley just a week before that he could not lead those who were looking to him to throw out a measure on which he had swallowed his own feelings in order to keep Liverpool's cabinet together. As one who had always acted openly and fairly, he could not now 'commence cheating and truckling about the support of a measure to which, from circumstances, he is a party, although he disapproves of it!'[21] In the interval he had apparently found a way to reconcile rejection with his conscience. In fact he had been discussing with Huskisson, still President of the Board of Trade, how to combat the iniquitous practice of grain merchants driving up the price in towns where the averages were taken in order to release the foreign grain they had in warehouses. To curb this profiteering the Duke had proposed that no grain be removed until the price reached 70s.; Huskisson would not accept this but said that he would not personally object to such a restriction at 66s., though such an amendment would probably be fatal to the bill in the Commons.

Thinking that anything on which he and Huskisson agreed would be acceptable to Parliament, Wellington moved his amendment. Lord Goderich, formerly Frederick Robinson, who had just arrived in the House as Leader, announced that this would destroy the bill. The Duke threw him into confusion by producing Huskisson's letter, and the House gleefully passed the amendment. An acrimonious correspondence ensued between Wellington and Huskisson, who had neglected to keep a copy, to determine exactly what had been written, on the propriety of quoting private letters in Parliament, the evils of warehousing and the consistency between the Duke's amendment and his acceptance of the bill in cabinet. Wellington had honestly misunderstood Huskisson's none too clear words, but he refused to give up his amendment and the government was forced to abandon its only major piece of legislation.[22] Canning was furious. Ill and overwrought, he denounced the sacrifice of the prosperity of the country to the interests of faction and told an astonished House of Commons – on Waterloo Day – that the Duke was 'a tool in the hands of more crafty intriguers.'

Despite this hostility, new efforts were made to get Wellington back to the Horse Guards when Parliament rose at the beginning of July. Sir William Knighton worked on Charles Arbuthnot, asking him what his friend's terms were. When he was told, reparation 'as clear to the world *as the sun at noon day*,' Knighton grumbled unconvincingly about Canning and the Whigs, claimed that it was impossible to manage the army without the Duke, and dilated on the necessity of having him close to the King in order to protect him against the 'cursed crew' with which he was surrounded.[23] The King and Lady Conyngham tried a more direct approach by persuading Lord Maryborough to have his brother call at the Royal Lodge. When this was conveyed to Wellington at Stratfield Saye, he cagily told his brother that he could not presume to go to Windsor without a formal invitation. The monarch professed himself unable to understand this excessive punctiliousness from his old companion and asked why he could not simply visit Maryborough and they could meet as if by chance in Windsor Park. '"In short," he said clapping Maryborough on the shoulder, "my good friend, I put it in yr hands and you must get him to come over & see me."'

Concluding that this was as much of an invitation as he was likely to get, and being far from uninterested in influencing the King, the Duke rode over to Windsor the next morning, by happy coincidence the sixth anniversary of the coronation. His visit was like 'the return of the Prodigal Son ... the Pages and messengers grinned from ear to ear at the sight of him, pressed him to take luncheon, & ... the Lords in Waiting attended him to the door, & Ld Fife held his stirrup while he got on his horse.' The King greeted him warmly and treated him to a garrulous narrative of events since Liverpool's stroke. Although Wellington would not agree to resume the command, they parted on good terms after two and a half hours. The Duke then saw Lady Conyngham and abused Canning in terms that he knew would be reported to the King. He warned that the country was in 'a most confounded scrape, that they were in the hands of the worst part of the Whigs & that, both at home and abroad, they were in a most awkward position.' He was much elated by his visit, but Lord Bathurst, who arrived at Stratfield Saye a couple of days later, warned him not to go too fast, gathering from Maryborough that the King was anxious for good relations with Wellington as insurance against the collapse of Canning who had been in danger from a bowel obstruction.[24]

The worst fears about the effect of the visit were realized when exaggerated reports appeared in the London papers. Canning remonstrated with the King and Maryborough feared that he would be dismissed even from the dogs if he did not persuade his brother to go back to the Horse Guards without conditions. Lady Conyngham tantalizingly claimed that new arrangements to put the army under Sir George Murray, Wellington's former Quartermaster General, were ready for the King's signature, while Sir Herbert Taylor added to the clamour by raising once more the cry of the army in danger: 'We do want you sadly; we want you were it but to stem the torrent of military reductions with which we are threatened, and to place, or rather to maintain, that question upon the proper footing.'[25] But the Duke remained unmoved by this barrage, telling Bathurst that the only results of the excitement would be to ensure that the King did not seek a repetition of the visit and to define the political factions more closely.[26]

No one had to wait very long for the next turn of events for it was soon clear that Canning really was dying. After suffering agony from inflammation of the lungs and liver that baffled his physicians, he expired in the early hours of 8 August. Even the sharp-tongued Mrs Arbuthnot was moved by his final torment. But Wellington, who was just recovering from an illness that had confined him to his house, was made of sterner stuff: 'The Mischief he has done and was likely to do has not yet been made apparent to the World. The King has not yet felt all the inconveniences to himself of the Step he took in April.'[27]

The talk in the capital was that the Duke would be sent for, and certainly the ministry without Canning to lead it was not very impressive. But the King had had enough excitement for the moment and decided to continue the existing arrangement. He prevailed on the timorous Lord Goderich to become Prime Minister, laying it down that the cabinet was not to touch the Catholic question or parliamentary reform and not to take in any more Whigs. Goderich quibbled about the Catholic stipulation but finally knocked under. After some reshuffling the government continued on the King's terms. Now that the chief obstacle had been removed by death, a fresh attempt was made to get the Duke back to the Horse Guards to shore up this fragile coalition. A week after Canning's death, Lord Anglesey, Wellington's successor at the Ordnance, travelled through the night to bring the latest summons to his old commander who was visiting in Dorset. Bursting into the Duke's room at 7.30 while he was still abed, Anglesey announced that he had letters from the King and the Prime Minister. George IV's, addressed to his 'Dear Friend,' consisted of one sentence: 'I write for the purpose of again offering you the command of my army, and I sincerely hope that the time is arrived when the country will no longer be deprived of the benefit of your high talents.' Goderich added his hope that Wellington would accept, not from any consideration for him but because the appointment was 'of the last importance to the best interests of our common country, which can in no circumstances forget what she owes to your long and distinguished services.' With Canning gone and without the slightest hint that he would be expected to support the ministry, there was no reason for the Duke to refuse any longer. But the awkwardness of explaining this sudden acceptance was reflected in his markedly abrupt manner towards Anglesey. 'Well, you will at least say I am a good courier,' the latter grumbled as he set out for London.[28]

On the same day that he sent his brief replies to Goderich and the King, Wellington began the thankless task of justifying his ways to the Ultras. To Lord Westmorland, for example, one of those stern and unbending Tories who had followed him out of office, he explained that he could not have refused without advancing new reasons and exposing himself to great risks. 'I am aware of the delicacy of the position in which I shall be placed,' he told Westmorland. 'But I think I can overcome that difficulty more easily than I could the abandonment of my professional position, or any inconsistency upon the reason of my resignation.'[29] This defence was in perfect accord with his public character and many of his friends recognized that it was practically impossible for the great soldier to deny himself his heart's desire. Others, however, felt obliged to express their apprehensions. Lord Bathurst pointed out that his situation would be very awkward: even though he had not been offered a seat in the cabinet or asked for guarantees of support, 'there must always be great delicacy in taking a part against the existing government, as it will be difficult so to divest yourself of your official influence as not to make it bear somewhat against the government from whence it is derived.' The Duke confidently replied that he would demonstrate his independence when Parliament met in 1828.[30]

The most violent reaction came from Mrs Arbuthnot, with whom he had a 'desperate *scene*' two days after accepting the appointment. She charged that he had 'shewn more eagerness to resume the Command than was consistent with his character as a politician.' When he insisted that he was no politician but a soldier to whom the army looked as its defender, she burst out that it was 'ridiculous nonsense for him to stand up and tell he was *no politician* ... that he had taken a most active part in both our home and foreign politics; that a body in the State looked to him as their proctor against the political economists, and that he must be quite aware that they did not do so on account of his military talents.' He had struck a blow at those with whom he had previously acted and if he could not resist the appointment, he should at least have made it clear that he was not bound to the ministry. As for being the champion of the army, she bitterly reflected in the privacy of her diary that he had not hesitated to sacrifice its interests 'when he was in a huff with Mr Canning about a matter of personal dignity.'[31]

The emotional exchange which threatened to destroy his personal happiness did not increase Wellington's pleasure at returning to the Horse Guards. The following day he wrote Mrs Arbuthnot a long letter in his carriage while travelling to Windsor for the formal acceptance; and he told her husband: 'I don't want anybody to congratulate me upon this Event. God knows it is not one of Joy to myself, nor do I think or expect it can be one of Joy to others.' Mrs Arbuthnot, all passion spent, also wrote a long letter to the Duke saying that she would not discuss the matter further nor set her judgment against his, but she regarded his departure from politics as a great loss: 'in this country in a time of peace, a soldier, however great, was less important than a politician.'[32] Once more it seemed that Wellington's political interlude was over; but once again events drew him back.

Delighting in the joys of a weak Prime Minister, George IV was bullying his divided and embarrassed ministers like a stage tyrant. Huskisson, who had moved to the War and Colonial Office and become Leader of the House of Commons, discovered on his return from the continent that 'Goderich had completely spoilt the Game. The K had taken the measure of Him; and openly says he must do all the duties of *Premier* Himself; because G has no nerves!' He also learned that the King was agitating for reunion with the Ultras; but Huskisson warned that admitting those who had harried Canning to his grave would disrupt the cabinet even further: 'The Wound is too recent and too green.'[33] Such was the discord among the various factions, the vacillations of the high strung and lachrymose Prime Minister and the constant harassment of the King, that even Wellington's appointment made no significant difference. He was scrupulous in his loyalty and did nothing to hasten the government's collapse. But in the circumstances that was hardly necessary. From his eyrie at the Horse Guards he observed that the ministers were 'not very well satisfied with each other or with his Majesty, nor are they respectable or respected by the public, nor have they the experience of the habits necessary for the performance of the business of the government.'[34] He told Lord Eldon that the administration was '*falsehood personified*': to the world it was all liberality and was supported even by the Radicals; but to the King and those who supported the old order, it professed allegiance to those principles.[35]

Despite his contempt for the whole enterprise, the Duke stuck close to his official duties and gave the ministers no cause for dissatisfaction. The only important matter on which he pronounced in the autumn of 1827 was the proposal to economize by reducing the army. Surveying its resources and responsibilities, he predictably concluded that any attempt to cut down the military establishment would increase the risk of major disturbances in the urban areas of Britain and Ireland and endanger the security of the empire. He argued that reductions always turned out to be false economy and touched on a theme that was to become an obsession with him in the 1840s, the development of steamships, to justify a large concentration of troops in the ports to guard against invasion.[36] Fortunately for the Commander in Chief, the cabinet was too preoccupied with internal disputes to take issues with the great figure whose prestige they so desperately needed.

Wellington for his part took advantage of his indispensability to claim a peerage for his brother Henry, the ambassador to Austria. For the last eighteen years, with the exception of a single year, he told Goderich, his brother had served in the rank of ambassador as a commoner while less deserving individuals had been raised to the peerage. He assured the Prime Minister that he was not seeking any special advantage for his family and realized that he had no right to draw attention to this case of neglect.[37] Goderich acceded with alacrity, and three weeks later Sir Henry Wellesley became Lord Cowley. Only Gerald, now enjoying the fat slumbers of the Church, still lacked a title.

By the end of 1827 it was obvious that the ministry could not last much longer. The Prime Minister pleaded with the King to admit Lord Holland, the very embodiment of Whiggery, and Lord Wellesley, now returning from Ireland after a month-to-month extension to help his finances. But George IV would not hear of them. When Goderich begged permission to retire if the appointments were not acceptable, the King took him at his word and called on Lord Harrowby to form a government. But Harrowby was even more timid than Goderich; when he declined Goderich was prevailed upon to continue without new ministers.

By this time the members of the cabinet were manoeuvring for advantage in the next combination. When Goderich proposed the Whig Lord Althorp as chairman of a finance committee, he found himself between Huskisson, who insisted on it, and J.C. Herries, the Tory Chancellor of the Exchequer and the King's favourite, who would resign if Althorp were appointed. 'I understand that the Government is tottering to its foundations,' the Duke told Peel on New Year's Day. 'They are all going, for some reason or other.'[38]

This absurd spectacle did not last much longer. In his last tearful interview on 8 January Goderich told the King that the cabinet was fatally divided. George IV, finally tired of this feeble cipher, decided to let him go. The 'transient and embarrassed phantom,' as Disraeli later called him, flitted back into the shade, though emerging again as a minister in both Whig and Conservative governments for almost twenty years. His curious parting advice to the King was to send for Lord Anglesey, the new Viceroy of Ireland. The monarch instead summoned the impeccably Protestant Lord Lyndhurst, who in turn advised him to call for the Duke.

The morning after Goderich's resignation Wellington was awakened before eight with a note from Lyndhurst saying that he must come to Apsley House immediately with a message from the King. A few minutes later, before the Duke was even dressed, the Chancellor himself arrived to announce that the government was at an end and that the King wanted Wellington to form a new one.[39] After a year of turmoil and danger the Duke had no doubt about what was required of him, and what he required of himself. Permanent damage to the country's political and social system from the subversive Canning, the incompetent Goderich and their near revolutionary Whig allies, admitted to the councils of state after twenty years' unremitting effort by Wellington's friends to keep them out, had been avoided only because the construction of Canning's ministry had occupied much of the 1827 session and because Goderich had not even met Parliament as Prime Minister. The new session was fast approaching. But the Duke was confident that the hour and the man were matched. He would be the national saviour who would eject the Whigs and restore an improved form of Lord Liverpool's government.

When Wellington and Lyndhurst arrived at Windsor they found the King in bed, 'groaning and appearing very miserable and unhappy.' As he rambled on about recent events, however, his spirits lifted. He sat up and began mimicking his late ministers, 'exhibiting such a drama, so lively, so exact, and so amusing, that the D. never saw anything like it – Goderich, Lansdowne, and, above all Anglesey, whom he positively made himself look like.'[40] The point of this entertainment was to persuade Wellington to lead a new government. He did not refuse, but replied that his position as Commander in Chief made it necessary for him to consult others before committing himself. When he inquired about the nature of the ministry he was expected to put together, the King told him that the Catholic question must remain open but the Lord Chancellor and the Viceroy and Lord Chancellor of Ireland must all support the Protestant position. Lyndhurst, who was present throughout the interview, was to continue in office and Lord Grey was specifically barred. With these exceptions the Duke was free to choose from anyone who had served under Goderich, Canning or

Liverpool. 'Upon the whole,' Wellington told Peel, 'he left me a *carte blanche* ... and he repeatedly desired that I would form for him a strong government.'

On his return to London the Duke summoned Peel, the only Tory of commanding ability in the Commons, to discuss 'this interesting commission': 'I have sent for nobody else, nor shall I see anybody till you come.'[41] The next day he solicited Bathurst's advice. But even with these two congenial figures the task was more difficult than Wellington expected. Far from being able to pick and choose from politicians who would rally eagerly to his national standard, he found that he was closely circumscribed by factional considerations. Peel was above all anxious to enlist good speakers in the Commons and argued that the Canningites must be retained. Bathurst wanted simply to recall all those who had left with the Duke the previous spring, to which Peel responded: 'Very well! I will support you in everything, but I will not take Office!' This did not at all accord with Wellington's conception of his duty and unique position: for some inexplicable reason his colleagues regarded him as a mere politician like themselves. He told Mrs Arbuthnot that he could not bear the injustice with which he was treated, 'and the whole affair will end by my telling them one of these days that they must settle their matters as they can among themselves.'[42]

The indispensable Peel got his way and the Canningites, as they were called after their chief's death, were able to command a high price for their services. Huskisson, their leader, remained at the War and Colonial Office; Lord Dudley continued at the Foreign Office and Charles Grant at the Board of Trade; Lord Palmerston went on as Secretary at War, as he had almost beyond the memory of man; William Lamb, a Whig, was allowed to stay as Irish Secretary; and Lord Anglesey was confirmed as Viceroy. Once these major offices were filled, there was not much that remained for the Duke's friends when the Whigs were dismissed. Peel returned to the Home Office and became Leader of the House of Commons; Bathurst became Lord President of the Council; Lord Melville went to the Board of Control; and Lord Beresford to the Ordnance. Henry Goulburn, a Tory unabrasive enough to be acceptable to the Canningites, became Chancellor of the Exchequer, while J.C. Herries, whose antipathy towards the Whigs and low regard for the Canningites had precipitated the collapse of Goderich's ministry, was tactfully relegated to the sidelines as Master of the Mint. At Peel's insistence two new recruits were added to increase the debating strength in the House of Lords: Lord Aberdeen as Chancellor of the Duchy of Lancaster and Lord Ellenborough as Lord

Privy Seal. Lord Wellesley was easily passed over by his brother who wrote unconvincingly a few weeks later: 'It would have given me the greatest Satisfaction if circumstances had permitted me to ask for your Assistance in the difficulties in which I found myself; and to have been the means of giving the King and His Councils the benefit of your Powerful Services and able advice.'[43]

More remarkable than those appointed was the omission of Lord Eldon. Even the Duke felt that the inclusion of the very embodiment of stern and unbending Toryism would be an incitement to trouble with the Canningites. On the second day of cabinet making he went to see his former colleague and talked pointedly of the difficulties of deciding among the various candidates for office. Eldon insisted that he did not wish to be considered for the Chancellorship, which was in any event reserved to Lyndhurst, but he did not close the door to another office. With remarkable insensitivity, the Duke evidently considered that Eldon was reconciled to exclusion and left without saying a word. Two weeks later, however, he was back in response to rumours that 'a lady,' presumably Mrs Arbuthnot, had imposed her veto on Eldon. The Prime Minister tried to soothe the old man's feelings by claiming that the impossibility of forming a ministry acceptable to Eldon had led him to conclude that further communication would simply have caused Eldon 'unnecessary trouble.' Unmoved by this solicitude, Eldon replied that there was nothing in his previous record to indicate that he would have refused simply because he disapproved of some ministers. He insisted that he had been neglected; told Wellington that he would have been honoured to have been Lord President, though he would have given up even that if others had objected; but now refused to be mollified by some minor compensation. When he did mention that he would welcome the inclusion of that kindred spirit, Sir Charles Wetherell, however, the Duke lost no time in appointing him Attorney General.[44]

Charles Arbuthnot's claims were not fraught with the same political consequences as Eldon's, but satisfying them was closely bound up with the Duke's personal happiness. When the new Prime Minister explained that he could give his friend nothing better than his old post of Commissioner of Woods and Forests without a seat in the cabinet, Arbuthnot said that he would prefer no office if he could not be in the cabinet. Wellington was forced to point out that he could include in the cabinet only those who would defend the government in Parliament. Arbuthnot had no heart for this bold part and when he persisted in his demand, the Duke became greatly annoyed. A rupture was averted only when Arbuthnot relented.

'God Knows,' Wellington told him, 'that I have disgust enough in all these affairs to avoid the augmentation of that which must be the consequences of the break up of the only private & confidential Relation I have in Life.' To Mrs Arbuthnot he added that her husband could feel ill treated only by false comparison with others. He assured her that he would cut the tongue out of his head before making Arbuthnot a proposition to lower him in his own estimation, in hers, or in the eyes of the world.

Mrs Arbuthnot considered her husband's appointment a poor reward for his loyalty when such 'rif raf' were in the cabinet and she was dismayed that her hero had not taken the opportunity to construct a real Ultra Tory government. She conceded that the ministry was an improvement on Goderich's but thought it 'a bad moral lesson that those who behaved shabbily & shewed they had no political principle shd be rewarded, & that those who were honest should suffer.'[45] Many of Wellington's associates were of the same opinion, despite his pleas of necessity. 'We cannot form a Ministry as we do a Dinner or a party in the Country,' he felt obliged to tell Lord Londonderry. 'We must look to its Stability; and its capacity to carry on the King's Business in Parlt., carry with it the respect of the Country, and of Ireland; and of foreign Nations.'[46]

Much reservation was overcome by the great sacrifice that the Duke himself had to make. The new cabinet unanimously decided that he must give up the command of the army which he had hoped to retain as Prime Minister.[47] With a heavy heart he told the King that he would prefer to give up his political office if only he could see someone to take his place. To Lord Hill, who succeeded him at the Horse Guards, he said that he wished that he had made retaining the command a condition of becoming Prime Minister.[48] The Duke of Cumberland, the King's Ultra Tory brother, wrote from Germany that those of his persuasion could not now refuse their support. The new Prime Minister, he pronounced, 'though not so *eloquent* as Mr. Canning, still, believe me, he is in everything else far his *superior*.'[49] As for the army, Wellington could take some comfort in the fact that General 'Daddy' Hill, if not the cartoonist's 'Hill of Straw,' could be relied upon to do nothing contrary to his wishes and to make no important decision without consulting him.

Within the government feelings ran high about Canning's administration and the ministers treated each other with the courtesy of men who had just fought a duel.[50] But the Duke could take satisfaction in having put together a reasonable approximation of Liverpool's ministry and could expect that with good management and luck it would prove at least as efficient and harmonious as its predecessor. He certainly did not spare himself in his efforts. When Mrs Arbuthnot spent two weeks at his house, she scarcely saw him except at dinner; and as soon as that was over he would begin writing again until midnight.[51] Thomas Creevey, whose Whig principles had not prevented admiration of his political opponent since their meeting in Brussels at the time of Waterloo, told his niece: 'The Beau is rising most rapidly in the market as a practical man of business. All the deputations come away charmed with him. But woe to them that are too late! He is punctual to the second himself, and waits for no man.'[52] As he had in the field, the Duke wanted to see everything and do everything. If only his colleagues had been content cheerfully to accept his command while enjoying some tactical independence, all might have been well from his point of view. But they all had strong views which they wanted to express and impose on others. This was a great strain on one of Wellington's disposition and military habits, and within days he was comparing himself to a dog with a can tied to its tail and complaining in terms reminiscent of Lord Liverpool's after fifteen years. 'There,' he told Croker, pointing to a pile of green bags and red boxes, 'there is the business of the country, which I have not time to look at – all my time being employed in assuaging what gentlemen call their *feelings*. In short, the folly and unreasonableness of people are inconceivable.'[53] Nor were the backbenchers any more orderly than the cabinet ministers. As he searched for someone to move the Reply to the Address from the Throne in the House of Lords, he told Peel: 'We have the most zealous friends, till we ask them to do any thing; and then we find that they either cannot or will not.'[54]

The ministry thus painfully constructed was received in a hostile spirit by an opposition furious over the collapse of Goderich's administration, the dismissal of the Whigs, the clinging to office of the Canningites and the sinister appearance of an autocratic soldier as Prime Minister. A passage in the Speech from the Throne deploring the sinking of the Turkish fleet at Navarino by the combined squadrons of Britain, France and Russia as 'an untoward event' seemed to confirm the disposition of the new government. Great was the fury of those who regarded Navarino as a triumph for Greek independence and the cause of freedom generally. But this issue was simply one aspect of the bitter clash between Canningites and Whigs. Most of this took place in the House of Commons, but the Duke was naturally dragged in from time to time, as for example when Henry Brougham, on the grounds of his continuing as Commander in Chief until his successor was appointed, claimed that Wellington was aiming at becoming a military despot.

The discussion took a different turn when Huskisson, who had left at the meeting of Parliament to seek re-election on being appointed to a new office, assured his constituents at Liverpool that he had insisted on pledges from Wellington that the policy of his government would be the same as Canning's. In vain did the Colonial Secretary endeavour to extricate himself from this latest embarrassment by explaining that he meant simply that the continuation of the Canningites was a sign that policy would remain unchanged. The Ultras' suspicions were aroused and the Duke hastened to deny the apparent meaning of Huskisson's words and to defend his own reputation. He asked the House of Lords if anyone really believed that those who had joined his ministry had required a guarantee about the practical application of his well-known principles? Such a corrupt bargain would have tarnished Huskisson's reputation as much as his own: 'No guarantee was required, and none was given on my part.' He insisted that his administration was as mixed as Liverpool's and one in which discussion had never been so free.[55] The last was all too true as far as the Duke was concerned; and the fundamental differences which it indicated provided easy opportunities for its opponents.

Early in the session Lord John Russell on behalf of the Whigs introduced a motion calling for the repeal of the Test and Corporations Acts. In principle these prevented everyone except members of the Church of England, even members of the Established Church of Scotland outside that kingdom, from holding public office. In practice Dissenters and Presbyterians could escape the restriction by taking the sacrament of the Church of England before entering office, by hoping that the test would not be applied or, most satisfactorily of all, by relying on the Indemnity Act which Parliament had passed every year for almost a century. Despite the growth of Methodism since the late eighteenth century, the arrangement had been accepted fairly readily since the union with Ireland on the grounds that tampering with the Protestant laws would weaken the case for preserving Catholic disabilites. But in 1827 the Dissenters, increasing in numbers, wealth and confidence, demanded an end to their second-class status in return for their support of the Protestant cause in the 1826 general election. Canning had insisted that Catholic relief must come first. But in 1828, with a more Protestant government in office, Russell could appeal to their followers, exhibit his liberal principles, strike a covert blow for Catholic emancipation and divide the Tories and Canningites. The motion easily passed the House of Commons.

The instinctive reaction of the Duke and Peel, as pragmatic conservatives, was to defend a system that, however absurd in law, worked well in practice and the alteration of which was fraught with danger for the Catholic question. But when they looked about them, they found little support. The Dissenters were a force to be reckoned with in most constituencies and the question was evidently hopeless in the Commons. The universities would not stir. The bishops wanted a settlement that would end the abuse of the sacrament and feared for the peace of the Church if there was prolonged discussion and a difference between the Commons and the Lords on a religious question. Lay peers shared their sentiments. In these discouraging circumstances Wellington decided that it was better for the ministry to manage concession while it still had some initiative than have the issue forced by the opposition.

Only the most adamant defenders of the Church's constitutional position now opposed the bill. Foremost among them was Lord Eldon, who saw the foundations of the system he had fought all his life to preserve being swept away by the supposed opponents of reform. Their reasons for denying him office were now abundantly clear. In bitter tones he told the House of Lords that he had heard much of 'the progress of information, and of persons changing opinions which they had held for years; but he had not thought it possible that the march of the mind could have been so speedy as to induce some of the changes of opinion which he had witnessed within the last year.' He dismissed the government's defence of 'expediency' as 'a word used by those with nothing to say,' and invoked the familiar spectacle of the French revolution as a dreadful warning that interference with existing arrangements would weaken the foundation of the country and expose it to ruin and anarchy. This was a great embarrassment to the Duke, who had often used this line of reasoning and would often use it again. Rising immediately after Eldon, he insisted that the new dispensation would strengthen the Church's connection with the state and provide a better protection than annual suspension. Deploring the abuse of the sacrament and pointing to the petitions in favour of repeal, he implored the House to pass the bill in the interests of civil peace. Later in the debate he added the astonishing declaration that he was not one of those who considered the best means of preserving the constitution to lie in 'adhering to measures, which had been called for by particular circumstances, because they had been in existence for two hundred years, since the lapse of time might render it proper to modify, if not to remove them altogether.'[56]

The bill passed by large majorities, though Wellington had to endure much from the King who had no enthusiasm for the measure and whose inclination was strengthened by the Duke of Cumberland who had hurried back from Germany. When Wellington told George IV before one of Eldon's amendments that members of the royal household should attend the House of Lords, only Lord Maryborough and Lord Roden appeared, and the latter voted against the government. The Lord Chamberlain went further and sent his proxy to Eldon's group, provoking a rocket from the Duke intended for the monarch: 'If the servants of the Crown do not mean to support me, either I will retire, or those who will not support me must retire.' Having become Prime Minister in circumstances of 'an accumulation of difficulties of past years, postponed by the necessities and the procrastinating spirit of the times,' and having made great personal sacrifices, he had the right to expect that the old friends of Lord Liverpool's government would give him 'a fair and liberal support; and at least avoid *seeking for curiosities* in order to form a party against me.'[57]

The ministry was fairly well united on the Test and Corporations Bill, but on other issues there was no agreement. The cabinet accepted that there should be a corn bill on the same principles as the one that had come to grief on Wellington's amendment the year before, but the details provided ample scope for dispute. The Duke insisted on his warehousing provision and wanted the reduction in duty to begin at a higher domestic price, while Huskisson wanted to stand by all the terms of the earlier bill. A compromise was eventually devised whereby Wellington dropped the warehouse clause and the Canningites accepted a duty of 20s. a quarter when the price of corn was 66s., rising by a shilling for each fall of a shilling in the price, but falling rapidly as the price rose, so that at 73s. and above there would be only a nominal duty of 1s. This was not achieved without the President of the Board of Trade, Charles Grant, insisting on resigning, Huskisson saying that he could not stay if Grant went, and this being avoided only by Grant relenting while Huskisson was with the King. The measure that emerged from the emotional discussion was not what either side wanted, but both could claim success, the Canningites in getting the Duke to relent in his protectionism, and Wellington in getting a higher level of protection than the year before. The Prime Minister openly avowed in the House of Lords that the bill was a device for steering between extremes, conciliating all parties and establishing the corn laws on a lasting foundation.[58] On this basis it was accepted by all but the most determined protectionists. The legislation did little to curb the activities of speculators as a mere 6s. rise in price brought a drastic reduction in the duty; but no government cared to tackle further alteration until the 1840s.

Another legacy that divided the ministry was parliamentry reform. In the 1826 election two boroughs, Penryn in Cornwall and East Retford in

Nottinghamshire, had exhibited corruption that was flagrant even by the easy standards of the time. In 1827 the House of Commons got as far as passing a bill disenfranchising Penryn and giving second reading to one transferring East Retford's franchise to Birmingham. As soon as Parliament met in 1828 the Whigs introduced bills to transfer Penryn's members to Manchester and East Retford's to Birmingham. This brought gratifying results. The Duke thought there was 'no justice in taking a privilege from a body of 250 because 25 have been found to abuse it.' He and his fellow Tories considered it sufficient punishment to throw the boroughs into the hundreds – to extend their boundaries to the next territorial unit. The Canningites, however, wanted representation for some of the new industrial towns, an idea which the Tories considered sheer folly. Wellington's confidante, Mrs Arbuthnot, spoke with the true voice of Tory England when she pronounced that such a change would 'cause riots & loss of lives & property at every election & is not needed, for the great merchants get returned for the rotten boroughs & can attend to the interests of their town much better than if they were obliged to pander to the passions of an interested mob.'[59]

While the cabinet was busy quarrelling over this, the Duke fell on his nose getting out of his carriage and was so disfigured that he did not leave his house for some days. Peel meanwhile arranged a compromise whereby one of the boroughs would be thrown into the hundred and the franchise of the other transferred to a large town. This provoked further argument about which borough would lose its franchise. Huskisson favoured East Retford as the more corrupt, Peel Penryn as the more ancient offender in the county with most parliamentary boroughs. Finally Peel's choice was accepted. The House of Commons agreed to throw East Retford into the hundred and to give Penryn's representation to Manchester. When the Penryn bill went to the Lords, the East Retford one remained as a hostage in the Commons. The whole arrangement collapsed when the peers were so impressed by the solemn perjury of the Cornishmen who testified at the bar that the Whig lord in charge of the measure proposed the hundred in place of Manchester. On the day that debate on East Retford resumed in the Commons, Peel told the cabinet that he now felt free to vote as he liked, while Huskisson announced that he was committed to enfranchising Birmingham. Time was pressing and the ministers had to adjourn without coming to any agreement. When the vote was taken that night, Peel voted with the majority of eighteen to throw the borough into the hundred. Huskisson, after pleading for delay, voted to give the franchise to Birmingham.

As they walked home afterwards Joseph Planta, the Treasury Secretary, criticized Huskisson's vote in strong terms and told him that the only honourable course was resignation.[60] The Colonial Secretary thought this over and later that night wrote to Wellington offering to surrender his office, expecting that this fine gesture would appease those who had voted the other way and won. After his experience over the corn laws the year before, he should have realized the necessity of precision in dealing with the Duke. Wellington consulted Bathurst, who had objected to any enfranchisement of new towns and who advised taking Huskisson at his word since the Canningites acted too much as a party within the cabinet.[61] The Prime Minister decided to settle once and for all who was in control. He told the astonished Huskisson that he had considered it his duty to submit the letter to the King. Lord Ellenborough, the Lord Privy Seal, found the Duke 'completely roused, and seems to feel as he did at Waterloo.' Wellington told him that the Canningites had 'an erroneous and exaggerated view of their own consequence, which existed in the minds of none but themselves. They were always endeavouring to lord it. In this case, if he had solicited Huskisson to remain, Huskisson would have been Minister instead of himself.'[62] The only way for the Colonial Secretary to retain his office was formally to withdraw his resignation, which would destroy the independence of his group and acknowledge the Duke's supremacy.

This was totally unacceptable to Huskisson, who sent Dudley and Palmerston to remove the misunderstanding. Dudley told the Prime Minister that Huskisson had never intended to resign and urged him to talk to the unhappy minister. The Duke abruptly replied that he had no objection to seeing Huskisson, but as he had not requested an interview he did not see why he should. Palmerston pleaded to the same effect as he and Wellington paced up and down the Long Gallery of the House of Lords. The Duke pointed out that the matter was known all over town and was simply the last in a series of episodes that had offended the Ultras who, if the ministry was not careful, would abandon it at a time of difficulty and 'we should be at the mercy of our enemies.' Wellington was determined to avoid the situation of Lord Goderich. When Palmerston offered his own resignation it had no effect. The Duke told Ellenborough that Palmerston must go with Huskisson: 'he did *not choose to fire great guns at sparrows.'*[63] Nineteen years in the same minor office was no proof of indispensability in Wellington's eyes.

Further efforts were made by Huskisson's friends to get the Duke to relent, but he insisted on capitulation or resignation. He did not hurry the decision, arranging to see the King about a successor to Huskisson after church the following Sunday. Early that morning he wrote: 'My belief is that we shall be in a better position after this affair, be its result what it may, than we were before.'[64] There was no last minute appeal, and the Prime Minister was not downcast when Palmerston, Charles Grant, Dudley and William Lamb, the last two with great reluctance, followed Huskisson out of office.

If not actually dismissed, the Canningites had certainly left under a forced draught. The Tories were ecstatic. At their annual feast, the Pitt dinner, no less a person than Lord Eldon proposed an extra cheer for the Protestant ascendancy. Wellington was free at last to build the kind of government he wanted, and as the Canningites in his view had not lived up to their reputation as speakers in the House of Commons, he felt that he could take a chance on new blood. What he was looking for were men who would do their duty as he saw it; serve their country selflessly on lines laid down by him; administer their department efficiently; and not waste the cabinet's time in pointless disputation. Setting down his record of the events of Huskisson's resignation, he insisted that there had been no fundamental difference between them: 'Principles are brought forward solely to aggravate the consequences of these unfortunate difficulties.' There was much talk of

> Whig principles, and Tory principles, and Liberal principles, and Mr. Canning's principles; but I confess that I have never seen a definition of any of them, and cannot make to myself a clear idea of what any of them mean.
>
> This I know, that this country was never governed in practice according to the extreme principles of any party whatever; much less according to the extremes which other opposing parties attribute to its adversaries.

For himself he professed no interest in ideology. He sought simply to maintain 'the prerogatives of the Crown, the rights and privileges of the Church and its union with the State; and these principles are not inconsistent with a determination to do everything in my power to secure the liberty and promote the prosperity and happiness of the people.'[65]

But where were the sterling characters to be found who would see their simple duty exactly as the Duke did? Only among those rejoicing in the name of Tory, and perhaps only among those who also appeared in the Army List. Sir Henry Hardinge, one of Wellington's trusty military lieutenants, replaced Palmerston. Sir George Murray, his former

Quartermaster General, succeeded Huskisson. Neither took a prominent part in the formulation of policy and the opposition cries of military government were justified only to the limited extent that these two ministers were loyal administrative subordinates of the field marshal who commanded the cabinet. For the rest, Lord Aberdeen was promoted Foreign Secretary and replaced as Chancellor of the Duchy of Lancaster by Charles Arbuthnot, still without a seat in the cabinet. Lord Francis Leveson-Gower became Irish Secretary. And because he declared the original offer of the Secretaryship at War not worth the trouble of re-election, Vesey Fitzgerald was appointed President of the Board of Trade.

When his brother, Lord Cowley, wrote to convey Metternich's delight at the change, Wellington replied: 'We are going on well here. The Government is very popular; and indeed there is but little opposition.' Nor was the Duke's judgment blinded by his wishes: Charles Greville, despite his Canningite and Whig sympathies, saw the situation in much the same light.[66] Even Huskisson was soon regretting his departure as the ministry seemed to be getting along better without him and his associates than he had believed possible. But the strain of the last year and a half and the new issue that loomed over the cabinet took their toll on the Prime Minister. At the end of the parliamentary session in July, Lord Ellenborough thought that he was worn out. Mrs Arbuthnot observed that his 'amusements' consisted of 'going to the Treasury at noon, doing business till five, going to the House of Lords; dining – generally at dull places he don't care about – then reading and writing papers till he goes to bed.' But after seventeen days at Cheltenham he seemed restored to full health and ready to deal with a matter full of danger for the country, his political combination and his personal reputation.[67]

CHAPTER FOUR

A BATTLE LIKE WATERLOO

THE DUKE had no inkling of the consequences of appointing Vesey Fitzgerald to the Board of Trade. A popular Irish landlord and a supporter of Catholic claims who also enjoyed the confidence of the Protestant landlords, there was no reason to doubt that Fitzgerald would be safely returned for County Clare. But just ten days before the polls opened Daniel O'Connell announced that he would be a candidate in order to challenge what seemed like the extinction of Catholic hopes with the departure of the Canningites from the ministry. This unprecedented candidacy of a Catholic threw the whole of Ireland into a state of excitement. Thousands of troops were assembled in the neighbourhood of the poll, though the election turned out to be remarkably quiet as the priests marched the Catholic voters into Ennis in perfect order. The outcome was a foregone conclusion and when O'Connell was ahead by 2057 to 982 after five days, Fitzgerald abandoned the hopeless contest. But this was just the beginning of the problem. While there was no legal prohibition against candidacy, no Catholic could sit in Parliament. O'Connell, revelling in his new role and the embarrassment it caused the government, was in no hurry to claim his seat and decided to wait until 1829 rather than enlivening the dying days of the present session.

A month before O'Connell declared his candidacy, Wellington had to make a statement on Catholic emancipation when a bill proposing it reached the House of Lords from the Commons. There was no doubt that it would be defeated, but Peel had come to the conclusion that concession could not be resisted much longer. He urged the Prime Minister, who was less confined than he was by strong statements on the subject, to take a line that would leave him free to consider the entire Catholic and Irish questions after Parliament rose; but apart from pointing to his own disqualifications for managing a settlement and promising support from the back benches, he had no practical advice to offer.[1] The Duke knew that his ministry depended on Peel, but there was no time to discuss this before he had to speak. All he could do was temporize with the assistance of a bushel of papers from that staunch defender of Church and Tory causes Henry Phillpotts, then Dean of Durham. Phillpotts advised emancipation with safeguards for the Establishment, but without the papal concordat Wellington had advocated in 1825.[4]

Speaking immediately after Lord Wellesley, the Duke expressed his regret at having to differ from one 'whom I so dearly love, and for whose opinions I entertain so much respect and deference,' but hoped that in the end it would be found that they were not opposed. He told the House that although he believed the Catholic religion to be unfavourable to civil government anywhere in Europe, he had always considered emancipation a matter of expediency rather than doctrine. In the condition of Ireland, the admission of priest-ridden Catholics to public office would destroy the constitution and safety of the country. The repeal of disabilities would also require some control of the clergy, but an agreement with the Pope was impossible because no foreign ruler could be allowed jurisdiction within the kingdom. Above all, he pleaded for an end to emotional discussion so that the issue could be considered with care: 'if the public mind was now suffered to be thus tranquil – if the agitators of Ireland would only leave the public mind at rest – the people would become more satisfied, and I certainly think that it would then be possible to do something.'[2] O'Connell, interpreting this as a hostile statement, decided to contest the election in Clare. Charles Greville, on the other hand, reported that it produced bets that there would be Catholics in Parliament by the following year.[3] The Duke himself told the cabinet at dinner at Apsley House the next day that no one wanted to solve the Catholic problem more than he, but he could not 'see daylight.'[4]

Illumination came in the form of the election in Clare. The Duke concluded that the government of Ireland was effectively in the hands of O'Connell. A general or even a by-election would produce 'the same scenes ... that took place in Clare; in fact the King's Govt is paralyzed & his representative brought into contempt by the state of the Catholic body.'[5] If Catholics were not allowed to take their seats in the Commons when elected, those from Ireland might form their own assembly and plunge the country into civil war on any attempt to suppress it. The cabinet unanimously rejected Fitzgerald's advice that O'Connell's seat be declared vacant and a bill introduced barring Catholics from election as this would provide further provocation in a situation that Wellington at least thought was approaching that of the rebellion of 1798.⁶ From Dublin the Viceroy urged the government to find a solution to the Catholic question while he endeavoured to keep the country quiet. Within a week of the Clare election Wellington had decided that Catholics must be allowed to sit in Parliament under special oath. He told Mrs Arbuthnot that the enabling legislation should be passed annually, 'as a measure of precaution & not to let the affair out of our hands till we see how the Catholics behave.' Priests should be licensed and paid by the state; all communication with the Pope should pass through the Home Office; and the 40s. franchise in Ireland should be limited by requiring the payment of some specified amount of county rate.⁷

This proposal for carefully controlled Catholic emancipation required the full support of Peel and the King. Knowing all too well the strength of George IV's Protestant feelings, the Duke did not risk telling him what he had in mind but drew up a carefully crafted memorandum on the events and implications of the Clare election. Pointing out that the Catholics had not broken the law and that any attempt to suppress the Association by force would produce a clamour for emancipation from the House of Commons, he told the King that it was 'the duty of all to look our difficulties in the face and to lay the ground for getting the better of them.' By grimly stating, if not actually exaggerating, the dangers in Ireland, the Prime Minister persuaded the King to allow him, Peel and Lyndhurst to study the matter, though the monarch insisted that he was not committed to any alteration of the present system.⁸

Desultory discussions among the three ministers dragged on for five months without conclusion. Lyndhurst was willing to accept whatever the other two agreed on, and with remarkable patience the Duke laboured to find a way to keep Peel. Only he could make an effective case to the government's anti-Catholic supporters in the Commons. Even if he defended emancipation from outside the ministry, his resignation would encourage the Lords to reject it, and the King even to forbid its introduction as an official measure. But try as he might, it seemed that Wellington could find no way to prevent Peel from leaving.

Outside the tiny circle that knew of these discussions there were persistent rumours that the ministry was considering some great change. In August the King's erratic brother and heir presumptive, the Duke of Clarence, was dismissed from the post of Lord High Admiral, which had been revived for him as part of Canning's accommodation of the King the year before. In the ministerial shuffle produced by the appointment of a regular political First Lord of the Admiralty, the Privy Seal was kept suspiciously vacant. The Duke told Peel that he had to consider 'the not impossible case of your finding yourself obliged to leave us to ourselves. In this case I must have the command of all the means possible to make an arrangement to carry on the King's service, and I would keep other offices vacant if I could.'[9] The unsolicited gift of the new Bishop of London's former living to Lord Grey's brother also aroused much speculation.[10] But most startling of all was a speech by Peel's brother-in-law, George Dawson, a Secretary to the Treasury. Hitherto noted for his strong Protestant views, Dawson told his constituents at Londonderry, on the anniversary of the relief of that city in 1689, that it was time to give Catholics full political rights. The Orangemen were aghast, and it was naturally supposed that the speech was a stalking horse for the government. The Duke could not very well dismiss Dawson while trying to keep Peel, but once the Home Secretary had pronounced the speech 'unfair and impolitic in the extreme,' he could expostulate: 'Dawson should recollect that he is the servant of the government; that he is supposed as the Secretary of the Treasury to be in my confidence; and as your brother-in-law to be in yours. He should be a little more cautious.'[11] All these incidents added to Wellington's troubles by forcing him to go out of his way to convey the impression that he had not wavered in his devotion to the Protestant constitution.

The Prime Minister might have lessened his difficulties by taking the Lord Lieutenant of Ireland into his confidence. But he did not trust Anglesey, who had been openly supporting emancipation since the Clare election, and they spent the summer and autumn ostensibly working at cross purposes. The King wanted to dismiss the Viceroy at the beginning of August, but the Duke and Peel considered the timing wrong. Although he did not know it, Anglesey was being kept in office only so long as it suited their convenience. He attributed the refusal of his advice to pacify Ireland by concession to Wellington's incapacity. 'I am disposed to think that the Duke of Wellington would willingly adjust the question,' he told Lord Holland, 'but that he does not know how to set about it. I feel confident that I do, but he has not the nerves to put himself into my hands, & to open his heart to me.'[12] Anglesey informed O'Connell of his impending proclamation declaring assemblies illegal, thereby enabling the Catholic leader to issue his own address and take the credit for reducing tension, and he refused to arrest Catholic troublemakers. The Duke told Bathurst (who knew of his emancipation plans): 'Lord Anglesey is gone mad. He is bit by a mad Papist; or instigated by the love of popularity.'[13]

When the Viceroy went further, complaining that Wellington did not keep him informed on Irish policy, he was sharply reminded that it was his duty to enforce the law as it existed: 'You are quite mistaken if you suppose that you are the first Lord-Lieutenant who has governed Ireland with an impartial hand.' Anglesey's attempt to turn away this wrath by observing that Wellesley had also been conciliatory to the Catholics and that the King himself would approve his administration if he had the opportunity to observe the state of the country did nothing to diminish the Duke's anger. But the height of impertinence was reached when Anglesey demanded the right to publish their correspondence if necessary to defend himself.[14] Summoning the cabinet on Christmas Eve, Wellington read the Viceroy's letters and got his colleagues to agree to his dismissal.

Anglesey's successor was the Duke of Northumberland, whose strong Protestantism had given way to the pleasing conviction that the time had now come for a settlement of the Catholic question under the wise leadership of the Duke. But another development at the same time gave the transfer of authority a different appearance. A few weeks before Wellington had received a letter from Dr Patrick Curtis, the Catholic Archbiship of Armagh and Primate of Ireland, expressing the hope that rumours of an impending resolution of the Catholic issue were true. Perhaps recalling that he had received valuable assistance from Curtis, then Rector of the Irish College at Salamanca, during the Peninsula War, the Duke took the trouble to reply, saying that he would like to see the issue settled but could see no prospect of it. This was not much different from what he had told the House of Lords in June, but Curtis found in the letter some ray of encouragement and was soon showing it around ostensibly on the principle that it was better to reveal the truth than allow wild speculation about a letter franked by the Prime Minister. A copy eventually reached the Dublin newspapers and Anglesey, after inspecting the original, wrote to Curtis saying that although there seemed no likelihood of emancipation in the near future, Wellington was the best individual to bring it about. On New Year's Day 1829, the day after receiving the notice of his recall, Anglesey had the correspondence published in the newspapers to defuse Catholic anger at his dismissal.[15]

The Duke was furious. Parliament would assemble in a month. Peel seemed as determined as ever to resign. The King had agreed to nothing. And here was the departing Viceroy maniacally inflaming Protestant opinion. Anglesey was ordered home immediately and the government of Ireland entrusted to the Lord Justices until the new Lord Lieutenant arrived. To most people this peremptory summons was a clear indication that Wellington intended to stand by the penal laws.

Desperate for the right kind of strong allies in his emancipation venture, the Prime Minister turned to the Church, hoping that the Bishops would be as willing to give way on the Catholic issue as they had been on the Dissenters a few months ago. But the ecclesiastics failed him again, this time in the opposite sense. Not only were they hostile to Catholicism, as they had not been to Dissent, they also knew that concession would jeopardize the position of the Church in Ireland.

This adamant stand proved to be a blessing in disguise. Peel now accepted that a safe settlement of the Catholic question depended on him, and on 12 January he told the Duke that he would remain if necessary. Wellington was overcome with relief. He told the Home Secretary that even if the King accepted emancipation, the difficulties of getting it through Parliament would be increased tenfold by his departure, while his continuation in office would ensure that 'the means of getting the better of them will be diminished in the same proportion.'[16] But when Peel was converted, he was converted more thoroughly than the Duke, and the price of his services was to go far beyond what the Prime Minister considered a safe position. During their earlier discussions Peel had opposed the idea of an annual relief bill, preferring complete political equality except for certain sensitive offices; he had been sceptical of a change in the franchise that would give more power to those less dependent on the landlords; he had warned that state payment of the priests would lead to similar demands from Dissenters and even the established Church; and he had considered that licensing priests would be no more than a formality while giving them 'a sanction and authority derived from the Crown.'[17] With a heavy heart the Duke had to put aside most of his own convictions and accept Peel's.

With time pressing, the two turned their efforts to the King. Three days after Peel agreed to stay, George IV gave separate interviews to the Protestant ministers, Wellington, Peel, Lyndhurst, Bathurst, Goulburn and Herries, and to his dismay discovered them all convinced that Catholic emancipation must be granted. He had little choice but to allow the whole cabinet to discuss the matter, though he insisted that he was 'in no way pledged to the adoption of the views of his Government, even if it should concur unanimously in the course to be pursued.'[18] Two days later the Duke told the pro-Catholic ministers of the deliberations over the last few months and Peel announced that he would stay despite his previous record on the matter. Thereafter the cabinet met almost every day to work out the details of the Speech from the Throne. But when Wellington gave the King a preliminary report, he burst out: 'What, do you mean a Catholic to hold any judicial office? To be a Judge of King's Bench? . . . Damn it, &c., you mean to let them into Parliament?'[19]

Recognizing that managing the King and even its own supporters was not going to be easy, the cabinet decided to proceed in stages. First the Catholic Association would be suppressed. Then the voting qualification would be raised and the King given the right to prohibit unacceptable priests, to prevent the Catholic clergy from assuming titles held by the Church of England, wearing religious habits, worshipping in public and founding new religious houses, and to exercise some control over Maynooth College, which had been training Catholic clergy with government support since 1795. Once these securities had been accepted Catholics would be allowed to sit in Parliament and to hold all offices save Lord Chancellor of England and Ireland, Prime Minister, Secretary of State and all posts connected with Oxford, Cambridge and schools of royal foundation requiring the holders to profess the faith of the Established Church.[20] With Parliament asembling only a few days after these arrangements had been agreed on, the ministers did not risk telling the King about specific legislation but concentrated on getting his assent to a passage in the Speech commending the matter to the two Houses for consideration. Perfectly well aware of what was afoot, George IV did his best to avoid even formal approval. Only the firm resolve of the Duke got him to accept the Speech as drafted.

When the government announced its plans to the backbenchers the evening before Parliament met, there was no great beating of shields by those who had rejoiced in the departure of the Canningites as a sign that the Protestant constitution was safe in the hands of its strongest defenders. The peers who dined with Wellington at Apsley House were sulky[21] and it was hard to find individuals of standing who would move and second the Reply in the two Houses. In the Lords the Marquess of Salisbury practically abdicated as mover by mumbling that he could accept Catholic emancipation only if there were the fullest securities; in the Commons the seconder, Lord Curry, was no more enthusiastic.

The Whigs and Canningites were ecstatic at the announcement of Catholic emancipation in the Speech, though resentful that it should be brought about by the man who had driven them from office. But it was the Ultras who really felt betrayed. Lord Eldon launched a formidable attack, claiming as he had on the Protestant disabilities a year before, but this time with more feeling, that it was not only difficult but dangerous and unconstitutional to alter the Catholic laws. The Duke appealed in vain to the great jurist to assist the ministry with his learning and experience. In vain too did he try to convince his old friends that he had always been anxious to settle this issue. To allay their fears he assured them that measures to pacify Ireland would be introduced before emancipation. He maintained that the constitution would not be endangered because Catholics would never be in a dominant position. Without a trace of embarrassment considering his previous contempt for public opinion, he insisted that a majority of the people wanted a solution to the matter. And he appealed to the peers to refrain from further discussion until they saw the legislation.[22] But the Tory Lords had not the slightest intention of accepting such a self-denying ordinance. Nor were they mollified by Lord Anglesey's generous congratulations on Wellington's courageous stand.

Undismayed by this initial hostility, the Duke was confident that the Ultras would soon see the wisdom of this action and fall into line behind it. To hasten the process, he applied himself to personal persuasion. To the Duke of Rutland, for example, who arrived with a large petition against emancipation, he sent a long narrative of events, concluding that the alternative to himself was those who were less concerned about the interests of the aristrocracy:

> If this government is not supported by those highly respected
> individuals and parties in this country who are the main pillars of the
> monarchy, it is time that I should take my leave.
>
> I cannot submit to be the puppet of the rump of the Whigs and of
> Mr. Canning.

Rutland refused to commit himself to supporting Catholic relief, but he did modify his hostility to the extent of saying that Wellington's resignation would be 'the greatest calamity which could befall the country in this crisis.'[23]

Those Tories who felt awkward about attacking their hero found an easier target in Peel, who had always been identified with a strong Protestant position. When he sought vindication from the charges of apostasy, weakness and opportunism by submitting to re-election at Oxford University, he was defeated by a Protestant champion and forced to seek refuge in the rotten borough of Westbury, obligingly vacated by the owner, Sir Manasseh Lopes, a financier convicted of electoral corruption in another notorious rotten borough a decade before. Three voters elected Peel while others registered their objections in a shower of missiles and the poll closed while the Protestant candidate was still on his way from London. The defeat at Oxford and the manner of Peel's return did nothing to strengthen the moral case for emancipation or counter the insistence of the Ultras that the Duke and Peel were acting contrary to the wishes of the country.

The Tory opposition was strengthened by the Duke of Cumberland who hurried over from Germany as soon as he heard rumours of Catholic relief. Wellington had persuaded the King to write to dissuade him from making matters worse by coming to England and had added a message of his own pointing to the reasons against the third in line to the throne leading a partisan group.[24] These letters missed Cumberland on the road, but they would not have deterred him from his public duty. As soon as he arrived, he went directly to Windsor to keep his brother on the Protestant path. The value of the assurance that he would not put himself at the head of the Protestant party was revealed three days later when he violently denounced emancipation in the House of Lords. Despite Wellington's entreaties, he was also relentless in his efforts with the King. If Cumberland thought he could form a ministry, Wellington told him, he should do so; otherwise, 'defeating the measures of the present Govt was only harrassing the King & defeating his own object, for the King cd only fall back upon the Whigs.'[25]

The preliminary coercive legislation was welcomed by the Tories and acquiesced in by the opposition as the price of emancipation. But the obstruction, evasion and vacillations of the King made it seem that the relief measure might never even be introduced. Wellington, above all, but also his colleagues, had to devote enormous efforts to persuasion and endure interminable monologues. After one conference which went on for six hours, during which the Duke, Peel and Lyndhurst scarcely managed to speak for fifteen minutes, the King objected to every part of the bill and said that he would not hear of it. The three ministers then told him that they would announce to Parliament the next day that they no longer held their offices and would not proceed with the legislation.[26] An hour and a half after they left the King's resolve failed him and he sent a message retracting his veto: 'As I find that the country would be left without an administration, I have decided to yield my opinion to *that* which is considered by the Cabinet to be for the immediate interests of the country .... God knows what pain it costs me to write these words.' But whatever the pain, Wellington insisted on a more explicit endorsement. From his bed the next morning the monarch replied: '*You have put the right construction upon the meaning of my letter of last evening.*'[27]

After the strain of the last few months it is hardly surprising that the Duke's health collapsed when the King finally relented. He was confined to his house for several days with a bad cold and as usual was bled, which must have added to his exhaustion.[28] In the meantime Peel introduced the Emancipation Bill in the Commons. There was no doubt that it would pass by large majorities with the support of the Whigs and the Canningites. But the ministry was greatly embarrassed when those voting against it included Sir Charles Wetherell, the Solicitor General, George Bankes, the Chief Secretary of the Board of Control, Lord Lowther, the Commissioner of Land Revenue, and several minor officials. Catholic emancipation had been an open question in Wellington's government, but voting against it as an official measure was a different matter. When Mrs Arbuthnot, having swallowed her own fierce opposition, tried to goad the Duke into sacking the dissidents by telling him that the motto being applied to his government was 'Amnesty for enemies & oblivion for friends,' he angrily told her that he knew best and would do as he liked. The next day he added: 'I am fighting this battle, for it is a battle like Waterloo. I must look to the means of winning it and, to do that, I must keep the King quiet & the Tory Party in as good humour as I can.'[29] But his forbearance simply increased Tory boldness. The press heaped abuse on him; the King continued to receive anyone with petitions against the bill; and the Duke of Cumberland even had the idea of leading a mob to Windsor with a petition, which led Wellington to declare that he would have no hesitation in clapping Cumberland in the Tower.[30] The final provocation came when Wetherell, whose Protestant conscience had prevented him from drafting the bill, drunkenly launched a vicious attack on it and the Chancellor in the House of Commons. Despite Cumberland's boast to Lyndhurst that the Duke would not dare dismiss him, he promptly did.

While the Emancipation and Franchise Bills were in the Commons, the peers kept their anger warm by calling for information and presenting petitions. On 10 March, the first day that he had been out since his cold, the Prime Minister made an effective reply to the Earl of Winchelsea, the rising young Tory Hotspur of debate. Denouncing Wellington's conduct as arbitrary and predicting his early relief from the burdens of office, Winchelsea called for a general election and a reform of Parliament to make it more reflective of the real views of the country. Neither his suggestion of parliamentary reform, novel in the mouth of a Tory at the time, nor his blistering attack were particularly worthy of notice by the

Duke, but a few days later Winchelsea sent a letter to the secretary of the committee establishing King's College in London. A Church antidote to 'that Godless place in Gower Street,' the Benthamite University College, King's was a royal foundation and the Prime Minister a principal figure. Winchelsea suavely explained that he wished to withdraw his subscription as the institution was clearly part of Wellington's 'insidious designs, for the infringement of our liberties, and the introduction of Popery into every department of the State.'[31]

When the letter was published in a newspaper, the Duke, as Winchelsea intended, was goaded into defending himself. Since the courts were closed until May, he resorted to the private aristocratic code of honour. Winchelsea compounded his refusal to apologize by impertinently insisting that Wellington first deny that he had been contemplating emancipation when he presided over the meeting to found the college. The Duke angrily retorted that no man had the right 'to call me before him, to justify myself from the charges which his fancy may suggest.' Further correspondence through intermediaries produced no retraction and Wellington demanded 'that satisfaction for your conduct which a gentleman has a right to require, and which a gentleman never refuses to give.'[32]

The Duke did not approve of duels but ire and the unavailability of immediate legal recourse drove him to one. Winchelsea had sober second thoughts about killing or even wounding the great man. On the eve of the meeting he told his second, Lord Falmouth, that he would not fire at him, but after Wellington's shot would offer an expression of regret.[33] The next morning they met at Battersea Fields at eight o'clock. 'Well, I dare say you little expected it was I who wanted you to be here,' the Duke remarked to Dr Hume in great good humour. After loading the pistols and measuring off twelve paces with Falmouth, Wellington's second, Sir Henry Hardinge, the Secretary at War, read a formal protest against the duel and warned Winchelsea and Falmouth that they alone were responsible for the consequences. At the signal the Duke raised his pistol and seeing that Winchelsea did not follow, fired and missed. Winchelsea then raised his pistol over his head and fired into the air. It is impossible to tell whether Wellington fired wide or not. According to one account he told Hardinge: 'I only fired at his legs.'[34] But he was not a good shot and the result may have borne little relation to the intent. Out shooting ten years earlier he had emptied two and a half powder horns with little result apart from peppering a retriever, a keeper's gaiters and the arms of an old woman washing clothes at a cottage window.[35] There is no evidence that his aim had improved in the interval and Winchelsea should have considered himself lucky to have escaped unharmed.

The form of a duel having been enacted, Falmouth pulled out a prepared statement, but the Duke noticed that it did not contain the word 'apology.' Honour was satisfied when at Hume's suggestion the word was simply inserted. Hardinge then made a statement that Winchelsea and Falmouth were responsible for forcing Wellington to fight his first duel. Falmouth tried to reply, but the Duke interrupted: 'My Lord Falmouth, I have nothing to do with these matters.' Touching two fingers to his hat he bid the company 'Good Morning' and rode away with Hardinge.[36]

Most people admired Wellington's personal courage and blamed Winchelsea for the duel, but there was a general feeling that the Prime Minister should not have descended to Winchelsea's level. The Duke himself believed that he had cleared the atmosphere of slander and that 'intentions not short of criminal were given up in consequence of remonstrances from some of the most prudent of the party, who came forward in consequence of the duel.'[37] Even the King admired this chivalric conduct, prompting a wit to remark that he would want to fight a duel himself, and another to reply: 'He will be sure to think he has fought one.'[38] The most curious response came from the philosopher Jeremy Bentham who in a long diatribe to the 'Ill-Advised Man!' (his salutation) inveighed against the private law of duelling, advised Wellington to repent before the House of Lords and hailed the Duke as the indispensable reformer: 'Here am I, leader of the Radicals ... more solicitous for the life of the leader of the Absolutists than he himself is! What paradoxes, what prodigies, has not the field of politics given birth to of late!' But they were not paradoxes on which Wellington cared to dwell. His perfunctory reply did not save him from another tortured letter in which Bentham presumed to take a bolder line: 'I want to make you do what Cromwell tried at and found was too much for him. I cannot afford to lose you.'[39] But despite the provocation of this comparison with the destroyer of royal government, Wellington was able to resist the temptation of replying.

Whatever the duel did for the Duke's personal popularity, there is no evidence that it did much to help the emancipation bill in the House of Lords. The Ultras continued in their unrelenting hostility and the King did not cease to receive petitions. Wellington was so tired of the whole business that he threatened to resign as soon as it was over. He would not rely on the Whigs and he was tempted to tell the King that by encouraging his natural supporters against the government, he had destroyed the ministry and must make another as best he could.[40]

When he opened the debate on second reading, the Duke addressed himself primarily to the Tory Lords. He begged them to believe that his fundamental attitude was unchanged. Only a careful study of conditions while in office had convinced him that his former stand on the Catholic question was no longer tenable. Pointing to the state of Ireland, which the Ultras agreed had been on the verge of civil war for a year and a half, he argued that it was impossible to use the law against Catholic leaders because they were careful not to break it. Their activities were also widely dispersed. The government could not simply ask Parliament for stronger powers because a majority of the House of Commons was convinced that emancipation was the real remedy and using armed force without legal support would risk complete social collapse. But if nothing were done the skilful Catholic leaders would keep Ireland in chaos forever. Invoking his great authority, he told the peers that even if he had the military means, he still would not consider force the way to solve the problem. 'I am one of those who have probably passed a longer period of my life engaged in war than most men,' he reminded the House,

> and principally, I may say, in civil war; and I must say this – that if I could avoid, by any sacrifice whatever, even one month of civil war in the country to which I am attached, I would sacrifice my life in order to do it [cheers]. I say that there is nothing which destroys property and prosperity, and demoralizes character to the degree that civil war does: by it the hand of man is raised against his neighbour, against his brother, and the whole scene ends in confusion and devastation.

Turning to the idea that emancipation violated the sacred constitution established at the Glorious Revolution, he noted that the penal laws against Catholics had been altered as early as the reigns of William and Mary and Queen Anne, and as recently as 1817 when Catholic army and navy officers had been excused from taking the same oath as Members of Parliament – a change that had been supported by the then Lord Chancellor, Lord Eldon. The Church in Ireland could only lose in any upheaval and no Catholic securities could strengthen it. Countering his own earlier view, he argued that any agreement with the Pope would be an admission that he had some authority in the country and would weaken the position of the Church of England. He ended on the visionary note that religious differences and the political divisions based on them would disappear as a result of emancipation, but prudently qualified this by a solemn assurance that if this turned out to be wrong, he would not hesitate to ask Parliament to provide whatever was necessary to meet the danger.[41]

It is impossible to tell if Wellington's speech converted any inclined to rejection, but there was great surprise when second reading was carried by the wide margin of 217 to 112. The fate of the bill thus settled, the other stages were quickly passed and attention turned to the measure to raise the Irish franchise. The Duke pointed out that electoral influence had fallen from the hands of the landlords and large leaseholders who had created a mass of 40s. freeholders for life in order to increase their power to the Catholic clergy. Now that Catholics were to sit in Parliament, it was vital to ensure that they were not simply creatures of a Catholic organization.[42] Accepting the wisdom of this, the House of Lords had little objection to raising the voting qualification from 40s. to £10.

As these measures made their way through the Lords, the King was abusing his ministers in his worst style and threatening to withhold royal assent until after the Easter recess. The Prime Minister in turn stormed that George IV was 'the worst man he ever fell in with in his whole life, the most selfish, the most false, the most ill-natured, the most entirely without one redeeming quality.' He repeated his threat to resign as soon as emancipation was accepted and never to serve again, not even as Commander in Chief unless his services were required in the field outside the country. Mrs Arbuthnot tried with little effect to mollify him by pointing out that those who would suffer most would be the people: 'You have achieved a most brilliant victory, you have the prospect before you of giving permanent peace & tranquility to a country which has never yet known either.... Under these circumstances you have no right to resign yr office because you are bored with the labour & disgusted with the King.'[43]

Wellington was obviously in no mood to be trifled with. When the idea was revived of a procession from Apsley House to Windsor to present a petition to the King through the Duke of Cumberland, he warned that the proceedings would be illegal and told the King to accept the petition only through the Home Secretary. To make evasion more difficult Peel was dispatched to Windsor and instructed formally to repeat the advice. 'If the King will not take Peel's advice we go out' was the resolve of the cabinet. The procession turned out to be nothing more than a handful of people who travelled in carriages and who, when told by an equerry that they must go through Peel, went quietly away.[44] But the monarch took his petty revenge by holding up the commission for assent until an hour before the cabinet met to decide how it would deal with this latest obstruction.

By the time Parliament rose for Easter the Duke was exhausted and suffering from a bad cold. But he could take comfort in the reflection that he had solved the Catholic and Irish problems that had poisoned politics since the beginning of the century. Once the benefits of emancipation began to be obvious, the Ultras would return to his side, his wisdom confirmed by this latest success. Now that the issues separating the Canningites were also resolved, the way was open for them to return at his gracious invitation. Within a few months a government like Liverpool's, but free from the conflicts that had marred its last years, would be restored and the management of the country's affairs ordered and settled on the best and surest foundation.

Unfortunately Catholic emancipation turned out to be a Pyrrhic victory for Wellington and all he represented. Whatever it did for religious and political freedom, it did nothing for the peace and stability of Ireland. By giving Catholic Ireland an effective voice it markedly increased the agitation both there and at Westminster. The Ultras did eventually return to the Duke, but only in the face of a far greater danger produced in large part by their continuing hostility, and when it was too late for their restored champion to get the better of it. The Canningites, far from welcoming the opportunity to return with contrite hearts, would come back only as conquerors. Catholic emancipation was not the end of political controversy but the prelude to years of bitter conflict over the very reforms the Prime Minister had hoped to forestall.

The Duke could have reduced some of the tension in Ireland and in Parliament by using his influence to ensure a gracious handling of the way in which restrictions against Catholics were removed. When Parliament met after Easter, half a dozen peers of old Catholic families took the new oath and assumed their places in the House of Lords. No such tranquil scene characterized the House of Commons when O'Connell appeared on 15 May, having waited until Lord Surrey, the son of the Catholic Duke of Norfolk, had taken his seat. Since he had been elected before the Emancipation Act, he was told that he must take the old oath. When he refused he was ordered to withdraw. At the bar he insisted that nothing in the Act of Union prevented him from taking his seat and the spirit of the Relief Act favoured it. The Ultras were delighted to rally behind the ministry and humiliate their antagonist by ordering a new election, while the Canningites and Whigs in vain supported O'Connell.

No one doubted that the member for Clare would be returned, and no one dared oppose him. But O'Connell took advantage of his rebuff to revive the outlawed Catholic Association and travel around the country working up support for a new campaign to restore the 40s. franchise and repeal the union. The Protestants also organized and the summer of 1829 was marked by familiar scenes of violence and lawlessness.

Wellington believed that the trouble lay in the landlords' aim of embarrassing the government by neglecting their duties and refusing to enforce the law. When his old friend Lord Clancarty suggested public works to meet the unrest caused by the agricultural depression and collapse of trade that had reduced the demand for Irish workers in England, the Duke sharply replied: 'Governments have plenty to consider and to do in relation to Ireland without attending to schemes of this description, which can have only a partial operation.' He insisted that he would know the reason if the law were not fully enforced and pointed to the folly of landlords joining 'the party called the *King's friends* against his ministers, believing that is the way to save themselves, and to serve the country' while at the same complaining that 'Ireland is *banished from the consideration of government.*'[45] He told the Viceroy that the Ultras' efforts to bring down the ministry were 'a little manoeuvre which will answer no purpose.' If the authorities in Ireland would only assert themselves, no harm would befall the government.[46]

Despite his annoyance with the Ultras, the Duke worked with great patience to win them back. Those ministers who had voted against emancipation but not attacked the government were allowed to stay. The King naturally raised no objection when formally consulted; more to the point, the individuals themselves agreed to stay, though one of them felt obliged first to consult his mentor, the Duke of Cumberland.[47] After Peel's experience at Oxford, Wellington wisely waited six weeks until the end of the session before filling the two vacancies in the ministry and shuffling the minor offices. In the redistribution Lord Castlereagh, heir to the Ultra but pro-Catholic Lord Londonderry, became a Lord of the Admiralty and two conservative Whigs were also appointed: Sir James Scarlett, who had been dismissed to make way for Wetherell, now replaced him as Attorney General; and Lord Rosslyn, one of Grey's associates who had stood aloof from Canning's ministry, became Lord Privy Seal. No one outside the government was much impressed by the quality of those recruited or kept. The Whigs and Canningites were generally contemptuous of the additions, while the attitude of the Ultras was summed up by the Duke of Cumberland: 'it is all of a piece with that d—d rascal's (meaning the Duke of Wellington) conjunct! a junction with the Whigs & paving the way for Lord Grey.'[48]

Far from being appeased, the Ultras under Cumberland seized on every grievance until at last they found one which pulled down the mighty turncoat. A premonition of the final unlikely event appeared at the end of the 1829 session when the Marquess of Blandford, heir to the Duke of Marlborough, proposed suppressing the rotten boroughs in order to prevent them from being purchased as the foundation of a real Catholic party in Parliament. This was an indirect but telling thrust at the Duke's control of a solid block of seats through official patronage and influence as Prime Minister. It was an echo of what Winchelsea had said two months before, but even now the resolution caught the Ultras perplexed and unprepared. Few of them joined the Whigs, who were careful to distinguish their motives from Blandford's, in voting for it. But the virtues of a House of Commons free from government influence was something for Old Tories to ponder.

Wellington bore what he considered this passing mischief largely in public silence. The only time he lashed out was when the *Morning Journal* absurdly charged that he was aiming to become King and boldly declared that it would resist the attempt. The Duke insisted on prosecution and secured a verdict against the paper. But his outburst of anger did him little good. Many thought that he had demeaned himself even by noticing the article, while the press rallied to the defence of its freedom. For the most part he relieved his strain and frustration in private. When, as so often, he threatened to escape by resignation, Mrs Arbuthnot attributed it to overwork: 'He works like a dray horse, he cannot gain by it for he is as great as he ever can be.' She did not think that he would actually leave. As she pointed out, he always got his own way in the end but he was 'a sort of spoiled child. He wishes to be liked by everybody; he is by nine-tenths, but the *one* tenth irritates him.'[49]

When trade continued depressed through the winter of 1829–30 and the harvest proved disastrous, it was naturally supposed that Wellington would court some popularity, at least among his natural agricultural allies, when Parliament met in February. But he was convinced that conditions were not as bad as they were represented, and in any event did not think that there was much that the government could do. In October he told Charles Arbuthnot that the 'enormous extent of our manufactures, their constant increase, our improved agriculture, the increase of buildings in nearly every town in England and throughout the country, the increase of luxury in the middle classes, and the keeping up of the revenue' proved that the economy was sound. The various remedies proposed by the agriculturalists would do nothing to improve conditions. If there was a problem it was due to the 'high profits of the retail traders, and the state of luxury in which they live,' not high taxes, tithes or lack of employment.[50]

The Speech from the Throne three months later mirrored this view in blandly regretting that distress should prevail 'among the agricultural and manufacturing classes in some parts of the country' but feeling sure that the legislators would agree that this was owing largely to bad weather and other causes beyond political remedy and that they would not want to do anything to compromise public credit. Far from assuring members of both Houses about the ministry's competence, the statement produced an uproar that went beyond partisan considerations, though Wellington's erstwhile friends were prominently in the van. For the first time since the war amendments were moved to the Replies in both Houses. In the Commons the government came close to falling when Sir Edward Knatchbull, an agricultural Tory from Kent, proposed an amendment deploring the distress, which he insisted was general throughout the country, and calling on the House to consider ways to cure it. He was supported by other Ultras, the Canningites and Daniel O'Connell, who took his seat and made his maiden speech that day. The ministry was saved by Lord Howick, heir to Lord Grey, who argued that the Duke's legislative record entitled him to a fair trial. But help from that quarter simply increased the hostility of the Ultras towards the Prime Minister. In the Lords, Earl Stanhope denounced the Speech as the most inept and inappropriate ever delivered from the Throne; his amendment was defeated only by the Whigs and Canningites joining Wellington from fear that Stanhope would use a victory to press for his favourite project of suspending the convertibility of paper money for gold. This reinforcement also served to drive the Duke and the Ultras further apart. Wellington himself did not help the cause of reunion by insisting that he was concerned about the state of the country but considered that retrenchment and a steady reduction of the national debt provided the best remedies.[51]

True to its beliefs, the administration reduced expenditures, lowered the interest on some securities and abolished the taxes on leather, cider and beer, but not on malt which the agriculturalists most wanted. The Duke claimed that those taxes had been repealed which, 'as compared with others, would take the smallest sum out of the Treasury, and put the largest amount into the pockets of the people; he was satisfied that the repeal would be a great relief to the country.'[52] In line with his conviction that middlemen were profiting unduly, a measure was introduced permitting anyone on payment of two guineas to the Excise Commissioners to sell beer. This produced almost five hundred petitions from brewers who owned or controlled licensed premises; from local owners who feared competition; from agriculturalists who would have preferred the more direct benefit of remitting the malt tax; and from local politicians who objected to undermining the right of magistrates to license particular houses. The Ultras were the natural spokesmen for all these interests; but the protests simply confirmed Wellington's belief that there was a conspiracy against the welfare of the community. He was insistent that the new public houses would provide better surroundings and enable workers to enjoy 'a superior article at a much cheaper rate than they had been accustomed to do.'[53] His confidence was not long lived. A year later, when his political fortunes had changed, he complained that the measure had 'occasioned and encouraged extraordinary drunkenness. It has broken up the domestic habits of the people. It has brought many families upon the poor-rates. It has tended to promote disturbances. The public-houses are so numerous, that they cannot be under the control of the magistrates.'[54]

All of the ministry's financial legislation went some way towards pleasing some of its opponents. All of them wanted it to go further in some direction, but the government was safe so long as they remained divided and contradictory. The Duke could see in the diverse attacks confirmation of the wisdom of his moderate course, and could expect that in time even the obtuse would recognize his steady wisdom. But time was running out in the spring of 1830. The King was obviously failing. If he died, an election would have to be held within six months.

At the end of May George IV gave up signing documents, and on 26 June he died. Despite all that he had endured from him, Wellington managed a handsome tribute that did him no harm among those Tories who had fastened their hopes on the late King's opposition to change and who feared his successor's apparent liberalism. Fortunately not on oath while extolling the monarch's virtues, he told the House of Lords that his manners

> received a polish, and his understanding a degree of cultivation, which made him far surpass in accomplishments all his subjects; and made him one of the most remarkable Sovereigns of our time.... Up to the last moment of his life, no man ever approached his Majesty who did not feel instructed by his learning, and gratified by his condescension, affability, and kindness of disposition.[55]

William IV, despite having been dismissed as Lord High Admiral two years before and having supported Catholic emancipation, lost no time in assuring his ministers that they enjoyed his full confidence. Proposing the Duke's health at a banquet at Apsley House a month after his accession, he announced 'to all whom he saw around him, to all the Ambassadors and Ministers of foreign Powers, and to all the Noblemen and Gentlemen present, that as long as he should sit upon the throne he should continue to give him the same confidence.'[56] Wellington was too wise to put much faith in the spontaneous ebullition of an eccentric monarch, but he enthusiastically pronounced him 'so reasonable and tractable ... that he had done more business with him in ten minutes than with the other in as many days.'[57]

William IV's accession nevertheless meant an election while Wellington's old supporters were no closer to reconciliation than they had been at the height of the battle over Catholic emancipation. The death of George IV also removed the proscription on Lord Grey and increased the likelihood that he would become a rallying point for the variegated opposition. 'Lord Grey is certainly in himself a host,' Wellington gloomily reflected, 'and his active opposition in the House of Lords, as the leader, would render others active likewise, whose opposition is now so little so, and more personal than political.'[58] So impressed was the Prime Minister by this danger that in George IV's last days he considered resigning and entrusting the ministry to the fresh leadership of Peel.

Rather than waiting for its opponents to consolidate, the government decided to strike immediately and elections began at the end of July. The last stages of polling coincided with news of the revolution in France which drove the absolutist Charles X off the throne and touched off other uprisings on the continent; but this had little effect on the elections, which were mostly over by this time.[59] As usual only about a quarter of the seats were contested, but the ministry concentrated its efforts against those Canningites who sat for boroughs under government influence, thereby not only doing nothing to win them back but pushing them further towards parliamentary reform to free Parliament from the control of the cabinet. The gains against the Canningites were at least offset by losses in other boroughs. Two of Peel's brothers and his brother-in-law were defeated. In the counties the loss of prestige was even greater than the numbers; there was a general revolt against established interests, both Whig and Tory, and few were returned who were not in favour of some kind of reform.[60]

It was impossible to tell how the various factions stood until Parliament met and the ministry declared its intentions. With the revolutions on the continent and unrest at home, Charles Greville thought that the Duke's prestige might carry the government through the short autumn session necessary to settle the King's civil list, after which he would be able to negotiate with others from a position of strength. 'There is unquestionably a notion amongst many persons (of the aristocracy) that he is the only man to rely upon for governing this country in the midst of difficulties,' Greville thought, though it was hard to say on what the impression was based; 'not certainly upon any experience of his abilities for government either as to principles or the details of particular branches of business, or his profound, dispassionate, and statesmanlike sagacity,' but more upon 'certain vague predilictions, and the confidence which he has infused into others by his own firm, manly, and even dictatorial character, and the recollection of his military exploits and splendid career, which have not yet lost their power over the minds of men.' Pining for someone with the mastery of a Canning just a few days before, Greville had analysed what he considered Wellington's shortcomings as Prime Minister. His method was not 'patient investigation, profound knowledge of human nature, and cool discriminating sagacity,' but quick apprehension which deceived him into thinking that he knew more than he did. Greville thought his amazing confidence the product of his military successes, reinforced by the deference of his acolytes. Although usually right and sensible, he was nevertheless 'beset by weaknesses and passions which must, and continually do, blind his judgment.' Above all he lacked 'that suavity of manner, that watchfulness of observation, that power of taking great and enlarged views of events and characters, and of weighing opposite interests and probabilities' needed in the present delicate circumstances, in which 'one false step, any hasty measure, or even incautious expression, may be attended with consequences of immense importance.'[61] But even Greville must have been astonished at his own prescience when Parliament met.

The Duke was not downcast by the results of the election, but he did recognize the need to strengthen the ministry in order to defend the country's institutions against the various schemes for change that were likely to be proposed. Even before Parliament had been dissolved he had tried to detach Lord Melbourne, as William Lamb had become on the death of his father, from the Canningites and entice him back to office with urbane assurances that he perfectly understood that Melbourne had left from fear of personal embarrassment over a love affair in Dublin and not for political reasons. Melbourne churlishly replied that he had resigned over the Duke's treatment of Huskisson and would not return without some of his former colleagues, Whig as well as Canningite.[62]

Wellington had no intention of submitting to such a demand, but after the election he swept aside the unpleasantness of the campaign against the

Canningites and decided to make a direct approach to their leader. An ideal opportunity arose with the opening of the Manchester-Liverpool railway on 15 September. The Prime Minister was bidden as an honoured guest and Huskisson would be in attendance as MP for Liverpool and sponsor of the Railway Bill in Parliament. As the harvest was good, the price of food falling and industry reviving, Huskisson thought that the 'great Captain' would be able to throw him into the background and 'cater a little applause and bid for a little popularity before the meeting of the new Parliament,' though he thought that it would take great self-confidence for the Duke to claim any credit for the improved situation. In the same letter he also told the Whig, Sir James Graham, that Whigs and Canningites should not listen to separate offers but insist on a total reconstruction of the ministry, 'so as to exclude no one and to admit to a fair participation of influence and power in the deliberations and management of the State persons more competent than those who now have charge of some of the most important Departments.'[63]

With Huskisson in this unpromising mood, the railway expedition set out from Liverpool in fine style. The Duke and his party were provided with a special car of gilt wood and a scarlet awning. Their train ran on one track while the others ran alongside it. Mrs Arbuthnot wrote that she had never seen a more beautiful sight than when the train 'shot off' to the waving of a vast crowd. One of the trains on the other track passed and was passed by Wellington's for his amusement. After covering sixteen miles in forty minutes, they stopped to take on water. Despite warnings from the directors, the official party clambered out and walked about the tracks as they would have done if changing horses. Huskisson was talking to the Duke and Mrs Arbuthnot when George Stephenson's Rocket came hurtling down the track. The visitors fled to their carriages but Huskisson, always clumsy and still weak from a recent illness, was struck by the engine which crushed his leg and thigh. In the general alarm and dismay Lord Wilton managed to apply a tourniquet. Huskisson was hoisted into the music carriage which was attached to Wellington's engine and dispatched to the nearest town at the unprecedented speed of thirty-six miles an hour.

The official party was all for returning to Liverpool, but the directors advised going to Manchester to prevent the crowds from becoming violent. Reluctantly they continued and found the entire population out to see the Duke. People cheered and crowded around to shake his hand and Mrs Arbuthnot thought that she had never witnessed such enthusiasm, though she had seen him in many such situations. In the tragic circumstances the Prime Minister departed Manchester as soon as he decently could, stopped to inquire about Huskisson's hopeless condition on the way back, and left the train before it reached Liverpool to walk to the house where he was staying. The celebrations at Liverpool were cancelled; but early the next day he went to see its fine new docks and public buildings.[64]

Wellington was greatly impressed by his reception and what he had seen in the North. On his return he gave a glowing account of the condition of that part of the country to the cabinet. He admired the machinery and the canals but was understandably more restrained in his praise of the railway. 'The rapidity of motion is so great in the steam carriages that even the Duke with his quick eyes could not see the figures on the posts which mark the distances at every quarter of a mile,' Lord Ellenborough wrote, recording the Prime Minister's report, 'and when two steam carriages crossed no face could be seen. It was like the whizzing of a cannon ball. The cold is great, and they must have some defence against the wind, through which they pass so rapidly.'[65] When these changes were made and the railways spread, Wellington became a great traveller on them.

Reflecting on the consequences of Huskisson's accident, Charles Greville thought it another example of the fatality that attended the Duke: 'There were perhaps 500,000 people present on this occasion, and probably no one soul besides hurt. One man only is killed, and that man is his most dangerous opponent, the one from whom he had most to fear.'[66] Probably nothing would have come of the negotiations with Huskisson, and perhaps his death removed a barrier to reunion with the Canningites. A week later one of Huskisson's followers, Lord Wharncliffe, urged on the Prime Minister the necessity of strengthening a ministry that was generally beaten in argument if not in numbers. The revolutions abroad and the discontent at home pointed to a struggle in which

> the only hope of preserving what is vitally essential to the
> maintenance of the constitution, would appear to be the existence of
> an administrat'n, with strength and talent enough to rally round it the
> moderate and the sensible, and to enable it, without interposing an
> obstinate and useless resistance to real improvements, to resist
> attempts that are sure to be made and can only, if successful, lead to
> confusion.[67]

This welcome advice encouraged the Duke to make an indirect overture to Lord Palmerston, the new leader of the Canningites. Graciously observing that Palmerston's resignation in 1828 had not been accompanied by hard feelings and that there was no difference of policy to make a return discreditable, Wellington signified that he was willing to offer Palmerston high office.[68] But Palmerston was as insistent as his late leader on concerted action and would not join without others. When the Duke, in an interview at Apsley House on the eve of Parliament, agreed to include a couple of his associates, Palmerston held out for a total reconstruction that would have destroyed Wellington's dominance.

The appeals to the Canningites came to nothing, but they inspired both hopes and fears that the Duke would do something about parliamentary reform. The fact that he had been opposed to the enfranchisement of Birmingham in the last days of the old Parliament was no compelling evidence of his intentions.[69] Everyone remembered similar pronouncements before Catholic emancipation was proposed. By the time Parliament met in November there was a general feeling that some change was inevitable. Even many of the Ultras believed that concession was necessary to prevent the agricultural riots in the South and the industrial unrest in the North from developing into revolution like those in Europe. Other Ultras looked to parliamentary reform as a means of preventing Wellington from flouting the wishes of the country, as he had over Catholic emancipation.

But the Duke had no intention of proposing or encouraging any such change. Having seen for himself, he knew that the country was not in a serious condition. There was certainly much apprehension about events on the continent which had unsettled men's minds 'upon a variety of political questions, such as Parliamentary Reform, Tithes, Slavery, Taxation &c.,' he told the Irish Viceroy, but he hoped that the meeting of Parliament would 'tend to tranquillize and . . . we shall get through our difficulties.'[70]

With the Prime Minister in this optimistic mood, Parliament was opened by the King on 2 November. There was no mention of parliamentary reform in the Speech from the Throne but the Whigs raised the issue immediately. Linking the revolutions in Europe and the disturbances in Britain with his great eloquence, Lord Grey proposed a simple remedy:

> You see the danger around you; the storm is in the horizon, but the hurricane approaches. Begin, then, at once to strengthen your houses, to secure your windows, and to make fast your doors. But the mode in which this must be done, my Lords, is by securing the affections of your fellow-subjects, and – my Lords, I will pronounce the word – by reforming Parliament.

Wellington in reply concentrated on foreign affairs and on Catholic emancipation, which he denied was responsible for the continuing lawlessness in Ireland. Only at the end of his speech did he take up Grey's challenge in order to reiterate to his supporters and the Ultras that he had no intention of altering the admirable composition of the House of Commons. He told the peers that he had 'never read or heard of any measure up to the present moment which could in any degree satisfy his mind that the state of representation could be improved, or rendered more satisfactory to the country at large than at the present moment.' Such an uncompromising statement in the political climate of hostility and apprehension even in the House of Lords was bad enough, but he proceeded to compound his difficulties by delivering a memorable panegyric to the existing arrangement. Confident that his natural allies were looking for assurance that he would not be moved by any passing clamour to alter the basis of the constitution, he told them that the country possessed

> a Legislature which answered all the good purposes of legislation, and this to a greater degree than any Legislature ever had answered in any country whatever.... He would go still further and say, that if at the present moment he had imposed upon him the duty of forming a Legislature for any country, and particularly for a country like this, in possession of great property of various descriptions, he did not mean to assert that he could form such a Legislature as they possesed now, for the nature of man was incapable of reaching such excellence at once; but his great endeavour would be to form some description of legislature which would produce the same result.

He not only had no intention of introducing a measure of reform, but announced that it would be his duty to resist any brought forward by others.[71] In the House of Commons the mover of the Address in Reply was assuring the MPs that the ministry would not be found wanting in the reforms demanded by the spirit of the age.

When he sat down the Duke is supposed to have turned to Lord Aberdeen and asked: 'I have not said too much, have I?' The Foreign Secretary, a proponent of moderate reform, replied: '*You'll hear of it!*' When another peer came into the House and asked Aberdeen what Wellington had said, he replied: 'He said that we were going out.'[72] Greville thought, 'Never was there an act of more egregious folly, or one so universally condemned by friends and foes.'[73] The Duke's adamant stand drove the Whigs and Canningites together in insisting on some degree of parliamentary reform, without achieving its chief object of conciliating the Ultras, who were also willing to accept some change in the Commons. Calling for a small measure of parliamentary reform to conciliate the confidence of the country two days later, Lord Winchelsea told his duelling opponent that if he was looking for support among 'the high-minded gentlemen' with whom he had formerly associated, he might as well 'attempt to take high heaven by storm.'[74] Peel's refusal to commit the government to tax reductions added to the political disaffection, but the real battle lines were drawn on parliamentary reform. Despite the feelings of some ministers, the cabinet was prepared to stand firm when the issue was debated in the Commons on 16 November.

In the meantime, the ministry had an opportunity to demonstrate its determination to take strong measures against popular disturbances on the occasion of the Lord Mayor's procession and banquet on the 9th. The Prime Minister would attend, along with the King and Queen. As the date approached rumours circulated that an attack would be made on him. In the Rotunda, a meeting house near Blackfriars Bridge, Henry Hunt and William Cobbett were haranguing crowds on the iniquities of the government, denouncing the Duke's opposition to reform and inveighing against the restrictions on popular liberties by the new and efficient Metropolitan Police instituted the year before. On the 6th the Lord Mayor-elect wrote to tell Wellington that he had heard of designs against him and advised bringing an escort of troops. The Duke had also learned of plans to attack the police, to extinguish the lights in the banquet hall and other schemes that would precipitate riot and disorder. The cabinet finally advised the King not to attend. Wellington also decided not to go rather than seeking protection 'from the civil and military power in such a way as would be likely to produce that very disturbance which all men were so anxious to avoid.'[75] This prudence was seized upon as an admission of the government's unpopularity and proof that a more responsive one was needed. Lord Wellesley did not help matters, or relations with his brother, by pronouncing that decision 'the boldest act of cowardice he had ever heard of.'[76]

Despite the cancellation, there was a feeling that something would happen that night. The troops in the capital were reinforced and three divisions of police kept in reserve. The Duke carefully secured Apsley House. The gates into the stables and yard were locked and armed guards were stationed at the windows; no one was to fire unless the garden was broken into, but in that event, 'every effort must be made to prevent the approach to or entry of the house.'[77] Wellington dined at home and shortly before eight wrote to tell Peel that he would join him soon at the Home

Office to superintend operations.[78] But apart from a few clashes with the police, the night was remarkably quiet.[79] Far from gaining credit for its careful handling of a potentially dangerous situation, however, many people thought the ministry had over-reacted to an imaginary threat. A more reckless government might have let the festivities proceed in the hope of violence and a chance to demonstrate its capacity; but this would have been completely out of character for the Duke, who always feared that no one could tell where unrest would end once it had been allowed to begin.

After this excitement, attention turned to the debate on reform the following week. The Prime Minister let it be known that he would continue if he had a majority as low as twenty. As the time drew nigh he asked his chief supporters whether they would prefer a coalition with a group that could supply speakers in the Commons or resignation.[80]

On the eve of this momentous discussion, the House of Commons debated William IV's civil list. On an opposition motion to refer the matter to a select committee, the government was beaten by 233 to 204. Many of the administration's supporters were absent, and only that morning had the Whigs, Canningites and Ultras agreed to vote together on an issue that involved less soul searching than parliamentary reform.

When the vote was taken, the Duke was giving a dinner at Apsley House for the Prince of Orange. A message was sent up telling what had happened. Whispering the news to Mrs Arbuthnot, Wellington hurried out to see Peel, Arbuthnot and others who were waiting downstairs. Mrs Arbuthnot could hardly wait for the other guests to leave. When they did, she thought she had never seen a man as happy as Peel, who had been in a state of nervous anxiety for days: 'He said, when the Opposition cheered at the division that he did not join in it but it was with difficulty he refrained, he was so delighted at having so good an opportunity for resigning.' With the pillar of his ministry in the Commons in this mood, the Duke had no alternative but to take advantage of this fairly honourable defeat to avoid humiliation the next day.[81] William IV was greatly distressed and wanted Wellington to attempt a coalition. But when Peel insisted on resignation, the King summoned Lord Grey.[82]

Most of the ministers were relieved to be leaving before being defeated on a major issue. Peel in particular was elated to exchange the Leadership of a minority government for that of a strong opposition. The Duke did not share or understand this attitude and never got over the casual way in which Peel had thrown up the defence of the country's institutions. At the time he tried to hide his anger even from Mrs Arbuthnot, who was not deceived; but a month later, on Boxing Day, he complained that apart from himself, 'there was no Man in our Cabinet who cared one pin about Parliamentary Reform, or anything else excepting a quiet life.' A couple of days later he reminded Mrs Arbuthnot that he had been perfectly willing to go on: 'I did not break up the Government. To use a vulgar expression, I did not dirty my own Nest by way of excuse for quitting it.' Before the former ministers decided what they were going to do, they would have to see how 'the Gentleman' – Peel – was 'disposed to act who did these things, and who must have it in his Power to choose whether he will do them again.'[83] Now that the only person who really understood the interests of the country, and those of the aristrocracy in particular, had been driven from office by a perverse combination of Ultras bent of revenge and weakness within, everything was in jeopardy. The way was open for the destruction of the citadel of order, for anarchy and ruin. Wellington had seen the danger, but no one heeded him. When the new government's intentions became all too clear, he pronounced of his defeat: 'the nobility and gentry and Royal Family will yet bit their thumbs for it. Rely upon it we are in a scrape, and that is scarcely in the power of human ingenuity, prudence, or fortitude, to get us out of it.'[84]

CHAPTER FIVE

MAN'S SECOND FALL

A FTER HIS departure from office, Mrs Arbuthnot was delighted to find her friend enjoying his freedom and 'the power of sitting in the *dolce far niente.*' She thought he would never be bored for he read a great deal, had bought hunters and was busy setting his own county to rights: 'Time does not hang the least upon his hands.'[1] But the amusements of country life, the satisfaction of dealing with the rioters in Hampshire and the solace of the printed page were no substitute for the great affairs to which he was accustomed. He told Croker that he was 'essentially, and by his position and his duty, a public man, and will continue so long as life and intellect last.' Unlike Peel, who was professing a desire to retire to private life, the Duke saw it as his essential task to 'keep the *party together*; not to oppose – nay, to support – the King's Government in all that may tend to the public safety, but to *observe* them, and if they attempt any thing hostile to our institutions, to oppose.'[2] At a banquet for the fifty odd members of his administration at Apsley House, he expressed the hope that those who had turned him out would soon rally behind him once more. When the Duke of Gordon, proposing his health, looked forward to the command, 'As you were!', Wellington replied: 'No, not as you were, but *much better!*'[3]

The Ultras, having as they thought administered a salutary lesson to their misguided champion, were mostly willing to take him back in order to destroy the new ministry before it embarked on any dangerous course and to construct another in harmony with their principles. But far from being a chastened penitent, the Duke demanded that the Ultras accept the wisdom of Catholic emancipation before he took them back. He told that would-be remote wirepuller, the Duke of Buckingham, that scarcely had his government ended than those who had destroyed it were proposing that he form another on a broader basis: 'Would this be fair to the King? Would it be consistent in myself? Could such a scheme succeed, if I was capable of thinking of it?'[4] As he put the matter more succinctly to Mrs Arbuthnot, the Ultras wanted him to accept the Duke of Cumberland: 'This is a Burthen that I will not take upon me.'[5]

For the moment it was not clear what the nature of Grey's coalition of Whigs, Canningites and a few Ultras was going to be. The administration was aristocratic enough to seem proof against any extensive change of anything; and although it was committed to parliamentary reform, not much was heard of this for a few months while a cabinet committee worked on the matter in great secrecy. Meanwhile the government concentrated on financial retrenchment, discovering that it could not reduce the civil list, on which it had defeated Wellington, without offending those supporters who were clamouring for pensions on finally entering the promised land. On law and order the reform ministry rather surprisingly showed itself more vigorous than the Duke's. O'Connell was arrested for agitation against the union and the new Home Secretary, Lord Melbourne, was far more ruthless than Peel in crushing agricultural disturbances. Proceeding by proclamation rather than legislation, the Lords Lieutenant were reinforced and special commissions were established to try offenders in the counties most affected. A few were executed and several hundred were transported.

All of this was good in the eyes of the Lord Lieutenant of Hampshire. Two weeks after leaving office he wrote with satisfaction: 'Not a life has been lost, but little concession has been made, and little property destroyed by open outrages. In the mean time those who have something to lose have learnt how to associate and resist, and they will be better prepared for what we may yet have to do.'[6] He ascribed the disturbances to the numerous class of men, 'well educated, who have no means of subsistence, and who have no employment ... who go about in gigs' financed by the revolutionary bankers behind the new government in France.[7] This was not exactly how Grey's ministers perceived the situation, but they were impressed by Wellington's efficiency and perhaps in the hope of enlisting his goodwill they allowed him to name three of the special commissioners.

While engaged in these local difficulties, the Duke's great fears were of parliamentary reform. It was at first generally expected that this would not extend beyond the modest suppression of a few boroughs and the enfranchisement of a small number of industrial towns. But as time went by Wellington's apprehensions increased. At the end of January he told Croker, who found him in low spirits about politics, that he believed that the King, 'from pique or fright or folly, will consent to some sweeping measures of reform, and when the Crown joins the mob all balance is lost.' This gloomy assessment was supported by Lord Rosslyn, one of Grey's associates before joining the Duke, who considered the Prime Minister, 'with all his high airs ... as timid and irresolute as any man I ever knew, and more under the influence of people about him that you might imagine, and those are the very people who are now for the most violent measures.'[8]

The Duke's worst expectations were amply confirmed when Lord John Russell unveiled the government's proposals to the House of Commons on 1 March. Electoral boroughs with fewer than 2000 inhabitants at the 1821 census were to be totally disenfranchised and those with less than 4000 were to lose one of their two representatives. Of the 168 seats – one quarter of the total – thus eliminated, fifty-five were to be added to the English counties, forty-four to unrepresented English towns, five each to Scotland and Ireland and one to Wales, leaving fifty-seven to be abolished. In the boroughs the vote was given to all £10 householders, with those who had the franchise under the present arrangement retaining it for life as long as they remained resident. In the counties £10 copyholders (practically freeholders) and £150 leaseholders for at least twenty years joined the ancient 40s. freeholders. Similar changes were made in Scotland – which had only about 4500 voters in what were in effect 45 pocket boroughs – giving that country some real political expression for the first time since the union of 1707. In the Irish counties the £10 freeholder qualification established by Wellington two years earlier was supplemented by the addition of some leaseholders; in the boroughs the requirement was set at the level of £10 householders. Irregularities and disturbances at elections throughout the United Kingdom were to be reduced by dividing the large counties, requiring the residence of voters, establishing a permanent register that would be revised annually, increasing the number of polls and confining voting to two days in each constituency.

When Russell read out the list of boroughs to be wholly or partially disenfranchised, there was 'a sort of wild ironical laughter, mixed with expressions of delight from the ex-Ministers, who seemed to think themselves sure of recovering their places again immediately.' But Peel looked 'serious and angry, as if he had discovered that the Ministers, by the boldness of their measure, had secured the support of the country.'[9] He at least knew that any hope of exposing the shortcomings of the ministry's proposals and demonstrating his own competence to bring in a superior measure of moderate reform had disappeared with the announcement of this extensive change.

The Duke of Wellington told Lord Ellenborough that he was thinking of adding a clause abolishing the House of Lords, 'for it was far better that it should be done at once than as the ultimate result of a protracted struggle.'[10] He told the Duke of Buckingham that the changes would destroy the country and that he favoured opposition without compromise in both Houses. Disenfranchising boroughs without proving delinquency or overpowering necessity would give 'a shake . . . to the property of every individual in the country.'[11] The MPs for rotten boroughs, whatever party they belonged to, were men

> who would preserve the state of property as it is: who would maintain by their votes the Church of England, its possessions, its churches and universities; all our great institutions and corporations; the union with Scotland and Ireland; the dominion of the country over its foreign colonies and possessions; the national honour abroad, and its good faith with the King's subjects at home.

But Wellington rejected the imputation that his objection to this particular measure meant that he was automatically opposed to all change. Denouncing 'the greatest reformer on earth' as the enemy of reform was 'neither more nor less than one of the lying cries of to-day.'[12]

When Sir Robert Peel – he had succeeded to his father's baronetcy the year before – shook off all thought of retirement and reasserted his position as leader of the opposition to the Reform Bill, the Duke rejoiced in the prospect of its defeat and swallowed some of his resentment of Peel's conduct when they had left office to congratulate him on his initial speech condemning the measure: 'It is impossible that it should not produce an extensive and lasting Effect upon the Political Mind.'[13] Wellington was convinced that 'well judging people' all over the country opposed the bill and reaction was bound to increase with reflection. The bill must be delayed as long as possible in the House of Commons; but if it survived all the hurdles before a majority of that House came to its senses, it must be rejected by the Lords.[14]

After only two nights' debate the Commons hurried to the division on second reading. The young Whig Thomas Babington Macaulay, honing his literary skills in a letter to a friend, described the division as one of those occasions 'like seeing Caesar stabbed in the Senate House, or seeing Oliver [Cromwell] taking the Mace from the table; a sight to be seen only once, and never to be forgotten.' In the largest vote ever taken in the House, the bill passed by 302 to 301. When the numbers were read out, Macauley continued, 'the jaw of Peel fell; and the face of Twiss was as the face of a damned soul; and Herries looked like Judas taking his necktie off for the last operation.' The government MPs poured into the lobby in noisy excitement and were greeted by the cheers of an equally delirious crowd outside.[15]

The Duke was taken aback by this victory for 'the principle of a measure of revolution' and declared that if it succeeded he would never again enter the House of Lords, though the force of this was contradicted when he added that after forty-five years in the service of the monarch he could not retire and would continue to serve as long as he could with honour, 'that is to say, as long as I may not be insulted by the servants of his Government.'[16] His determination to resist the bill to the utmost made the Ultra Tory lords, who were under less pressure to concede than their counterparts in the Commons, eager to range themselves behind his banner. But Wellington remained cool to the idea of a close alliance, telling Lord Falmouth that those who were working for rejection would have much more freedom 'if they should have formed no combination for ulterior measures, and most particularly none which might be supposed to have in view objects of personal ambition.'[17] He flatly refused to gratify the Ultras by giving any undertakings on men and measures if he were called on to form a ministry, but he was willing to work with them and advised that the best course for everyone was 'to bury in oblivion their differences, to co-operate in destroying an evil of which, in my opinion none, have seen clearly all the immediate dangers; and then to see what course it will suit them to take thereafter.'[18] In this amicable spirit he even made up his differences with the Duke of Cumberland.

After the bare majority on second reading, Grey's cabinet had the Easter recess to consider how it would proceed when detailed consideration began in committee. To meet an amendment that would be proposed by General Isaac Gascoyne, the Ultra member for Liverpool, to maintain unchanged the total number of English and Welsh seats, thirty-one of those scheduled to be eliminated were restored, all but two of them going to England. The Prime Minister was also wise in preparing for dissolution. Despite the government's concession, Gascoyne's amendment carried in the early hours of 20 April by 299 to 291. The Duke thought this defeat too narrow to do the ministry much harm, but any hope that it would produce further concession disappeared when the government, after being assured by O'Connell that Ireland would remain quiet, decided on a general election. William IV considered 'dissolution tantamount to revolution' in the agitated condition of the country and agreed to it only because there seemed no possibility of an administration strong enough to resist the demand for the whole bill. On the same day Lord Wharncliffe gave notice in the House of Lords of a motion for the following day asking the King not to dissolve. His intention was to demonstrate the moderation of the Tories and their willingness to form a ministry to carry a restricted measure. The debate would probably have served only to reveal the divisions of the opposition but it was forestalled when the government, defeated in a vote on the estimates in the Commons, sought dissolution the next morning.

As the House of Lords had the right to dispose of business at hand before admitting commissioners, the King had to go in person to prevent Wharncliffe's motion. Fortunately for the cabinet, and to the astonishment of the Tories, William IV regarded the motion as an interference with his prerogative. Both Houses were in an uproar when he arrived at the Palace of Westminster, and only his entry restored some seething sense of order to the Lords. Wellington thought the monarch's submission to the ministers the most fatal step for the monarchy since Charles I gave up the power to dissolve the Long Parliament.[19]

The angry peers met afterwards at Apsley House. Wharncliffe was so incensed that he wanted to call a meeting of the members of the House of Lords to discuss the dissolution. The Duke promised to consult some of the leading peers in order to pacify him; but the next day wrote a careful letter pointing out to Wharncliffe the dangers in what he proposed. As Parliament had been dissolved by the King, the Lords could meet only 'without his authority, and contrary to his inclinations, to discuss his last act in relation to ourselves.' It would not look well for 'the conservators of the Constitution' to act in this way. Outside Parliament peers were 'no more than others of his Majesty's subjects, excepting that we possess the privilege of being exempt from arrest; and we have titles of honour and rank and precedent in society.' Their very station in life should make them examples of loyalty and submission to authority, avoiding even the appearance of anything contrary to this, particularly in the critical times that were approaching.[20]

This was a well-timed homily for the aristocracy. The general election produced fresh outbursts of support for a measure that even some of those who would still be excluded from the franchise pathetically believed would improve their position in society and reduce the price of food. In London the Lord Mayor ordered an illumination for 27 April, five days after dissolution. It was only to be expected that Apsley House would be a target. But on this occasion the Duchess lay dead inside.

She had been ill for some months but her death had not been expected so soon. A few days after the excitement in Parliament, Wellington wrote to Mrs Arbuthnot: 'The Poor Duchess died at half past ten this morning. She suffered some pain in the night. But none this morning.'[21] Her death seemed to affect the Duke no more than the passing of an official colleague. If he experienced any remorse it was not evident. But their lives had been connected for half a century and perhaps her passing gave Wellington occasion for reflection on his own. It may also explain his gloomier view of the political scene.

He duly observed proprieties by withdrawing from social life for a month, assuring Mrs Arbuthnot from Stratfield Saye that he was not in the least distressed by his enforced idleness: 'I walk, play at tennis and ride and read all day, so that the Hours do not at all hang heavy upon my Hands.'[22] Nor did he cease from political vigilance. Even before the Duchess was in her grave he was expressing fears that the ministers would try to persuade the King to grant a second dissolution if the reform bill were defeated once more: 'This would be indeed a *Coup d'Etat!*'[23]

The Duke had left London by the time of the illumination and the defence of Apsley House was left to the servants. After thirty windows had been broken, one of his servants climbed onto the roof and fired two blunderbusses into the air. Persuaded that the house was well protected the crowd went away. 'They certainly intended to destroy the House,' Wellington wrote, 'and did not care one Pin for the Poor Duchess being dead in the House.' As the local authorities had permitted this outrage, he ordered the parish to be sued for damages.[24]

The substantial gains of the reformers plunged the Duke into a depression as deep as any in his life. 'Matters appear to be going on as badly as possible,' he told Mrs Arbuthnot.

It may be relied upon that we shall have a Revolution. I have never doubted the Inclination and disposition of the lower Orders of the People. I told you years ago that the people are rotten to the Core. You will find that it is true. They are not bloodthirsty, but they are desirous of Plunder....

I told you likewise that the Upper Orders and the Gentry were not prepared or in a State to resist the attack upon Property which would be made. They are ... Timid, and excited alone by a thirst for Popularity. Even those defeated at this moment in their objects would walk on all fours to please the Mob and regain their Seats![25]

The only ray of hope, he told another correspondent, was that the elections had been 'decided by terror': 'It is impossible that there should not be a reaction. The only doubt is, whether it will be in time, or sufficiently strongly pronounced, to influence the decision of Parliament.'[26]

Wellington must have been aware that the King was urging modifications on the cabinet and that even some ministers were having second thoughts about reform. But the government decided to stand by 'the bill, the whole bill and nothing but the bill,' which was reintroduced into the Commons with only minor changes. On 8 July after little discussion it passed second reading by 367 to 231. This large majority ensured its eventual success, though the opposition persisted in criticism for another forty nights. A few more seats were restored and an amendment to enfranchise £50 tenants at will was carried against the ministry. The point of this weary course of objection was to gain time for the expected reaction and to pave the way for rejection by the House of Lords. A week after the vote on second reading the Duke was convinced that the change of opinion had occurred. He told Lord Cowley that nine-tenths of the property holders and all the members of the learned professions and the financial community looked with dread to the consequences of the measure, as did even many of those who in public supported it. Only Radicals and Dissenters welcomed it as the beginning of a new era of destruction and plunder. For his part, recognizing that it would ruin 'all our establishments, institutions, fortunes, and power,' Wellington declared that he would rather 'fall in defence of the constitution and institutions as now established than by the lingering operation of a modern revolutionary system to be established by the Reform Bill.'[27]

The bill was finally carried to the House of Lords on 22 September. The night before the Duke invited the leading opposition peers to dine at Apsley House. They agree to allow first reading, but to make every effort to defeat the measure thereafter. The meeting was thrown into some confusion by the arrival of Lord Eldon and Lord Kenyon roaring drunk from dinner with the Duke of Cumberland, but Wellington was able to tell his guests that he would never be responsible for introducing a Reform Bill. This was substantially qualified by the warning that those who might be asked to take part in an administration after the defeat of Grey's should not pledge themselves in advance on the issue: 'If called upon by the King they would first learn what his real views were on the subject of this Bill and of Reform, & then they would have to decide whether they should take the Govnt. or not. They would be much embarrassed by premature pledges.'²⁸

Debate on second reading in the House of Lords was a great occasion, with galleries erected to accommodate the large number of peers. Grey in a magnificent oration defended the bill as incorporating the principles of his whole political career. The Duke, speaking on the second night, denounced it as a measure that would overthrow the whole system of representation. He charged the government with unconstitutional practice at the last election in calling for delegates pledged to a particular piece of legislation rather than MPs free to deliberate with their colleagues and decide according to their own judgment. He claimed that the new franchise would chiefly benefit shopkeepers, 'a class of persons of all others the most likely to combine in political views.' The domination of urban interests over rural would continue. But the greatest evil would come in trying to carry on a ministry under a system in which 'persons in the lowest condition of life, liable to, and even existing under the most pernicious influences, are to have votes.' The House of Commons would be 'a democratical assembly of the worst description;' other radical measures, including the secret ballot, would be passed; overseas territories would be lost; all authority would cease; and finally a military dictatorship might arise, as it had at the time of the Civil War, when the country was last subjected to an unchecked House of Commons. But while arguing for rejection, Wellington did indicate a willingness to accept some small alteration when he advised the peers to leave themselves free to adopt another measure that would secure 'the blessings of a Government. By doing so, you will perform your duty to your country, and will deserve its thanks, and the gratitude of posterity.'²⁹ The next night he intervened briefly to protest the efforts of political unions to force the bill on Parliament, suspecting that the ministry was deliberately encouraging agitation in order to strengthen its case for concession. To a London magistrate who agreed, he wrote that the government wanted 'enough of a mob to create terror, but not enough to do serious mischief.' Since all the arguments were against it, the ministers were determined to carry the bill by physical force 'operating upon the terrors of those who are to decide the question.'³⁰

After five nights of exceptional rhetoric and the spectacle of Lord Chancellor Brougham on his knees begging the House to pass the bill, it was defeated by 199 to 158. When the House of Commons resumed two days later, Lord Ebrington proposed a resolution of confidence in the government and support for the main features of the Reform Bill. When this carried by 329 to 198 Grey persuaded the King to grant a short propagation for the cabinet to consider its course.

The rejection of the bill touched off great demonstrations against the House of Lords. But the Duke was unmoved. He was sure that enthusiasm was waning and that the disturbances were worked up by agitators who did not represent the true feelings of the country. He considered some reform inevitable by this time, but the vote had gained time for moderates, including those in the government, to gain the upper hand.[31]

The protests were certainly strong enough. In London speakers addressed two or three thousand people in Regent's Park, who then marched on St James's Palace. The streets were filled and Wellington prudently decided to stay at home. 'A Charming Life, this!' he wrote to Mrs Arbuthnot. 'However, I am convinced that we are right, and that we have taken the Course which we ought to take.' A few hours later he added that his house had been pelted with stones for an hour. Many windows had been broken before help arrived, but the attackers had not tried to enter the garden where armed men were posted. As it was five o'clock and beginning to rain, he concluded: 'the Gentlemen will now go to their Dinners!'[32] In other towns the demonstrations were greater and more violent. At Birmingham the Political Union claimed 150,000 at a meeting to express thanks to the ministry and vote a tax strike if the Reform Bill were not passed; at Derby people were killed in the riots when prisoners were freed from the jails; at Nottingham the castle, owned by the Duke of Newcastle, was burned to the ground; and at Exeter Henry Phillpotts, appointed Bishop by the Duke at the end of his government, was besieged in his palace. But the greatest eruption was touched off at Bristol a couple of weeks later by the arrival of the Ultra Tory Recorder, Sir Charles Wetherell. Rioting, looting and arson continued for three days; by the time it was over, the mansion house, the bishop's palace, the jail and various other buildings were in ruins and the city bore the appearance of one that had been sacked.

After this, even Wellington thought it prudent not to reveal the time of his arrival at Dover the following week. He told the Deputy Governor of the Castle that those who wished to insult him were perfectly free to do so, but he would attend his court as usual and expect the municipal authorities to provide adequate protection. The mayor hurriedly swore in 200 special constables. But to everyone's surprise the Lord Warden was greeted in a friendly manner when he drove into town. As he walked around the streets he was pleased to observe that every respectable man took off his hat, 'and I did not hear a Word of Reform or a whisper of discontent or disrespect.'[33]

Whatever the sentiment in the ancient port of Dover, there was widespread apprehension about a demonstration of the National Union of Working Classes planned for London on 7 November. Rumours circulated that weapons were being purchased, raising the prospect that London might share the fate of Bristol. Elaborate preparations were made at the Horse Guards and completely revised by the Duke, who was happy to help even a Whig ministry meet civil disturbances. As usual he emphasized that the troops should be kept in reserve until they were needed. The Tower, the Bank of England, Whitehall and the Palace of Westminster were to be secured and provisioned and lines of communication maintained by the police who would control the major buildings. Eighteen pound carronades, which could 'lay open, in a minute, any house or church,' should be available to regain any building essential to the movement of troops which fell to the mob. As always he stressed the importance of ample provisions for the soldiers: 'Plenty of biscuit and cheese will be sufficient, with the porter, which will not be found wanting anywhere.'[34] But the plan was never put to the test. Two days before the meeting Lord Melbourne managed to persuade the leaders to postpone it on threat of prosecution for treason.

The challenge from workers demanding a democratic Parliament raised the prospect of better-off individuals forming a national guard to protect themselves and their property. Wellington warned the King that this was leading the country to a great crisis. He believed that arrangements had been made to supply arms to the Birmingham Political Union while the government stood idly by, and observed that there had never been such a self-armed force which had not tried to control the government or seize supreme power.[35] This made a great impression on William IV, who raised the matter with Lord Grey. The Prime Minister with some asperity asked the Duke to substantiate his claim about a contract to arm the Birmingham Union. When Wellington made further inquiries, he discovered that his information was based on hearsay. Only slightly abashed, he shifted his complaint to the character of the Union: 'If not armed, they are prepared to receive and to use arms whenever it may suit the purpose of those at the head of the union that they should take arms in their hands.'[36] Despite Grey's defensiveness when the Duke probed his motives in relation to the Union, the government did ban the military organization of political groups.

Impressed by the violence of the reaction to the defeat of the Reform Bill, waverers among the Tory peers, fearing that continued resistance from the House of Lords would jeopardize the entire structure of the country, entered into negotiations with the ministers for a more limited measure. But the government could not make enough concessions to satisfy the waverers without losing the support of the reformers, and there was no assurance that the waverers could persuade enough of their colleagues to let the bill become law. The Duke, who wanted far greater concessions than would satisfy the waverers, gave them no encouragement. He told one of their leaders, Lord Wharncliffe, that it might be possible to consider some small measure of reform if the political unions were suppressed,[37] though he considered that the ministry had no intention of doing that. It would simply use the failure of discussions with the waverers to persuade the King to create enough peers to carry the unaltered bill and then suppress the unions.[38]

After a two-month recess, Parliament was recalled on 6 December. A few days later Lord John Russell introduced the third version of the Reform Bill in the House of Commons. The number of boroughs to be totally disenfranchised remained the same but the number to lose one member was reduced from forty-six to thirty. The criterion for disenfranchisement was also changed from the population at the 1821 census to households and taxes at the 1831 census. The franchise was further restriced by requiring householders to be ratepayers not in arrears in their assessments. And in keeping with General Gascoyne's amendment, the House of Commons was kept at 658 members, preserving the proportion of English seats and pleasing the reformers by permitting the enfranchisement of more towns. These concessions, combined with the disturbances of the autumn, induced more MPs to vote for the bill than the last time.

The problem for the ministry was not the House of Commons but the House of Lords. The Leader of the Opposition there was in a low mood at the beginning of 1832. Physically he claimed to be suffering no more than 'a bad feverish cold, occasioned by neglect of and an endeavour to bully slight colds.'[39] But the effects lasted a couple of months and perhaps contributed to his pessimism. In the middle of February he told J.W. Croker that he was disenchanted with life in London, where he could not go out without risking insult. Even Croker had to point out that this amounted to no more than 'occasionally a blackguard hoots or says something gross.'[40]

The proposals of some of his colleagues did nothing to lift Wellington's spirits. The Duke of Buckingham suggested that he counter the threatened creation of peers by racing to Brighton, throwing himself at the King's feet, and offering to form a government on the principles that had established the country's greatness and agreeing to enact some measure of parliamentary reform. 'Fail to do this,' warned Buckingham, 'and you will have on your mind to the last moment of your existence the pain of thinking that you have missed taking a step which at least might have had the effect of saving us from a revolution.' With remarkable forbearance, Wellington explained why, even apart from his present indisposition, he could not consider such a step. He could not work with the present House of Commons but neither could he recommend dissolution as a new Parliament could not meet in time to pass the annual Mutiny Act. The King would be obliged to 'shake off' the Duke and would become even more dependent on the Whigs than before. The time was coming, he told Buckingham, when the Tories would have to regard themselves as being on a battlefield and be prepared to make sacrifices for the public interest, but in his position he had carefully to consider the consequences of every step.[41] He even went to extraordinary lengths to avoid being alone with the King for fear of an appeal for rescue or even the rumour of it. When he had a couple of petitions against reform to present, he did not request an interview but made an abstract which he read at a royal levée. The cabinet ministers present were annoyed, and even the King inquired about the state of his health.

As the time for considering the Reform Bill in the Lords drew nigh once more Wellington made it clear that he would take the same firm line as before. He encouraged the faint-hearted not to be deterred from their duty by threats of physical intimidation. 'Let noble Lords only look back at the consequences of their last vote,' he told Lord Aberdeen: 'A few windows were broken, and other outrages committed; but we have gained six months of time, during which there has been a remarkable alteration of sentiment in the country.'[42] He tried to dissuade the waverers from supporting the bill by telling Lord Wharncliffe that the opposition would finally have to accept some reform, but the passion for an extensive measure had passed. If and when the present bill became law, it would be necessary to force it on the country. Voting for it would destroy the House of Lords and other institutions as effectively as a large creation of peers. The waverers should follow his example and not commit themselves to anything until they saw the actual bill in the Lords.[43]

But the waverers were not to be deterred. As soon as the bill was introduced in the Lords on 26 March they and some of the bishops announced that they would support it on second reading. Wellington briefly countered the idea that the bill was substantially different from the earlier ones, insisted that it would produce a revolution in the constitution and gave notice that he would propose considerable changes if it survived into committee.[44] On second reading he elaborated his position and, while not condemning reform outright, insisted that it was a matter to be approached with caution, gradually and in a piecemeal fashion. He even admitted that in time all the details of the bill might be implemented,[45] though no doubt he hoped to be spared that in his lifetime. The vote was taken after four nights' debate and the success of the waverers was reflected in the majority of 184 to 175.

The Duke was not cast down by this victory and in the three-week Easter recess he had time to consider his amendments. He told Lord Bathurst that he would try to reduce the number of boroughs scheduled to lose both members and restore the second member to those scheduled to lose one, in the hope of arriving at something like the present House of Commons with the addition of the proposed forty-five new seats.[46] The government heard of this through the waverers. When the House moved into committee on 7 May and Lord Lyndhurst, in a taunting speech, moved that the first clause listing the boroughs to be totally disenfranchised be postponed to the last, Grey announced that this was a matter of confidence for the government which would either demand a creation of peers or resign if the amendment were carried. The waverers regarded this as an empty threat and voted with the opposition to carry the motion by 151 to 116. During the division the Tory leaders held a hasty conference and decided to prevent the ministry from taking advantage of the defeat by announcing that the motion was not designed to destroy the bill. When debate resumed Lord Ellenborough told the astonished ministerialists and Ultras that the opposition was willing to accept the abolition of all the seats in the postponed clause in due course. The Prime Minister understandably complained that it would have been better to announce this before the vote.

Despite Ellenborough's announcement, the cabinet insisted on a creation of peers or resignation. In his interview with the King, Grey talked of fifty new peers and Brougham of sixty, while William IV expressed his reluctance to go beyond twenty. Later he sent word that he had decided to accept the ministry's resignation. He summoned Lord Lyndhurst from the Court of Exchequer and told him that he was looking for someone who could form an administration that would carry an extensive measure of reform without creating new peers.

Lyndhurst went immediately to the Duke. But Wellington had concluded from his experience in office that the Prime Minister must be in the House of Commons and decided that Peel was the person for the job. Peel refused to have anything to do with parliamentary reform, insisted that it must be settled on the basis of the present bill, and took a stand on consistency and disinterestedness that would be forever lost if he changed on this as he had on Catholic emancipation. Croker, who was present at the interview, fully supported Peel and recommended the waverer, Lord Harrowby, as the natural Tory to carry reform. Harrowby had great oratorical gifts but the Duke was suspicious of such compromisers and opposed pressing him into service. He doubted that the Ultras would serve under Harrowby, but as a meeting of Tory peers had already been set for the next day, he warned Lyndhurst to say nothing to him in the interval.[47]

As Peel and Lyndhurst walked away from Apsley House, Peel suggested Charles Manners-Sutton, the Speaker of the House of Commons, who by virtue of his office had never uttered a word on reform. But Lyndhurst was not impressed. Later in the day he wrote to tell Wellington that he 'must consent to be *the minister*, or everything will fail.' Lyndhurst was confident that they could manage the matter; in any event 'it is *our duty to try*.' This exciting challenge spoke to all the Duke's instincts never to be wanting when duty or danger called. He eagerly replied that they should certainly exert themselves to enable the King to shake off 'the trammels of his tyrannical Minister.' He was 'perfectly ready to do whatever his Majesty may command me. I am as much averse to the Reform as ever I was. No embarrassment of that kind, no private consideration, shall prevent me from making every effort to serve the King.' But nothing should be decided until the peers met the next day.

When the Tory Lords gathered at Apsley House, Wellington addressed them on their duty to lay aside personal feelings and interests and assist in the task of averting revolution. With two or three exceptions they agreed to support any government that could be formed, even if it enacted a Reform Bill similar to the one they had just been opposing. Lyndhurst departed to report to the King, though there was not much specific information to convey. Both Harrowby and Manners-Sutton refused to lead an administration. When Croker went to see the Duke the next day, the latter conceded: 'Well, we are in a fine scrape, and I really do not see how we are to get out of it.' If no one else would do his duty, it was up to the national saviour to step into the breach once more: 'he had passed his whole life in troubles, and was now in troubles again, but ... it was his duty to stand by the King, and he would do so.'[48] William IV may have created his own difficulties by allowing the wrong impression to get about on his attitude to reform, but whatever evils this had produced Wellington believed it was now up to him to come to the rescue and minimize the danger to the country and its institutions. The King accepted the offer with gratitude and relief.

The Duke's problems were overwhelming. Apart from Peel's refusal, which would have been enough to convince most people that the enterprise was hopeless, the incumbent ministry was supported in the Commons by a vote of confidence of 288 to 208. The Common Council of London presented a petition to the Commons calling on it not to pass the budget until the Reform Bill became law; monster petitions to the same effect arrived from Manchester and Birmingham; and others were being prepared in towns all over the country. There were plans for a tax strike and a financial crisis by withdrawing funds from the Bank of England. 'To Stop the Duke, Go for Gold' appeared on placards all over London. Nathan Rothschild, the banker, sought out Charles Arbuthnot to tell him that the only way of preventing violence was for Wellington to announce as soon as he met Parliament as Prime Minister that he would not allow his personal opinions on reform to disappoint the expectations that had been raised.[49]

The Duke did not have much luck in persuading his old associates to see their duty as he saw his. Lord Bathurst repeated his decision taken in 1830 not to return to public life; Croker stood with Peel in refusing, despite Wellington's warning that 'in such a crisis as this, if a man put himself on the *shelf*, it might not be so easy to take him off the shelf when he perhaps might desire it;' and Herries, Goulburn and Alexander Baring also refused. Only Generals Hardinge and Murray, who had learned their duty in a harder school stood by their old chief in the face of overwhelming odds in the House of Commons. The King tried to help by summoning Peel, but to no avail; he then entreated Manners-Sutton to become Leader of the Commons by offering compensation for the claim to a peerage and the pension usually given to the Speaker on retirement, but again without effect.[50] Despite these setbacks, Lord Ellenborough found the Duke full of fire when he was called to Apsley House. His eyes flashed and he repeated his determination to form a ministry that would save the House of Lords: 'he should be ashamed to walk in the streets if he did not.' But Ellenborough also refused to resume his place at the Board of Control.[51] Negotiations dragged on for three days, with Wellington finally pinning his hopes on Manners-Sutton as Prime Minister, Baring as Chancellor of the Exchequer, and himself serving in any useful capacity. But Baring would not act without Manners-Sutton, and the weakness of that vessel was glaringly apparent. After he had dithered and bored the Duke and Lyndhurst with a three-hour speech on the state of affairs, Lyndhurst went home, flung himself into a chair and declared that he would not endure 'such a *damned tiresome old Bitch.*' The next day, pleading for more time, Manners-Sutton nervously told Wellington that 'if *no other* arrangement can be made, I must give way, though with fear and trembling.'[52]

Monday, 14 May provided the first opportunity for the House of Commons to discuss the King's commission to the Duke and MPs made the most of it. The crowded and excited House heatedly debated the propriety of the proposed new ministers abandoning their previous opposition to reform for the sake of office. An onslaught from the Whigs was only to be expected, but far more damaging were the attacks from a couple of Ultras. Sir Robert Inglis, the Protestant champion against Peel at Oxford in 1829, declared that he could see no difference between a public and a private code of ethics and could not with honour support Wellington's effort. At ten o'clock Hardinge wrote to tell the Duke that the proposed administration would produce all the evils of reform with the added sacrifice of political character. Peel and his followers would stand smugly aside while Wellington's course was violently attacked. The Duke must consult the friends who had attended the debate before going further.

Wellington was puzzled by this letter, having understood that the debate had begun well. He replied that he would be glad to see any MP, but 'I confess that I can't see very clearly how speeches or a vote in the House of Commons can prevent me from pursuing the course on which I have entered, unless it should be found that a government cannot be formed for the King in the House of Commons.' Baring meanwhile, unable to gain any control of the House, accepted the Whig proposal that the old government be confirmed in office with a promise that the opposition in the Lords would allow the Reform Bill to pass. When the Speaker, Peel, Hardinge and Croker arrived at Apsley House shortly after midnight, Wellington had already heard from Baring, who said that he would rather face a thousand devils than such a House of Commons. After much discussion Peel's recommendation that the Duke should inform the King that the state of the Commons made it impossible for him to form a ministry was accepted. The monarch was to be left to do as he saw fit, but the meeting agreed to withdraw from active opposition to the Reform Bill in order to prevent the House of Lords from being swamped by new peers.[53]

Early the next morning Wellington and Peel conveyed their gloomy news to the King. He in turn had to invite Grey to return and tried to persuade him to modify the bill in order to make it acceptable to the opposition. But Grey had no need to agree and insisted on securities that the measure be passed as near as possible to its present form. The only way to avoid creating peers was for the leading opponents in the House of Lords to announce that they would end their resistance. The King endeavoured to persuade the Duke to make such a statement and have his followers accept it; but this was too much for Wellington's pride. He told the King's secretary that he and Lyndhurst would, as they had promised, not attend any further discussion of the bill, but he could not publicly declare this without becoming a party to the ministry's proceedings.[54] Apart from his own sensitivity, any such announcement would cost him dearly with the Ultras, some of whom were already complaining to the Duke of Buckingham that Wellington had thrown up the task too easily without seeking their valuable advice. 'Meetings are talked of,' Buckingham warned, 'which may become more eager, and express their opinions more strongly than you would like.' The Duke was roused to an immediate defence of what he had done and sharply told Buckingham that he was acting for no group of individuals, but for the King: 'I informed certain Peers of what I was about to do in order to conciliate their confidence, but I was not acting for them, or under their direction; or, in respect to details, with their knowledge.'[55] He was able to persuade a meeting of peers that he had taken the right course, but in the strained circumstances it was out of the question for him to go further and ask them to let the bill pass.

When the House of Lords next met, on 17 May, Wellington presented an account of his efforts to form a government. He ended with a strong denunciation of the Reform Bill as unnecessary and injurious but offered no indication of his future course. Whatever this did to reassure his followers, the ministers regarded it as intolerable. The next day they obtained a written promise from the King to create enough peers to pass the bill. That afternoon it was announced in the Lords by the Prime Minister, to deafening cheers from members of the House of Commons who crowded the steps of the throne.

The rest was anti-climax. The ministry accepted a few minor amendments from the diehards who persisted in their resistance, but the preparations for armed resistance out of doors melted away. The Duke steadfastly refused to return to the House of Lords until the measure had passed and most of the leading opponents followed his example. But he had the darkest misgivings about what was happening. 'We shall have the bill in its worst form,' he concluded. 'In the meantime we have no government. God knows whether this country can have one again without passing through a crisis in its affairs.'[56]

CHAPTER SIX

THE DARK DEFILE

THE PASSAGE of the Reform Bill, the failure of his friends to support his heroic attempt to temper and control parliamentary change when it had become inevitable, and the reaction from the intense political activity of the last six years, plunged the Duke of Wellington into a depression from which he did not easily recover. 'It is terrible how all our friends croak,' Charles Arbuthnot told his son almost a year later:

> Between ourselves, no one is worse than the Duke. To hear him, there is no hope of our being saved from revolution. I trust he is wrong: but wrong or right, the hearing from morn till night that we are going fast the way the French went 40 yrs. ago is very painful, & it makes me very much wish to live at Woodford.

A few months later he added to his wife: 'Our political state hangs heavy on my mind. The last talk with the Duke depressed & oppressed me. He certainly is Job's comforter.'[1] So desperate was Arbuthnot to revive his friend's spirits that he even enlisted the unlikely aid of J.W. Croker, who had left the House of Commons forever when the Reform Bill became law. Croker promised to help but pointed out that the Duke's assessment was preferable to false confidence, 'by alarming men who really do not seem to suspect the mine over which they are walking.'[2]

Wellington even complained that social life was not as enjoyable as it had been before the reform of Parliament. He told Mrs Arbuthnot at the end of 1833 that society was becoming more demanding: 'Everybody required infinitely more attention, particularly from me, and is infinitely more difficult to please.' He grumbled that for a whole week at Stratfield Saye he had been unable even to read his letters, 'much less the newspapers, or any other of the Numerous papers, documents &c. which are sent me' because he was compelled to be 'literally a *Slave* – the *Master of the Ceremonies*' for a house full of guests who refused to do anything without him. Other men, who did not have the world on their shoulders or were obliged to receive a steady stream of applications 'from all Mankind upon all descriptions of Subjects,' had wives and sons to assist them; but he was forced to bear it all alone. Leaving undone all he decently could, he still had to write fifteen or twenty essential letters a day.[3]

Although he always affected indifference towards public opinion, the plunge in his personal popularity during the Days of May did nothing to improve his estimation of human nature and the tone of society in the new age. On Waterloo Day, 18 June 1832, just two weeks after the Reform Bill received royal assent, he was pursued by a mob in the City as he rode away from the Tower. An attempt was made to drag him off his horse and at Holborn the growing crowd began throwing stones and mud. As calm as ever in the face of personal danger, he rode into Lincoln's Inn where he had business with Sir Charles Wetherell, the Ultra Tory he had dismissed as Attorney General at the time of Catholic emancipation. The gates of the Inn were secured against the Duke's pursuers and the lawyers made preparations for the rest of his journey. A short while later he rode out of the west gate and made his way to the iron shutters and still broken windows of Apsley House. 'So passeth away the glory of this world,' commented Lord Eldon, who had long since got over his hostility towards Wellington.[4]

But as the great hopes for the reform ministry quickly evaporated, the Duke's reputation for honest if misguided conduct soon restored him to the national pantheon. Riding with him in St James's Park a year later Charles Greville was pleased to see 'everybody we met taking off their hat to him, everybody in the park rising as he went by, and every appearance of his inspiring great reverence.'[5] The Duke even repaired the windows of Apsley House, left broken for a year and a half as an expression of his contempt for efforts to intimidate him, ostensibly to honour the King's attendance at the 1833 Waterloo dinner, but at least tacitly in recognition of his restored public standing. Slowly the gloom that had hung over him since the Reform Bill lifted.

Even at his lowest ebb, Wellington was convinced that it was his duty to remain at his post to save what he could from the general wreckage of reform. When an Irish clergyman wrote to seek his advice on emigrating to Canada at the end of 1832, the Duke exhorted him to stay where he was in terms that reflected his own sense of what was expected of him in difficult times. 'You are a minister of the Church of England,' he reminded his correspondent: 'You have, I understand, the cure of souls. Can you abandon your post in a moment of crisis and danger for worldly objects?' In a burst of uncharacteristic optimism he told the clergyman to expect better times, assuring him that he might prosper in Ireland if he made the same sacrifices that would be required in 'the forest or swamp, or in a desert' of North America.[6]

Surveying the terrain on the morrow of reform, the Duke saw the House of Lords as the only safeguard of the constitution. The King was well-meaning but weak, as his conduct throughout the Reform Bill had shown, while the next general election would produce a House of Commons worse than any elected under the old franchise. He expected a dissolution before the new voters' registers were complete and the long foretold reaction had time to occur. From all parts of the country he received the same reports: 'gentlemen of local position will not stand for the towns which are left with representation in Parliament. Lawyers, physicians and shopkeepers will be the members for these places.'[7] The elections were not in fact held for six months and polling, now restricted to two days, was more orderly than before. There were more reformers than in the old House of Commons and almost half of the MPs were new to Parliament, but most of the leading figures reappeared and the social composition of the House was not much changed. Wellington, however, insisted that the revolution was made: 'that is to say, that power is transferred from one class of society, the gentlemen of England, professing the faith of the Church of England, to another class of society, the shopkeepers, being dissenters from the Church, many of them Socinians, others atheists.'[8] Only about 150 of the 658 MPs were Conservatives, as those who had opposed the Reform Bill were coming to be called, while the rest were generally allied to the ministry. The Duke was not alone in thinking that the government would adopt extreme measures in order to conciliate the fifty or sixty Radicals and the thirty-nine members of O'Connell's party.

The House of Lords, with its huge Conservative majority, was a source of strength for the preservation of traditional institutions and privilege, but it could be a great source of danger if the Conservative peers used their majority to provoke the government to destroy it and other established bodies. As Wellington told Charles Greville at the beginning of the first reformed parliament in 1833:

> The first thing I have to look to is to keep my house over my head,
> and the alternative is between this Government and none at all. I am

therefore for supporting the Government, but then there is so much passion, and prejudice, and folly, and vindictive feeling, that it is difficult to get others to do the same.[9]

The Ultra Tories were eager to revenge themselves for the Reform Bill by throwing out every piece of legislation that came to the House of Lords, in the hope that this would defeat the ministry and pave the way for a restoration of the old House of Commons. Wellington was able to make only a limited impression on them with his argument that discussion in an assembly composed of men of 'education, of habits of business, and of talent,' must be opportune in order to have a moral effect on society, the legislature and the mob. Debate in the House of Lords, 'which still possesses a legislative power but no political influence, ought to be very cautiously managed.'[10] He tried to keep peers away from the House until late in the session when legislation arrived from the Commons and could be carefully considered and judiciously amended, instead of attending early in the session and seeing occasion for antagonizing the government. He also warned against forming Conservative organizations outside Parliament. It was all too easy to turn the best society to the worst purpose; and in any suppression of political bodies constitutional ones would suffer the same fate as the subversive.[11]

This cautious advice hardly provided the battle cry for which the Tory Lords were yearning. They were much annoyed at the Duke's seemingly supine immobility at Stratfield Saye at the beginning of the 1833 Parliament. Lord Londonderry complained to that other perennial malcontent, the Duke of Buckingham, that Wellington's 'total secession' was making the House of Lords what the Radicals claimed it was, 'of *no use* to the country.'[12] Later in the session, when he was active, the Ultras were annoyed that he did not take their advice, while he angrily expostulated that they would not follow his orders. Not for the first or the last time, he asked Mrs Arbuthnot how he was supposed to guide to any good purpose a party that refused to consider the nature of the House of Commons, 'One which will go by its own Road under the Direction of the duke of Cumberland, Duke of Buckingham, & Lord Londonderry.' 'Of course,' he said, 'I am no longer *their* Leader. Am I to become their Follower?'[13] He particularly resented the Ultras holding their own meetings and then coming to the assemblies of Conservative peers at Apsley House claiming to speak for a distinct group within the party. He warned the Duke of Buckingham that he was 'a Person quite independent of any Society or Association.' Even if the Ultras sent him to Coventry they would find that they could not destroy his influence: 'nobody could put me down excepting myself, and ... it was more probable that the Tory Association would suffer than that I should, either in Character, in efficiency or in any other manner.'[14] Lord Rosslyn, at whose house the offending meetings were held, assured Mrs Arbuthnot that Wellington had got the whole thing out of proportion. The Ultras might be sulky and abusive about his refusal to wreck the ministry's legislation, but his standing among them was as great as ever and 'when the time comes when exertions are to be made with any prospect of ultimate success, the greatest part will come in.'[15]

In restraining the Tory Lords from their suicidal course, the Duke was following the same course as Peel in the Commons. Peel may have disgusted the Ultras by announcing at the beginning of the 1833 session that parliamentary reform was finally and irrevocably settled and that he was prepared to consider other changes provided that they were carried out gradually, dispassionately and after careful deliberation, but he had no difficulty in asserting his ascendency over the reduced and largely inarticulate Conservative MPs. His policy of supporting the principle of reform while criticizing specific aspects of the Whig proposals was so effective in attracting those who wanted change but feared the government's susceptibility to the demands of the Radicals that within a year and a half of the general election the ministry's majority had disappeared and coalition with the Conservatives seemed the only hope of salvation.

But while working to the same end, there was little consultation between Wellington and Peel. The Duke did not easily forgive Peel's refusal to help him form a government in May 1832, which he saw as being of a piece with his eagerness to break up the ministry in 1830. In private he could be as scathing as any of the Ultras; when Lady Salisbury questioned him about Peel's cautious strategy, he told her: 'Nothing but weakness.... He is afraid – afraid of everything.'[16] In public, however, he scrupulously avoided any hint of criticism. He knew that Peel was the best hope in the House of Commons for a Conservative government, and for two years after the Reform Bill they maintained correct if not cordial relations. To outward appearances all was well between them. They met socially from time to time and may have discussed politics; and in the small world in which they lived there were various intermediaries, as well as those who tried to poison feelings between them. Even before Parliament met in 1833 J.C. Herries sent Wellington extracts of a letter from Peel to Henry Goulburn warning against trying to defeat the ministry by allying with the

Radicals and stressing the importance of conciliating the goodwill of 'the sober-minded and well disposed portion of the community.'[17] Their only exchange of letters in the whole of 1833, in July when Peel warned of the danger of defeating the Irish Church Bill in the Lords, revealed that they understood each other's position well enough. The Duke agreed with Peel about the danger of destroying the government in the Lords and provoking a disastrous general election, but pointing to his problems with the Ultras told Peel that it was 'not so easy to make men feel that they are of no consequence in the country who have hitherto had so much weight and still preserve their properties and their stations in society and their seats in the House of Lords.'[18]

Wellington may not have been aggressive enough for the Ultras in 1833 but he conscientiously attended to matters that came to the House of Lords on the lines that he had made clear to his associates. As so often, the main source of contention was Ireland, which despite Catholic emancipation had been in a state of exceptional lawlessness for two years. The Whigs applied the time-honored formula of coercion and conciliation, giving the Lord Lieutenant special powers but also redressing one of the principal grievances by reforming the Church of Ireland. The cess (an Easter rate) was to be abolished; ten of the twenty-two bishoprics suppressed; livings suspended in parishes where no services had been held for the last three years; and a graduated tax levied on benefices worth more than £200 a year. The savings would be applied to the building and upkeep of churches, better salaries for the poorest clergy and general charitable purposes.

This was as bad a start to the new age as the Duke had feared. Interfering with the independence of the Church in Ireland was serious enough, but it was clearly just one step in a process that had begun with parliamentary reform and would end with the destruction of the Church in England, the monarchy, the independence of all privileged institutions, even polite society. Charles Arbuthnot wrote that it broke Wellington's heart not to throw out 'the Church Robbery Bill,' but the nature of the Conservative party in the Commons made the risk too great.[19]

Peel did not object to the basic principle; in turn the government surrendered the provision that revenue from the suppressed bishoprics be used for secular purposes and agreed that the clerical tax would not apply to incumbents. These were significant concessions, but not enough to satisfy the Duke, much less the Ultras. But unlike his friends who were clamouring to defeat the bill entirely, Wellington would not risk the House of Lords by opening a breach with the Commons on this measure.

When it reached second reading on 19 July he appealed to the peers not to reject it but to allow it to go to committee for closer examination. The example of his absention allowed it to pass safely into committee. There his stock among the Ultras rose as he supported an amendment that appointments in parishes where services had not been held for three years not be suspended without authorization from the bishop, and revenues from suspended parishes be used to build churches and rectories. This ran exactly counter to the bill's intent, and a political crisis was avoided only when the ministry decided to accept defeat on these matters for the time being in order to save the measure. The Duke convinced the Tory Lords to rest content with their considerable victory and allow the mauled bill to become law.

The Ultras were in a solemn if not mutinous mood when the Duke, after all his pronouncements about the pillage that would follow parliamentary reform, refused to lead them in total rejection. But lacking organization, numbers and the taste for day-to-day business to form a ministry of their own, they recognized that their only prospect of success lay with Wellington, whatever exhortations were necessary to keep him on the straight and narrow. He in turn regarded the Ultras as fearless but impetuous cavalry, ready to charge on any occasion but needing his restraining hand to prevent their quixotic efforts from leading to disaster.

Some of the Ultras' discontent with the Duke's conduct on the Irish Church was allayed by his pleasing orthodoxy on a couple of other matters that came before the House of Lords in 1833. Many of Grey's supporters in 1830 had been in favour of the abolition of slavery. Crown slaves had been freed in 1831 but the general issue had been neglected in the long struggle over the Reform Bill. In 1833 the cabinet finally produced a measure providing for total abolition at the end of a seven-year transitional period. Wellington had taken a prominent part in the negotiations to end the slave trade after the war and had been a party to the parliamentary resolutions of 1823 calling for abolition, but he took the gravest view of what he regarded as this precipitate freeing of the slaves. He denied that the intention in 1823 had been emancipation in the near future and argued that a long period of education was necessary to prepare the slaves for their new place in society. Without that they would not work; the sudden change would be disastrous for British trade and revenue and the livelihood of free workers; property would be threatened by the breakdown of society; and in all this haste the wishes of the colonial legislatures were being ignored.[20] These fears had little effect on the bill, as even in the House of Lords only a tiny minority opposed it, but their expression undoubtedly did much to reassure the Ultras about their leader's soundness.

On the proposal to allow Jews to sit in Parliament, the Duke staunchly insisted that the country and legislature were Christian and challenged the government to demonstrate the necessity of a measure which 'at first blush appeared to invade the principles by which the Legislature had been hitherto guided.' He denied the analogy with Catholic emancipation by observing that the Jews had never enjoyed privileges and could not therefore claim their restoration. He acknowledged the 'respectability and propriety of a large proportion of the Jewish nation' and recognized that their lot had improved greatly in the last two centuries but he could not 'as a member of a Christian assembly, advise the Christian King of a Christian country to pass such a bill.'[21] His attitude was not eccentric and the bill was rejected by 104 to 54. Not for another quarter of a century did the peers change their mind on this issue.

A considerable amount of legislation had reached the statute books in 1833, too much for those who feared what might follow if not enough for those who wanted more fundamental change. Wellington and Peel could congratulate themselves that their strategies were helping the reaction against reform. As the ministry's fortunes declined even further in 1834, the Duke remained steadfastly at his task, confident that it was surely if slowly working. Once again the Ultras were eager to destroy the government in the House of Lords as soon as Parliament met, and once again Wellington had to remind them: 'We must be very cautious in our measures. A false step might do the greatest injury to the institutions and interests of all descriptions which it is our duty as well as our object and our inclination to support and maintain.'[22] He did not envisage the collapse of the administration, of which others claimed to detect signs, and told the Ultras that even if it did happen it would not be the great blessing they imagined unless it was also accompanied by a general conviction that the Reform Act should be undone. 'The truth is,' he gloomily informed the Duke of Buckingham,

> that all government in this country is impossible under existing
> circumstances. I don't care whether it is called monarchy, oligarchy,
> aristocracy, democracy, or what they please, the Government of the
> country, the protection of the lives, privileges, and properties of its
> subjects, and the regulation of the thousand matters which require
> regulation in our advanced and artificial state of society, are

impracticable as long as such a deliberative assembly exists as the House of Commons, with all the powers and privileges which it has amassed in the course of the last two hundred years.[23]

As the parliamentary session wore on and the House of Lords waited for legislation from the Commons, the tension between Wellington and the Ultras increased and the Duke's anger with it. When those two perpetual *frondeurs*, Lord Londonderry and the Duke of Buckingham, tried to goad him into what they called a 'stand up fight,' his patience finally snapped. He angrily reminded Londonderry:

> I am also for a fair *stand up fight*. Such has always been my practice. It is not that of the Duke [of Buckingham]. In the last session of Parliament I fought several fair stand up fights throughout the dog-days, and till the end of August, with the support of not more than ten or a dozen peers, upon questions of the greatest public and personal interest even to the Duke of Buckingham himself, but I do not recollect that I had the advantage of the Duke's support on any one of these occasions.[24]

Two days later he terminated the exchange with a mighty rocket. Confidently hurling the stone from his own glass house, he insisted that if he were to carry on a war with Buckingham, the latter must write legibly: 'I can scarcely read one word of his letter, indeed not one word beyond the first page.' He added that talk of himself as leader, 'or anything but the slave of a party, or in other words the person whom any other may *bore* with his letters or visits upon public subjects he pleases is just what I call *stuff*. I beg therefore to have no more of the duke's letters.'[25] Fortunately Buckingham's glaring inadequacies, the least of which was his hand-writing, provided Wellington with plenty of grounds for defence. But keeping such restless troops in line as the government really did crumble in the summer of 1834 taxed all his diplomatic and authoritarian skills.

By the time political events reached a crisis the Duke had received another great honour in becoming Chancellor of Oxford. When it became obvious in the autumn of 1833 that Lord Granville did not have much longer to live, the Conservative interest in the university, after searching in vain for a suitable peer of outstanding literary or academic attainments, gravitated to the Duke of Wellington. Their advocate with the Tory hero was Lord Sidmouth, who had already persuaded him to sit to Sir Francis Chantrey for a bust commissioned by members of the university who wished to commemorate his noble attempt to form a government in May 1832.[26]

The overture must have come as a considerable surprise to Wellington. Only eight years before he had removed his two sons to Cambridge after Lord Charles had been sent down for compounding the mischief of helping to paint the doors of the dons of Christ Church red by breaking out of the gates one night. As a further disqualification, he told Lord Bathurst: 'I had not received a university education; that I knew no more of Greek or Latin than an Eton boy in the remove; that these facts were perfectly well known; and that I must be considered incapable and unfit.' When the emissaries came from Oxford he urged that they consider Bathurst, the Duke of Beaufort, Sidmouth or Lord Talbot. But they were not put off by this, nor by the Duke's observation that 'it would occur to every body that I was an example of success in life without academical education and an example to be avoided, rather than an example for the university to hold forth to the youth of the country.' But he did add that, 'in all cases of this kind I considered myself as an Instrument to be used by the publick when it was deemed necessary.'[27] Despite his elaborate parade of modesty, he was as proud of this recognition of his achievements by one of the great centres of learning as he was of his success in the field with little formal military education.

At the same time that Wellington was being approached, another group at Oxford was anxious to expunge the humiliation of the by-election of 1829 by getting Peel to accept nomination. Peel would have been delighted by this vindication of his political integrity, his intellectual ability (he had taken a double first) and his position in the Conservative party. But a ruinous contest with the Duke would divide the organization he was trying to build, further antagonize the Ultras, and mean great loss of face in the party if he were defeated. One of Peel's sponsors tried to get Wellington to withdraw, but the Duke saw no reason why Peel's feelings or their political relationship should enter into the matter. But if he would not stand down Peel must. When he did, on 17 January, the Duke was elected without opposition.[28]

Although he was informed that Wellington had at first attempted to have the Chancellorship offered to him, the matter rankled in Peel's sensitive mind and did not improve relations between them. On 1 May, which the Duke always celebrated as his birthday by dining with the Arbuthnots, the well-meaning Charles Arbuthnot tried to use the occasion for a reconciliation. Peel accepted the invitation but Arbuthnot told Lord Aberdeen that he did not think that he and Wellington exchanged a single word.[29] Aberdeen then tried his hand at mediation. In a long interview

Peel admitted that he was not as close to the Duke as he had been. He traced this partly to Wellington's pointed complaints that not all his friends had shared his willingness to stand by the King in May 1832, but also to the matter of the Chancellorship in which he thought it strange that the Duke should have agreed to the nomination without any communication, direct or indirect, 'without an attempt to ascertain whether I had a wish to renew with the University of Oxford that connection which had been severed solely through the performance of a public duty, and through fidelity at a trying time to the Duke of Wellington.'[30]

The Duke could not afford to have Peel nursing such grievances and he repeated to Arbuthnot and Hardinge, in the sure and certain knowledge that it would be conveyed to the right quarter, that in the event of a Conservative ministry the Prime Minister must be in the Commons. He also disclaimed any office for himself. When Arbuthnot pointed out that he could not be excluded and that his influence in the House of Lords was indispensable, Wellington pointed to the Horse Guards and asked why he should not return there.[31] Heartening as this news must have been to Peel, it was not sufficient for him to swallow his pride and go to Oxford when Wellington was acclaimed by the university in June.

Charles Greville, who preferred to spend his time at Ascot, dismissed the Duke's installation as 'a complete Tory affair, and on the whole a very disgraceful exhibition of bigotry and party spirit; plenty of shouting and that sort of enthusiasm, which is of no value except to the foolish people who were the object of it, and who were quite enraptured.' But even Greville had to exempt Wellington from his general condemnation for remaining 'quite unconcerned at the applause with which he was greeted; no man ever courted that kind of distinction less.'[32]

The Duke invited Croker to accompany him on the journey. When Croker inquired about the mode of travel, Wellington replied, 'I am the Duke of Wellington, and bon gré mal gré, must do as the Duke of Wellington doth.' He would send an appropriate equipage to Oxford but he would enter the city 'as I have always entered that and others – as an individual.' So unprepossessing was their open carriage and pair that forty of the hundred young men who rode out to greet them went by before Croker, realizing what was happening, pointed out that this was the great man. As they rode into town, Croker could not get Wellington to take off his hat even to ladies. He saluted everyone like a soldier, and Croker reflected: 'he is a sad hand at popularity hunting.'[33]

The installation ceremonies, the conferring of honorary degrees on platoons of the Duke's military companions and Ultra Tory friends and the related festivites, lasted for four days. Among the attendants was Lady Salisbury, the niece of General Gascoyne of anti-Reform Bill fame, who felt herself almost too liberal for the admirable spirit of the place: 'nothing but Ultra Toryism and Ultra Protestantism will go down. It was quite delightful to find oneself in such society.' The undergraduates in the gallery of the Sheldonian Theatre occupied their time each day until the ceremonies began by calling out names for approbation or censure:

'Whigs and Pickpockets', 'Tories and Honest Men,' 'French Allies' (hissing), 'French wines' (applause), 'A laugh for the Dissenters' (upon this there was a long and universal laugh, the most ludicrous thing I have ever heard), 'Lord Grey and his return in office', 'Parliament as it is' (hissing), 'Parliament as it was' (vehement applause), 'The present House of Commons' (hisses), 'The House of Lords' (great applause), 'The memory of George 3rd' (great applause) . . . And after having exhausted every possible subject at last somebody called out, 'The whole human race.'

The Duke of Cumberland entered the theater with some trepidation on the first day, but this was not the comparatively radical atmosphere of the House of Lords. The whole arena rang with acclaim which he rose repeatedly to acknowledge. When the Duke of Wellington himself entered the whole building shook with applause. 'He looked gratified,' Lady Salisbury wrote, 'he could not do otherwise – even he must have been flattered by such a reception from such an assembly.'

The conferring of degrees was in Latin and the Duke had applied to Sir Henry Halford, as famous for his Latin poetry as for his medical skills, to translate his discourse. Everything he did delighted the assembly. When the Newdigate Prize Poem was read by its author and he reached the lines,

> And the dark soul a world could scarcely subdue,
> Bent to *thy* genius, Chief of Waterloo!

the whole audience rose and applauded the deliverer of Europe for quarter of an hour. Wellington himself later said that he had never seen anything like it, but as the versifier was on his deaf side he did not understand what had produced the uproar. He remained impassive throughout the demonstration, but when he finally took off his cap and pointed it at the speaker to continue, this simply increased the excitement which ended only with 'the mere exhaustion of our animal power.'

When the Duke left the theater on the last day, the cheers were almost as great again. He told Lady Salisbury: 'If I could be spoilt by this sort of thing, they would spoil me here.' As he walked around All Souls with her after the last banquet, while Scottish reels were being performed in the Codrington Library, his thoughts turned to the reformers he had left in London: 'And they would destroy all this!'[34] The exclusiveness and abuses of the universities were already under attack in Parliament and Oxford was being riven by the Tractarian controversy, but the university was to find in its Chancellor a vigorous external defender and an energetic arbiter of its internal disputes to the day of his death.

Even as Wellington was travelling back to London the government was being shaken to its foundations. Badly needing the support of O'Connell's MPs, the cabinet narrowly agreed to a commission to examine the revenue of the Irish Church to see if there was a surplus that could be used for lay purposes. This was too much for Edward Stanley, the Irish Secretary, Sir James Graham, Lord Ripon (formerly Goderich) and the Duke of Richmond (the last of Grey's Ultra Tory ministers), who promptly resigned. The Prime Minister himself was barely persuaded to stay and Lord Althorp, the seemingly indispensable Leader of the Commons, also expressed his desire to leave. This convulsion was followed by far worse when the renewal of the Irish coercion legislation prompted O'Connell to reveal a sordid bargain between him, the Viceroy (since the autumn of 1833 once more Lord Wellesley) and some cabinet ministers to keep Wexford quiet during a coming by-election in return for removing the restrictions on public meetings. This time Althorp, who had been a party to the negotiations, decided that he too must resign. So great was his anguish that the Duke of Wellington thought he was on the verge of suicide. 'Mind what I say,' he told Lady Salisbury. 'If that man goes they cannot last.'[35] On 7 July he left, and the following day Grey also resigned.

The day after that Grey gave a final, emotional account of his forty-year career to the House of Lords. The Duke was quite unmoved by this sentimental performance. As soon as Grey sat down he was on his feet, ostensibly to defend Peel against some pointed remarks in Grey's speech but really launching a general attack. He accused Grey and Althorp of deserting the King and vigorously defended his own ministry against the charge of having left the country in an unmanageable state by the time the Whigs came to power. He claimed that 'during the three years and a half that the noble Earl has presided over his Majesty's Councils, there had been more blood shed in this country than there was from the year 1780, the time of Lord George Gordon's riots, down to 1830, the period when the noble Earl accepted office.' None of the responsibility for this could be laid at the opposition's door; he himself had never objected to the ministry's proposals on partisan grounds and he had supported Grey whenever possible.

Even the members of Wellington's party were embarrassed by the vehemence of his speech.[36] Perhaps he should have repressed his feelings, or at least saved them for another day and let Grey depart in peace, but the long, complacent justification of a career that he considered to have been dedicated to the subversion of an excellent order was more than he could bear. All his pent up hatred of the Whigs as traitors to their order and his contempt for those who boasted of their ability to carry out a task and then ran away from the responsibility and blamed others for their own failings welled up and found expression in an outburst that was impulsive but not unprepared.

Alarmed at the prospect of what might follow Grey but cheered by his departure, the King summoned Lord Melbourne, the most conservative of the remaining ministers, and instructed him to try to form a government including Wellington, Peel and Stanley. But these individuals were no more eager to enter such an arrangement than Melbourne. The Duke told the King that he agreed with Melbourne that no coalition was possible; a ministry not based on principle could not control Parliament or benefit the royal interests. He insisted that this was not a partisan view but one grounded in his view of the constitution of the country and the importance of maintaining 'the authority of the crown, of the privilege of both houses of Parliament; of the Church of England and its privileges as established by law, particularly in Ireland; and of the rights and property of all corporations and of all descriptions of Your Majesty's subjects in all parts of the world.'[37] Peel took the same position. The two Conservative leaders showed each other their letters and were so satisfied with them that neither could suggest a change in the other's. Both were determined to attempt only a real Conservative administration with the right to dissolve Parliament in order to seek a majority in the Commons. But the King feared to dismiss the Whigs and embark on such an adventurous course at the moment. Instead he trusted Melbourne to keep the Whig government going on moderate lines, a task helped by Althorp's reluctant withdrawal of his resignation in response to a letter from 200 of the ministry's supporters.

The price of Althorp's return was soon revealed. Three days after forming his government Melbourne told the House of Lords that he was dropping the prohibition on public meetings and the establishment of courts martial in disturbed districts from the Irish Coercion Bill. This capitulation was more than Wellington could bear. He poured scorn on Brougham's flagrant inconsistency in claiming that it was impossible to get the measure through the House of Commons when only a few days ago, while Grey was still Prime Minister, the Lord Chancellor had been using all his eloquence to defend the necessity of military courts. The Duke added to the ministry's embarrassment by demonstrating from the Lord Lieutenant's official reports that the number of outrages in Ireland had diminished by three-fifths since the previous Coercion Act had come into force; that crime had practically disappeared in the disturbed area; and that those charged with keeping the peace were anxious to have the special powers renewed. He told Melbourne that he would support whatever Coercion Bill was proposed, but if a less effective bill than the expiring one was enacted, 'he would tell the noble Viscount, and he would tell his Majesty's Ministers, that for such a measure he and they alone would be responsible.'[38] As the Conservatives in the Commons were not in a position to insist on a stronger bill or form a government, the Duke did not feel that he could press the omissions on the ministry in the House of Lords and risk its resignation. When the legislation reached the Lords at the end of July he again registered his objections by introducing an amendment to restore the vital clauses, but he did not insist on a vote. After the bill was passed, he and a number of Ultras recorded a written dissent, declaring that firmer measures were needed to keep Ireland tranquil.

On the bill to admit Dissenters to degrees at the two ancient universities, the new Chancellor of Oxford was not so hesitant. Pointing out that the universities were chartered corporations, he challenged Melbourne to vote with him as he had declared on becoming Prime Minister that he would uphold the institutions of the country. Wellington insisted that admitting Dissenters would destroy the system of college discipline and stoutly defended the Anglican monopoly in the two universities:

> It was not only that young gentlemen were educated there in literature and science, but they were taught their duty towards God and man, by learning the religion of the Church of England, by being taught what Christianity was, by learning their duty towards their Maker and their fellow man. Would any man tell him that those studies would not be interrupted by the admission of Dissenters into those institutions?

He begged the peers not to force the measure on the King, who was authorized to prevent 'schism, dissensions, and disorders' and to see that 'the true doctrines of the Gospel, the doctrines of the Church of England, were maintained and taught, and nothing else.'[39] The Lords had no difficulty in accepting this argument and the bill was easily rejected by 187 to 85.

The legislation amending the poor law system, on the other hand, had the Duke's wholehearted support. He was not alone in believing that the structure of society was being sapped by the present arrangement, which he considered made overly generous provision for those who did not really need it, kept wages too high and forced local poor rates up to an intolerable level. After 1795 the practice of subsidizing wages of agricultural workers in relation to the price of corn and the size of the labourer's family had spread through the south of England. This form of guaranteed annual wage had helped to prevent agricultural uprisings in times of bad harvests, low wages and revolution across the Channel, but its continuation and spread after 1815 raised the spectre of an endless cycle of idleness and improvidence among the workers and ever-increasing poor rates. The activities of 'Captain Swing' in smashing machinery and burning ricks and barns in 1830 also called in question the sedative effectiveness of the subsidy. The new system, proposed after two years' investigation by a royal commission, ended the practice of subsidizing wages and allowing people to enjoy poor relief in their own homes. Only the truly indigent would henceforth be maintained at public expense, in workhouses where the standard would be kept below that of labourers outside in order to make the system self-enforcing. All this was good in the eyes of the Duke, even though it meant the invasion of local custom for centralized uniformity. He was not one of those who saw any virtue in 'a system of administration which differed in each and every one of the 12,000 parishes in this country, and in each of which different and varied abuses had crept in.' Addressing himself primarily to the Ultras, some of whom were eager to challenge the Whigs on the issue of local autonomy, he insisted that no scheme had been proposed 'which in his judgment at all equalled the present, and for it he must return the noble Lords opposite, with whom it had originated, his sincere thanks.'[40]

The Duke was in great form in the last days of the parliamentary session. After the defeat of the bill to admit Dissenters he went to Hatfield to celebrate the large majority with Lord and Lady Salisbury and other Tory friends. There he received the terrible news from Sir Henry Halford that Mrs Arbuthnot had died of cholera that morning.

He threw himself on the sofa in great agitation and walked about the room almost sobbing before going to his bedroom. Mrs Arbuthnot had been unwell for some time, and even at Oxford where her husband had received one of the honorary degrees she had been markedly subdued and had not taken her usual place at Wellington's side. But the Duke had left for Hatfield thinking that she was somewhat better. Death at least came with merciful swiftness and she was spared much suffering, keeping her spirits and mental vigor to the day before she died, reading newspapers and even joking with Halford about her altered appearance. But the very suddenness of her death made it all the harder for the Duke to bear. 'It is a dreadful loss to him,' Lady Salisbury wrote, '... her house was his home, and with all his glory and greatness, he *never had a home!*'[41] The next morning he sent a note to Lord Salisbury and left Hatfield at 8.30 to comfort Charles Arbuthnot at Woodford.

The great pillar of his life was gone, but Wellington felt that he had to bear his sorrow in private. In public he kept up appearances, if only to counter the general impression that she had been his mistress. Three days after her death he was back in the House of Lords speaking on foreign policy. Some thought this showed lack of feeling, but Charles Greville at least admired 'the good taste and sense to smooth his brow and go to the House of Lords with a chearful aspect.'[42] Adhering rigidly to what he saw as his duty however trying the circumstances had always been one of the Duke's characteristics, and the orderly structure of his daily routine probably helped him to deal with the strain better than withdrawing from public life to the agonies of introspection and reappearance later.

Charles Arbuthnot, who had been almost pathetically dependent on his wife, collapsed under the shock of her death. Wellington cared for him through his nervous breakdown and took him to live with him for the rest of his life. They had been close personal and political friends for fifteen years, but their common loss brought them even closer together. To a greater degree than before, Arbuthnot became the Duke's chief political agent and public guardian.

Wellington was able to bear Mrs Arbuthnot's death better than her husband, but he never found anyone to take her place. Lady Salisbury, of whom he had become fond in recent years, assumed the position to some extent. She was a charming companion and a good listener, but she could not take the same part in political discussion; and she had children to compete with the Duke for attention. In time this friendship might have developed into one like that now so abruptly ended, but only five years later Lady Salisbury also died at the early age of thirty-seven.

In the aftermath and probably in reaction to Mrs Arbuthnot's death, Wellington embarked on the strangest of his romantic adventures. At the beginning of 1834 a Miss Anna Marie Jenkins, a woman of strong religious convictions who had brought a murderer to repentance in his death cell a year before, wrote to the Duke about the state of his soul. A bible and an invitation to visit followed at intervals. Wellington was always interested in religion and theology and in November, seeking consolation for his loss or merely out of curiosity, he called on Miss Jenkins. He can hardly have expected her to be an attractive woman of twenty. So overwhelmed was he that, according to her account, he burst out: 'Oh, *how* I *love* you! how I *love* you!' He assured her that the feeling was inspired by God Almighty. After their next meeting, which did not take place until 23 December, Miss Jenkins decided that his words did not quite mean what she had imagined. The second round of protestations convinced her that the Duke was not proposing marriage but seduction. Great were the outbursts of indignation and accusations from the injured saint, who may not have been as free from social ambition as she insisted. Wellington refused to reveal his real intentions but pointed to the impossibility of marrying someone nearly fifty years younger (and almost as far apart socially, he tactfully refrained from adding) while continuing to express admiration for her.

There matters might and probably should have ended. But Miss Jenkins persisted in her correspondence and the Duke, whether from guilt, because he feared exposure or because he could not resist the pleasure of replying, continued to write sporadically and even occasionally to meet Miss Jenkins for the next seventeen years.[43] Sir Herbert Maxwell, the first of Wellington's biographers to read and use these letters, dismissed them in the 1890s as 'twaddle.' So in a way they are, though they do indicate the Duke's great loneliness and lack of satisfactory female companionship in the last decade and more of his life. The powerful reaction to Mrs Arbuthnot's death had made him susceptible to Miss Jenkins, and the failure to find anyone to take her place made him reluctant finally to cast her off. Many others were also encouraged, if less abruptly and forcefully; but no one ever possessed all of Mrs Arbuthnot's qualities, and after Lady Salisbury's death no one even came close. For the most part after 1839 he had to fight loneliness and depression by exhausting attention to work, restless journeys and his endless correspondence.

In the time immediately following Mrs Arbuthnot's death and while he was caring for her husband, there was not much political activity that called for the Duke's attention. The parliamentary session ended on 15

August and a week later he wrote with considerable satisfaction that the destruction of the House of Lords was out of the question: 'we have only now to follow a plain course with moderation and dignity in order to obtain very great, if not a preponderating influence over the affairs of the country.'[44] No one expected any great political change until Lord Althorp was called to the Lords on the death of his father, when there might be a reconstruction of the ministry. But as Earl Spencer's death was not considered imminent, Peel felt quite safe in leaving for an extended journey to Italy in the middle of October.

In fact Spencer died on 10 November. Four days later, as he was about to go out hunting at Stratfield Saye, Wellington was summoned to the King at Brighton. On his arrival he discovered that the government had been dismissed when William IV refused to accept Lord John Russell as Althorp's successor as Leader of the House of Commons; the other candidates proposed by Melbourne were even worse. Pointing to the divisions within the ministry, the monarch told the Prime Minister that it would be unfair to ask him to continue in his precarious position. Melbourne took this ejection from office with his usual equanimity, even agreeing to carry the messages to the Duke back to London, whence they were forwarded to Stratfield Saye.[45]

Wellington could hardly refuse a commission he had undertaken in more difficult circumstances in 1832. But as he had long ago firmly decided that the Prime Minister in modern times must manage the House of Commons, he told the King that he could only undertake a provisional government until Peel returned from Italy. Late that night the Duke wrote to Peel from the Royal Pavilion advising him to hasten back as quickly as possible. In another short note he sketched out the political situation, telling Peel that the King had seized on Spencer's death to dismiss the ministers instead of waiting for them to discover that they could not continue. He also pointed out that the ministers, particularly Melbourne, were quite willing to leave rather than be pressed to stay when trouble arose in the next parliamentary session. Wellington emphasized that he had refused to become Prime Minister, insisting that this be offered to Peel, and would not even assemble a ministry until he returned. In the meantime he would conduct the business of government himself with the help of a few temporary assistants who would prepare for the general election. Even the Great Seal would be put into commission under Lyndhurst.[46]

These letters, the formal summons from William IV and copies of the letters exchanged between the King and Melbourne were given to James

Hudson, the Queen's gentleman usher, who set off through France and Italy in search of Peel. He found him in Rome on 25 November. Preceded by Hudson, Peel posted back to England at the same speed as the Emperor Hadrian fifteen hundred years before, arriving in London early in the morning of 9 December.

Two days after the interview at Brighton, the King came to London to transfer power from the Whigs to the Duke. He told a hastily assembled group of Conservative Privy Councillors that he had already appointed Wellington Lord High Treasurer, was now conferring the Home Office on him and that he would also hold the seals of the Colonial and Foreign Offices for the time being. All other posts would remain vacant. After this brief business, William IV entertained the assembly to the inevitable and tedious justification of his actions.[47]

Once entered into the plentitude of power the Duke lost no time in enjoying his temporary kingdom. He rode straight from St James's Palace to the Home Office, thence to the Foreign Office and the Colonial Office to deal with the business of those departments. Greville observed that he was clearly enjoying the part of Richelieu in running the entire government, but some not unfairly complained of the 'unceremonious and somewhat uncourteous mode in which without previous notice he entered into the vacant offices, taking actual possession, without any of the usual preliminary civilities to the old occupants.' After this initial tour, Wellington conducted business from the Home Office and only occasionally visited the rest.[48] Most people were impressed or amused by the Duke's conduct of the whole administration of government and had no reason to think he was acting unconstitutionally; but the Whigs, if only to divert attention from their own failings, affected to believe that he was trying to become a military dictator. Creevey thought it would have been one thing for the Whigs to die a natural death, but it was quite another to have them 'kick'd out of the world by this soldier, and to see him stand single-handed on their grave, claiming the whole power of the nation as his own.'[49] But there were no riots as there had been in 1832 and Wellington was able to tell Peel that the country had never been more tranquil: all attempts at demonstrations had failed and addresses were pouring in thanking the King for dismissing the Whigs.[50]

This optimistic assessment was not entirely true. The City of London voted an address to protest entrusting the government to those who had opposed the reform bill and defended every abuse in the institutions of the country. Even the Duke had to admit to Peel that there were other similar addresses, though 'principally from Scotland, from places of inferior importance.'[51] But the criticism was directed more against the King than the individual who had responded for his request for help. As Wellington told one correspondent: 'I may be Constitutionally responsible for enabling the King to carry on a Govt. without the aid of his popular Ministers. But the Quarrel is His. I have nothing to say to it; excepting that I facilitated His Changing his Ministers.' As for the Whig complaints that they had been turned out of their offices with indecent haste, as each of the Secretaries of State had equal power to convey government orders, it would have been ludicrous to have had individuals contradicting each other for a few weeks. Arrangements might be a bit unusual at the moment, but everything was going on well and no one was the worse except himself who was worked as no post horse ever was: 'However I have settled every depending Question and have set right some which my Predecessors had left wrong.'[52]

The most tiresome part of his duties was not day-to-day administration, in which he revelled, but having to deal with the garrulous William IV. After one performance, on the occasion of finally wresting the Great Seal from the reluctant Brougham, the Duke wrote: 'He is in great spirits; but He is thank God! between ourselves gone out of Town. He was becoming a little in a hurry; and I am afraid that I should not have kept him quiet.'[53]

As well as dealing with the King and keeping the wheels of government turning, Wellington was also carefully preparing for Peel's return. After two weeks he sent him a list of candidates for office and the places available. He emphasized that this was entirely for Peel's convenience, not an attempt to impose his own judgment. But part of the point of this memorandum must have been to convince the cautious and hesitant Peel of the practicality of a Conservative ministry and the eagerness of all to serve. The Duke also reported that Wellesley would be resigning as Viceroy and that an account of Irish affairs would be drawn up as soon as possible; there were hopes of attracting disaffected Whigs; and the Ultras were 'very well disposed to go all reasonable lengths in the way of reform of institutions. I have their letters to show you. I have been astonished at their being so docile.'[54]

Wellington had issued a circular to his political associates explaining his own refusal to form a ministry and his recommendation of Peel. When Charles Greville asked him if the Ultras were ready to put themselves into his hands and agree to whatever he considered necessary, he replied without hesitation: 'I think they are; I think they will do anything.' Greville could hardly disapprove of a government which was prepared to tackle the country's problems in a spirit of reform, but he was offended by the Duke's 'revolting inconsistency' in changing his tune: 'he gave no indication of such a disposition during the last Session; it is all reserved for the period when he is possessed of power.'[55]

There was much to what Greville said. But Wellington firmly believed that while any ministry of which he was a member might propose careful and well-regulated reforms, it would not be characterized by that precipitancy and love of change that he considered the hallmark of the Whigs. And in contrast to the late ministry, it would take a strong stand against civil disorder. He told Lord Londonderry: 'the Existence of the Country turns upon the Elections. It is quite wonderful what a Number of Persons there are who are looking to Plunder. They will plunder if we don't get a Parlt returned which will support a Govt which can, and will restrain them.'[56]

As soon as Peel arrived in London on 9 December he sent a message to the King requesting an interview and closeted himself with the Duke. Later in the day he kissed hands as Prime Minister and accepted the Chancellorship of the Exchequer. At a Privy Council meeting the next day, William IV announced Peel's appointment and thanked Wellington on his own behalf and that of the country for the way in which he had conducted business since the Whigs resigned.[57]

Peel's first task was to fill the government offices in a way that would increase his strength in the House of Commons. He made overtures to Sir James Graham and Lord Stanley (as he had become on the death of his grandfather in October), but the renegade Whigs, while promising support from outside, refused to join the ministry. Ostensibly this was owing to the Duke's violent speech at the time of Grey's resignation, accusing the government of which they had lately been members of failing to keep order in the country and of general incompetence; but the real reason was that they doubted the success of the Conservative enterprise. Wellington offered to stay out of the ministry in order to secure Graham and Stanley, and later was willing to leave if Stanley would come in. But apart from the fact that the Duke's sacrifice would not achieve its object, Peel knew that without Wellington in the cabinet there would be little hope of controlling the Ultras.

Trouble, as was only to be expected, was already brewing in that quarter. Lord Londonderry was demanding a suitable appointment and the Duke of Buckingham was contemptuous of the office of Lord Steward that he was offered. With a blunt asperity that would have been fatal from Peel, the Duke told Londonderry that he could understand Buckingham refusing the offer:

> But I cannot understand His being Offended; or thinking of any thing excepting how best to support the Effort that is making.
>
> I hope that the least result of it will be to get the Gentlemen of England again upon their Legs! No man would like to hang behind in such a Struggle.

For his part, Wellington added, he would give up his office at any time and lead the House of Lords out of office or in, whatever would facilitate getting a majority in the House of Commons; but 'till Great Men as the D. of Buckingham view matters in this Light we shall not be safe.'[58]

Buckingham insisted on standing aloof, nursing his injured pride, but other Ultras were conciliated with office. Buckingham's relative, Charles Wynn, became Chancellor of the Duchy of Lancaster; the Earl of Wilton took the despised Lord Stewardship; and the Earl of Rosslyn became Lord President of the Council. A couple of weeks later it was announced that Lord Londonderry would go to Russia as ambassador. Apart from this, the most surprising appointment was that of Sir Edward Knatchbull, whose motion had brought down the Duke's ministry in 1830, as Paymaster General. But while the Ultras were amply rewarded, most of the major offices went to more moderate individuals. Wellington became Foreign Secretary; Lyndhurst Lord Chancellor; Aberdeen Colonial Secretary; Goulburn Home Secretary; and Lord Ellenborough President of the Board of Trade.

After putting together a ministry, Peel had next to face the general election for which the Duke had begun preparations. The process had already taken on a momentum of its own and in the excited atmosphere of November and December every political faction was eager for a contest. Wellington himself had heartily supported local initiatives in this matter, telling the organizer of a Conservative dinner at Ipswich a few days before Peel's return: 'We are embarked in a great cause, and we must make every exertion to save our Constitution, and all that is valuable to Us as a Nation and as Individuals in a Social State.' He thought that nine-tenths of 'the Property the Education the Talent and Intelligence of the Country' was behind the enterprise, but the task was to ensure that a majority of the Commons reflected this opinion.[59]

Peel, who had worked hard to form Conservative constituency organizations, was not likely to overlook the value of energetic partisans. But if the Conservatives were to win a majority, or even substantially increase their number of seats, they needed to go beyond the ranks of the committed and appeal to those who had supported the Whigs in 1832. To attract those disposed to reform but disillusioned with the former government, Peel presented the cabinet with a statement of principles. Ostensibly an address to his own electors at Tamworth, this was really a party programme. He emphasized his record as a reformer in the 1820s and the legislation he had supported since 1832; repeated that he accepted the Reform Act as a final and irrevocable settlement of that issue; and declared that he would never oppose the correction of proved abuses and the redress of real grievances. As proof of this he announced that the commission on municipal government established by the Whigs would be allowed to continue and its report would receive full and unprejudiced consideration. A commission would also be appointed immediately to study Church reform and the distribution of its property. This Tamworth Manifesto certainly caught public attention when it was rushed to the press following a cabinet meeting that lasted until midnight. It was hard for the Ultras to swallow after their high hopes of a ministry that would reverse reforms, but the presence of the Duke and some of their colleagues in the government helped to convince them that this was the high price of keeping out the Whigs.

Following the generally encouraging response to the Manifesto, the ministry decided on dissolution at the end of December. As usual only about a quarter of the seats were contested and polling was remarkably quiet. The results, however, were not as satisfactory as the government had hoped. The Conservatives did well in the counties but not in the boroughs. The Whigs claimed a majority, but whether or not this was the case no one could tell until Parliament met and the ministry announced its intentions.

When Parliament did assemble on 19 February, it was in some physical discomfort. A few months before, in order to find temporary quarters for the bankruptcy court, the Treasury had cleared the old tallies (notched sticks formerly used to keep accounts) from their storage room in the Palace of Westminster. On 16 October workmen began burning them in the stoves of the House of Lords. Over the protests of the housekeeper, who smelled burning in the medieval structure, they kept at their task until half past five in the afternoon. An hour after they left the ancient dry timbers of the building were in flames. The firemen managed to save Westminster Hall, but most of the rest was destroyed or badly damaged. Only William IV saw a ray of hope in this disaster, magnanimously offering Buckingham Palace, much enlarged by his extravagant predecessor, as Parliament's new home. But despite his pertinacity, both

Houses were united in insisting on remaining where they were. Ultimately Charles Berry's new gothic structure rose on the site of the old; in the meantime the House of Lords was patched up for the Commons and the Painted Chamber for the House of Lords.

These makeshift arrangements reflected all too well the precarious fate of the ministry. There was an unpromising beginning in the Commons when Charles Manners-Sutton, the Speaker since 1817, was challenged by a Whig candidate on the grounds of his partisan activities outside the House since Wellington had taken over from Melbourne. The election in a full House of James Abercromby by a majority of six was a palpable defeat for the new government. The Conservatives met at Lord Salisbury's for what had been intended as a celebration, but which turned out to be more of a wake. Peel would not attend and the Duke refused any comfort that things would turn out for the best, gloomily insisting that 'it was as bad as could be; and the thing appeared worse because they had all been led to feel so secure.' He even ordered his secretary to have everything ready to leave the Foreign Office at a moment's notice; but within a few days his pessimism had lightened at least to the extent of thinking that, bad as things were, the country was 'on its legs again.'[60]

At first glance it is hard to see on what this judgment was based. In the Commons the government suffered another embarrassing reverse when the opposition carried an amendment to the Address in Reply by a majority of seven and then launched attacks on Wellington's assumption of total power before Peel's return. Charles Arbuthnot told his son that the object of focusing all criticism on the Duke was to destroy the ministry by forcing him out.[61] At the first meeting of the House of Lords, Melbourne absurdly accused Wellington of having advised the King to dismiss his former ministers. The Duke insisted that he had had no contact with the court for over three months before the summons to Brighton caught him by surprise; if there had been anything improper in his assistance, he tellingly asked, why had Melbourne agreed to take the King's letter to London? He defended himself against the charge of holding more than one office by observing that Melbourne's former leader, Canning, had begun by holding both the Foreign Office and the Prime Ministership; and Wellington challenged anyone to show that his conduct as caretaker had produced any untoward results.[62] This was enough to meet Melbourne's mild accusations, but in the Commons more ardent spirits were preparing to launch a vote of censure on the Duke's supposed dictatorship if the ministry lasted long enough. But the opposition's strategy of concentrating

153

on Wellington also drove the government's supporters closer together and reconciled some of those who would otherwise have been critical of its reform plans. When Lord Stanley, though standing aloof from the Whigs, joined the assault Charles Greville pointed out that the Tories would 'not endure that a youth like Stanley shall avail himself of his accidental advantages to treat their great man with levity and disrespect.'[63]

There was not a great deal for the Duke to do at the Foreign Office, and foreign policy was one area in which William IV had approved of the Whigs' conduct and specified that the Conservatives were to follow the same course. He was besieged by the usual requests for a patronage and replied to them in his customary brisk fashion. But there was one powerful claimant who could not easily be dismissed. Lord Londonderry, a leader of the Ultras and a former diplomat full of grudges at not receiving a pension for his former services or office in the Duke's administration, might without careful handling become the danger to the ministry he had been in 1829 and 1830. He would be intolerable in the cabinet, but at the moment one of the best diplomatic posts, the Russian embassy, was vacant. Londonderry unfortunately held strong pro-Russian views while the Foreign Office was supporting Turkey, but he could not be passed over and offered a lesser post without risking loud Tory disaffection. Despite the treachery he had endured from Londonderry in the Peninsula, at the Congress of Vienna and on numerous occasions closer to the present, Wellington decided to give him the appointment. One of the attractions must have been the great distance of St Petersburg.

Making this great Tory ambassador to the most autocratic court in Europe did nothing to placate the friends of liberty in Europe. But when Londonderry referred to the Poles who had risen in revolt at the beginning of the decade as the Tsar's rebellious subjects in the House of Lords in the . middle of March, the opposition raised a storm of protest in the Commons that Sir Robert Peel could not meet. Many thought that this was the issue that would force the Duke to resign. The next day Wellington defensively told Charles Greville that he was not 'particularly partial' to Londonderry but insisted that he had great abilities, 'was an excellent Ambassador, procured more information and obtained more insight into the affairs of a foreign Court than anybody, and that He was the best relater of what passed at a conference, and wrote the best account of a conversation, of any man he knew.'[64] It was nevertheless clear that if the government were to survive Londonderry would have to resign or have his appointment cancelled. To the great relief of the ministers he resigned. The Duke, paying tribute to his high qualities and 'that delicacy of feeling which belongs to his character,' took full responsibility for the appointment but observed that the country must be deeply obliged to Londonderry for resigning in order to avoid a vote in the Commons that would endanger the balance of the constitution by questioning the royal prerogative of naming ambassadors.[65]

Londonderry's sacrifice did nothing to increase the strength of the government, but it did encourage the Whigs, Radicals and Irish Repealers who had been meeting at Lichfield House since the beginning of the session to find some common ground on which to defeat the ministry. So hostile was this Lichfield House compact to the Conservatives that the Duke of Bedford declared that if the choice lay between despotism and anarchy, he would take anarchy; to which Wellington responded: 'I can tell Johnny Bedford, if we have anarchy, I'll have Woburn.'[66] In vain did Peel try to save his administration by introducing legislation acceptable to the Whigs, if not entirely satisfactory to the Radicals and the Irish. The opposition did not object to his bill for civil marriages as demanded by the Dissenters or his long list of English Church reforms, but in its present united state it could insist on the appropriation of part of the revenue of the Irish Church for secular purposes, which was anathema to the Conservatives.

Faced day after day by defeats in the House of Commons and grumblings from his Ultra supporters about abandoning his principles, Peel became disheartened and anxious to abandon the hopeless enterprise. The Duke, smothering an imminent major embarrassment by persuading the Tory Lords to refrain from a Protestant debate while Church matters were being debated in the Commons, tried his best to keep him at his post. On 24 March they had a 'terrible scene,' with Peel in a state of high excitement, his features 'working and twitching in a thousand ways,' while Wellington, according to his own account, was 'as cool as possible.' The Prime Minister wanted to resign and wanted the Duke to agree that that was the right thing to do. But Wellington would not. He told him:

> Nobody has a right to desire you to remain longer than you think fit; but I implore you for the sake of the country, for the sake of your own credit, do not resign without you have made a clear case for it that your party and country may be satisfied it is *impossible* for you to do otherwise.[67]

The next day Peel sent a circular to members of the cabinet saying that with no majority in the Commons in prospect, accepting repugnant legislation in order to win the transient support of the opposition and continue in office without power could only bring discredit.[68] Wellington agreed that mere office was 'a post of trouble, of difficulty, and of danger' and wished that it was in his power to relieve the Prime Minister; but he urged him to remain and contend against the mischief of the opposition for as long as possible. 'A week more or less cannot signify much either way in any view whatever,' he exhorted him, 'excepting to your high character, and to the contentment of those who had supported you; and I earnestly recommend to you to bear with the evils of your position, till the conviction will be general that you cannot longer maintain it.'[69] But the Duke knew that there was little chance of preventing Peel from leaving soon and concluded that the best hope for the country was a coalition of Grey and Stanley and Peel and their followers: 'And yet that is a dream – a mere vision.'[70]

The end came after two more discouraging weeks, during which it was amply demonstrated that the government could not carry even trivial matters in the Commons. When the division came on Lord John Russell's motion that Irish tithes be appropriated to lay purposes, Lord Lyndhurst promised to send Lady Salisbury immediate news. But Wellington, knowing what the news was likely to be and what Peel would insist on doing, pronounced himself satisfied to know the result when the newspapers arrived at ten the next morning: 'If I could do any good by having it before, I would; but as I can't, I had just as soon wait.'[71] The division was carried against the ministry by the decisive majority of 285 to 258. The following morning Peel resigned and the King had no alternative but to bid farewell to his beloved Conservatives and recall the Whigs he had united and whose hand he had strengthened by his precipitate dismissal five months earlier.

CHAPTER SEVEN

HOLDING THE LINE

A S SOON as the formalities of resignation were over, Wellington hurried out of the capital as he had in 1830, 'out of spirits and annoyed at all that had passed', to attend to business at Dover and Stratfield Saye. Despite the succession of defeats in the Commons, he thought that the ministry had given up too soon, 'but Peel would not stay, there was no persuading him.'[1] The immediate loss of three by-elections in widely scattered counties by the Whigs when Lord John Russell took office and two MPs went to the House of Lords supported his view that the country was coming around to the Conservatives against the Whigs, Radicals and Repealers; but it took an act of greater faith to believe that the Conservative government could have hung on until this was reflected in the numbers in the House of Commons. It would be more difficult to achieve a majority out of office, but the prospects were infinitely brighter than three years before. The problem in the House of Lords was to avoid provoking the temporarily strengthened Whigs into a direct attack on it; but the Conservative peers could at least afford to take a bolder line in the defence of traditional institutions and privilege than the Duke had considered safe after 1832.

Wellington's task was to prevent this defence from getting out of hand. Once again the Ultras dreamed impatiently of destroying the Whig government in the House of Lords and establishing a real Tory ministry. The Duke of Buckingham, reflecting on the course of modern history, insisted that the Lords should stand by their principles and not give way to the Commons: 'By not acting upon these principles the Country was exposed to the Miseries of the Great Rebellion, & her Sovereign lost his Crown & Life. By similar blindness the French Revolution was brought on & convulsed all Europe.' He insisted that as the Conservatives were hourly increasing in strength, it would be weakness not to fight for their principles where they could be brought to bear: 'By not following this line we should crush the reviving hopes & feelings of the Country & materially strengthen the power of the Enemy.'[2] But unhappy as the Duke of Wellington was with Peel's conduct, he had to point out once again that he was the key to Conservative fortunes and that to defeat the government in the Lords without some assurance of a majority in the Commons would be absurd. As he told Lyndhurst: 'Can we or can the Duke of Cumberland, the Duke of Buckingham and the Marquess of Londonderry form a Govt. for the King?'[3]

Despite this initial testiness on both sides, Wellington and the Ultras were soon working together in remarkable harmony. As the year was well advanced by the time Melbourne's government settled into office, the cabinet announced at the end of May that it would proceed with only two major items of legislation, municipal reform for England and Wales and reform of the tithe for Ireland. Perhaps it could not do less than provide one measure each for the Radicals and the Irish, but these bills would have constituted an ambitious programme for a full session. Both aroused the strong hostility of the Duke and the Ultras.

Municipal reform was the local counterpart of the 1832 parliamentary Reform Act and stirred much the same emotions. Scotland had been provided with municipal institutions for its new parliamentary boroughs almost silently in 1833, with the franchise set at the parliamentary level of £10 householders. But in England town governments generally remained in the hands of self-perpetuating corporations which managed the property and patronage at their disposal to their own advantage and, despite the repeal of the Test and Corporations Acts in 1828, were still largely unsympathetic to Dissenters. The Conservatives had accepted the principle of municipal reform in the Tamworth Manifesto and the royal commission reported on the subject just before they went out of office. Wishing to reassure the urban voters, Peel wrote to Wellington hoping that they could co-ordinate their activities and limit the opposition of the Ultras. Both, Peel was sure, were 'looking to the same objects, and feel much more interested in protecting the monarchy, and the public interests involved in its security, than in fighting a mere party battle.'

But the Duke was at one with the Ultras in regarding the municipal corporations as bastions of order and political support whose destruction would pave the way for the abolition of the House of Lords and other privileged institutions. He was willing to concede that there should be some improvement in the financial administration of the towns and that they should be provided with efficient magistrates, but he warned against any increase in 'the Political Interference of the Democracy; that is of the ten pounders' and was opposed to any uniform principle of reform unless it should be one favourable to the influence of the crown. In a statesmanlike manner he added that he was willing to make some sacrifices on small points for the sake of party.[4] Peel decided that there was nothing to be hoped for from Wellington and thereafter kept his own counsel. The Duke concluded that the abrupt end of the discussion meant that Peel had not made up his mind on the issue. 'Just shows you what the man is,' he told Lady Salisbury, '– can decide nothing.'[5]

Peel of course knew exactly where he stood on the matter. When Russell introduced a bill abolishing the existing corporations and replacing them by 183 borough councils elected by ratepayers of three years' standing, he supported the principle of a large measure of reform and allowed the bill to pass second reading with a division after very little debate. In committee he failed to secure a property qualification for councillors; another Conservative was defeated in his attempt to preserve the parliamentary franchise of the freemen; and Stanley lost his bid to have the elections held every two years instead of annually. But after relatively harmonious debate on such a great issue the bill went to the Lords at the end of July.

The Conservative peers were determined to fight the measure tooth and nail and their great leader seemed fully with them. He was not far off the mark in considering that the royal commission had set out less to inquire into the state of the corporations than to destroy them and the last vestiges of the old system of representation which had existed before 1832. He thought the charges of corruption exaggerated and based on gossip and scandal. Any changes to the present excellent arrangement should benefit the inhabitants, and those who would manage their affairs must meet a high property qualification. As the charters were so diverse, the Duke believed that each corporation should be dealt with individually, a procedure that would have the happy effect of keeping Parliament busy for years to come. But above all, considering the low estate to which all authority was reduced, there must be no increase in the power of democracy.[6] This attitude diverged from Peel's on every point, but it was by no means extreme among the Ultras and Wellington was soon trying to restrain the more eager.

A meeting of seventy or eighty Conservative peers at Apsley House on 27 July decided to allow the bill to pass second reading, provided that counsel for the corporations were heard at the bar. They also agreed to restrict themselves to moderate amendments in the expectation that Peel might soon be called to office and have to introduce a bill of his own.[7] But one of the two lawyers chosen to present the consolidated petitions against the bill was that steadfast defender of old corruption Sir Charles Wetherell. For three days he and his colleague requited the trust in them by whipping the Ultras into a frenzy against the bill. At a dinner on the third night Peel, who had tried to calm the peers the day before, got into a heated argument with Wetherell. Seeing that things were getting out of hand, the Duke tried in vain to dissuade his colleagues from hearing further evidence against the general principle of the bill, but finally relented at the insistence of Lyndhurst.[8] Facing the prospect of endless delay, there were rumours that the government would resign or at least that Parliament would be adjourned. Peel, in disgust, dissociated himself from the Lords by leaving town without even telling Wellington.

When the Tory Lords realized that the testimony at the bar was not strengthening their case for the probity and exemplary administration of the corporations, they were not at all averse to ending the hearing of evidence. The more ardent spirits wanted to defeat the measure immediately, but they were outnumbered at another meeting at Apsley House which decided to turn it into a truly Conservative bill, leaving the responsibility for rejection or abandonment to the Commons or the ministry. When Peel sent word that he disapproved of wrecking the bill and would take no responsibility for forming a government if the Whigs resigned on the issue, Wellington and other moderates began to think how they could avoid antagonizing him without sacrificing the amendments they had agreed on with their colleagues. It was finally decided that the Duke would make a conciliatory speech on the general principle before Lyndhurst tackled the legal complexities of the bill's 200 clauses.

Wellington's statement did not bring much comfort to those who supported the bill, but its primary purpose was to reconcile those who were adamantly opposed to some revision of chartered rights. After paying his respects to those who felt compelled to reject it entirely and reviewing the shortcomings of the legislation, he observed that while he had no quarrel with the present arrangements, he could not conceal from himself that 'in the course of a very few years the people of this realm have advanced greatly in riches, in knowledge, and in luxury, and that in proportion to that advance it is natural they should wish to have participation in the administration of Government.' In that spirit he urged the House to remove the evils, 'in some instances justly complained of,' of the corporate system and to delete the defective parts of the proposed measure in order to secure 'the rights of the Crown, the privileges of the people, of the officers of the Corporation, and of all who are entitled to any participation in the Corporation funds.'[9]

These general principles were applied so thoroughly in Lyndhurst's amendments that in the end the bill was scarcely recognizable. The property and parliamentary franchise of the freemen were preserved forever; the councils were to be elected only by those who paid rates at the highest level of assessment; there was to be a property qualification for councillors, one-third of whom would be elected for life as aldermen; town clerks would hold office like judges on good behaviour; the management of Church property would be restricted to Anglican councillors; and much more. The majorities for these amendments were so large that the government soon ceased to divide the House. When it was pointed out to Lyndhurst that he was striking out clauses that Peel had accepted in the Commons, the happy warrior allegedly replied: 'Peel! What is Peel to me? D—n Peel!'[10] The Radicals clamoured for an attack on the Lords and for stopping supplies until the bill was passed; the Ultra peers talked excitedly of giving no quarter, despite Wellington's advice to refrain from further discussion. Peel remained in the country, disapproving of the amendments and of the Lords' holding up other bills, but refusing even to commit himself to returning to London when the Commons took up the amended bill on 31 August. At the last moment, and without notice, he did return. After paying deferential tribute to the independence of the House of Lords, he threw over his aristocratic associates by agreeing to the concession made by the government, defending a few minor amendments of the Lords, and offering to negotiate other differences. The question was, what would happen when the bill went back to the Lords?

The night before, eighty peers met once more at Apsley House. The Duke announced that he would hold his opinion until the last. Although he did not reveal it, he had received a letter in the name of the King urging him to use his influence 'in checking any Ebullition of feeling which should produce the Risk of a serious Collision between the Two Houses of Parliament and increase the Embarrassment of His Majesty.' Holding up a bill when even the Conservatives in the Commons wanted to bring the matter to a satisfactory conclusion could only shake the strength and consistency of the party to which the King looked as a rallying point for all moderates in the event of an emergency.[11] Although the Ultras were all for sticking to what the Lords had already decided, it was Wellington's statement, pronounced with authority and regret, along the lines of the King's appeal, that carried the meeting. He would not change his mind on having aldermen as well as ordinary councillors, but in the present difficult circumstances he advised accepting the bill substantially as agreed to by the Commons. Any other course would certainly involve the Lords in great danger.[12]

It was the end of the parliamentary Reform Bill all over again in miniature, but this time with no serious prospect, though some heated talk, of civil unrest to force the measure on the Lords. The Duke and Lyndhurst publicly hauled down their colours in the House of Lords; the Duke of Cumberland, perhaps on the urging of the King, left town; and the Ultras remained quiet as the final terms of the bill were worked out between the two Houses.

The resistance of the House of Lords could be represented as something of a triumph for Conservative interests as the measure that was enacted was much more restricted than that originally proposed. There was a property qualification for councillors, elected for three years by those who had paid rates for three years; the councillors in turn elected one-third of the council as aldermen for six years, one-third retiring every two, and the mayor annually. The parliamentary franchise, but no other privileges, of freemen would continue for life. And to dispose of the issue of a religious test for Church matters, municipal Chuch patronage was to be sold on the open market under the direction of the Ecclesiastical Commission, the proceeds going to the common use of each town. No new municipalities were created and the bill applied to 178 existing boroughs rather than the original 183; but others could apply for incorporation, as Manchester and Birmingham did in 1838.

For the Duke of Wellington the extensive nature of this reform was a bitter defeat for his most cherished principles. He told Lady Salisbury that the bill created 'a little Republic in every town, possessing the power of raising money. In case of anything like a civil war, these would be very formidable instruments in the hands of the democratic party. Charles I was ruined by the money levied by the City of London.'[13] He never ceased to bemoan this change in the same terms as the Reform Bill of 1832. When the industrial towns of the North were the scenes of great unrest in the next few years, he had no difficulty in tracing this to the new municipal councils.

Wellington and the Conservative peers were afforded some compensation for municipal reform in defeating two other pieces of legislation. When a bill arrived commuting the Irish tithe to a rent charge to be paid by the landlord and reducing the number of Church benefices in order to produce a surplus revenue for education, they struck out the appropriation clause which had been opposed by Peel in the Commons. The ministry promptly abandoned the measure for the present and cast the blame for non-payment of the tithe on its opponents. The measure to provide Dublin with an efficient police force like the one Peel had devised for London in 1829 contained nothing to which the Conservatives could object. It was nevertheless thrown out, ostensibly because the Lord Mayor and Corporation had not been consulted and because it was unseemly for the Lords to be hurried at the end of the session, but really to spite O'Connell, who was expected to enjoy the patronage of it.

The Duke was full of apocalyptic gloom in the autumn of 1835. Municipal elections for the new councils were held up and down the country and O'Connell embarked on a furious campaign against the House of Lords, characterizing Wellington as 'a stunted corporal' and Peel as being 'as full of cant as any canter who ever canted in this canting world.' The Duke told Lady Salisbury: 'We are on the eve of a great change in society. I am one of those who think the change had better be gradual than sudden: if gradual, we all (the aristocracy) may find our places in it. We may not be what we were, but we shall be something.'[14] When Henry Goulburn tried to convince him that the outlook was improving, he gloomily conceded that the gentleman of the country were beginning to rally, 'but a political Power has been established in the Country which is too strong for them.' That democratic power prevented the aristocracy's nominees from governing: 'Who will govern? How long can the Country go on without a Govt? How are it's growing Difficulties to be met and got the better of?'[15] But despite his pessimism, the House of Lords in 1836 was able to hold the line on two issues Wellington considered vital without the political crisis that had arisen over English municipal reform.

At the beginning of the year the Duke and Peel met at a number of country houses, including Peel's, where they smoothed over sore feelings about the Corporations Bill and discussed the outlines of their policy for the coming season. They agreed that neither should move an amendment to the Address unless some objectionable principle were included. Wellington told Lord Aberdeen that the House of Lords should lie low and not take the initiative in anything: 'My Determination is if possible to keep them quiet till we shall have before us a Bill which it will be our Duty to amend or reject, and to proceed vigorously, and to act upon a broad intelligible Principle which every body will understand.'[16]

Despite this resolve, matters got off to an acrimonious start when the Address recommended municipal reform for Ireland on the same basis as

Scotland and England. Taking a stand on the strict usage that it was not the function of the crown to suggest principles of legislation but simply to refer issues to Parliament, Wellington immediately moved an amendment committing the Lords only to remedying just causes of complaint. Seeing himself outnumbered and realizing the immense difficulty he was going to have with the measure, Melbourne wearily accepted the rebuke and allowed the amendment to pass without a division. Even though an Irish municipal bill had passed the Commons late in the previous session and then been dropped, Peel felt obliged to move the Duke's amendment in that House and was humiliatingly beaten by 284 to 243, the largest majority the government had ever had on a major issue.

The commissioners who investigated the Irish corporations discovered the same abuses as in England. The ministry proposed councils elected by £10 householders in the seven largest boroughs and £5 householders in the others. Wellington and Peel realized that they could not possibly defend the Irish corporations – 'I am afraid there is too much evidence of malversation and misgovernment to enable us to leave the Corporations as they are,' sighed the Duke – but even though this measure was more restricted than the English one, they were determined that local government should not fall from the Protestant ascendency to the Catholic repealers. 'It is impossible to deliver the population of the Irish corporate towns to the government of those whose conduct is described in the evidence taken before the Intimidation Committee of the House of Commons,' Wellington told Peel. 'We are trying an experiment in England and Scotland, but we have evidence sufficient to show us that we ought not to try it in Ireland.' The Conservative leaders agreed that the best course was to move for the abolition of all corporations, even Dublin's, and to have the towns administered (as many in England still were) by sheriffs, magistrates and commissioners appointed by the crown. But the Duke had no great hope that Peel could get the House of Commons to accept this.[17]

His assessment was correct. When a motion to this effect was proposed in the Commons it was defeated by an even greater majority than the amendment to the Address. A small group of MPs and peers meeting at Peel's house nevertheless decided to continue the struggle in the Lords.[18] Lyndhurst was again entrusted with the detailed management, this time with the advantage of working in harmony with Peel. Wellington did not play a major part in the debates, but he did point out that the whole history and condition of Ireland proved that English forms could not be transplanted to the other side of St George's Channel. He insisted that the corporations were not as bad as they were represented and warned against throwing power to the Catholics, who would most probably use it to avenge the past. He told the House that he could not consent to this 'revolution of power' and could see no reason for it, 'unless to gratify the ambition of some at the expense of the interests of all.'[19] By the time the bill emerged from the Lords it had predictably been reduced to one simply for the abolition of municipal corporations.

The Irish MPs were furious at this treatment of the measure and at statements such as the Duke's. Caught between the peers and the Irish, the government tried to devise a compromise by proposing elected councils for the twelve largest boroughs and total abolition elsewhere. But the Conservatives would not concede the basic principle. The revised bill passed the House of Commons but was firmly rejected by the Lords. Wellington rehearsed his earlier arguments and exhorted his colleagues to stand by their resolve.[20] Faced with this impasse the ministry decided to drop the measure for the present and municipal reform was added to the lengthening list of perennial items of Irish legislation.

The Irish Tithe Bill also received its annual hearing, and was condemned to its annual fate. By 1836 the matter had increased in urgency as Evangelical members of the Church of Ireland formed themselves into a Lay Association to recover the tithes by means of court orders supported by writs of rebellion. But the government would not drop lay appropriation and the Conservatives would not accept it. As the House of Lords prepared once more to excise the clause for the spoliation of the Church, Wellington went out of his way to praise the Lay Association, though not by name, claiming that after its long difficulties and privations the Irish Church was in a better position than before, 'owing to the protection which had been afforded to the clergy by enforcing the law in that country.' If justice were properly done by the Church, there would be no magnificent surplus to dispose of; and he advised the Lords to improve the bill to the benefit of the Church and people.[21] But striking out appropriation was no improvement in the eyes of the ministry and the measure joined its companion for municipal reform in the special limbo for Irish legislation.

There was nevertheless some hope that these Irish matters, and the new item of a poor law that was added at the beginning of the session, might be resolved in 1837. The Whigs were looking for a compromise that would enable them to save their honour, places and the support of O'Connell while the Conservatives, convinced that the ministry could not last much longer, did not want to come into office committed to some awkward position like the Whigs on appropriation that would prevent them from finally settling Irish problems without sacrificing principle and consistency. The Conservatives were willing to concede a poor law that would provide workhouse relief for the destitute at a modest cost to the landlords, as this rating would provide a better basis for a municipal franchise than perjured statements about real and movable property; they were also happy to settle the tithe, so long as all revenue remained in the Church; and once these matters were satisfactorily arranged they were prepared to compromise on municipal reform as councils with a high property test for the franchise would be no great threat to the Church and Protestant property. But they were insistent that Ireland be dealt with precisely in this order. The Whigs, on the other hand, were above all determined to secure the principal Irish demand of municipal reform; then they were prepared to compromise on the tithe as O'Connell, if not the English Radicals, was willing to abandon appropriation; and they were least concerned to provide a poor law, for which the Irish showed no great enthusiasm as they witnessed the workings of the English system.

The obvious course for the government, as the Duke told Lord Roden, was 'to force on the discussion of the Irish Corporation Bill in the H. of Lords as soon as possible. Our Game is to postpone it as long as possible.'[22] Although they were excited by the prospect that the ministry would resign if it did not get its way on this bill, Wellington assured Peel that the Tory Lords were perfectly docile and amenable to the direction of their leaders, having 'given up their opinions; ... sacrificed their Influence in the Country; their Interests; the Interests and the Influence of their adherents and Party, the Interests of the Church of Ireland; all to promote the general objects of the Country and to preserve Peace.'[23] The news of this selfless renunciation and new eagerness to obey must have come as a revelation to Peel, particularly as he and the Duke were having trouble in getting large numbers to town to follow them in delaying Irish municipal reform so that the three bills could be dealt with by the House of Lords in the prescribed order. When Bishop Phillpotts of Exeter, perhaps not appreciating that the general orders had changed from previous sessions, wrote that he would prefer to stay in the country until after Easter when legislation generally began arriving in the Lords, his great patron sharply observed: 'It is impossible for me to express a wish which shall tend to conflict with the Convenience of any Noble Lord .... The Reputation of the House & the Safety of the Publick Interests depend upon Noble Lords doing their Duty. I only entreat them to give their attendance.'[24]

Whether the government would resign or whether there would be a compromise on Ireland in the summer of 1837 no one could tell. When the Municipal Bill arrived in the Lords Wellington summoned his followers to Apsley House and persuaded them to allow second reading but to delay further consideration until the other two bills were before them. On the motion to go into committee on 5 May, he made a long speech about his concern for the security of the Church and the necessity of examining the other two measures to see how they would affect the Church, and moved that the committee stage be postponed until 9 June.[25] This was carried by a large majority. When the other bills had not arrived on 9 June, the committee was again postponed until 3 July.

The ministry endured this obstruction and the abuse of the Radicals with remarkable equanimity only because a new element had entered the political calculations with the illness of the King. After the second postponement of the Municipal Bill it was clear that he would never recover. 'Doctor, I know I am going,' he said, 'but I should like to see another anniversary of the battle of Waterloo. Try if you cannot tinker me up to last out that day.'[26] At his express wish the Duke held his annual dinner on 19 June (the 18th fell on a Sunday), and the King died during the night.

When the tributes were paid in Parliament to the late monarch, Wellington claimed to have found in all his dealings with him 'a firmness, a discretion, a candour, a justice, a spirit of conciliation towards others, and a respect for all.' He thought that there probably never was a sovereign 'who in such circumstances, and encompassed by so many difficulties, more successfully met them than he did upon every occasion that he had to engage them.'[27] In private, however, the Duke scathingly characterized him as 'the most ignorant Man ever placed in a great situation' and his reign as 'a most unfortunate one for Himself, His Country and the Family': 'He had an unfortunate facility or rather weakness of Character; which enabled every *Charlatan* to prey upon Him. This Country will long suffer from the Measures of His Reign.'[28]

Wellington was greatly impressed by the young Queen Victoria's conduct at the first Privy Council meeting on the morning of her accession. He told Charles Arbuthnot that 'he could not have been less alarmed & nervous than she was, &... he would not but have been present for the whole world.'[29] But he feared for the consequences of the accession of a woman of eighteen. 'Supposing her to be an angel from Heaven,' he told his niece Lady Burghersh, 'she cannot have the knowledge to enable her to oppose the mischief proposed to her.' She would not even have the strength for

Melbourne to use her as he had William IV, 'as a sort of *bugbear* to frighten his supporters by telling them the King will take the Conservatives if pushed too hard. We are governed by a corrupt and ignorant faction,' he lamented; 'not supported by a corrupt court, but forced upon the court by the democracy. God help us!'[30] The Prime Minister took good care to surround the Queen with attendants of his own political persuasion and within a few weeks the Duke was complaining that she was encompassed by 'Whigs and Whigling Male and female; and Nobody knows anything excepting Gossip.'[31] Melbourne further increased his political advantage as well as indulging his passionate temperament by acting as her secretary, tutor and confidant. This was one of the great romances of history, which cooled only when the Queen married three years later, but it was firmly based in the first instance on political considerations. After condemning monarchical power and influence time out of mind the Whigs now found themselves basking in royal favour while the Conservatives were unwelcome at court for the first time in living memory.

As well as the Queen's political captivity, Wellington was soon decrying the personal independence that was to cause him so much discomfort in the next fifteen years. When she insisted, even against the advice of Lord Melbourne, on attending her first military review on horseback rather than in a carriage with her ladies, he observed to Lady Salisbury: 'I could not wish ... a better subject for a caricature, than this young Queen, alone, without any woman to attend her, without that brilliant *cortège* of young men and ladies who ought to appear in a scene of that kind, and surrounded only by such youths as Lord Hill and me, Lord Aberdeen and the Duke of Argyll.' As to the soldiers, 'I know *them*; they won't care about it one sixpence.' It was all a childish fancy based on reading about Queen Elizabeth at Tilbury: 'But *there* was a threat of foreign invasion, there was an occasion which called for display *then*. What occasion is there now?'[32] Despite this grumbling the Queen rode as she intended.

Eager to escape from its political embarrassments and hopeful that the manifest favour of the Queen, and the mulish obstruction of the House of Lords would do it some electoral good, the government embarked on the general election in July. The Conservatives hoped that their record of support for moderate reform and the reaction against the Radicals and the Irish would tip the balance in their favour. They continued to gain in the English counties and small boroughs, but lost seats in Ireland, for an overall increase of about thirty-five.[33] With the support of O'Connell's party the Whigs still had a slim majority. The Duke took some small comfort in the results – 'Those who were Radicals remain Radicals, but the difference in the elections arises from the number of Conservatives who have been awakened to a sense of danger' – but he expected further trouble from the 'Destructive party': the Dissenters; 'the atheists, and the republicans in principle, who are prepared to ally themselves with the papists as a means of bringing about a revolution;' the Catholics; and the Whig aristocrats, 'who are induced by party feeling to patronize measures they cannot approve.'[34]

Finding himself bound more than ever to the Radicals and the Irish, Melbourne sought to escape through William IV's dream of a coalition with the Conservatives. He approached Wellington through Lady Burghersh, but the Duke's response was not encouraging. With the position of the Conservatives in the Commons somewhat improved he saw no reason to relieve Melbourne from the responsibility of managing a situation brought about by the Reform Act which had thrown power to 'masses of men, whose object is to pull down the Church' in alliance with 'the Great Families & Proprietors, who in all times have made use of any Instrument to oppose the Throne & Establishments.' He agreed that the election results made the management of the country 'by what is called Government' very difficult but he advised the Prime Minister to follow a responsible course and take a chance on support from moderate men of all sides, 'if there are any such.' This might eventually lead to coalition, and would certainly give people time to consider, but 'All previous understanding upon the Questions must be out of the Question!' Through Lady Burghersh Melbourne responded that he intended to take a moderate line in Parliament but could not go back on any issue without losing his own position.[35]

The Queen's beloved uncle, King Leopold of Belgium, meanwhile supplemented Melbourne's efforts with a direct approach. Wellington made it clear that the Queen could count on him in any difficulty, though he warned that frequent consultation would be resented by the ministers. He repeated his satisfaction that the election would force the government to be more moderate in its policies, especially as they affected the Church, for 'the Security of all Property in England particularly of those great landed Properties possessed by many depended upon the maintainance of the Church.' Like Melbourne, King Leopold wanted to know what attitude Peel would take when Parliament met. The Duke could only reply that he did not know, that he had little communication with him, but that they generally agreed without consultation.[36] At the end of October Wellington told Lord Wilton that he had not seen Peel to talk to or heard from him since the death of William IV, but he was sure that the numbers he commanded in the Commons would enable him to prevent, 'and particularly may enable the H. of Lords to prevent a great deal of Mischief.'[37]

Peel, about whose intentions there was so much curiosity, was as eager as Melbourne to reach some accommodation on the everlasting Irish issues now that the chance of office with a majority in the Commons seemed within his grasp. But even though the Duke was the key to his aim, as the only person who could get the Lords to support a compromise, Peel remembered all too well the experience of the English Municipal Bill the year before and did not confide in him in advance.

When Parliament was summoned in the autumn, principally to deal with the new monarch's civil list, the Ultras were eager to strike a fatal or at least a telling blow at the Whig government. But they were deprived of one of their great champions. The Duke of Cumberland became the King of Hanover on the accession of Queen Victoria who could not succeed to that throne. When William IV lay dying Wellington's advice to Cumberland was: 'Go instantly ... and take care that *you don't get pelted!*' But the new King insisted on staying to swear allegiance as an English peer to his niece, even though he was warned that this would be resented in Hanover. Once arrived there, Ernest Augustus immediately put into practice the sound principles on which he considered a country should be governed, suspending the constitution granted in 1830, persecuting the professors at the University of Göttingen and conducting himself practically as an absolute ruler. Even the Duke was taken aback by this, not so much on account of the propriety of such actions in Hanover as on the impression they would produce in England, 'where it ought to be a paramount interest with him to preserve or acquire as good a character as he can.'[38] The King was still next in line for the throne and returned from time to time to his apartment in St James's Palace; encouraged the Ultras from afar; and occasionally threatened to resume his seat in the House of Lords. But he was no longer there to give his close attention to legislation and intrigue. The Old Tories were the weaker for it, and for the death of Lord Eldon in 1838; but Wellington's task was immeasurably easier and his position as the Conservative leader in the Lords clearer.

The first ritual clash in the House as the peers awaited business from the Commons occurred over Ireland. Both sides staked out the ground for what they imagined would be the major issue of 1838. The Duke did not gain much praise from his followers by rising above partisan considerations to congratulate the Lord Lieutenant for enforcing the law and giving proper protection to the Protestants. But when the civil list was discussed he redeemed himself by protesting the reduction in the annual allowance for royal pensions to a mere £1200. Many service officers of modest means who had been waiting for some reward since 1815 would find their hopes dashed by this woefully inadequate sum; but he refused to defy constitutional usage by holding up financial provisions voted by the Commons.[39]

Having settled the financial provisions for the monarch, the government intended to adjourn Parliament for six weeks until the usual meeting time at the beginning of February. But on the very day of adjournment, news arrived of a rebellion in Lower Canada (Quebec). On the basis of slight information the Radicals immediately blamed it on the ministry's tyrannical administration of the colony while the Conservatives charged that it had been produced by weakness and inappropriate concessions to appease the Radicals in England. In the face of this double onslaught and with no certain knowledge of the seriousness of the revolt, the adjournment was shortened to the middle of January. By that time news had arrived of another uprising in Upper Canada (Ontario). In military terms these were small insurrections and fairly easily suppressed; but the situation was all too reminiscent of that in the other American colonies in 1775 and was readily transformed into familiar contemporary terms by analogy with events in England and Ireland. In both colonies reformers were demanding government more responsible to the local inhabitants; in both there was a clash between the elected assembly and the legislative council chosen by the governor from the local elite; and in Lower Canada the assembly was predominantly French while the council was British.

Most Conservatives were delighted at the government's latest troubles and some would have been happy to have the rebels seize Montreal if that would have brought down the Whigs. But the Duke of Wellington refused to take any party delight in this serious threat to imperial interests. Believing that the insurgents would be supported by the United States and other friends of republicanism, he told Charles Greville that the government should exhibit its determination by sealing the St Lawrence 'so as to prevent the ingress of foreigners, Belgians, French and others, who would flock to Canada for employment against us.' He busied himself writing papers on the military situations as conscientiously as if he had been in office. Delivering one of them to the Horse Guards he remarked in high good humour to General Hill: 'Why it looks as if we were at our old trade again.'[40]

As soon as Parliament met in January he inquired what the government intended to do. Foreseeing the possibility of international war, he entreated the Lords in a famous phrase to remember that 'a great country like this could have no such thing as a small war.' He advised the ministers to embark on the enterprise 'upon such a scale, and in such a manner, and with such determination to the final object, as must make it quite certain that they would succeed, and that, too, at the earliest possible period after the [shipping] season opened.'[41] His fellow Conservatives were hardly prepared for such disinterested statesmanship in the Whigs' hour of need and great was the dismay over this speech. But as Charles Greville observed, the Tory Lords had to confine themselves to 'a sort of undergrowl and with rueful faces, for they stand in awe of the great man, and don't dare openly to remonstrate with him or blame his actions.'[42] When he spoke again two days later they hoped he would make some amend; but he simply reiterated his views, though he did criticize the ministry for not taking effective action following its refusal of responsible government the year before and claimed that the troubles in Lower Canada stemmed from the decision in 1831, which he had opposed, giving control of the revenue to the assembly.[43] This was no better. In an unusual reversal of roles it was now Peel who more aggressively challenged the government.

The Duke was distressed by this divergence, which he interpreted as criticism of him by Peel. But he was even more alarmed when it seemed that the Conservatives in the Commons might go to the lengths of supporting a Radical motion condemning the ministry's handling of Canada. At Lady Salisbury's he sat angrily in his chair, his fingers between his teeth, scarcely looking at her: 'I should like to know, when they have carried the motion, and turned Ministers out, what is to be the next step? Eh? What is to happen then?' When Lady Salisbury, caught between her strong Tory sentiments and her love for Wellington, ventured to suggest the importance of holding the party together, he burst out: 'The party! What party? What is the meaning of a party if they do not follow their leaders? I don't care sixpence if they split! D—m! 'em: let 'em go!'[44]

A few days later he wrote more temperately to Peel agreeing that he might be forced to support the Radical motion but urging him to find a course that would at least enable him to demonstrate that he had not created the crisis and had done everything to avoid it. If a Conservative government came to power with Radical support, it would be said that the Conservatives' course was as bad as the Whigs' in bringing down Peel's ministry in 1835; and Peel would have to deal with a situation in Canada that would occupy all the country's forces for two years during which O'Connell might well plunge Ireland into turmoil for repeal. He warned that a political party 'must look before it, must consider the consequences of the steps about to be taken, and must make it certain that even the first will not be ruinous.' Peel tactfully replied that he agreed in the main but stressed party considerations.[45] Fortunately he was able to devise an amendment that united the Conservatives but was unacceptable to the Radicals, allowing the Whigs to stay in office.

To deal with Canada the ministers decided to suspend the constitution of Lower Canada and to despatch Lord Durham as Governor General of all the colonies, with special powers in Lower Canada. Conservatives were appalled that 'Radical Jack,' one of the architects of the Reform Act, a ceaseless advocate of Radical causes and a colleague so irascible that Melbourne refused to have him in the ministry, should be entrusted with such a delicate mission. In the Commons Peel managed to scale down his powers, and in the Lords Durham was attacked by his arch-rival Brougham, whom Melbourne had also refused to have as Chancellor when he returned in 1835, and by Lord Lyndhurst. Wellington, however, refused to object to the individual or to the powers entrusted to him.

With Canadian problems apparently out of the way for some time to come, Parliament could turn its attention to reaching some agreement on Irish matters. The proposed poor law was opposed by some Conservatives on the grounds that the English one was provoking such resistance that its extension to Ireland would be disastrous. But in contrast to Peel, who was endeavouring to maintain a discreet silence on the subject, the Duke firmly supported the bill in the House of Lords. The Irish tithe was settled in a manner even more pleasing to all Conservatives when the Whigs finally abandoned lay appropriation; the remaining simple conversion to a rent charge of 75 per cent of the nominal value of the tithe was essentially the proposal that had brought down Peel's ministry three years before.

Irish municipal reform did not share the happy fate of its companions. The government was prepared to limit elected councils to the eleven largest towns and allow a majority of electors in others to petition the Viceroy for incorporation, but it insisted on a £5 householder franchise. In the Lords, Lyndhurst had no difficulty in raising this to £10. He was warmly supported by the Duke, who repeated that he would have preferred simply to abolish the old corporations but was prepared to accept a new system of municipal government so long as it would give security to the Protestant ascendency. He hastened to add that he was no great admirer of the new corporations in England. The increase in law and order that apparently characterized them had been produced only by the police at great expense. Social tranquillity, which had formerly made England one of the most desirable places to live, was fast disappearing in the corporate towns, where there was 'nothing but political squabbling and agitation from one year's end to another ... and he sadly feared that before long the increase of political agitation would put in hazard the capital which was in existence in this country.'⁴⁶ When the bill returned to the Commons the ministry agreed to an £8 franchise but this compromise was unacceptable to the Lords and the measure had to be abandoned once more.

In the midst of these political labours the Queen's coronation at the end of June provided some relief. But when it was decided that the occasion would be less grand than the standard set by George IV, those Tories who had little reason to feel attachment to the Queen or her advisers but who exhibited a lively regard for the institution of monarchy professed themselves scandalized that there would be no banquet after the ceremony. They were probably also not delighted that there would be instead a long procession for the benefits of the inhabitants of the capital and the crowds which came by the new railways. Wellington had no patience with such grumbling and sensibly pointed out that as the Palace of Westminster had been in ruins for four years there was no suitable place to hold a banquet.⁴⁷

The Duke was one of the centres of attraction at the coronation. There was great applause when he paid homage to the Queen and again when he left the Abbey. That night there was a great ball at Apsley House and Wellington was still apparently untired when Lady Salisbury left at 2 a.m. To spare the feelings of his old adversary Marshal Soult, who attended the coronation as the French representative, he instructed Gurwood to hold back publication of the volume of his despatches on the battle of Toulouse in 1814, at which he had beaten Soult. When he gave a dinner at Apsley House for the foreign representative he also did his best to remove from his table the trophies marking his victories over the French. This magnanimity was not shared in other quarters. Croker insisted on publishing an article on the battle of Toulouse, which Wellington pronounced inaccurate in parts, in the *Quarterly Review* on the very day of Soult's arrival. 'I am a very clever man,' the Duke complained of his failure to dissuade Croker from publication, 'a very clever man indeed, except when any gentleman happens to differ in opinion with me on any point – and then I am not a clever man at all.'⁴⁸

Wellington would not have missed the endless round of dinners, balls and receptions at which he was such a great ornament for anything, but they must have been a great strain for him. In May he suffered one of his periodic bouts of deafness that lasted for several weeks. 'I suffer Torments in the House of Lords, at Meetings etc. etc.,' he wrote, 'where I am obliged to talk after listening to [and] endeavouring to hear and understand what others say.'[49] He was so plagued with rheumatism that he declared that he would prefer to be rid of it than he would 'all the libels of all the Jacobins, Bonapartists, Radicals, Reformers, and Whigs in all Her Majesty's dominions, including her ancient kingdom of France, and her colonies in N. America.'[50] Charles Greville, saddened by the great strides that old age seemed suddenly to have made on him, elegiacally if prematurely wrote that it was a fine sight to behold 'the noble manner in which he is playing out the last act of his glorious life.'[51] But not everyone was saddened by this decline. The Tory Lords continued to be restive at his forbearance towards the ministry, though there was no one else they could look to as leader. They were particularly annoyed when, after being rounded up by the whips, the Duke changed his mind about supporting one of Brougham's attacks on his former colleagues and swept out to dinner with Lord Aberdeen after advising them not to divide the House. Brougham gave lapidary expression to the rage of the Ultras: 'Westminster Abbey is yawning for him.'[52]

The sounds of the coronation revelry had scarcely died on the air before news arrived that Durham had taken full advantage of his great powers to banish eight rebels to Bermuda without trial and issued an ordinance that they and fifteen others who had fled to the United States would suffer the death penalty if they returned. Although legal opinion differed on the correctness of Durham's acts, Conservatives and Radicals were at one in denouncing his high-handed conduct. In vain did Melbourne try to enlist the support of Wellington by pointing out that he had not objected to Durham or his commission a few months ago. The Duke sternly replied that he had not considered it his duty to excite opposition to a measure the government felt appropriate; the cabinet presumably knew who was best qualified to deal with the situation; and it was the ministry that had failed to supplement the general legislation with specific guidance. He also denied Melbourne's ridiculous charge that he had deliberately set a trap for the government by agreeing to Durham's appointment and then later criticizing his actions. But despite provocation from the Prime Minister, Wellington separated himself from his own eager followers by announcing that he had no wish to push the government beyond setting illegalities to right and preventing their recurrence.[53]

When Durham was required to proclaim the disallowance of his ordinance and announce that those who had acted under it would be indemnified, he issued a long justification of his administration; before the rebuke for this arrived he had resigned. The Duke thought this must have been the first time that a colonial governor had abused the administration by which he was employed and excited discontent and insurrection against the sovereign authority. He prophesised that the end was nigh for British possessions in North America: 'An Angel from Heaven would not be permitted to settle the Colonial Question, either by the people of England or by those in the Colonies, after Lord Durham's Proclamation.'[54]

At the beginning of 1839 Col. Gurwood reported from Stratfield Saye that Wellington was in better health than he had been for some time. He was riding every day for an hour, walking for another, rubbing himself with Indian gloves for rheumatism for three separate half hours, 'and thus takes what he calls, his five doses.' He was rather feeble in his gait, though Gurwood thought no more so than any man nearly seventy. But although his mind and spirits were good, his view of public affairs, particularly the recent agitation for the repeal of the corn laws, was as gloomy as ever: '"Oh! poor country!" is often his exclamation, when talking of our foreign and domestic politics.'[55] A month later, on 22 February, he suffered what was almost certainly a stroke. Not many knew about it. Lord Mahon who did thought the Duke in the House of Lords ten days later looked 'very pale and worn, his voice loud at some intervals but very low and indistinct at others, and the loudness or emphasis not according to the points he wished to urge.'[56] Throughout the rest of the session there was concern that he was failing.

When Parliament assembled some days before the Duke's stroke it was expected that the leading issues would be Canada and the corn laws. But although Durham had produced his famous report early in the year, domestic preoccupations and protests from Upper Canada against union with Lower Canada meant that it was postponed until the following session. The corn laws were not so easily dispatched. Urban agitation had increased as the price had almost doubled from 35s. to 73s. between 1835 and 1839, a hardship compounded by industrial collapse since 1837. Numerous groups had been formed to work for the repeal of import duties on grain, but all were overshadowed by the Anti-Corn Law League founded in Manchester in 1839. Most of its evangelistic activity lay in the future in the spring of that year, but feelings had reached such a pitch that they were of vital concern to Parliament. The House of Commons defeated a Radical motion for abolition. During a more general debate in the Lords, Wellington expressed his clear and conventional convictions on the subject. The strength and prosperity of the country must be founded on agriculture; any reduction in the duty might make it unprofitable, 'thereby ruining a vast class of industrious and, at present, happy people ... it was impossible to say what might be the extent of the alteration, nay of the revolution of property which would follow.' He reminded the House that a quarter of a century of protection had witnessed not only the repayment of a huge war debt but also the production of such a supply of wheat that even 'the very lowest orders of the people subsisted mostly upon it, which was not, he believed, the practice in any other country.'[57]

The social composition of the House of Lords guaranteed that the discussion of this topic would be fairly amicable. The same could not be said of Irish affairs. Following the last rejection of the Corporations Bill, O'Connell had founded a new society, the Precursors or 'Cursers,' dedicated to municipal reform, the extension of the franchise and increased representation in the House of Commons for Ireland. This latest challenge was scarcely organized before Conservative feelings were inflamed by the unsolved murder in broad daylight of Lord Norbury, an inoffensive resident landlord, on New Year's Day. Conservatives also saw in the new Viceroy, appointed before Parliament assembled, further clear evidence of the government's truckling to O'Connell. Lord Fortescue, whose son had been one of O'Connell's sponsors when he entered Parliament and one of the chief assailants of the House of Lords at the time of the Reform Bill, had himself in 1838 used the word 'war,' always inflammatory in an Irish context, in a speech opposing the claims of the Irish Church. The Duke was not reassured by Fortescue's statement in the Lords that he would maintain the law in Ireland, and demanded to know if he was going 'to administer the law as it stood, or did he mean to carry on a war for the alteration of the law?' Observing that the Lord Lieutenant would have great patronage in a Church which he had claimed was too large for the Protestant population, but which Wellington insisted was no more than adequate for its duties, he claimed that the House should have specific securities in this matter.[58] With these and similar wiggings, Fortescue departed secure in the knowledge that the watchful eye of the Conservative peers would be on his every step.

A couple of weeks later the Tory Lords carried a motion for a select committee to inquire into the state of Ireland. The ministry seriously considered resigning on this issue, which would keep its followers together and leave to the Conservatives the embarrassment of trying to do better in Ireland. Peel anxiously asked the Duke, who only shortly before had been warning against a minority Conservative government, why he had allowed the vote to take place. To Peel's surprise he replied that he had been led to believe by one of the Orangemen in the Commons that Peel agreed to it. The leaders had been outwitted. Wellington told Peel that the incident was typical in showing that their followers did not care a pin about their opinions and thought they knew what ought to be done better than the leaders. Yet these were the individuals on whom they would have to rely in forming a ministry: 'I cannot adequately express my disgust with such people.'[59] Peel was able to escape his embarrassment when the government appealed to the Commons by an amendment criticizing the ministry but declaring that the vote in the Lords was not one of censure. But with emotions so high over Ireland, when the Lords once more raised the franchise requirement in the Municipal Bill, the ministry again decided to drop it for the year.

The end for the government came when its majority in the Commons was reduced to five on a move to suspend the constitution of Jamaica after the legislature refused to act as a protest against British interference. Conservatives and Radicals combined on the morning of 7 May, and the ministers decided that they could continue no longer. In an emotional farewell Melbourne advised the Queen to send for the Duke. Wellington expressed his willingness to help but declined to form a government on account of his age and also because the Prime Minister should be in the Commons. When he recommended Peel, the Queen pressed him at least to agree to become Foreign Secretary. But the Duke insisted that the Prime Minister must be free to make his own appointments.

Peel's stiffness was a great contrast to Melbourne's urbanity, but he listened patiently as the Queen explained that the Duke must be in the cabinet, that she was not in favour of a dissolution and that she intended to continue her friendship with Melbourne. Within these limits the arrangements for the new ministry proceeded smoothly enough. Stanley and Graham agreed to join, Wellington took the Foreign Office and the principal posts were filled within a few days. The sticking point came when Peel raised the issue of changing some of the notoriously Whig Ladies of the Bedchamber as a sign of confidence. The Queen, encouraged by Melbourne who understood that she was being asked to give up all the ladies, blankly refused. Peel then returned with the Duke, who was more of a man of the world in such matters. But he had no more luck. The

Queen pointed out that the Ladies could not support the government in Parliament and insisted that she did not talk politics with them. Peel summoned his proposed ministers who agreed that they would not take office without some sign of royal approval, particularly as they would not have a majority in the Commons. The Whigs, not realizing until the last minute that only a partial change was required and then concluding that all or some of the principle was the same, stood gallantly by the beleaguered Queen and sloped back into office as her trusted servants.[60]

Political feeling over the Bedchamber Crisis was reinforced by its coincidence with another matter concerning the royal attendants. At the beginning of 1839 Lady Flora Hastings, a pious, unmarried High Tory Lady in Waiting to the Queen's mother, the Duchess of Kent, began to show signs of pregnancy. Suspicion pointed to Sir John Conroy, the Duchess's lover, with whom she had travelled from Scotland alone in a post-chaise. The Queen, who regarded Lady Flora as her mother's spy, believed the rumours. Melbourne was cynically amused. Lady Flora eventually agreed to a medical examination, which seemed to establish her innocence though the doctor had reservations. But by this time her brother, the Marquess of Hastings, was demanding to know what foul Whig had begun the slander. Hastings, the Duchess of Kent, Melbourne and the father of one of the Queen's Ladies in Waiting all appealed to the high authority of the Duke. His advice was the same to all: in the interests of the Queen and Lady Flora they should say nothing of the matter. When it reached the press in the weeks before the Bedchamber Crisis he counselled everyone to carry on as usual. But Lady Flora's condition continued to deteriorate. When she died in July the incompetence of the royal physician was disclosed at the autopsy which revealed a tumour on the liver. The monarchy was once more the target of popular abuse. But Wellington did not let his feelings about the Queen's refusal of the Conservatives affect his high regard for the institution. He was instrumental in removing the greatest problem by persuading Conroy to leave the country, thus paving the way for better relations between the Queen and her mother.

In the aftermath of the Bedchamber Crisis it was obvious to all but the extremists that until the political situation was changed by a general election or some sudden alteration of fortune, the Whigs could not resign but neither could they legislate without the support of the Conservatives, while the Conservatives could enjoy a share of power but not office until they acquired a majority in the Commons. This was perfectly acceptable to the Duke, who preferred controlling the Whigs from his strong position in the

6 Wellington and Peel at Windsor Castle in 1844 – at the time of the Bedchamber crisis five years before the Duke had observed of their difficulties with the Queen, 'I have no small talk, Peel has no manners,' but by 1844 both were in high favour with the Queen and Prince Albert (painting by Franz Xavier Winterhalter, Windsor Castle; reproduced by gracious permission of Her Majesty the Queen)

House of Lords to taking part in a government weak in the Commons; less so to Peel; and intolerable to those of their supporters who were clamouring for office and a chance to put their principles into practice.

A couple of weeks after the impasse over the Ladies, Melbourne acknowledged the conditions on which he was allowed to remain in office in an elliptical statement to the House of Lords that he did not intend to go further in matters of reform than his ministry was already committed. To the great annoyance of those peers who were looking to the imminent defeat of the Whigs, Wellington responded by saying that he had never seen any reason why the government should have resigned because the particular form of one piece of legislation had not found favour in Parliament. He recommended that the Prime Minister stick to his duty and trust to the good sense of the legislature and the country for support: 'And although certainly I have the misfortune of differing from him on many subjects, I think I may venture to tell him that he will not find Parliament fail him if he will honestly and sincerely perform his duty.'[61] There was the usual talk in the clubs of the Duke's decay after this pronouncement, and even his defenders thought he had gone too far; but Wellington told his secretary that he had considered it necessary to nail Melbourne down to his statement and to promise Conservative goodwill in order to protect the monarchy from danger.[62]

This did not mean, as some feared, giving the ministry uncritical support. As well as wrecking the Irish Municipal Bill, Wellington led the Lords in removing the extraordinary powers for the governor from the new Jamaica Bill, which also dropped the suspension of the legislature. He warmly supported the bishops in opposing features of the government's increased grant for education that might benefit Catholics and Dissenters, particularly the provision for a non-denominational teachers' training school which was eventually dropped. He did grudgingly endorse the new penny postage system, that great feature of Victorian civilization, but only because as a money bill the House of Lords could by convention only accept or reject it. From his own experience in the army, in which soldiers could send letters for a penny, he doubted that there would be the dramatic increase in correspondence necessary for the innovation to pay its way. He considered, rightly in the short run, that the cost of opening new post offices and the decrease in revenue would simply add to the budget deficits of the last few years.[63] Behind the figures he produced to support his argument lay the suspicion that some new form of land tax would be needed to get the country out of financial difficulties.

But the Duke's great concern in the summer of 1839 was not so much legislation, which he was in a good position to control, as Chartism. This demand for political democracy was produced by the collapse of trade since 1837, the high price of bread, and the extension of the new poor law to the industrial North, inflaming the endemic discontent with wages, hours of work and conditions in the factories and rapidly expanding towns. A petition purportedly bearing 1,200,000 signatures was ready for presentation to the House of Commons by the National Convention or 'People's Parliament' at the moment of the Bedchamber Crisis. Faced with the prospect of a Conservative government, the Convention withdrew to the safer ground of Birmingham. The petition was not introduced until 14 June and debated on 12 July, when it was summarily rejected. Disturbances broke out in several towns. Most of them were easily suppressed, but in Birmingham, where vast crowds had been assembling in the Bull Ring for the past two weeks, there was rioting and destruction on 15 July on a scale that had not been seen since the days of the Reform Bill.

The next day Wellington rose in the House of Lords full of wrath. All his fears of revolution and his pent-up anger against the incompetence and neglect of the Whig administration found expression in a short, fierce speech. On the basis of newspaper reports he declared with all his military authority that Birmingham had been treated worse than a town taken by storm:

> I have been in many towns taken by storm, but never have such outrages occurred in them as were committed in this town only last night ... property was taken out of many houses and burnt in the public streets, before the faces of the owners, notwithstanding the presence of the police and troops with ample means of putting an end to these disgraceful disorders.

The problem was lack of authority, 'a deficiency on the part of the magistrates to keep the peace.' He demanded to know who was responsible for such magistrates and charged that no municipal council should have been established without a full investigation of the town and the specific consent of Parliament. The ministry had not only granted a council under the general terms of the Municipal Corporations Act but had also permitted the Home Secretary, Lord John Russell, to appoint magistrates on the recommendation of this council, rather than having them appointed by the Lord Chancellor without local consultation. These magistrates had sided with the rioters and refused to interfere in the outrages. 'It would have been impossible formerly, that these things could have gone on in this great country, once so peaceable and happy,' he pronounced; 'but the peace, the honour, and the best interests of the country have been sacrificed by these disgraceful proceedings.'[64] The government now deplored the Duke's sad decline, while his friends rejoiced in the recovery of his powers.

Order was quickly restored by the magistrates, who were more inexperienced, unprepared and confused than in sympathy with the rioters; but two nights later Wellington returned to his basic charge by repeating that the ministry had practically allowed the election of magistrates.[65] When he was accused of exaggeration by Russell he repeated, on the authority of 'certain other transactions of which certainly he had more knowledge than most other noble Lords in that House,' that 'the peaceable inhabitants of the town of Birmingham were worse treated upon that occasion than the inhabitants of any town he had ever known or seen taken by assault.' This was the result of nine years of liberal rule in a country that had fought a war for twenty-two years, 'and had carried it on with circumstances of glory and success in all parts of the world, in order to avoid these miseries, as it was hoped, so that no such mischiefs might ever approach her shores.' Melbourne, sensing the Duke's unease at having to defend his original impulsive judgment, responded that if Birmingham was in the condition Wellington represented, 'then must war be a much milder affair than he had imagined,' and suavely inquired why the Duke had not alluded to the riots in Bristol following the rejection of the Reform Bill by the House of Lords in 1831.[66]

The Duke had certainly got the whole matter out of perspective, as he had not twenty years before at the time of Peterloo when he had had confidence in a better system of government directed by sounder individuals. But he was consistent in his fears for the safety of the political and social order, and he could scarcely believe that peers were drifting away to their rural pleasures in the midst of this national emergency. When even the faithful Aberdeen prepared to leave for his home in Scotland, he burst out: 'It may be best to let the Country go to the Devil its own way; or according to the guidance of the Gov't the Political Unions the Chartists. With all my Heart be it so! I will not drive any Body to stay!' But one member of the opposition at least could be counted on to remain: 'I have before now stood alone; and I can stand alone! And Please God! as long as I have strength and voice they shall hear of the Mischief which they have done and are doing!' Aberdeen's plea that he was leaving only because he had business to attend to in Edinburgh and that he had been in the House every day but one since the beginning of the session was not much solace to the defender of rectitude in his present mood.[67]

The outburst of Chartism vindicated all Wellington's predictions about what would follow the Reform Bill. 'Gentlemen would have an alteration of their Constitution & Govt,' he observed with dark satisfaction, depriving property of 'its fair Share & that proportion of political Power which was necessary in order to keep the Machine of Gov't. its balance in Motion.' They forgot that 'all Gov't. even that of Self is restraint, and that it is not safe to entrust the Powers of Restraint solely to the hands of those who ought to be restrained.' Nothing but a bounteous Providence could now restore peace, happiness and tranquillity and he could only hope that this would be achieved without the usual course of plunder, murder and civil war.[68] When a deputation from Manchester came to see him, he earnestly advised preventing the destruction of the town and its industry by getting rid of the corporation and even the borough, and reverting to the manorial system 'in which Manchester was opulent, respectable and in the enjoyment of Social Happiness and tranquillity ... and of the Reputation and credit of the finest Mercantile and Manufacturing Town and the greatest Encouragers of the Arts in the civilized World.'[69]

Far from wanting to reverse the Municipal Corporations Act, the ministry sought to strengthen it by providing better means of maintaining law and order. The army was increased by 7000 and new police bills for Birmingham and Manchester were introduced to provide for local needs and to relieve the London police from being rushed around from crisis centre to crisis centre at great expense and risk to the capital. At Peel's suggestion the police were put under commissioners responsible to the Home Office rather than the town councils. County magistrates were also empowered to establish rural police forces. These measures were supported by Conservatives in the Commons but the Duke at first wanted to reject the Manchester Bill on the grounds that it was less adequate than the existing legislation covering local police. He reluctantly agreed to support it after discussions with Lyndhurst and the Manchester delegation, but he resented criticism of his original view and continued to suspect the motives of those Conservatives in the Commons who only a few months before had been combining with the Radicals against the ministry. 'I have all my life found myself under the necessity of being quite right,' he grumbled to Lord Francis Egerton. 'But I find it more difficult at this moment than ever. All Mankind in the Country including the Gov't. are invariably acting upon some erroneous view of Popularity. The H. of Commons is rotten to the core.'[70]

At the end of the parliamentary session in late August he told the Prime

Minister that all he had wanted for years was 'to see the country governed; he wished he could see that.' Having followed the conduct of affairs in recent years, he advised Melbourne to 'turn over a new leaf, and really govern the country in future.' Generously he spelled out in detail how this could be accomplished by increasing the authority of the central administration, taking early notice of what was happening in the country, enforcing the law against those engaged in illegal proceedings and combinations and choosing better magistrates. He also warned that the military establishment should be further increased and the ministry should ensure that those who were tried, convicted and sentenced were actually punished.[71] Only a few days before some individuals at Warwick had been pardoned. Wellington told Lord Londonderry in despair: 'Punishment for offence the old Practice of the British Gov't. is now discontinued.'[72]

Shortly after Parliament rose, the Duke decided to make a personal investigation of Chartism by attending a meeting in London. Far from being alarmed at what transpired, he considered it wonderful that he was not thrown out of the window as a spy. 'I was alone there, the only one of my Caste!' he told Lord Francis Egerton. Despite the hard things that he had said about the Chartists lately, their treatment of him showed that they were at least 'better people than their fellows in the U. States who threw a Stranger over the bannister of the Stairs and broke his Ribs.'[73] What the Chartists made of this surprising appearance of their unmistakable arch-enemy is hard to say; evidently they were more amused than alarmed. But at least one person seems to have taken Wellington's attendance for genuine conversion, and the following spring wrote to solicit his support for the cause. He was promptly assured that there could be

> nothing in common between the Duke and Chartists or those who combine to commit outrage and plunder against person and property; and to overturn the Gov't. and to destroy its force and Happy constitution in Church and State; and to usurp the Gov't. with their own Hands.
>
> There is no part of the conduct of the Administration of which the Duke disapproves more than he does that in relation to the Chartists.
>
> But His disapprobation of the conduct of the Administration does not bring them nearer to the Chartists.[74]

Wellington's authentic view was expressed on the last outbreak of the movement in 1839, when 3000 miners attacked Newport in South Wales on the morning of 4 November to free one of their companions and give the signal for a general uprising. The assault was beaten off by a handful of soldiers, but all the Tory suspicions were aroused by the revelation that one of the principal leaders was a magistrate appointed by the Home Secretary, though later struck off the list for seditious language. 'Oh! if I were twenty years younger!' the Duke exclaimed, throwing up his hands with feeling.[75]

CHAPTER EIGHT

INTIMATIONS OF MORTALITY

T HE ULTRAS were delighted at their champion's excoriation of the Whigs in the last part of the 1839 parliamentary session. At the end of August the greatest Tory feast since his installation as Chancellor of Oxford was held to honour him as Lord Warden of the Cinque Ports. About 3000 people attended. Lord Brougham, rejected by the Whigs and trying to ingratiate himself with the Tories as well as the Radicals, managed to insinuate himself into the proceedings and improved the occasion with one of his celebrated orations. Charles Greville, reading it in the *Times* to which Brougham had characteristically sent a copy in advance, thought it 'tawdry . . . stuffed with claptraps and commonplaces,' but the Duke pronounced it one of his best speeches.[1]

Despite the Chartist threat and the incompetence if not complicity of the ministry, Wellington rejoiced in the esteem of those whose opinion he regarded most highly. But within a few weeks he was plunged once more into the depths of personal grief. Lady Salisbury had been in failing health for a year and an invalid for six months (apparently, though this was not understood at the time, suffering from diabetes). Her death on 15 October was nevertheless a great blow for the Duke. Another light of his life had gone out; and he was physically and emotionally less able to bear it than the greater loss of Mrs Arbuthnot five years earlier.

When the news reached him at Walmer Castle he concealed his feelings as best he could. He put on mourning and sealed his letters with black wax. But, as he had in the case of Mrs Arbuthnot though this time with less need, he avoided grounds for gossip by carrying on as usual, going as arranged to review Lord Cardigan's regiment at Canterbury. He was still in mourning a month later when he collapsed of a stroke at Walmer. Lord Mahon rushed to the castle on hearing the news and found Wellington on his camp bed, 'apparently insensible; his face like monumental marble in colour and in fixedness, his eyes closed, his jaw dropped, and his breath loud and gasping.' The local doctor attributed the attack to a long cold ride in the rain after almost starving himself for two days and not eating much for a couple of months. Fortunately he decided not to take blood. At first it seemed that the Duke might lose the use of his left side, but gradually it returned along with his sight and speech. As he recovered his faculties he recalled that he had been unable to hold a newspaper earlier that afternoon and had tried to conquer his affliction by exercise; while out riding he had felt a cramp in his side.[2]

In London the cabinet discussed the ceremonies to be held in the event of his death. But the discussion was premature. Within a couple of days he was out of bed and back at his correspondence, writing seven or eight letters the first day. Just four days after the seizure he attended a Privy Council meeting at Buckingham Palace where the Queen particularly looked for him. Charles Greville, the Clerk, thought him 'very old, very feeble, and decrepit ... but he was chearful as usual, and evidently tried to make the best of it.'[3]

Within a couple of weeks he was bravely but unconvincingly insisting to Peel that he was 'as well at this moment, as strong, and as well able to bear fatigue, as I was twenty years ago. I must continue for some time longer to be careful about catching cold. But I shall be out hunting yet before Parliament meets.' All too soon for Peel's comfort, he was exhibiting undiminished concern for the political state of the country and warning of the dangers of a premature Conservative ministry. He wished he were able to take the labouring oar from Peel, but alas he could not. With great patience Peel explained to his invalid colleague the danger of refusing to take office once the party had a majority in the House of Commons. But Wellington remained unconvinced: 'If I had to decide upon this question, as upon one in war, I should avoid, if possible, to take any course which should force upon you the occasion to decide to undertake the Government for some time longer.'[4]

Whatever the Duke struggled to believe, the stroke had taken a great deal out of him. It was the second within a year, and not the last. The illnesses of 1839 and 1840 marked the onset of old age as clearly as those of 1822 and 1823 had marked the end of the robust health that had characterized his youth and early middle age. His physical decline had been commented on for the past couple of years, but suddenly it became more pronounced. In addition to deafness and rheumatism, he became more tired, excitable and irritable; more suspicious, secretive and unwilling to see people; more resentful and outspoken against the demands placed on him, though no more willing to give them up. His speeches were slower in delivery and less coherent in form; if they continued to read as well as before this was, as Charles Greville noted, because the Hansard reporters 'lopped off the redundancies and trimmed them according to their fashion.'[5] He became physically smaller, more emaciated and shrunken within his uniform on state occasions when those who saw him only infrequently noticed the change. And his correspondence mirrored the physical deterioration: the handwriting becoming smaller, the tone more abrupt, emphatic and abusive, the punctuation and use of capitals more erratic and the exclamations even more frequent than before.

But in the private world of his mind there was no change. To demonstrate his undiminished powers he was readier than ever to perform any duty, to attend any function and to give advice on any subject. The principles that had guided him for a lifetime were still applicable to the troubles of the 1840s; he saw as clearly as ever what was wrong with the country and what was required to put it right. He was certainly remarkably energetic for a man in his eighth decade and determined to keep going to the limits of his capacity. But his illnesses, his deafness, his tendency to fall asleep when seated for any length of time, his return to the Horse Guards in 1842 and the restoration of sound government in 1841, increasingly removed him from day-to-day involvement in policy and the business of the House of Lords. Thereafter his speeches, except on military matters, were generally confined to pronouncements on major issues. His authority among the Conservative peers was nevertheless as great as before and his services as essential to keep them in order. And as he withdrew from daily public controversy his stature increased. After fifteen years in the forefront of politics, declining powers were returning him to the position he had held when he first came back from France in 1818. But in this long last phase his standing was higher than earlier. He was the Nestor of his country, cheered, honoured and appealed to as the source of wisdom on every topic.

That there was still plenty of fire in the old man was amply revealed immediately after the Privy Council meeting that followed his stroke. The Queen had assembled her trusty and well-beloved advisers to announce her forthcoming marriage to her cousin, Prince Albert of Saxe-Coburg-Gotha. Not everyone was delighted. The Tories were suspicious of Prince Albert as a German, a reputed intellectual, probably a Radical and possibly even a secret Catholic. The Queen's close association with the Whigs and her refusal of a Conservative ministry earlier in the year did nothing to dispose them to smooth the path for the arrival of the betrothed of 'our Gracious,' as Wellington had taken to calling her. Melbourne prudently rejected the Queen's proposal to make Albert King Consort or even an English peer, on the grounds that either would be resented and provide too many opportunities to interfere in constitutional matters. But he saw no difficulty in granting precedence next to the Queen, the matter on which she was most insistent.

In this, however, the Prime Minister did not reckon on the legal precision of those true friends of monarchy who saw it as their duty to protect the institution even against the incumbent. A clear indication of what was to follow occurred when the assurance of Albert's Protestantism, a necessary condition for the marriage, was omitted from the declaration to the Privy Council and again from the Speech from the Throne in January. The Duke, with concerned punctiliousness, insisted on inserting an amendment in the latter. In the teeth of humiliating defeat, Melbourne conceded. In the Commons the opposition, with many government MPs absent, cut the Prince's annual allowance from £50,000 to £30,000. Wellington, as Gurwood told Lord Liverpool, did not care 'one fig' about the allowance, but he was greatly exercised about the precedence, 'which he says is contrary to all that has been done in this country.'[6]

Precedence was established by statute and the Tories affected to believe that changing it for Prince Albert would be unjust to the royal dukes and to any future Prince of Wales. Two of the Queen's uncles were reluctantly persuaded to yield, but Wellington and his friends were cheered by the adamant refusal of 'our beloved Ernest,' the King of Hanover. Taking their stand with this congenial companion once more, they forced the ministry to abandon the precedence section of Prince Albert's naturalization bill. The Queen was furious, most of all with Wellington whose professed devotion to duty and the monarchy and good sense had led her to expect better things. But the old soldier was unrepentant. 'I stand where I believe I ought to be always – in the breech!' he proudly told Lady Wilton. '... I told those who spoke to me, "The House of Lords must not commit an Injustice. It must not consent to deprive any Man of his Birthright. At all events I will not consent. If I stand alone, I will protest."'[7]

The Queen wanted to repay this churlishness by refusing to invite the Duke to the royal wedding on 10 February. But Melbourne, who had a more sophisticated understanding of political dispute and who was far from blameless in the Bedchamber matter, told her that the country would not stand for the exclusion of the national hero.[8] Not that Wellington found many of his friends in the Chapel Royal. Allowing for the vastly different surroundings, he was almost as isolated at this Whig feast as he had been at the Chartist meeting a year before.

The Queen managed to get most of her own way on the precedence issue simply by declaring Prince Albert's standing next to her everywhere except in the Privy Council and Parliament by royal prerogative after the marriage. And in spite of their clash of wills the Duke soon stood high in royal favour. This was partly because the Conservatives supported the Regency Bill in favour of Albert in the event of the Queen's death and the minority of an heir, but also because with the prospect of war with France looming in the summer of 1840 everyone wanted to be on good terms with the great commander. 'I was never so well received,' he wrote after a visit to Windsor in August. 'I sat next to the Queen at Dinner. She drank wine repeatedly with me; in short, if I was not a Milksop I should become her Bottle Companion.' Prince Albert and King Leopold visited him in his room and he even had some discussion with the Prime Minister.[9]

On a more mundane level, the government was saved from the necessity of introducing much risky legislation in 1840 by the House of Commons's long preoccupation with parliamentary privilege. The House of Lords meanwhile occupied its time in discussing the menace of Owenite socialism, particularly the settlement of Queenwood in Wellington's own county of Hampshire. The Duke expressed his gratitude to that kindred spirit, the Bishop of Exeter, for bringing this matter to the attention of the House, as even he had not realized that socialism had made such progress in rural areas. While he doubted that it was possible or expedient to prosecute all who belonged to such societies, he hoped that the ministry would take notice of their activities and ensure that the magistrates carried out their duties in a manner less partial to these dangerous individuals than at present seemed to be the case.[10] Wellington as Lord Lieutenant followed his own advice, instructing the justices of the peace near Queenwood to 'observe and take Cognizances of the Proceeding of such an institution; more particularly as this Association has commenced and Published that it has objects inconsistent with the Doctrines of the Christian Religion, with the Duties of Christians with Morality and with the very existence of Society.' They were to take immediate notice of any breach of the law and draw the attention of the 'Influential Classes' to 'the Danger and Mischief which will probably result from the establishment of this Institution among them, and to induce them to refrain from giving their Attendance upon its Meetings and to persuade their Servants and Dependents to follow their example.'[11]

He told the Lords in the second debate that he had been studying the Owenite publications and Bishop Phillpotts had not exaggerated the viciousness of the system. Owen's doctrines were spreading rapidly and it could not complacently be assumed that they would collapse of their own absurdity. 'Some step must be taken,' he warned:

> The people must be made to understand that neither the legislature nor the Government looked upon this institution in any other way than with disfavour – that they were determined to discountenance it – and that wherever, in the promulgation of its doctrines, there should be a breach of the law, that breach should be punished.

Not only did the ministry disregard this sterling advice, but Lord Lansdowne, the Lord President of the Council and Lord Lieutenant of Wiltshire on which Queenwood also bordered, dismissed the danger by observing that the settlement consisted of a mere thirty or forty people. As those who joined had to pay £20, socialism would be more effectively curbed by having poor people duped of this sum than by any action of the Attorney General.[12] And certainly for the few years of its existence the Utopian community did not prove the centre of discontent or disaffection.

Just a week after the last discussion of this godless heresy, the Duke was stricken once more. He had dined early – at two o'clock as had been his custom since his illness in November – and had ridden out to visit Lady Wilton and Lady Burghersh. He felt a chill in his hand and could not make out the numbers on the houses so that he rode by Lady Burghersh's several times without being able to recognize which one it was. She was concerned and as he left her footman told his groom to pay close attention to him. He sat peculiarly in the saddle and as he approached Apsley House the reins fell from his left hand, though he was able to pick them up with his right. His servants, seeing that he was unable to dismount, helped him off and sent for Dr Hume. Wellington staggered into his sitting room where Hume found him groaning near the chimney piece. He was immediately put to bed and three other doctors were summoned. By 1 a.m. he had had eighteen convulsions, suggesting that the stroke was accompanied by epilepsy, his arm was affected and he was unable to speak.

Once more it seemed that he might die, or at least never fully recover. The next day Lyndhurst told Charles Greville that the Duke should retire from public life: 'Above all things to be deprecated is, that he should ever become a dotard like Marlborough, or a driveller like Swift.' As no one could replace him or keep the Conservative peers in line in the same way, the consequence would probably be the break-up of the party; but

Lyndhurst darkly added: '*there are many who would be glad of an opportunity to leave it.*' In three days, however, Wellington was out of danger and his doctors were declaring that they had never seen such marvellous powers of recovery. All London sent to inquire about his condition save the Queen who, on her honeymoon and with the precedence issue not yet resolved, took not the slightest notice until Greville reminded the Prime Minister that people would not endure her treating the Duke of Wellington with disrespect: 'Everybody knows her Father was the greatest rascal that ever went unhung, and they will say that it is the bad blood coming out in her.'[13]

Within a month the Duke was back in the House of Lords going about his business much as usual, though people were shocked by his appearance. Another month later Lord Mahon recorded at Stratfield Saye that he was well enough but grown very old: 'He is now extremely thin – stoops a good deal on one side, his countenance careworn and pale, and the fire of his eagle eye much quenched.' He would fall asleep even in the morning, he could not read easily without glasses – that was hardly surprising – and he found riding difficult and perhaps even painful. But he could still walk firmly an astonishing four or five miles a day, his spirits were good and his mind seemed as clear as ever, though he was slower to grasp and express ideas. 'It is a victory of mind over matter,' concluded Mahon.[14]

Given his conscientious attention to business, it was fortunate for Wellington's recovery that the main business of the 1840 session did not arrive in the House of Lords for almost four months after his stroke. But whether the Tory peers would have been more or less obstructive to Peel's aims without his lead is a good question.

For the sixth year in succession Parliament took up Irish municipal reform which both the government and the Conservative leader in the Commons were anxious to settle by compromise. The latest bill provided for the suppression of all existing corporations and for councils elected by £10 ratepaying householders only in the ten largest towns; in others a majority of £8 ratepayers could apply to the Viceroy for incorporation. This encountered no difficulty in the Commons. In the Lords the Duke delivered a menacing speech, repeating his familiar objections to elected councils in Ireland, and his doubts, based on the experience of the recent poor law in that country, that the valuation of property would be honestly carried out, and giving notice of wrecking amendments in committee.[15] This surgery was again entrusted to Lyndhurst, who restored the vote of the freemen and raised the qualification for those towns to be incorporated by the Viceroy to £10. But even with these improvements it was by no means certain that Wellington, who had been much impressed by the counsel for the corporations at the bar, would not persist in attacking the measure or at least refuse to support it. Peel did not risk a direct confrontation, but on his behalf Sir James Graham appealed to Charles Arbuthnot. At first the Duke seemed impervious to his friend's reasoning, but as Arbuthnot patiently explained the view of the leaders in the Commons that the matter must be resolved once and for all, he saw Wellington's mind 'turning by degrees' to a recognition that his duty lay in doing what was required of him. So confident was Arbuthnot of this process that he told Lord Aberdeen not to talk to him, 'but leave it all now to the workings of his own mind.'[16] Arbuthnot's confidence was justified, though the Commons had to accept the Lords' amendments in order to enact a pale shadow of what had originally been proposed in 1835.

On Canada, a more recent issue, there seemed less prospect of convergence between the Duke and Peel. The leader in the Commons accepted the ministry's proposal to unite Upper and Lower Canada, but Wellington did not waver in his conviction that union would pave the way for separation. He would not, 'at the close of a life passed with honour, take upon himself the grave responsibility of inflicting a heavy and fatal blow on England, when he knows that he had the power to prevent it.' Arbuthnot, who was again engaged to persuade him, pointed out that union was supported by the Lieutenant Governor of Upper Canada, the former Governor General and by the inhabitants of both colonies. The Duke responded with dark suspicions that opinion in Upper Canada had been tampered with by Poulett Thomson, a senior member of the government who had been despatched as Governor General the previous autumn. When Arbuthnot tried to argue that no better solution than union had been devised, Wellington replied that he would unite Montreal to Upper Canada and rule the French population of Lower Canada by means of a governor and council. This authoritarian solution commended itself neither to Peel nor the Whigs. Arbuthnot urged Graham to get Peel to discuss the matter directly with the Duke,[17] but Peel was no more eager for controversy with his counterpart on this than on Ireland.

When the bill arrived in the House of Lords Wellington attacked it with great vehemence. He denied that union would provide a safe settlement of the issue, claiming that the temper underlying the rebellions of 1837–38 and encouragement from the United States had not been brought under control. He denounced the desire he had sensed for some time to get rid of the North American colonies and let them become republics, warning the peers that the resources and power of the colonies were such that Britain would suffer 'a loss indeed.' He charged the ministry with purchasing support for union by offering the local population responsible government, even though it was incompatible with British sovereignty, and gave notice that he would attempt considerable amendment in committee. But if after full and impartial consideration the government still accepted responsibility for this measure, 'in God's name let them do so, but for himself say "not content" to this bill.'[18]

The speech was heard in breathless silence. The peroration in particular produced a great effect when, 'with an energetic gesture he threw off all responsibility of the measure from himself, and left it "in the name of God" upon the Ministers. As he stood erect, his figure looked very thin – wasted and shrunken with in his clothes; but his countenance beamed with noble expression.'[19]

It is not clear what the Duke intended next. But a few days later, seeing that neither Peel nor Stanley would be responsible for the fall of the government which would certainly happen if the bill were rejected or mutilated, he summoned the Conservative peers to Apsley House to tell them that he intended to give way. 'His conduct was magnanimous,' Aberdeen told Arbuthnot, 'and in fact he made a great personal sacrifice for the party.' Aberdeen added that this was the most impressive pronouncement Wellington had ever delivered at such meetings:

> The effect of the address was like magick; and although we had many
> present who were obstinate, violent and wrong-headed, not a syllable
> was said in opposition to the Duke's suggestion. He treated the whole
> subject with the utmost dexterity and skill; and when he spoke of his
> own position, it was beautifully done, and the effect was irresistible.[20]

The Duke could not surrender his criticisms of the bill but he did advise the peers not to reject it if the ministry insisted. On this basis it was accepted on 13 July, with Wellington formally recording his objections in a twenty-seven-clause protest.

The strain of reconciling his conscience to the necessities of party unity may have contributed to some kind of seizure a couple of days later. Like the others, this began with a disorder of the stomach, at the same time – in the late afternoon – and exhibited the same symptoms, though in a less severe form. But on this occasion Wellington felt it coming on and was able to send for the doctors in advance. Within two days he was practically back to what was now normal, and after five days Lord Mahon met him coming out of the House of Lords in good spirits and physical condition.[21]

Despite the Duke's compliance with Peel's wishes on two important pieces of legislation and the state of his health, Peel showed no sign of gratitude. It grieved their followers to see relations between the two vital leaders of the party so cool, and it did nothing to increase the respect of the Ultras for Peel. But in the autumn, with no issues to divide them and with both alarmed by Palmerston's reckless diplomacy in the Near East which seemed to be driving the country to war with France at the same time that it was embroiled in China and Afghanistan and facing the possibility of war with the United States, Arbuthnot was pleased that he could act as the agent through which each expressed his high regard for the other. Peel assured Arbuthnot that 'nothing in private life gives me half so much satisfaction as communicating freely and unreservedly with the Duke of Wellington' and assured him that he would not commit himself without previous consultation. Wellington repeated his customary observation that he and Peel generally found themselves on the same ground without discussion. He solemnly affirmed that he had always found Peel ready to discuss things with him, though being in different Houses, 'constant communications upon every particular is impossible, and can only be recurred to when the business in both Houses requires communication, or is likely to clash.' Pleading deafness, he claimed that it would be useless for him to attend the business meetings of Peel and his associates; but he would always talk to Peel. All this was considerately transcribed from the Duke's handwriting by the anxious Arbuthnot.[22] It did not take any great insight for Peel to recognize that the Duke had no intention of compromising his independence beyond what was absolutely necessary. But if relations were not cordial they were, as 1840 ended, at least correct and based on mutual understanding and respect.

Towards the end of January 1841 Wellington unconvincingly told J.W. Croker that he had never felt better. 'You know,' he assured him,

I have never been well since that fellow poured liquid fire into my ear, and electricized not only the nerves of the ear, but all the adjacent parts, and the injury extended in all directions, sometimes to the head and then down to the stomach, then to the shoulders, and then back again to the head, and so on; but I outlived it, and have, in fact, worn it out, and am now, thank God, as well as ever I was, and in all respects. I eat as well, I sleep as well, I walk and ride as well, I hunt and shoot as well as I have done these twenty years.[23]

A week later, however, he was stricken once more in the House of Lords.

He had been out walking on a bitterly cold day, eaten his early dinner, gone out walking again with Lady Douro and then gone to the House of Lords in an open carriage. Brougham, who was treating the House to one of his orations directly opposite the Duke, noticed that his face was drawn and distorted. He staggered out of the chamber and walked the length of the gallery supported on either side; then he returned in Brougham's carriage to Apsley House where the doctors once more rallied around. Lord Mahon hurried there from the House of Commons and learned that he was suffering a strong convulsion. The alarm was as great as ever, but once more he was out of his bedroom within three days, '*pronounced himself as well as ever*' as Greville observed, and was busy working at his papers, though Lord Mahon noticed that he was weak and languid and had hardly any appetite.[24]

Even or perhaps because of his debility, he was determined not to falter in the high matters required of the Duke of Wellington. When the Rev. G. R. Gleig suggested reading for amusement, he replied that no one would allow him to read anything but their own letters:

> In the old world from the Pillars of Hercules to the Indies; and from thence to the North Pole, and thence in the new to Cape Horn; and the cape of Good Hope & to the Antipodes of England in the southern Hemisphere; there is not an Individual who wants any thing of any description; particularly money who does not apply to me for it. If a church or chapel, Glebe or school House or even Pagoda is to be built; I must patronize and subscribe for it: the same for Canals; Rail Roads; Harbours; and works for the promotion and protection for commerce.

> The Publick business of parliament – even the activity with which I enter into the transactions thereof are nothing in comparison with the perpetual private correspondence with which I am loaded.[25]

The area of his concern extended even to a maritime accident at Liverpool. He did in the course of his reply to the letter conveying the news observe that there was 'no occasion to call His attention to such melancholy Events as occurred within these last few days off Liverpool,' but this slight concession did not prevent him from responding and drawing a general moral from the incident: 'Till the people of the Country will again feel Respect for Law order and publick Authority, No regulation can be enforced. Such Misfortunes must happen.'[26]

In fact, as Greville noted later in the year, there was nothing in

7 The Duke of Wellington at 75, white-headed, stooped with arthritis, the Nestor of his country (pencil and watercolour portrait by Charles Robert Leslie, British Museum; reproduced by permission of the Trustees)

particular that Wellington was obliged to do; but he considered himself so busy, principally with his correspondence, that he could see no one, not even his closest relatives, except Lord Wilton who was permitted to bore him by the hour on the strength of the Duke's friendship with Lady Wilton. The replies he dictated to requests for interviews were so brutally uncivil that Algernon Greville was constantly employed in toning them down.[27]

Wellington eventually made a good recovery from the series of attacks he had suffered in the last couple of years, but he was definitely more irritable, liable to be confused and apt to get things out of perspective. It was well for him, and certainly for his historical reputation, that he was not called on to play any strenuous part in Parliament at this time. But even his confusion could not be depended upon by those who wanted to use it to their advantage. When the Bishop of Exeter tried to enlist him in a scheme against the Roman Catholic seminary in Montreal, he duly delivered a hot speech on the subject; but he then read the material, discovered that the ministry's line was perfectly in accord with that of previous ones including his own, and announced that he was withdrawing his support of the motion.[28] Great was the rejoicing among Phillpotts's enemies to see this proud prelate overthrown by his patron.

In the middle of May the government was decisively beaten in the Commons on a proposal to reduce the duties on foreign sugar, one of many tariff adjustments in the budget, by a combination of those favouring protection and those objecting to encouraging foreign, slave-grown sugar. The administration decided on a general election, but first to air in Parliament what it hoped would be the winning proposal of replacing the sliding scale of duties on corn by a fixed levy of eight shillings a quarter. Peel had no intention of being caught on this potentially destructive issue and refused to commit himself further than saying that the interests of both agriculture and industry must be considered. On a direct vote of confidence the ministry was defeated by a majority of one. But if Peel was discomfited by a corn debate on the eve of an election, the Duke had no hesitations. He robustly assured the peers once more that he would continue to defend the corn laws as long as he was capable of addressing them. The wise system of protecting grain had been devised, and amended during his administration, not simply to provide the aristocracy with high rents but to support agriculture and to preserve the country's independence for its subsistence.[29]

As the election results came in, it seemed clear that the Conservatives had a majority in the Commons. But following the customary practice, the Whig government met Parliament on 24 August. Amendments to the Reply expressing lack of confidence in the ministry were moved in both Houses. In the Lords, Wellington availed himself of the opportunity to deliver a wide-ranging denunciation of the Whigs' mismanagement of finance and the economy and to condemn their corn law proposal with a ringing endorsement of agricultural protection.[30] The amendment was easily carried by 168 to 96. In the Commons, where Peel was displaying a more flexible attitude towards the corn laws, the process took a little longer; but there too the amendment passed by 360 to 269. The Queen had no choice but to summon Sir Robert Peel, but at least this time there was no difficulty over the Ladies of the Bedchamber. The efforts of Prince Albert at the time of the debate on the sugar duties in May had produced an agreement that the leading ladies would retire with the ministers and Peel would signify to the incoming ladies the Queen's intention of appointing them.

In May, too, Peel had been turning his mind to the Duke's place in the ministry. He was the only person who could control the Tory Lords, but Peel was not alone in thinking that he was no longer equal to the duties of a major office. Under Arbuthnot's skillful management Wellington, spontaneously as far as he knew, came to the conclusion that he could be of greatest service as Leader of the House of Lords and a member of the cabinet without office. He pointed out with some satisfaction that this would enable the Prime Minister to tell disappointed claimants to office that even the Duke had stood aside in the interests of government, while leaving him 'leisure to assist with his advice all other offices which might require it.' Reporting this happy result, Arbuthnot told Peel that he should not reply to his letter as the post was brought in while he and Wellington were at dinner, and it was better that the Duke know nothing of their discussion.[31]

Totally unaware of this manipulation, Wellington a few days later told Peel of his decision at great length, insisting that all he wanted was to be 'as useful as possible to the Queen's service – to do anything, go anywhere, and hold any office, or no office, as may be thought most desirable or expedient for the Queen's service by you, and by those with whom you will think proper to consult upon the subject.' Given the general situation, it was best that he should be held in reserve. O'Connell would probably cause trouble in Ireland: 'If such be the case, you may rely upon it that I shall be required to settle the affair.' A general war with France had just been avoided; if that had occurred he would now be Commander in Chief of the allied armies in Germany, in each of which he was field marshal: 'God send that such an event may never occur! But considering the state of France, there can be no certainty.' In North America there would probably be fighting before the Maine-New Brunswick border was settled: 'In this case also you will require that I should give as much of my attention as possible to the operations of the war.' And in order for his good offices to be available to ensure amicable relations between the Palace and the ministry, he should not be tied down by 'the trammels of an office, however able I may be still to conduct the business with perfect ease to myself.' Peel had no difficulty in assuring the Duke in fulsome terms that he was exempt from the usual rules and should be kept free for any action. The essential point was that he should be in the Lords, as 'the organ, not of this department or of that, but of the whole Executive Government, and that Foreign Countries and this Country and Her Colonies should know and feel the Influence of your great authority in all their various Concerns.'[32]

On this happy note the workhorse of state was appointed Leader of the Lords and a member of the cabinet without department when the Whigs went at the end of August. His only hesitation about taking office, he told Lord Wellesley, to whom he was now reconciled, was based on the desire 'at my Age to make way for Younger Men, better qualified in every way excepting perhaps in practical experience. However in this respect as in every thing else; I will do what is best in the publick Service.'[33] Not everyone exhibited this same sense of selfless sacrifice and Wellington told Lady Wilton in some astonishment that he did not think it possible that 'Men could think so exclusively of themselves and their Individual objects':

> Everybody who has ever been employed heretofore thinks that he
> ought again to be called into the Highest and most active
> employment, however old he may have become. Then some are
> looking forward to personal objects of aggrandizement, which cannot
> be granted without injustice to and the supercession of others, and
> exciting Complaints on the parts of these and the claims of Many.[34]

The Duke himself received a flood of applications from those who wanted him to promote their interests with the Prime Minister. He told Lady Burghersh that he had received fifty such letters in one day and scarcely had time for meals and repose for writing to decline his assistance. 'That which people will not understand is that the whole Labour and Business and ceremony and every thing else of the World; cannot be thrown upon one Man; and that an old one!!' he complained. 'I'll do what I can. But I really think that people now and then should apply in the proper quarters; and not come to me.'³⁵

How he was going to add cabinet meetings and increased duties in the House of Lords to his present burdens was a good question. Col. Gurwood told Lord Liverpool after a few weeks of office that by the time Wellington got to the House of Lords in the late afternoon he had already been at work for ten hours: 'he gets up at 6 o'clock, and although he has no particular official duty to transact, he is writing letters and papers all the morning. This labour is beyond his strength, and consequently when you see him in the House of Lords, he is knocked up.'³⁶ A few months later Lord Fitzgerald, the President of the Board of Control who was as close as any peer to Peel, was expressing the gravest apprehensions about the Duke as Leader in the Lords. He feared that his temper, his deafness and his reliance on his own unaided judgment might lead to some serious embarrassment for the government, especially as he was always surrounded by people who praised everything he said. Fitzgerald thought it would have been much better if he had retired from active politics. But the object of this concern was confident that he could manage well enough with the assistance of another secretary. Certainly he was not impressed by the capacities of his colleagues. 'I never saw our Nervous people so nervous and irritable as yesterday,' he told Lady Wilton a few weeks after they had entered the promised land: 'I have received not less than a dozen Boxes and Notes from Sir Robert since the Cabinet of yesterday, and have not read less than the contents of twenty since I saw you on Wednesday night. I only hope that my eyes will hold out.'³⁷

There was not much opportunity to judge Wellington's performance in Parliament in the brief session following the defeat of the Whigs as important business was postponed to 1842. But despite the fears of some ministers, he performed surprisingly well as Leader, restricting himself far more than he had in opposition to matters of his own particular concern and interest and leaving the rest to other members of the government in the House. His prestige and the ministry's overwhelming majority in the Lords ensured that most legislation would have an easy passage. The main problem was to convince Conservative peers that their services were still required now that their party was in office. Soon he was complaining, as he had before when in office, of the difficulty of getting people to stand up and move and second the Address in Reply: 'I cannot solicit each man to perform those duties, each as a personal favour to myself: nor can I go lecturing from one to another upon his duties as a Lord of Parlt.' If all else failed, he told Lord Aberdeen, he would do it himself to excite in the peers 'a sense of publick duty, and of shame for forcing upon a Man of my Age and Station the necessity of moving the Address; as I certainly will not conceal the Reasons for which I take a course so unusual.'[38]

In cabinet the Duke was treated with great deference and attention by his colleagues who were eager for his support. He always sat in the same place and each minister who had something to say would sit next to him so that he could hear the main part of what was being discussed. The ministers were willing to modify their proposals to ensure endorsement, but even this did not protect them from his asperity when he disagreed or misunderstood what they were about.[39] Peel usually did not discuss the details of legislation and parliamentary business with him, preferring to communicate what he wanted through Arbuthnot to running the gauntlet of prejudice, deafness, failing memory and irritability.

The great topic of 1842 was the new ministry's budget. Having derived so much credit from criticism of the financial irresponsibility of the Whigs which had produced large deficits every year since 1837, the Conservatives were under a heavy obligation to demonstrate that they could do better. In place of the fixed duty on corn proposed by his predecessors, Peel recommended that the sliding scale be amended to a duty of 20s. a quarter when the price stood between 50s. and 51s., falling to the nominal duty of 1s. at 73s. a quarter, but with pauses between 52s. and 55s. and 66s. and 69s. to discourage holding imports in bonded warehouses in order to drive down the duty. Customs duties were also drastically reduced on a wide variety of raw materials and manufactured goods. To cover the temporary loss of government revenue until it was increased by this stimulus to trade and also to pay off the accumulated deficits, Peel introduced a tax of 7d. in the pound, or 3 per cent, on incomes over £150.

These provisions looked suspiciously like the Whig programme of the previous year, and the second Duke of Buckingham (who had succeeded his father in 1839), the president of the Society for Protection of Agriculture, immediately resigned the Privy Seal in protest against what he saw as an attack on the landed interest. But the 1842 budget could be defended as a continuation of the trade and financial policies of the Tory governments of the 1820s. Despite the grumbling of the agriculturalists and his own staunch defence of the corn laws in the state of perfection they had reached under his administration in 1828, no one professed more delight than Wellington at these measures for 'getting the Country upon its Legs.' This was what he had been looking to for years:

If our foolish Predecessors had not destroyed the Revenue as well as
everything else; or having destroyed it, had adopted [an income tax]
and augmented their Army five Years ago; we should now find
ourselves in a very different Condition.... But very possibly they
might still have been governing the Country and not we![40]

The distance that the Duke had travelled on the corn question during a
few months of office may be seen in the memorandum he drew up to
organize his thoughts while the cabinet was deliberating on the issue. He
conceded that complaints against tariffs on food had been increasing lately
and that even some friends of protection wanted a more gradual sliding
scale. Agriculture was becoming so efficient in Scotland that it no longer
required protection, while in Ireland the change to flax, cattle and sheep
farming would soon produce a demand for cheap corn. MPs for
manufacturing districts were bound to reflect the distress of their areas and
no one could read the reports of the suffering of the hand loom weavers
without feeling anxious to do something for their relief. It was necessary
to increase British trade, but rather than generally freer trade to
encourage other countries to admit British goods in return for their own
exports, Wellington proposed bilateral treaties modifying the corn laws in
return for trade concessions.[41]

This was not exactly the policy adopted by the cabinet, but it is clear
that the Duke was no longer the stern and unbending defender of the 1828
system. When he had to defend the government's legislation in the House
of Lords he used some of the arguments in his memorandum, but the main
force of his case was that the new sliding scale would give more secure
protection and encouragement to agriculture. A rapidly growing
population made it impossible for the country to produce all the food it
needed, but he must have reassured many landlords when he warned
against becoming dependent for grain on 'the state of tranquility of the
people residing upon two or three of the large streams running to the
Baltic' and on other countries always having a surplus. The landed interest
must also have felt confident that the government would stop with this
alteration when he declared: 'If the Corn-laws were repealed tomorrow,
not a yard more of cloth, or a pound more of iron, would be sold in any
part of Europe or the world, over which this country does not exercise
control.'[42]

Even as these important commercial and financial provisions were making
their way through Parliament, Wellington was turning his mind to another

responsibility. At the beginning of April it was learned that Lord Hill would not be able to continue much longer as Commander in Chief. The Prime Minister immediately asked Arbuthnot to find out if the Duke would return to the post he had left with such regret in 1828. Arbuthnot's reply was swift and predictable. Wellington not only wanted the appointment but considered himself the only fit person for it, though he thought it must mean resigning the cabinet. Peel, however, was not about to lose this valuable icon. He instructed Arbuthnot to tell the Duke that his departure would greatly distress him as his presence in the cabinet was of the greatest importance to the government. Wellington recognized the justice of this, but considered that he should at least be allowed to give up the Leadership of the House of Lords, which he now claimed was wearing him to death. But as no one else could keep the Conservative peers in line, even this relief was denied him.[43]

When Hill did resign in August, Peel told the Duke that his colleagues in the cabinet had received the news of his intended appointment 'with the utmost satisfaction, and have desired me to express their decided and unanimous wish that you should remain a member of the Cabinet and continue to conduct the Business of the Government in the House of Lords.' Wellington replied that he had only wanted to resign from the cabinet in order to remove any suspicion of bias in army patronage and because deafness made his attendance at its meetings a waster of time. 'I am and always have been the object of the Malevolence of Party,' he warned; 'and you may rely upon it that you will feel the Inconvenience of not taking the course which I recommend.' But having stated his objections, he loyally professed his willingness to do whatever the Queen commanded, even if it should eventually lead to his resignation. In suitably emollient phrases Peel assured him that the Queen concurred entirely in the combination of the command of the army with his present position in the cabinet and in the Lords.[44]

There was one other matter to be settled before Hill took his leave. After fourteen years' good and faithful service, it was proposed that he be promoted to field marshal. The Duke was naturally consulted; but he would not hear of a breach of the sacred principle of seniority. Apart from members of the royal family there was only one exception to the rule of promotion by seniority above the rank of colonel. After the battle of Vitoria, Wellington had sent the Prince Regent the baton of Marechal Jourdain. In return the Prince sent him a letter and 'the Baton of an English Field Marshall: and I was promoted to a Field Marshall in the Army; over the Heads of half the *Lt. Generals*; and of all the *Generals* in the

Service.' But Vitoria had been the great event of the day and was no precedent for the present case. Lord Hill was the nineteenth general on the list and it could be relied upon that all those ahead of him would also claim promotion, 'as there is No Man so old in uniform who does not think himself entitled to an Honorary Distinction or advantage to which the Ordinary Rules of promotion in the Profession would give Him a Claim.'[45] No one dared contradict this solemn counsel and Hill was instead advanced a step in the peerage to viscount. By the end of the year he was dead and the title passed to his nephew Rowland Hill, the deviser of the penny postage.

CHAPTER NINE

THE DEFENCE OF THE REALM

B ACK AT the Horse Guards once more, the Duke found himself in familiar surroundings. There was his old aide, Lord Fitzroy Somerset, beavering away as Military Secretary where Wellington had left him fourteen years before. The soldiers, particularly those autocratic, high-strung brothers-in-law, Lord Lucan and Lord Cardigan, may have been as troublesome and as difficult to manage as the Tory Lords; but in the army, in refreshing contrast to the House of Lords, even cavalry officers had, in the last analysis, however grudgingly and perfunctorily, to abide by the decisions and orders of their chief.

Unless there was pressing business the Duke customarily arrived at his office about one o'clock and stayed until five if the House of Lords was sitting, six or seven if it was not. He would first see all the heads of departments individually with their reports and other matters. For each case he received a precis with the documents attached and an indication of how similar cases had been dealt with before. He drafted his decision in the half-page margin, usually adhering strictly to precedent. He also worked on army business at Apsley House, in the House of Lords and wherever else he happened to be. If he often dozed at the Horse Guards, he had no difficulty in rousing himself to assert his unquestionable authority whenever it was required.

Lord Hill, who was three years younger than Wellington, had worn himself out by patient and tactful administration. The Duke had been consulted on all major issues, and their conclusions been couched in suitably tactful terms. Now that he was in complete command Wellington did not deny himself the efficient luxury of irritability and sharp replies to keep at bay the endless demands that encroached on his valuable time. But in military as in civilian matters, he could rarely resist the opportunity of dealing personally with impertinence and anything that brought into question his great public position. When a woman at Dover was so bold as to ask him to investigate the conduct of an officer in the local garrison who had seduced her daughter, now pregnant, he wrote her a stiff reminder of their respective duties:

> The Duke of Wellington presents his compliments to Mrs. Landall.
> He is the Commander in Chief of the Army. His daily experience
> shews him that there is nothing so easy as to call for the interference
> in every social Case in which the Conduct of an Officer of the Army
> is disapproved of! But the Commander in Chief has no jurisdiction
> excepting in cases referred to in the Mutiny Act. There is not in that
> one word about the Chastity or good conduct of Young Ladies. These
> are under the guardianship and protection of their Parents; and
> particularly of their Mother.
>
> If an Officer of the Army be guilty of any violation of the Law of
> good manners or if he should do any Injury to any Young Lady; or
> through her to Her Relations, he is equally with all Her Majesty's
> Subjects accessible to the Law; and Mrs. Landall would do well to
> proceed in the Regular course against Captain MacDonald of the 89th.
> Reg't. and to lose no time if he is going away. It is more easy to
> complain to the Duke of Wellington! But he positively and distinctly
> declines to interfere in any case; until it is brought clearly under His
> jurisdiction as established by the Mutiny Act![1]

Despite the volume of his correspondence, the number who felt the lash of his pen or tongue was small. For those who saw him only at a distance his reappointment as Commander in Chief was simply the latest step towards immortality. He was one of the last prominent survivors of the great struggle against France that with the passage of time and the influence of romanticism was taking on mythic proportions. People marvelled that a man in his seventies who was visibly feebler than just a few years before should be so indispensable that he was taking on new responsibilities. But they were reassured that in the twilight of his life the great soldier was at the head of his profession. This was not just a fitting honour; as long as he was at the Horse Guards the country would surely be safe from danger. His judgment was respected as oracular and his characteristics, as far as they were known, were hailed as a model for dedicated and patriotic conduct.

As it seemed that he did not have much time left, people gathered wherever he went for one last look at the legendary hero. When he came in towards the end of a choral concert in June 1842, the singing stopped, 'the whole audience rose, and a burst of acclamation and waving of handkerchiefs saluted the great old man, who is now the Idol of the people.' It was a grand and affecting gesture, Greville wrote, and moved everyone but the Duke himself.[2] A year later, walking home with him, Lord Francis Egerton noted the usual signs of recognition and reverence: 'Hats were taken off; passers made excuse for stopping to gaze. Young surgeons on the steps of St. George's Hospital forgot their lecture and their patients, and even the butcher's boy pulled up his cart as he stopped at the gate of Apsley House.'[3]

The Queen, her annoyance over Prince Albert's precedence long forgotten, not only gloried in the attendance of her famous subject but favoured him with the dubious honour of two visits to his residences. In the autumn of 1842 she borrowed Walmer Castle for a holiday by the sea with her family as there was scarlet fever at Brighton. From the Ship Hotel, to which he had been displaced, Wellington grumbled that the castle had to be 'pulled to Pieces' in preparation for the royal visit.[4] But worse was to follow. Two years later he told Lady Wilton: 'Alas! it is but too true: the Queen is coming to pay me a visit at Stratfield Saye. I did everything I could to avoid the Subject: never mentioned the word Stratfield Saye, and kept out of Her Way.' Not to be put off by the Duke's modest protestations that the house, 'however comfortable as Gentleman's Residence,' was 'small and inconvenient as the Residence of H. M.'s Court,' the Queen simply smiled graciously and gave no hint of changing her mind. Extensive preparations and alterations had to be made – 'Bells must be hung from H. M. Apartments into those for Her Attendants, Walls broken through &c.' – but when the visit occurred both the Queen and Wellington were much pleased. The Duke was particularly flattered that the Queen had shown the good taste of preferring his house to the Duke of Buckingham's at Stowe.[5]

As well as his return to the Horse Guards, 1842 also marked a stage in Wellington's personal pilgrimage with the death of the brother who had overshadowed the first half of his life. The Marquess Wellesley had not represented any threat to the Duke's identity for years and recently, on the initiative of Wellington's old love Lady Wellesley, they had been on close terms, with the Duke clearly in the dominant position. Although he had been ill for almost a year, Wellesley's death on 26 September was a great strain for Wellington, perhaps reminding him in his weakened condition that his own end could not be far off and recalling all that he owed to the overbearing Governor.

The funeral at Eton, the scene of Wellesley's earliest triumphs but hardly of his own, was too much for his famous reserve. When the ceremony was delayed for an hour he became very angry: 'He complained loudly of it and was evidently becoming much excited. He had previously shown much feeling, being pale and thoughtful and depressed.' When the party was finally marshalled, he burst out to the undertaker: 'Sir, I don't know how it is, but these things – are never done with punctuality in England. Had you informed *me* that the funeral would not take place till eleven I could have been doing *other* THINGS!'[6] He managed to control his feelings for the rest of the ceremony but he travelled back to London alone rather than with his three brothers; stamped around Apsley House chanting that he would give the Provost of Eton no help to a bishopric if he had any pretensions to one, to the annoyance of his brothers who nevertheless prudently remained silent; and finally departed for Walmer.[7]

The summer of 1842 was not the most peaceful time to be returning to the Horse Guards. The war in China was coming to an end but another was threatening in North America, and in India the new Governor General, Lord Ellenborough, seemed to most members of the government and the East India Company to be acting like a rogue elephant. Perhaps because his conduct was reminiscent of Wellesley's and his own forty years before, the Duke took a keen interest in Ellenborough's operations in Afghanistan and Scinde. He publicly defended his old colleague's actions and bitterly denounced the Court of Directors in the House of Lords when he was recalled two years later,[8] though in private he was more critical of Ellenborough's imprudence.

Of more immediate concern was the revival of Chartism and the related disturbances which reached their height when Wellington took up the command of the army. Chartism had never died out, despite the repression of 1839 and 1840, and it made rapid advances in the distress of the winter of 1841–42. A second petition, purporting to bear over three million signatures, was presented to the Commons at the beginning of May but was rejected as summarily as the 1839 one, with the House refusing those who presented it permission to plead at the bar. An attempt to reduce wages in the coal mines and cotton mills touched off a wave of desperate strikes in the North and parts of Scotland and Wales; plugs were pulled out of the steam boilers to stop the machinery; and there were riots and clashes with the police and troops as the strikers looked for food and tried to persuade others to join them. Parts of Staffordshire and the West Riding of Yorkshire were in a state close to insurrection and the Chartist leaders tried to mobilize support for a national strike to last until the demands of the Charter were granted.

All the Duke's fears for the constitutional order were aroused by this challenge. The power and responsibilty to deal with it called forth a burst of energy that would have done him credit at the height of his powers. The Home Secretary, Sir James Graham, was no doubt glad of the steadfast support of this seasoned colleague, but his feelings must have been more ambiguous as he received a never-ending stream of advice on every aspect of the situation. Wellington thought that the strikers would at first be able to keep going on the contributions of sympathizers, but as their numbers grew they would have to turn to other means, 'as after all Men must eat & drink. Then commences Plunder: of the Houses of Individuals of Shops: etc. etc. Next will come the Roosts Farm yards, Fields' until at last the mobs became revolutionary armies living off the land by violence and intimidation. It was some protection that the strikers so far did not have 'the Discipline Subordination and Order of Armies: nor the regularity and economy in the distribution of the Plunder, and of course the Resources of any district of Country will not last very long for their Subsistence.' But these skills would be acquired in time. An effective blow must be struck immediately so that 'all Ranks and Classes should see that it is against the Law that they are contending and that the Government is too strong for them not only by it's Executive Means. But by means of the Law.'

As for the instrument of restoring order, Wellington considered that years of maintaining the armed forces at the lowest possible level had rendered them unequal to emergencies. He advised swearing in special constables in the disturbed districts and putting the yeomen under arms to reinforce and protect the police. As he had twenty years before, he warned against exposing the soldiers to danger and temptation and recommended that yeomen not be used in their own neighbourhoods. A few days later he added that half-pay officers and military pensioners should be enlisted as special constables and a list drawn up of those willing to aid the civil authorities. But above all he urged every effort to discover those involved in the disturbances so that their names could be published on placards in order to shake the confidence of the strikers in each other:

> It would prove to them that they were observed & watched and that some among them gave information to the Magistrates; & you would find that men would be much less likely to involve themselves in such illegal transactions; when made aware that the Magistrate would be informed. Such a feeling would greatly aid the operations of any repressive forces wch it might be possible to collect.

Studying the reports from the North, the Duke found good reason to doubt that the civil authorities there could be trusted to carry out their functions properly. The Lords Lieutenant of Lancashire, Cheshire, Staffordshire, Warwickshire and Derbyshire were well-intentioned but either not well enough or not sufficiently energetic to perform their duties efficiently. Many of the urban magistrates were opposed to the corn laws and were willing to tolerate disturbances in the hope of strengthening the demand for repeal; in any event they were not eager to expose themselves to attack in the House of Commons for using their powers to restrict the liberties of subjects. Wellington recommended that stipendiary magistrates be despatched to all centres of disorder and wherever outbreaks of violence were expected to require local authorities to discharge their duties and discourage disturbances by appearing with the constables and warning the inhabitants orally and by proclamation. Once in control of the situation the government should send out a special commission to try those charged and to impress the population by carrying sentences immediately into execution.[9]

Bad as the state of the country was, not everyone saw it in the same dark shades as Wellington. The determined assertion of order by troops moved by railway, the use of paid informers, the suppression of large meetings and the arrest of the leaders broke the movement within a few weeks. Writing to Ellenborough in India at the beginning of September, the Duke expressed his satisfaction at the crushing of the disturbances and hoped that Parliament would take steps against the unions when it met in the new year.[10] Having restored an uneasy peace, however, the ministry was not eager to encourage a fresh outburst by provocative legislation and did not even press for heavy penalties when those who had been arrested were brought to trial. But just as this threat faded another arose in Ireland. 'Monster meetings' were attended by hundreds of thousands in the spring and summer of 1843, which O'Connell confidently announced would be the year of victory for repeal.

The Commander in Chief was in good form to deal with the latest danger from that familiar quarter. He had suffered no recurrence of the attacks that had plagued him between 1839 and 1841 and had evidently made a good recovery. At the opening of Parliament in early February 1843 Charles Greville observed that he spoke with a force that surprised everyone. A month later he added: 'Nothing is more extraordinary than the complete restoration of that vigour of mind which for the last two or three years was visibly impaired. His speeches this Session have been as good, if not better than any he ever made.'[11]

But even in his relatively restored condition Wellington was thoroughly alarmed by the situation in Ireland, telling Graham that it was 'no longer in a social state. There is neither property nor safety for life except in the ranks of the Repealers of the Union.'[12] To the Colonial Secretary, Lord Stanley, he wrote that the Chartists, France, the United States and the democratic element in Canada all supported the repeal movement, and warned that 'Any Misfortune ever occurring in Ireland, Canada or Great Britain and attended by our being in a State of Military Naval Weakness would be attended by Consequences of which the Contemplation even is painful.' No one was less disposed than he to advocate government by the sword, but 'every Body must see that we have impending over us a Contest in Ireland; which must have an Influence over our disaffected parties in this Country and over the State of our Difficulties in Canada.'[13] It was only to be expected that the commander would advise an increase in the army, but his proposal to put the Protestant yeomen of the North of Ireland under arms was rejected by the Home Secretary as an 'awful one' that would impose on the ministry the responsibility for making any conflict a religious one from the beginning.[14]

By the end of the summer Wellington was complaining of 'murders unnoticed, of illegal combinations excited by priests and demogogues to refuse to work for individual landlords and farmers.' Processions led by priests and too large to be dealt with by the local authorities were terrifying the country, threatening what remained of the social order and tying down the whole disposable army and navy. Since the Irish executive was timid about enforcing law and order he expected the uproar to lead to civil war; but once again he warned that even a successful military operation would not settle the country if the centre of the disturbance was not immediately crushed.[15] The only solution was for the Duke to sacrifice his own ease and comfort to the proper government of Ireland.

Arbuthnot conveyed this hint to Graham who in turn informed the Prime Minister of Wellington's apparent conviction that 'the winds and the waves will obey him, and that his presence there will be a great calm.' Graham had no doubt that the Duke's iron hand could crush a rebellion but his actions would not be 'of a soothing character.' Peel, unconsciously echoing Wellington's own view twenty years before, agreed that he should be sent only if there was widespread insurrection or if the loyalty of the troops seemed in question.[16] The ministry meanwhile was working to ensure that this would not occur by increasing the number of troops and warships. In October it banned the final monster meeting of the year. A week later O'Connell and six others were arrested on charges of conspiracy. The following May they were sentenced to a year's imprisonment. When the decision was appealed to the House of Lords the Tory peers were only with difficulty persuaded to leave the case to the law lords. To general astonishment the appeal was upheld by three to two. This triumph of British justice, which did much to reduce tension in Ireland, was produced by three Whig judges voting against Lyndhurst and Brougham.

The decision of the Lords, announced at the end of the specially prolonged session in September 1844, did nothing to reassure the Duke. He kept on about the military deficiency in Ireland and even though Peel and Graham judged the threat to have receded, they felt obliged to pay patient attention to his advice. When the Home Secretary elaborated on the dangers of arming the Protestant yeomanry, Wellington became more violent, hotly denying that he had ever said anything about a religious restriction and stormed that if the occupiers of the land could not be trusted how much less could the Irish police, especially the officers, 'men recommended to the late Government by demogogues, members of Liberal Clubs, and members of Parliament in favour of Repeal, recommended to their constituents by O'Connell.' His chief fear was insurrection combined with invasion. 'I have some experience of war,' he sharply reminded the civilian Graham, 'and know what military operations are.' At the time of the Reform Bill, when Graham had been a Whig minister, he had trained his servants at Apsley House, 'some to the use of muskets, others of boar-spears, which I happened to have, or other arms. I besides strengthened my house and windows, in order to prevent the destruction by stones of my property in pictures within.' No member of the government had criticized him for that, and what had been legal in London in 1831 then must surely be permitted in the present condition of Ireland. Wearily the Home Secretary explained that taking steps to defend a house was not the same as applying for permission to train servants to arms, which Wellington had grudgingly to concede.

Turning to Protestant sympathy for an Irish parliament within a federal United Kingdom, the Duke recalled that when he had been Chief Secretary in Portland's government the Protestants had been separated from the Catholics by patronage. In the changed conditions since the Reform Bill he recommended 'Croker and the scribbling set. Let them dissect and discuss the speeches, and the plans proposed.' Once such authors demonstrated how close the Irish parliament had come to independence in the late eighteenth century, how a separate parliament would exclude Protestants, how it would seize the property and tithes of the Church of Ireland, pay salaries to Catholic priests and appropriate the property of absentees, even of those who favoured repeal, the Protestants of Ireland would cleave to the union as their only hope.[17]

Wellington may, as he saw it, have been carrying the whole world on his shoulders, but his parliamentary duties at least were lightened at the end of the 1844 session. Partly owing to his deafness, as Greville pointed out, his hold on the House of Lords was not as strong as it had been. Nor did he receive much support from his colleagues: Ripon, the President of the Board of Control, seemed worn out; Wharncliffe, the Lord President of the Council, did not do much; Lyndhurst, the Chancellor, was no help; and the government found itself in the degrading position of being 'constantly nursed and dandled by Brougham, who sat on the Woolsack and volunteered to speak for them on all occasion.'[18] A year before, the Duke had complained bitterly that he was not kept properly informed by departments of matters under discussion and unlike the Lord Chancellor had no secretaries or lawyers to turn to, while everyone looked to him for advice. As far as he was concerned, he burst out,

> I do not desire more than to go to the H. of Lords; and sit there from it's meeting till it's Adjournment without uttering one Word. But if I am to take part in Debate: I must be informed and must have time to seek for Information; if the Department in question does not think proper to supply that which is necessary! If I should not have the Information in time: I shall do no more than say that I have not the Information; and let the matter take the course which the Dept. choses it should take.[19]

This particular eruption was smoothed over by the ministers concerned, but the difficulty of the Leader of the House of Lords's temperament did not go unremarked. Stanley, the former Rupert of debate, chafing with boredom at the Colonial Office while Peel and his colleagues in financial departments posts dominated discussions in the Commons, told the Prime Minister that his office could be as well filled by any member who would vote when required. Casting his eye to an arena where he might shine, he pointed out that in the Lords he would be able to take part in general administration as well as rescuing that House from 'the state of inanation into which it has fallen.' He did not intend to challenge Wellington's position but thought he could be of some help in taking over the burden of debate. Under this seemingly generous offer was the scarcely veiled threat that when he succeeded as Earl of Derby he would refuse to serve under anyone but the Duke. If Peel intended him someday to be Leader, it was

8 A miniature of the Duke from a daguerreotype taken in 1844 (Stratfield Saye, reproduced by kind permission of the Duke of Wellington; photograph by David Carey)

best that he go now as Wellington's second in command.[20]

Concerned above all not to lose Stanley but unwilling to deprive anyone else of a more desirable portfolio, Peel hastened to secure Wellington's agreement. Having pleaded for relief, the Duke now had no choice but to welcome it. He did so in cool tones, observing that as the Colonial Secretary would eventually succeed to the Lords, it would 'undoubtedly be desirable in that view of the question alone that Ld. Stanley should be called to that House, at an early period: if his talents can be spared from the House of Commons: and his early removal to the House of Lords should not be disagreeable to him.' But while grudgingly admitting that it would be an advantage to have Stanley beside him, Wellington assured Peel that he was as well as he had ever been in the last twenty-two years, 'ready to do anything, or nothing; in order to promote the views of Government.' Peel swiftly and deftly praised the Duke's skill in managing the peers and assured him that Stanley's principal desire was to benefit from working with him and under his direction.[21]

Summoning Stanley to the House of Lords certainly made Peel's life easier, but it did not diminish Wellington's importance in getting the Conservative peers to accept legislation to which many of them were instinctively opposed. Most of this concerned Ireland as Peel and other ministers tried to remove the causes of the repeal movement by redressing grievances. In 1844 Catholics were permitted to hold gifts and property in trust for religious and charitable purposes and the Charitable Bequests Commission was reconstituted with equal numbers of Protestants and Catholics and a Catholic secretary. But in 1845 a modest measure of compensation for improvements for evicted tenants, which seems to have been entrusted entirely to Stanley, produced such an outcry in the Lords that the heir to great Irish estates deemed it prudent to withdraw it for further consideration, a process that took twenty-five years.

The proposal to increase the grant to Maynooth College, which trained the Catholic clergy, was hardly more popular. Thousands of petitions against it rained on both Houses of Parliament and at the Board of Trade the young William Gladstone, following the tortuous dictates of his conscience, supported the bill but felt obliged to resign because it contradicted his published views on the state's relations with the established Church. After long and acrimonious debate the bill passed the Commons with the support of the Whigs. But the real danger lay in the House of Lords where only the Duke of Wellington had a chance of persuading the Conservative peers to accept it.

He can hardly have been enthusiastic about this task, but in two long speeches he made a powerful case for the bill. He pointed out that the principle of supporting a Catholic college in Ireland as a more desirable alternative to relying on priests from abroad in a time of revolution had been accepted in 1795 by that Protestant hero George III, by the British government headed by Pitt, by an exclusively Protestant Irish Parliament, and had been confirmed by the Act of Union. Given the interest in Irish repeal in other countries, it was no more desirable now than it had been fifty years before to import foreign priests. He denied that there was any danger to the established Church in the bill or any grounds for thinking that it would lead to other measures undermining the Protestant position in Ireland. The question was not one of religion but of expediency. The population of Ireland had risen from three to eight million in the last fifty years; if an institution were to be maintained by a great country it should be one worthy of it. The professors should be better paid than clerks; servants should not have to be dismissed with the students during vacations; and the students should have the comforts belonging to 'men of their class, and fitted for that situation in life in which they are to be placed' including sufficient books and apparatus for instruction in literature and science as well as theology. If there was no religious principle involved in increasing the grant, there certainly was the great Christian one of 'abstaining from persecution; and if you are strong, I say it is your duty not to persecute the weak.'[22] With this powerful endorsement only the most determined Protestant peers persisted in voting against the measure.

While most cabinet ministers were directing their attention to Ireland and financial matters, Wellington was concentrating on the problems of defence. He had always considered the size of the army inadequate, but since the war scare of 1840 he had been focusing on the development of steamships, which was already providing the sinews of British commerce but which he saw only in terms of increased danger of invasion from France. At the end of the 1844 session he told Peel that the country should take advantage of the formidable speed of the new ships to train a special group of officers and devise a new code of signals. The French government could not be trusted to maintain peaceful relations and it was essential for Britain to be strong in every part of the world as an incident anywhere might touch off a general war. The only way to control France was by

> our certain and decided Naval superiority not only to their own; but
> to that even supported by the United States! As for my part, I have

long ceased to consider our present state as one of Peace!

Peace will not be secure until we shall be in a state to command it. [23]

The Duke kept up a steady stream of such letters, provoking an unusually sharp exchange between him and Peel in August 1845. To the Prime Minister's embarrassment Palmerston was saying the same from the opposition benches in the House of Commons. Peel could at first put off the Duke by facile agreement with his alarm, but when he countered Palmerston's arguments in the Commons, Wellington wrote to protest this repudiation of the views he had repeatedly expressed to Peel and Stanley. He also disclaimed any responsibility on his part for leaving the country defenceless 'under the circumstances of danger of invasion in an unprecedented degree existing on account of the comparatively modern invention and practice of the application of the power of steam to propel vessels of the largest size, and with the heaviest ordnance likewise of modern invention.' With steamships practically forming a series of bridges between France and England, every aspect of the country's military policy needed to be considered. And whatever was decided would take a year to become effective. 'I have done my duty to my own satisfaction in submitting these papers to you,' he righteously concluded. 'There my responsibility ends; you must decide the rest.' [24]

This formal protest from his loyal but fierce colleague, which he had been warned about by Arbuthnot a few days before, called for Peel's careful attention. He replied in a letter of twenty-seven sides pointing out that to accept Palmerston's public declaration that the country was defenceless would simply encourage a war policy in France. He agreed that the country must be ready for war but there were 'limits to the extent of that preparation. There are dangers in an opposite direction which it will be prudent not to disregard.' The choice of evils was between running some risks in the empire and rapidly accumulating more debt. He readily admitted that Britain itself could not be exposed to the same risk as the colonies, but the best course was a quiet increase in the country's strength while avoiding any gesture that could be seen as provocative. Reviewing what had been done since he had become Prime Minister he reminded Wellington that the navy was larger and more effective than the French one and that the army at home had been increased from 44,000 to 53,000, though it was still below the 100,000 that the Duke considered necessary to defend the country. Adding another 50,000 would violate important constitutional, financial and diplomatic considerations, but he promised to raise the matter with the Queen when she returned from the continent.

Wellington was not at all mollified by this statement and repeated that in the event of war, 'which sooner or late must occur, it will be the object of every Frenchman from King to the Peasant to make this Country the seat of the War; and to bring to a conclusion in this Country the long contest between the two Nations.'[25] After inspecting the defences of the south coast at the end of the summer he sent Peel a copy of a long memorandum to his old Peninsula comrade, now Master General of the Ordnance, General Sir George Murray. Perhaps for the benefit of third parties he wrote:

> You and I are old my dear Murray! and in the common course of things we can scarcely expect that the Almighty will spare us to perform this great Service!
>
> But any body could now save Portugal! and let us endeavour to place the defensive system of this Country on such Grounds, as that any body can safe this Country, when it shall please the Almighty to take us away.
>
> I thank God that I am in such good health and so strong and able to do anything; and you may rely upon my giving you every assistance in my Power.[26]

This unrelenting barrage from the Commander in Chief drove the Foreign Secretary, Aberdeen, to the brink of resignation and came close to destroying Peel's composure. In exasperation he wrote to Arbuthnot, who was endlessly urging him to communicate more with the Duke, that the demands on the Prime Minister made him feel that the office was 'above all human strength – at least above mine.' He had no intention of leaving the Commons for the Lords, but the problem must be solved somehow: 'The failure of the mind is the usual way, as we know from sad experience.'[27] The confidential defence issue was by no means resolved or even over, but at this very moment it became overshadowed by a more pressing and public crisis that was developing on the other side of St George's Channel.

While Wellington was obsessed by the country's military posture, the government was receiving disturbing accounts from parts of England and the continent about a disease affecting the potato crop. The worst fears were realized when it appeared in Ireland, where half of the eight million inhabitants lived exclusively on potatoes. At first the reports were so mixed that it was difficult to tell how bad the harvest was going to be, but by the middle of October the prospect was grim and Peel summoned the cabinet for the end of the month. He did not neglect to pay special attention to the Duke, whose attitude and influence would be crucial in any interference with the corn laws to admit food for the hungry in Britain and the starving in Ireland. Perhaps to test Wellington's thoughts on the matter as well as to set his mind on the same path as his own, Peel sent him a letter from Sir James Graham pointing out that a temporary suspension of the corn laws would be an admission that they aggravated scarcity and make it impractical to reimpose them.[28]

Wrapped up in his military concerns, Wellington took no alarmist view of what was probably a passing misfortune. He warned that importing other food to replace the destroyed potatoes would not be a complete remedy as the population did not buy its food in the markets but raised it on land provided in return for labour. He agreed that the cabinet should discuss the matter but optimistically believed that oats, the most suitable substitute for potatoes, were plentiful in Ireland as well as in England and Scotland.[29] As late as the end of November, when the full effects were clear of the disease that was spreading like wildfire in the wet weather that also produced a poor grain crop, high prices, the opening of ports to food and the prohibition of potato exports all over Europe, he continued to believe that the main problem in Ireland was social unrest, 'a consequence & symptom of the Disease, and not the disease itself! which is Popery in a Country governed according to the Principles of the British Constitution, that is by the People themselves!'[30]

Like most other ministers, the Duke had not followed the harvest in Ireland and elsewhere with the close attention of Peel or the Anti-Corn Law League, which redoubled its efforts in the face of high prices and the threatened scarcity of food. When the cabinet met on 31 October the Prime Minister told his colleagues that there would be great shortages in all parts of the kingdom in the new year. For Ireland, which would be most severely affected, he proposed a commission under the Viceroy to provide wages for food through a system of public works and direct relief where necessary. He did not think that they could ask Parliament for funds for this purpose without altering the corn laws, but to give others time to consider it was agreed to adjourn for a week.[31]

At the second meeting Peel recommended that the grain in bonded warehouses be admitted without duty and the ports opened at a reduced tariff. The government should meet Parliament at the end of November to secure authority for this and give notice of a bill to reduce further the scale of grain duties established in 1842. Only three ministers supported this drastic step; the rest, including Wellington, remaining unconvinced that a real crisis had been demonstrated.

Perhaps hoping that deteriorating conditions would convert his colleagues more effectively than argument, Peel proposed that the cabinet continue its discussion at the end of November. In the meantime efforts were made to save the potatoes by chemicals and drying; the Admiralty was instructed to buy oats in various ports; and large quantities of maize and meal were purchased secretly to avoid panic in the United States. Apart from humanitarian concerns and a desire to keep society together, Peel was clearly also hoping to take advantage of the situation to continue tariff reduction with no special exemption for food. This was powerfully assisted when the Whig leader, Lord John Russell, publicly declared himself in favour of total respect of the corn laws on 22 November. Three days later Peel told the cabinet that opening the ports would have to be followed by a review of the whole issue of agricultural protection, and while it might be better that this should be done by others, the present emergency made him willing to accept the responsibility. Still divided on the enormity of any such change, the ministers could only agree that Parliament should be summoned for early January.

A few days later Peel circulated a statement of the problem to the cabinet, asking whether the corn laws should be modified, maintained or suspended for a limited period. He repeated his own opinion that they should be suspended, but that would raise the general issue of protection. The Duke promptly replied in a memorandum for general circulation that he was one of those who considered the corn laws 'essential to the agriculture of the country in its existing state and particularly to that of Ireland, and a benefit to the whole community.' He thought that the whole country, even Ireland, was in a better state to bear the potato famine than any in Europe and repeated that the real evil in Ireland was not the immediate shortage but the system whereby people consumed all the food they produced, ensuring that they were always destitute and had neither money nor the habit of buying food in the marketplace. He urged the ministers not to be mesmerized by the immediate situation but to look to the future and not to destroy the corn laws unless absolutely necessary. If suspension would relieve the scarcity they should not hestitate; but they should first be fully convinced of the necessity and then make every effort to convince others. The main point, however, was to ensure that Peel continued as Prime Minister. 'A good Government for the country is more important than the Corn Laws, or any other consideration,' he pronounced in what was to be his attitude throughout the crisis, 'and as long as Sir Robert Peel possesses the confidence of the Queen and of the public, and he has strength to perform his duties, his administration of the Government must be supported.'[32]

Most of the cabinet shared Wellington's attitude, but Peel insisted on some clear decision before Parliament met. Summoning his colleagues once more, he proposed an immediate lowering of the 1842 sliding scale and the gradual elimination of the corn laws over a period of eight years. Stanley and the Duke of Buccleuch, the Lord Privy Seal, announced that they would resign rather than be parties to such a measure. The ministers in the House of Commons considered that it would be impossible to carry the legislation after these two resignations. Peel agreed and the following day travelled to Osborne to tell the Queen that the government could not go on. He advised her to call on Russell whom he would support in any alteration, including repeal, of the corn laws. Russell arrived from Edinburgh five days later, on 11 December. On the same day Peel's ministers resigned and received their seals back as a caretaker administration.

The next day the Queen told Wellington that whatever the results of Russell's efforts, she had a 'strong desire' that he should remain Commander in Chief: 'The Queen appeals to the Duke's so often proved loyalty and attachment to her person, in asking him to give her this assurance. The Duke will thereby render the greatest service to the country and to her own person.' In the dreadful collapse this was the most that could be saved; but Wellington cautiously advised the Queen to consult whomever was to lead the ministry as the Commander in Chief had to deal in confidence with the Prime Minister and other members of the cabinet. He could not form a political connection with his old opponent – 'Such arrangement would not conciliate public confidence, be considered creditable to either party, or be useful to the service of your Majesty' – but neither would he act with the opposition. To allay Russell's doubts he pointed out that during the whole period that he had been in opposition while Hill was at the Horse Guards he had given disinterested advice on military matters. He eagerly assured the monarch that he would 'cheerfully devote his service to your Majesty's command upon receiving the official intimation thereof, and that he will as usual make every effort in his power to promote your Majesty's service.'[33]

Russell had no wish to add to his problems by depriving the national hero of his rightful position and driving him into opposition, particularly after receiving such guarantees of neutrality and goodwill. In a minority in both Houses of Parliament he was having enough hesitations about forming a government, and the assurances of support for a Corn Bill from some Conservatives were not very comforting. After a week he was relieved to find an excuse in the internal dispute over Palmerston's return to the Foreign Office to hand back what Disraeli called 'the poisoned chalice' to Sir Robert Peel. There would be ample time for the Whigs to take office when the Conservatives had torn themselves apart on the issue of agricultural protection.

With an excitement heightened by the desperation of the venture on which he was about to embark, Peel agreed to continue and told his cabinet that he intended to meet Parliament with whatever measures were necessary for the emergency. Stanley stood by his resignation and was replaced by Gladstone, whose conscience now dictated his return; Buccleuch, after some hesitation, decided to stay. Peel's resolve communicated itself to the cabinet. Wellington pronounced the corn laws a subordinate consideration and Peel reported to the Queen that he had expressed himself '*delighted* when he received Sir Robert Peel's letter that day, announcing to the Duke that his mind was made up to place his services at your Majesty's disposal.' A few days later Arbuthnot told Peel: 'You can have no notion how much the Duke suffered, when he thought we were to be cursed with a Whig-Radical Government.' The Prime Minister in turn assured their intermediary that Wellington's conduct, 'from first to last was – I can pay it no higher compliment – consistent with the past.'[34]

At a meeting of the Privy Council on Christmas Eve, Prince Albert told the Duke, who was in excellent fighting spirits: 'You have such an influence over the House of Lords that you will be able to keep them straight.' Wellington loyally replied: 'I'll do anything: I am now beginning to write to them and to convince them singly of what their duty is.' While Peel worked on a scheme to replace the corn laws with incentives to efficient agriculture, the Duke went about his appointed task. But it was with a heavy heart. He told Lady Charles Wellesley's father: 'rotten potatoes have done it all; they put Peel in his d—d fright.'[35] He saw in the low price of potatoes, caused by panic selling before they became diseased, evidence that conditions even in Ireland had been much exaggerated rather than a sign of the dreadful suffering to come. But with all his doubts he was prepared to accept Peel's judgment, trusting him within the necessities of politics to preserve as much as possible of traditional institutions, privilege and the social structure of the country. By December 1845 it was clear that alteration of the corn laws could only be delayed by a revolt of the House of Lords, which might prove fatal to both. As he had at the time of Catholic emancipation, in May 1832, and on many lesser occasions, Wellington maintained that it was better for inevitable change to be carried out by a sound ministry that would control and limit it than by one eager to push reform as far as possible. His own obvious reluctance and agony were valuable in persuading others. If the great Duke of Wellington, the very symbol of the old order, judged that the corn laws had to be surrendered and that the consequences would not be calamitous, they too would accept the decision.

The Duke was well aware of the dimensions of the undertaking. Since just before Peel's resignation he had been carrying on a correspondence with Lord Redesdale, who rightly claimed to speak for many in saying that he could under no circumstances consent to the abolition of the corn laws. When Russell had been trying to form a ministry Redesdale had written to ask what course Wellington was going to take now that the Conservatives were apparently going into opposition. He compared the party to 'an army more numerous than any that could be brought against it, and confident of victory under any circumstances, whose staff and materiel have been surrendered to the enemy by their commander in order to prevent their fighting.' As whip in the Lords he claimed to be 'in a position of one in charge of a very large and important division of that army, which I am confident is well inclined to fight to the last, but which is at a loss to know to whom it is to look up as leader.' The situation appeared more complex to the Duke, and it is doubtful that he was much pleased by Redesdale's sneer at Peel or his claim to speak for the Conservative peers; but until Peel agreed to return he gave only evasive if lengthy replies.

Once Russell had failed he told Redesdale that 'the Question of forming a Ministry now rests between Sir Robert Peel & Cobden! There is no chance of any other Conservative coming forward! and the Whigs have declared themselves not able to form an Administration. We are very sick! God send us a good deliverance.' When Redesdale said that he would wait to see what Peel proposed before deciding whether to support him or to rally his friends independently, Wellington reminded him that the position was quite different from what it had been before the Conservatives resigned. With change now unavoidable, 'The object of all must be to render it as little injurious to the public Interests, nay more beneficial to the public Interests as possible.' He could only speak for himself and every individual must make up his own mind, but he warned: 'That which is to be apprehended is that new combinations might be formed upon the notions of the weakness of a Gov't. from which so many respectable Persons have kept aloof.'[36]

As he laboured to convert the peers, the Duke's essential message was the same to all, though each letter contained carefully designed variations to appeal to individuals. His method and arguments may be judged from his letter to the Duke of Beaufort. Beginning with a long narrative of the deliberations in the government, he pointed out that after the negotiations between Russell and Peel it was impossible for the Conservatives to stick to their former position on the corn laws. The choice was now the stark one between the dreaded Cobden and Peel, whose attachments to agricultural interests no one could doubt:

> himself a great Landed Proprietor, his social habits of intercourse with the Landed Interest, parliamentary consistency, and the Interest and power of the administration depending upon the Support of that Interest in the House of Commons, it is impossible that Sir Robt. Peel should not make every effort to propose a Settlement of this affair which should be just and fair.

Despite his own personal conviction that only a small adjustment to the corn laws was necessary to meet the present circumstances, he told Beaufort that he had 'never been insensible to their Inconvenience; the violent and constantly renewed opposition to them, occasions at least the inconvenience of uncertainty as to their duration, and affects more or less every negociation for letting land in the Country.' He claimed that he had always believed that the great benefit of the corn laws was to provide the opportunity to improve agriculture to the point that they would not be necessary. Others, however, believed that the landed interest had simply enacted and kept them for its own selfish advantage. But the corn laws were not the only interest of the country, and it was worth some sacrifice to preserve good government. Even if a protectionist ministry could be formed that would be able to resist the pressure for repeal in the Commons, 'what is to become of the other Questions of external and internal Policy, commercial, financial, Colonial, Irish which press upon the consideration of the Govt. every day?' He advised his noble friend to ponder these matters and see what Peel proposed before making his final decision.[37]

Only a determined sense of duty kept Wellington at this painful task. The replies were predictably no source of comfort. The Duke of Rutland, the greatest allotment owner in Ireland, wrote to say that the potato famine had been greatly exaggerated, 'and I am very happy to think, with a trifling Assistance at the seed time, very little of any inconvenience will be experienced by the Occupiers.' He did not doubt the government's sincerity in abandoning agricultural protection but thought that any change would be regarded as a triumph by the Anti-Corn Law League, 'a species of Genuflexion to them from those who have hitherto so zealously and steadily opposed their pernicious Doctrines. And it is a dangerous lesson to teach any Society, which seeks to accomplish an object by unconstitutional means that by preserving clamour and by incessant Brawling they can secure success.'[38]

While such discouraging responses, all too reminiscent of terms the Duke himself had used on previous occasions, were coming in, J. W. Croker of the *Quarterly Review* was wrestling for Wellington's conscience and trying to break Peel's government or at least throw a powerful obstacle in the way of repeal by persuading the Duke to resign. 'I firmly believe that the only trust of the country is in your Grace's consistency and firmness;' he wrote in flattering tones,

> and I confess I cannot see what right Sir R. Peel can have to drag your Grace through the mire of his own changes of opinion. He may say with truth and candour, that *his* opinions are changed, but can your Grace say so? Why should not he have the whole responsibility of his own conduct? What has your Grace to do with the affair? . . . Your Grace's resignation of the cabinet key might embarrass Sir R. Peel, but the difficulty is of his own making, *not yours*; and he before he made it, ought to have known how he was to *unmake* it.

But much as the Duke valued Croker as a friend and as a propagandist, and partly for that reason kept on writing to justify his course, he was not to be deflected from his duty by one of the 'scribbling sort.' He told Croker that he was 'the *retained* servant of the Sovereign of this empire.' Whatever Peel proposed, he would do his best to minimize the effect on the landed interest, but he would not be instrumental in placing the government 'in the hands of the League and the Radicals.'[39]

As he contemplated the ineffectiveness of his efforts, he told Lord Ellenborough that it was 'impossible to describe the want of confidence and misunderstanding which prevails.' It was the end of his own government all over again, and those Conservatives who would withdraw their support on this occasion would be 'acting over again the scene of 1830, some of them with the same intentions as in 1830, expose themselves and the Country to the same dangers over again.' This was 'a melancholy reflection to one who has served the Country for fifty years! who has seen the approach of this danger and has made every effort in his Power, and every sacrifice to avoid it! I confess that reflection on this state of things annoys me beyond measure!'[40]

When Parliament met on 22 January Peel outlined the recent course of events and announced his change of opinion on the corn laws since the experiment with freer trade in 1842 and the failure of the potato harvest. In the House of Lords Wellington at first refused to make a statement, seeking refuge in the plea that he did not have the Queen's permission. But four days later he gave an explanation that contained few surprises for those he had tried to persuade during the last few weeks. He told the House that he had not considered it necessary to open the ports, believing that there was no shortage of grain in the country and in any event the present corn laws automatically provided for the admission of grain at a nominal duty when the price was high; but he had felt obliged to give way in order to fulfill his primary obligation of preserving the ministry: 'I was of opinion that the formation of a Government in which her Majesty would have confidence, was of much greater importance than the opinions of any individual on the Corn Laws, or on any other Law.' He assured the peers that Peel would not betray the agricultural interests; but for his own part,

> whatever that measure may be, I must say this, that situated as I am in this country – highly rewarded as I have been by the Sovereign and the people of England – I could not refuse that Sovereign to aid Her, when called upon, to form a Government, in order to enable Her Majesty to meet Her Parliament and to carry on the business of the country.[41]

Peel was much pleased by this generous defence and the next day Lady Peel called on Wellington in tears to tell him of the impression that his speech had made on her husband.[42] The encouragement was certainly timely. That night the Prime Minister informed the House of Commons that he intended to continue the work of his 1842 budget by lowering or abolishing duties on a wide range of manufactured goods, raw materials and foodstuffs; but the item which attracted all attention was the one to reduce the duty on corn over the next three years to 1s. a quarter. As compensation some local rates were to be assumed by the national government and loans for drainage were to be provided at low rates of interest. But burying the abolition of the corn laws in this manner and offering paltry recompense did nothing to diminish the sense of betrayal and insult felt by the defenders of agricultural protection. The Conservative party, which Peel had striven to build and hold together since the Reform Act, was split into two hostile camps, with over 200 protectionists turning to Lord George Bentinck and Benjamin Disraeli and just over 100 standing by Peel.

In the House of Lords, where the protectionists were led by the bitter and formidable former Colonial Secretary Lord Stanley, the prospects of defeat seemed distinctly brighter than in the Commons. Two weeks after the legislation was introduced into the Commons, where Whig support ensured its eventual passage, the Duke told Lady Wilton that he could not predict the result in the Lords.[43] The next day Stanley sent Wellington a long letter saying that he could no longer serve as his deputy, though he would not oppose him any more than necessary. Stanley doubted that even the Duke could get the Lords to accept repeal; but whatever the outcome, a Whig ministry was inevitable and the Conservatives could unite only in opposition. There was no obvious person to reunite the party in the Commons but in the Lords there was Wellington. Probably looking to the Duke's support for him as his successor, Stanley pointed out that his influence and authority were and must remain paramount. However much his followers regretted his decision to part from them on the corn laws, 'they still regard you with undiminished personal respect and attachment; and with you at their head, will follow no other Leader, if any were ill-judged enough to set himself up in opposition to you.'[44]

There was a chance that Stanley's hopes of victory in the House of Lords might be realized when a group of Whigs proposed to join the protectionists in amending the measure to provide for a small fixed duty. But this devotion to Russell's proposal of five years before brought a sharp rebuke from the leader now. He told the Whig peers that he would not accept responsibility for any amendment and would not form a government if Peel resigned on the issue. This settled the fate of the bill.

The Duke's speech just before the division following three days' debate on second reading, memorable as it was as a statement of his own by now familiar position, almost certainly did not change any votes. Advising the peers for what he thought might be the last time, he expressed his regret at having to urge support for a measure disagreeable to many of his political friends. But however painful this parting of the ways, he had no choice but to support Peel's ministry and the present legislation as the servant of the crown, 'bound to Her Majesty and to the Sovereigns of this country by considerations of gratitude of which it is not necessary that I should say more to your Lordships.' He appealed to the confidence his friends had reposed in him for many years and to which he modestly affected to have no real claim:

> Circumstances have given it to me; in some cases the confidence of
> the Crown, and, in others, the zeal with which I have endeavoured to
> serve your Lordships, to promote your Lordship's views, and my

desire to facilitate your business in this House; and I shall lament the breaking up of that confidence in public life.

Recalling that he had persuaded the House to change its opinion on Catholic emancipation, he now urged it to consider the consequences of rejecting the present bill. The Lords would find themselves alone and exposed to the attacks of their enemies. They might have vast influence on public opinion and confidence in their own principles, 'but without the Crown or the House of Commons you can do nothing – till the connexion with the Crown and the House of Commons is revived, there is an end of the functions of the House of Lords.'[45]

Immediately after Wellington's speech the House divided and the bill was carried by 211 to 164, a majority sufficiently large that the protectionists allowed the bill to pass third reading without a division on 25 June, formally recording their protests in the *Journal of the House*. A few hours later the ministry was defeated in the Commons on an Irish Coercion Bill by a combination of Whigs, Irish and protectionists. As the Duke had predicted, it was 1830 come again. Rather than trying to fight a general election with a divided party Peel decided to resign. Even Wellington, who had been all for dissolution a few days before, agreed that in the state of the party, even in the Lords, retirement was the better course.

On 29 June Peel delivered his famous farewell address in the Commons, attributing the triumph of repeal to the influence of Cobden, delivering a parting blow to protection and trusting that he would be remembered 'in the abodes of those whose lot it is to labour, and to earn their daily bread by the sweat of their brow, when they shall recruit their exhausted strength with abundant and untaxed food, the sweeter because it is no longer leavened by a sense of injustice.' As Greville pointed out, almost every part of this speech offended someone. Wellington was particularly wounded by the tribute to Cobden.[46] Having defended Peel as the only alternative to the great apostle of repeal, it was gall and wormwood to hear the retiring Prime Minister praising the enemy of the landed aristocracy and glorying in the destruction of principles dear to Tory hearts.

The repeal of the corn laws and the resignation of Peel's government in a way marked the end of the Duke's political career. Never again did he speak in the House of Lords as a minister or leader of a party. More than at any time in his life, including the three years following his return to

England in 1818, he was truly independent, the most independent figure in the country, whose advice and authoritative support were sought by every individual and group. For all his earlier fears of Lord John Russell and a Whig ministry, he was remarkably friendly to the administration that endured for most of the time that was left to him. This was partly because he was Commander in Chief; partly because Russell and his ministers went out of their way to cultivate his goodwill; but also because, with the Conservative party hopelessly divided, the Whigs offered the best prospect of orderly government and the defence of institutions. His attitude was practically the same as Peel's, though arrived at independently. Indeed the only time he met Peel for a long time after the end of their administration was three weeks later when they encountered each other riding in the park. Wellington later complained to at least two people that he had told Peel all he knew, his reflections on events and what he intended to do in future. Peel did not respond, 'made no remark, and when they reached the House of Lords he said something about being happy to see the Duke in such good health and then rode off – evidently glad to get rid of him.'[47] Perhaps Peel was relieved that his political association with this angular figure was over, or, sensitive to the Duke's sense of betrayal in his praise of Cobden, was even more cautious than usual.

Relations between the two resumed their customary cool and awkward nature when they were out of office, but the Duke gave no encouragement to the vindictiveness of the protectionists to whom he was temperamentally closer than to Peel and his followers. He wished Stanley well as the protectionists' leader and assured him that he wanted to see a reunited Conservative party ready to serve the country in the danger ahead; but that could be achieved only by forgiving and forgetting the passions that had been aroused by the repeal of the corn laws.[48] This spirit of charity and reconciliation was rejected by politicians with their ways still to make and the protectionists and the Peelites remained bitterly divided. The Duke nevertheless continued to put his trust in Stanley to revive the Conservative party. At the end of 1847 he told him that there was nothing he wanted more than

> a cordial Union of the Influential Proprietors of the Country, the Mercantile & Manufacturing Interests, the Learned Professions the heads of the Professions of the Law and Church and in Short the Education and good Sense for the Support of good Gov't. and everything that is valuable to us as a Nation.

There are formidable obstacles to the attainment of this Object.

> But you have in your Hands a Nucleus! and I earnestly urge you to
> persevere. You will certainly in the end succeed![49]

Wellington did live to see Stanley as Prime Minister, but only of a
minority government without the Peelites; and neither he nor Stanley
survived the twenty-seven years that elapsed before there was a majority
Conservative government.

In the meantime the Duke's dealings with Russell's ministry were in
many ways smoother than they had been with his colleagues in Peel's
cabinet. When Russell formed his government he expressed his desire in a
personal interview that Wellington should remain at the Horse Guards. He
reported to the Queen that the Duke not only agreed but volunteered to
abstain from all political discussion: 'That he should attend very seldom in
the House of Lords, and then only to express his own opinion as an
Individual.'[50] Wellington was as good as his word, if not about seldom
attending the House at least about speaking there and taking part in
political discussion anywhere. When Lord Londonderry and Lord
Lyndhurst looked to him for advice in the weeks after the Whigs took
office, he told them that he could not be part of the opposition; they must
make up their own minds on political matters. To the annoyance of some
Conservatives the Duke also confined himself to private criticism of
legislation which the ministers hastened to accommodate – at least when
they understood what he wanted. Late in 1848 the Colonial Secretary told
the Prime Minister: 'I have just received your note, but the enclosure from
the Duke so entirely defies my power of decyphering it, that I can only
make a faint guess at his meaning.'[51] But until 1850 the ministers, like their
predecessors, could depend on the services of Charles Arbuthnot.

Now that the distraction of the corn laws had been removed, the matter
uppermost in Wellington's mind was once again defence. Scarcely had the
new ministers settled into office than he was drawing their attention to the
need to strengthen the south coast against invasion from France by
steamships. Perhaps hoping for better things from a government in which
Palmerston was Foreign Secretary, he sent Russell a memorandum similar
to the one he had sent to Peel the year before, ominously assuring the
Prime Minister: 'I shall be ready to give Your Lordship and your
Colleagues the same assistance as I gave to Her Majesty's late Servants:
and I shall consider that I am equally performing my Duty to the sovereign
and the Public.'

The Duke kept assiduously to this throughout 1847, as he had when the
Conservatives were in power. In February he warned:

little time will elapse between the first announcement to the public of
the prospect of hostilities; and the declaration of War; and still less
time between the declaration of War; and the necessity for the
defence of the Country against the attack of our formidable
neighbour; and the defeat of his armament at Sea; or a contest and
Battle on English Land for the possession and Sovereignty of the
Country; a trial to which our adversaries and Enemies have long
boasted that they have been looking forward; and from which they
anticipate the triumphant attainment of Vengeance for all their
former defeats and misfortunes; and that of all their ambitious objects
in Europe and the World.

The French would not find that the men of the country had degenerated in
half a century, but it was imperative to improve the fleet, to strengthen
the coastal defences, to embody and train the militia and to increase the
army by 20,000. It would take a year and a half to raise and train these
troops and he advised carrying out the preparations quietly, by degrees and
economically.[52]

Russell no more believed that war was imminent than Peel, and his
response was no more satisfactory. In April Charles Arbuthnot appealed to
Charles Greville to use whatever influence he had to get the ministry to
take up the issue that haunted the Duke and deprived him of his rest: 'night
and day he was occupied with the unhappy state of our foreign relations,
the danger of war, and the defenceless state of our coasts.' As a result of
this intervention Russell agreed to meet the Commander in Chief.
Wellington was not much reassured but Greville believed that with at least
two ministers urging the same thing, 'John will act, though not so rapidly
as the Duke wishes.'[53]

The issue developed into an embarrassing crisis at the end of 1847 when
a long letter which Wellington had sent to Major-General Sir John
Burgoyne, the Inspector General of Fortifications, at the beginning of the
year reached the press. Burgoyne's daughters had copied the letter and
distributed it to an ever-widening circle of friends until at last Lady
Shelley saw it as her patriotic duty and the best service she could render
her old friend to inform the public through the press. 'We are in fact
assailable, and at least liable to insult, and to have contributions levied
upon us, on all parts of our coasts,' it was revealed, 'that is the coasts of
these, including the Channel Islands, which till this time, from the period
of the Norman conquest, have never been successfully invaded.' The Duke
believed that,

excepting immediately under the fire of Dover Castle, there is not a spot on the coast on which infantry might not be thrown on shore at any time of tide, with any wind, and in any weather; and from which such body of infantry thrown on shore would not find within the distance of five miles a road into the interior of the country through the cliffs, practicable for the march of a body of troops.

But even such lurid revelations and detailed elaborations were less annoying than the blunt criticism of present and former ministers. Wellington insisted that he had

in vain endeavoured to awaken the attention of different administrations to this state of things; as well known to our neighbours, rivals in power at least, former adversaries and enemies, as it is to ourselves....

I am bordering upon seventy-seven years of age, passed in honour.

I hope that the Almighty may protect me from being the witness of the tragedy, which I cannot persuade my contemporaries to take measures to avert.[54]

Lady Shelley was at first delighted at her part in drawing attention to the dangers facing the country. But the Prime Minister was furious; the political world outraged or delighted; Burgoyne mortified and sure that he had lost the Duke's confidence forever; and Wellington beside himself that his private opinions and efforts to influence policy should have been ventilated in this manner. In a series of angry rockets he told Lady Shelley:

Notwithstanding the delight with which you, and the ladies and gentlemen, your friends, have annotated and at last published my confidential letter ... the course which you have taken has been most distressing, painful, and grievous to me, on account of the injury which such publication is calculated to do to the country....

It is quite delightful to live in times with your Ladyship, with Sir John, Lady and Miss Burgoyne!...

I do not know who is the legitimate Commander-in-Chief of the Army! I write confidentially to the Chief Engineer comments on a subject on which he has sent me a confidential paper. From him, his family, and your ladyship, this paper reaches the publick newspapers, and I am to be abused, and to bear the blame! Is this just? Ought not those to be censured who were the instrument of circulating, and finally publishing, this paper?[55]

But furious as he was with this publicity, it did at least increase public alarm and in the short run pushed the cabinet in a gratifying direction. In the budget presented in February 1848 expenditures on the army, navy and ordnance were increased and funds were provided for raising the militia which had been abandoned after Waterloo. Debate on the budget that year, however, was unusually protracted and disputatious and by the time of the last adjustment in June most of the increases had been revoked and the item for the militia dropped entirely. The danger of invasion seemed to have vanished in the French revolution of that year and even the danger closer to home had apparently been mastered.

All the Duke's prophecies about the collapse of European civilization seemed about to be fulfilled in the spring of 1848. In February the revolts in Italy spread to Paris, and France once more became the centre of revolution. Writing to the admirably firm King of Hanover – no long sarcastically 'our beloved Ernest' – Wellington recommended that if each ruler would organize his affairs and resources, the monarchs could 'rely upon their success in repelling every attack and finally of getting rid of this Monster in it's new Shape, as they did in it's former one!'[56] In his own country the Duke spared no effort in preparing to meet the challenge.

The most likely place for an outbreak of rebellion was Ireland where the Young Ireland movement, made up of the more romantic and extreme successors to O'Connell, who had died the year before, hoped to take advantage of revolution on the continent and Chartism in England to restore the Irish parliament. But with the French republicans refusing support, the Catholic clergy antagonized by the anti-clericalism of the movement and the population ravaged by continuing famine, disease and emigration, the country was not the most fertile ground for revolt. The Viceroy, however, was convinced that there would be an uprising and persuaded the government to take effective action. 'There can be no doubt now of the object of the disaffected in Ireland.' The Duke told the Earl of Glengall who was considerately providing him with stories of horrors to come: 'To deprive The Queen of Her Crown! and to establish a Republick! To attain this object they are to arm! and to attack the Castle of Dublin! God send us a good deliverance!'[57]

Learning that the Irish repeal leaders had sent people to Paris to learn the construction of street barricades, Wellington drew up a memorandum on the defence of Dublin. The fact that he had not been there for forty years was no hindrance to describing in detail how the castle, the barracks and other important buildings and the lines of communication could be secured. The inhabitants were to be warned to stay in their houses and heavy carriages and omnibuses, which could be overturned and covered with stones to form barricades, were to be kept off the important streets. In case of barricades, three or four heavy cannon were to be kept in readiness to breach them. The barricades and the houses on their flanks should then immediately be stormed, 'and care should be taken to have a body of Troops so placed as to be ready to fall upon those flying from it, in order to make those who engage in such operations feel, that it is [not] safe to carry them on opposed by Her Majesty's Troops.'[58] The Duke's advice turned out to be unneccessary. The vaunted revolution amounted to no more than a pathetic attempt to raise a ragged army in the famine-ravaged South West. This was easily met by the constabulary; those leaders who were caught were transported while others fled to the United States. But the Commander in Chief was at least prepared for insurrection in that familiar quarter.

The revolutions of 1848 did not find much greater echo in England itself. The Chartist leaders, excited by events on the continent and hoping for mass support from the large number of people thrown out of work by the collapse of trade in the previous year, decided to present a third monster petition to Parliament; to overawe the House of Commons it would this time be accompanied by a procession of half a million people.

When the government learned from advertisements just five days before the event that 500,000 people would gather on Kennington Common on 10 April and then march on Westminster, it was galvanized into action. It formally warned that it was illegal to organize an excessive number of people to present a petition to Parliament and two days before the gathering the cabinet discussed plans to meet the demonstration. The Commander in Chief was summoned and entered the room bowing respectfully to the ministers. Looking at the map on the table he gave the imprint of his authority to the proposal for preventing the crowd approaching Westminster. He advised keeping the troops concealed until they were to be used and leaving the Chartists plenty of room to run away. He thought the best place to stop the procession was the bridges over the Thames, though it might as easily be stopped at the end of any street before it reached the river. The great thing was to keep the parks and public buildings clear.[59]

Following his recommendation, troops were brought into the capital to fortify such important buildings as the Bank, the Mint and Somerset House and to restore order if the crowds got out of hand. Guns were placed near Westminster Bridge, but only officers were authorized to fire them. The first line of defence would be the regular police who would prevent the Chartists from crossing the river. To protect property and order in other parts of the metropolis 170,000 special constables, including Sir Robert Peel and Louis Napoleon, soon to be President and then Emperor of France, were sworn in. Practically every gentleman of property heeded the call to defend the constitution and his possessions and to play a part on the great day. Civil servants were also enlisted. Charles Greville at the Privy Council considered the preparations 'either very sublime or very ridiculous ... We are to pass the whole day at the office tomorrow,' – evidently an unusual demand – 'and I am to send down all my guns; in short, we are to take a warlike attitude.'[60]

On the day itself the Duke was at the Horse Guards by ten, receiving the latest intelligences and prepared to issue whatever orders were necessary. He recorded his impressions through the day in a running letter to Lady Wilton. In the course of the morning he reported:

> The Parks and this neighbourhood are as quiet as on any day in the whole year. But the whole town is in commotion and alarm! I will remain here till it will be time to go to the House of Lords in the afternoon ....
>
> The Accounts from the Country are very uncomfortable. In short, if these Mobs are permitted, we cannot go on as we are.

By one o'clock he had heard that Feargus O'Connor, the fiery Chartist leader, had decided to abandon the procession which, if all those assembled on Kennington Common had participated, would have amounted to 150,000 according to the Chartists, 25,000 according to Wellington's information, but certainly no half million and fewer than the number of special constables alone. O'Connor was called from the meeting by the Commissioner of the Metropolitan Police and informed that the procession would not be allowed. He readily acceded and urged the multitude to disperse. He told the Home Secretary that the demonstration was over and thanked him for the government's restraint. The Duke heard that O'Connor had said that the ministry treated him better than his friends on the common, who 'trod on His Toes and Picked His Pocket!'

At 1.45 one of his officers told Wellington that the petition was coming across Vauxhall Bridge in a cab; the crowd on the common was dispersing in all directions; and there was now 'a considerable Body in Palace Yard, and a Mob coming over Westminster Bridge.' But although there might be large numbers of people about for the rest of the day, 'there will be no more than giving the Police a little trouble. I consider the *Affair* broken, and I am already proceeding to have the orders made out to send the Troops to their Barrack.' By half past three he added: 'It has commenced to rain, and the troops are ordered to return to their stations. In short the War is over, and the Rain will probably keep the Town quiet this night.' At half past four, with 'the Monarchy is still safe on this day!'⁶¹ he left for the House of Lords. The following day the Queen wrote in her own hand to thank the old veteran for his services to her and to the country at this critical moment.⁶²

The petition ignominiously conveyed to Parliament in a cab was subjected to close scrutiny. It turned out to have not the boasted six million signatures but only about two million, including evidently those of the Duke, the Queen and various other prominent and fictitious individuals, as well as a variety of unflattering remarks. This provided ample grounds for rejection. But Wellington had particular as well as general reasons for thinking that this was not the end of the matter. On the evening of the demonstration an informer, who had made it his business to mingle with the crowd, began a letter to the Duke, telling him that he had heard many Chartists expressing themselves with violence that they would be revenged on Wellington and his associates and 'despatch them quick the first and the earliest opportunity.' Wilder spirits, apparently army veterans of fevered imagination, talked of securing a large number of cannon 'to be worked upon Swivels and those are to be planted at the various Barracks in the dead of the night to sweep the Army away without any notice.' Vitriol in thin glass bottles was to be thrown from rooftops onto the troops and horses in order to break their ranks and fireballs were to be tossed into the houses of prominent citizens.⁶³ The very absurdity of these proposals, so reminiscent of the Cato Street conspiracy almost thirty years before, must have persuaded even the Duke that they were not to be taken seriously; but this reinforcement of his natural fears served at least to keep him on the *qui vive* for fresh outbursts of violence.

Nothing so dire as his informant predicted occurred, though there were further demonstrations in London and elsewhere two months later on 12 June. These collapsed entirely in a combination of torrential rains, careful preparations of the troops and police and the arrest of a number of Chartists since the earlier attempt. 1848 marked the end of Chartism as a political force, though it lingered on for another decade as a utopian movement endeavouring to settle industrial workers on the land. Most politicians were soon congratulating themselves on their skill in guiding the country through two generations of potential civil war and revolution to an age of relative tranquillity and unprecedented prosperity. But

Wellington was never convinced that the danger had passed. Conscious that he could not expect to be spared much longer, he turned his mind to securing the forces of order on a firm foundation that would serve as adequate defence in the hands of lesser individuals after he had gone.

CHAPTER TEN

APOTHEOSIS

I N THE last six years of his life and for thirty years afterwards, the great symbol of the Duke of Wellington's standing in the hearts and minds of the country was the huge equestrian statue that stood opposite Apsley House. Sixty-two of his friends and former comrades in arms had formed a committee to subscribe and arrange for it at the beginning of 1838 and the Queen had given permission for it to be placed on the triumphal arch by Decimus Burton recently erected opposite the central arch of his screen at the entrance to Hyde Park beside Apsley House. After eight years of acrimony, only to be expected in a group chaired by the Duke of Rutland and including such disputatious worthies as Lord Londonderry, J.W. Croker, the Duke of Richmond and Lord Anglesey, the bronze statue by Mathew Cotes Wyatt was finally ready; not as had been hoped by Waterloo Day, 1846, but at least by September.

At noon on the 28th, a military procession set off from Wyatt's foundry in the Harrow Road to Hyde Park Corner to the strains of 'See the Conquering Hero Comes'. A special carriage pulled by twenty-nine horses wreathed in laurel was constructed to bear the casting, which stood about thirty feet high and weighed forty tons. The journey took an hour and a half and huge crowds were attracted by the memorable spectacle and the lively prospect of disaster. At Apsley House Lord Charles Wellesley and the Rev. Gerald Wellesley acted as hosts for a group of foreign and domestic royalty including that staunch Tory, the dowager Queen Adelaide. As the light was fading by the time preparations for hoisting were complete, the statue was not raised and bolted into place until the next day.[1]

The arguments that had gone on in the organizing committee were a pale shadow of the controversy that erupted once the statue was in place. Even before its completion it was agreed that it would be only on probation for three weeks. The scaffolding was left in place and disapproval of a monument grotesquely large even by Victorian standards was almost universal. But removing a statue from in front of the house of a hero still very much alive was no easy matter. The Duke was much pleased by this massive tribute, but recognizing that not all his friends were of the same mind he maintained an elaborately ostentatious and ominous silence. When Lord Clare told him in May that he and others did not approve of placing the statue on the arch and intended to raise the matter in both Houses of Parliament, Wellington replied that this was a subject on which he was 'and always had been, a *caput mortuum*. That I could say nothing about it.'[2]

He made a point of being at Walmer Castle when it was erected and did not return to London for a month. He then evasively pronounced that the forest of scaffolding preventing him from making a judgment.[3] But the decision of the government and the Queen shortly thereafter to remove it was a great strain on his resolve to remain 'Dead!' on the subject. He told the Chief Commissioner of Woods and Forests that

> the Statues of Many Men had been removed during their Lifetime from the Pedestals on which placed; that I had known of one Instance in Modern Times. But that I should be a singular Instance of a Man whose Statue would have been removed from its Pedestal during His Life Time, before it could well be seen! I added that it must be a matter of Indifference to me what should become of the Statue, excepting that its removal from its pedestal would annoy those who had subscribed to erect it; who had invariably testified their desire to shew that they held me in Honour! because in fact there was the greatest difference between a Statue to commemorate actions, and the actions themselves. These were the facts and must be accepted.[4]

Even the most obtuse minister must now have seen that the course of wisdom lay in removing the scaffolding and leaving the statue of the government's new ally where it was. When this was done Wellington was one of the few to pronounce his delight with the total effect: 'the colossal size of the Statue, so remarkable when near the Ground, has disappeared, and in fact it now appears small for the Height of the Arch on which it is placed.'[5]

The row over the statue continued through the first half of 1847. The government, the Queen and Prince Albert insisted that it should come down while the Conservative protectionists, appointing themselves the misguided Duke's champions, worked him up for their own advantage. In June Wellington gave Croker great pleasure by telling him that the cabinet was quite mistaken in taking his silence for indifference about removal. The ministers must be 'idiots to suppose it possible that a man who is working day and night, without any object in view excepting the public benefit, will not be sensible of a disgrace inflicted upon him by the sovereign and Government whom he is serving. The ridicule will be felt if nothing else is!'[6] Soon afterwards he told the Prime Minister that it might be impossible for him to continue as Commander in Chief if he received such a mark of disapprobation. Seizing delightedly on Russell's embarrassment, Lord George Bentinck was sure that the vote of £5000 for the removal would be defeated in the House of Commons: 'Do what they will, I think we have the Government on the hip now. If our people make anything like a muster, the statue is safe to stand for ever on its present pedestal.'[7] Russell was of the same opinion, telling the Queen that the Protectionists and the Peelites would combine to keep the statue and the ministry would be defeated. He added that he and Peel agreed that the best course was to announce that she had directed it to remain: 'The Duke of Wellington is reported everywhere to feel the strongest repugnance to the removal of the Statue – & this forms the best ground for retaining it as an eye-sore in its present position.'[8]

Russell came to a private agreement with Bentinck that the monument would remain where it was, '"unless the Duke should intimate to Lord John Russell that its removal to some other site would give him more pleasure;" and that "*the Duke's declining to give any opinion is to be construed as dissent.*"'[9] The Queen also reluctantly wrote a letter to soothe Wellington's feelings about the proposed removal:

> Although the Queen had hoped that her esteem & friendship for the Duke was so well known . . . & although she had thought that an other pedestal would have been more suitable for *this* statue & that the Arch might have been more becomingly ornamented in Honour of the Duke than by the Statue *now* upon it, she has given immediate directions that the Statue should remain in its present situation & only regrets that this monument should be so unworthy of the great personage to whose honour it has been erected.

In this moment of triumph Wellington could afford to reply in humble tones, expressing his 'sorrow and shame that your Majesty should be troubled for a moment by anything so insignificant as a statue of himself,' though he did not conceal his satisfaction at the outcome.[10] This happy issue may have provided some consolation for a victory on the other side at the end of 1846 when the ministry had invoked the Queen's assistance in getting his agreement to a general medal for all Peninsula veterans, a proposal he had resisted for thirty years. In answer to the latest rehearsal of objections, the Queen expressed her appreciation of 'the delicacy of the Duke in not wishing to propose himself a step having reference to his achievements,' but she could not 'on that account forgo the satisfaction of granting this medal as an acknowledgment of those brilliant achievements.' The best that Wellington had been able to manage in presenting his humble duty on that occasion was the hope that the medal would not be granted until it was convenient, though 'your Majesty and your Majesty's servants must be the best judges upon this point, as well as whether the medal in question shall be struck and granted at all or not.'[11] Those on whom the responsibility was thus imposed were not deterred by this grumbling and the medal with his name on it was duly struck and distributed.

As for the statue, it remained where it was for the rest of the Duke's lifetime. After his death its removal was once again considered, but this time rejected as an insult to the memory of the late hero. Thirty years later, when Hyde Park Corner was redesigned in 1883, the arch was moved to its present position closer to the wall of Buckingham Palace garden. After much deliberation the statue was dismantled and reassembled at Aldershot, where it still stands. In its place the present small, graceful equestrian statue by Sir Edgar Boehm was erected on a new and modest pedestal directly across from Apsley House.

To most people in these last years, the old hero was as grand as his statue. When he attended the installation of Prince Albert as Chancellor of Cambridge at the height of the political quarrel over the statue, the titular head of the other ancient university was received with even more enthusiasm than the Queen. 'It is incredible what popularity environs him in his latter days,' noted Charles Greville, 'he is followed like a show wherever he goes, and the feeling of the people *for him* seems to be the liveliest of all popular sentiments; yet he does nothing to excite it, and hardly appears to notice it.' But Greville also observed what his friends and the cabinet ministers knew only too well, that despite his physical stamina the Duke's mind was 'in a fitful and uncertain state, and there is no knowing in what mood he may be found; everybody is afraid of him, nobody dares to say anything to him; he is sometimes very amiable and good-humoured, sometimes very irritable and morose.' As a striking illustration of this lamentable decay Greville called in witness Wellington's 'strange intimacy' with Angela Burdett-Coutts.[12]

The daughter of Sir Frances Burdett, the Radical turned Conservative MP, and granddaughter of Thomas Coutts, whose bank she inherited in 1837, Angela Burdett-Coutts was forty-five years younger than the Duke. Plain, pious and devoted to good works, she consulted him on her business affairs and many charities and was obviously infatuated from their first meeting in 1839. At first he returned only polite attention but by the mid-1840s his feelings were growing warmer. Perhaps for this reason his correspondence with Lady Wilton came to an abrupt end in 1848. Fashionable society thought that Wellington would marry Miss Burdett-Coutts; but the intention was the other way round. In February 1847 she proposed to him. But what he wanted was not a wife but a sympathetic friend who would complete but not disturb his settled, familiar and, as he saw it, demanding routine. Miss Burdett-Coutts, however rich, was also not part of the Duke's aristocratic world.

The morning after the proposal he wrote that he had spent 'every Moment of the Evening and Night since I quitted you in reflecting upon our Conversation of yesterday.' He assured her that he would be her 'Friend, Guardian, Protector' but he could not be her husband. She had before her at least twenty years of happy enjoyment and he entreated her not to throw herself away upon 'a Man old enough to be your Grandfather, who, however strong, Hearty and Healthy at present, must and will certainly in time feel the consequences and Infirmities of Age.'[13]

The danger passed and the friendship continued at a less intense but nevertheless close level. Wellington entertained Miss Burdett-Coutts in an avuncular manner by recounting gossip and news of his activities in circles to which she was not bidden. But it was a peculiar relationship compared to similar ones he had enjoyed in the past thirty years. He never talked to Miss Burdett-Coutts about politics or revealed his feelings to anything like the same extent that he had to Mrs Arbuthnot and Lady Salisbury. It was a measure of his isolation in his last years that he was reduced to someone outside his own world as the principal female companion he so desperately needed. His only real confidant now was Charles Arbuthnot, but his true friend was work. As he told Angela Burdett-Coutts, with little apparent regret, on one of the many occasions that he begged off seeing her:

> The truth is that I am superannuated in reference to all that is
> required from me, publick as well as social, civil, military, political
> and Private; everything must come to me: I am always on the Gallop,

my recollection and thoughts constantly on the Screw; and I am obliged to seek Repose.[14]

The Duke also continued to be obsessed by domestic and foreign dangers. The failure of the Chartist demonstrations of 1848 provided a temporary reprieve but he told Lord Anglesey that he had been considering the fundamental issue of protecting the sovereign and monarchical institutions. Matters were well in hand at the moment as the Chartists were not yet armed and plans were ready for the defence of public buildings. But unfortunately the law gave the insurgents, 'even when organized for Military Operations, and with Arms in their hands, the initiative, and the power to carry on his operations, up to the point of a Magistrate reading the Riot Act; and ordering the Assemblage of people to disperse; and waiting the time required by the law.' The fact that mobs were illegal, he lamented, 'will not justify any person firing in upon one of these Bodies, excepting by orders of the Magistrate, given after the performance of the formalities required by the Law!' For those in authority it was always difficult to know exactly when subversive groups could be stopped in their progress towards rebellion. In the face of such limitations, the best that could be done was to reconnoitre and prepare for events. But whatever the difficulties, the formation of a national guard must be resisted as it would itself present the greatest danger of revolution.[15]

It was too much to expect a Whig ministry, or any in the leaden age since 1832, to repair the sad deficiencies in the law, but the present ministers could at least be expected to keep up the strength of the armed forces. Wellington had been much heartened by the increased sum for military expenditures in the budget in February 1848; but when the cabinet, judging that the danger had passed with the revolution in France, gave in to the Radicals by reducing the amount and eliminating the provision for the militia, his fears increased again. Worse was to follow. In December Lord John Russell wrote to inform the Commander in Chief that it would be necessary to make a considerable reduction in the army in the following year. The Duke immediately replied that the military establishments were already at a bare minimum; it was his duty to tell the Prime Minister that 'this country has not in its service a man not necessary for its service in peace.' Russell nevertheless insisted on reductions to ensure a balanced budget, claiming that raising taxes would endanger the country's political institutions. 'A gradual and prudent course of retrenchment,' he told Wellington, 'will satisfy the public mind, and enable us to preserve our present safe and enviable position.' Offering the cold comfort that the Colonial Secretary would endeavour to temper the effects of the reduction by cutting down the imperial garrisons as far as possible, he concluded that 'the system which will enable us to make the greatest and most speedy effort on the breaking out of war, without trenching too deeply on our finances in peace, appears to me the best.'[16] Despite protests from the Horse Guards, expenditures on the army and navy were reduced until new fears brought a reversal in 1852.

After a promising start Russell now seemed as indifferent to the dangers facing the country as Peel. As he brooded over his failure to convince two successive Prime Ministers of the urgent need for increased expenditures, the Duke turned his mind to ensuring that the direction of military affairs would not fall into the hands of such fickle politicians when he was removed from the scene. In the spring of 1850 the danger to order and authority increased when Parliament debated a proposal to save money by abolishing the office of Lord Lieutenant and administering Ireland as an integral part of the United Kingdom. The main argument for what Wellington regarded as a preposterous scheme was ironically a variation on his own fears: improved communications by steamship and railway had so reduced the effective distance between London and Dublin that a separate government was no longer required. The idea was defeated, but the Duke was shaken that it had even seriously been considered. Fortunately the death of the Adjutant General in March provided him with an opportunity to propose new arrangements for the security of the army. On 2 April Wellington took his scheme to Windsor Castle.

When Prince Albert visited him in his rooms shortly after his arrival, Wellington told him that that obsessive economist, Lord John Russell, wanted to combine the offices of Adjutant and Quartermaster General to save a salary. As the new officer would still have to operate two separate departments nothing would be saved and conflict might well arise between this new Chief of Staff and the Commander in Chief. But the Duke urged the Prince to consider the matter in a broader perspective; he himself was now almost eighty-two and although, 'thank God! very well and strong, and ready to do anything, but he could not last for ever, and in the natural course of events we must look to a change ere long.' Wellington then confided that he saw the greatest advantage in having a Chief of Staff to prepare the Prince to take over the army after his death.

Caught off guard by this astonishing suggestion, Albert replied that he would have to consider it carefully, that he lacked military experience and was not sure that he could take the command of the army in addition to his other duties. Not to be discouraged by such quibbles, Wellington insisted that the details could be handled by the Chief of Staff: 'he had thoroughly considered that and would make it work.' When the Prince raised the constitutionality of the matter, the Duke replied that that was exactly why the Prince must be his successor,

> as with the daily growth of the democratic power the executive got weaker and weaker, and ... it was of the utmost importance to the stability of the Throne and the Constitution, that the command of the army should remain in the hands of the Sovereign, and not fall into those of the House of Commons. He knew that as long as he was there the matter was safe enough; he had well calculated the strength of his position, and knew, he said, 'that the democrats would blow me up if they could, but they find me too heavy for them' ... But, were he gone, he saw no security, unless I undertook the command myself, and thus supplied what was deficient in the Constitutional working of the theory, arising from the circumstance of the present Sovereign being a lady.

The discussion continued in the evening with the Queen. By this time the royal couple was well prepared with objections. Albert pointed out that the responsibility for shedding blood in the event of a riot or revolution could not help but make the monarchy unpopular. But this did not have much effect on Wellington, who was concerned with just those situations in which it would be the sovereign's duty to direct the troops, not worry about popularity. The Queen added that the Prince already worked too hard in his anxiety to spare her as much as possible. The Duke could not dispute this and the conversation ended with an agreement that he would draw up a memorandum of the exact duties that the Prince would be expected to perform under Wellington's proposal.

Any calculation that this would keep the Duke occupied for a long time was destroyed when the Prince came to his room the next morning. The memorandum was already complete. After reading it Albert repeated his reservations about devoting himself to one branch of the government at the expense of the rest. His mind was made up and two days later he repeated his objections in a letter declining the proposal while expressing a desire for greater communication with the Commander in Chief and promising to read the papers that were sent to him, 'thus receiving instruction and tuition in military affairs from the greatest master of them.'[17] Both Russell and Peel agreed that he had taken the right course, but it was a heavy blow for Wellington. His great hope of safeguarding the country's institutions and checking the progress to democracy lay in ruins. The disappointment was not much softened by the Queen and the

Prince's flattering invitation to be godfather and naming their latest child, the Duke of Connaught, born on 1 May which he regarded as his birthday, Prince Arthur. If no one else would prepare to take up the burden when he was gone, the Atlas of the world would have to lose himself in work lest too much contemplation of the future drive him to despair.

Even apart from this bitter rejection of his plan to safeguard the army and the country, 1850 was a hard year for the Duke. At the end of June Peel was thrown from his horse at the top of Constitution Hill, not far from Apsley House, and died three days later. Wellington had never been close to him but they had been political associates for over thirty years and for most of that time the Duke had regarded him as the outstanding Conservative and great hope of the old order in the House of Commons. Peel had not always lived up to Wellington's expectations but his death, at the early age of sixty-two, would not make the Duke's task any easier. When, rather unusually, tributes were paid to him in the House of which he had never been a member as well as in the Commons, Wellington was his only constant ally to speak. Rising with great emotion immediately after Lansdowne, Stanley and Brougham, all past or present opponents, his mind fastened on the charges of deception and inconsistency which these three and many others had at one time or another directed at Peel. Delivering his brief statement through tears, the Duke affirmed: 'In all my acquaintance with Sir Robert Peel, I never knew a man in whose truth and justice I had a more lively confidence, or in whom I saw a more invariable desire to promote the public service.'[18] Even in his present condition he could have managed a more fulsome tribute, but he thought it important above all authoritatively to counter the criticisms which many present knew that he had also had of Peel and to ensure that the stateman went to his grave cleared of a charge about which both of them were so sensitive.

Far harder to bear was the death of Charles Arbuthnot in August. He had been in poor health for some time and his end was no surprise. In the course of a few days he grew rapidly weaker and when Wellington returned from the Sunday morning service at the Chapel Royal he found him very feeble, though still conscious and apparently without pain. The Duke could hardly hear him as he expressed 'his Thankfulness for the kindness with which he had been treated! and that his last moments were approaching. He expired without convulsions or pain! quite tranquil! as a flame extinguishes when the substance which keeps it alive is consumed!'[19] Charles Greville, who had noticed that Wellington had 'for a long time been growing gradually more solitary and unsocial,' more irritable and unapproachable, realized that without Charles Arbuthnot he would not have anyone to talk over past events and confide present grievances and would feel the passing of this old friend 'as acutely as at his age and with his character he can feel anything.'[20]

The Duke was affected more than Greville realized by the death of the steadfast companion who had shared his houses for sixteen years and so much of his life for over thirty. His thoughts must also have gone to Mrs Arbuthnot, who had bound them so closely together and for whose wonderful friendship he had never found even a remote substitute. A few days afterwards he told the second Lady Salisbury:

> I am grieved for the poor man we have lost! It is true that Life must
> have been a burden to him in these last days! But still we hoped to
> preserve it! and that he might have lived certainly not to be active,
> but to sit up in his chair and enjoy the society of his friends! I believe
> that I kept him alive when his poor wife died sixteen years ago![21]

With so many of his contemporaries gathered in, Wellington must have felt like one who walked alone some banquet hall deserted. He was certainly more hard pressed than ever for friendship. But he had long since got over his differences with Lord Anglesey and in his last years the two old survivors drew closer together, reminiscing, dining together and bringing debate in the House of Lords to a standstill as they staggered in, Anglesey on his artificial leg, Wellington stooped with arthritis, conversing in the loud and abrupt tones of the deaf.[22]

The Duke's brothers and sister were all gone and his vastly extended family seemed more a source of irritation than comfort. When he was invited to the wedding of one of Lord Wellesley's grandsons in London in October 1850, while he was at Walmer, he complained that this was 'one of the circumstances, which shew the exacting position in which I am placed. Everybody requires me to meet because I am an individual in some degree elevated, but they forget that they treat me worse than the Costermonger's donkey.'[23] To the bridegroom's unfortunate mother, mad in his estimation, who had written to tell him the time but omitted the place, he sent a blistering rocket:

> It is usual to indicate the place at which the Ceremony of the
> Wedding is to be performed when the Hour half past ten is named!
>   I conclude that it is not to be in the open space in Piccadilly
> opposite the Gate of my House! and that I must go to and be present
> at the place at *half past ten* on Thursday morning the 17th!

> If a Man eighty-two years of Age is thus to be required to give his Attendance, care ought to be taken to fix a Season for his Attendance which might be convenient to Himself and to avoid to receive at a few Hours notice to travel two hundred Miles at the end of the Autumn. . . .
>
> I cannot go about the streets on Thursday morning seeking for the place at which W. Wellesley is to be married to Miss Drummond.[24]

In addition to Angela Burdett-Coutts and his long, spasmodic and mainly epistolary friendship with Miss Jenkins, the Duke turned increasingly after Arbuthnot's death to the new Lady Salisbury (Lady Mary Sackville-West), fifty-five years his junior, and even to a Mrs Charlotte Jones of Pantglas, a society hostess even younger than Lady Salisbury. From his mother, one of Wellington's loves of thirty years before, Charles Greville also learned of his peculiar involvement with a social figure of the 1820s who had practically disappeared from view twenty-five years before. Perhaps Lady Georgiana Fane's appeal lay in the fact that she was a cousin of Mrs Arbuthnot, but Greville thought the elderly spinster now 'half-cracked.' After a flirtation and compromising correspondence lasting some years, the Duke abruptly decided to end the relationship. He refused to see her; but she persisted. The only place she could be sure of meeting him was at St James's Palace after the early service in the Chapel Royal (which he never failed to attend when in London, while rejecting the new fashion of demonstrating piety by attending twice on Sunday), where she succeeded in making a scene.

Greville summed up the situation: 'She is troublesome and He is brutal.' Hoping that the Duchess of Gloucester would help her cause, Lady Georgiana showed Wellington's letters to her Lady in Waiting, Lady Georgiana Bathurst, the daughter of the Duke's late colleague, who in turn confided in Lady Charlotte Greville. When the Duchess refused to read the letters, Lady Georgiana Fane consulted her solicitors who found in them grounds for breach of promise. Perhaps because Lady Georgiana had turned to friends of Wellington, the whole matter was somehow smothered. As Greville rightly said: 'It would be painful to see him an object of ridicule and contempt in the last years of his illustrious life.'[25] But considering some of those with whom he was and had been involved, the wonder was that he was able to end his life with dignity in this regard.

The approaching Crystal Palace Exhibition, that great celebration of the country's industrial, social and moral progress in the huge building of glass and iron erected in Hyde Park in 1851, did nothing to lift the Duke's spirits. He thought it madness to encourage millions of people from all over the country, to say nothing of foreigners, to flock into London on the pretext of attending the Great Exhibition of Art and Industry. His worst fears were aroused at the end of March by an informer, Thomas Paterson, who told Wellington that

> the disaffected of our own Country are acting in concert with the revolutionary refugees. I am also well informed that at *this* very *time* there is a deep laid plot going on in London to overturn the institutions of this country. Upon this subject I have been in communication with the Home office and the police but neither of the Functionaries at those Establishments seem to me sufficiently alive to the danger of the Times.[26]

Paterson did not need to fear that the Duke would be indifferent. But the government was in fact already preparing for the disturbances expected by many. A few days after Paterson's letter, the Prime Minister told Wellington that the Foreign Secretary had asked the ambassador in Paris to request assistance from the French police in identifying the 'red republicans' who might foment trouble in England during the exhibition. Russell thought there was good reason to think that 'some attempt at a Riot will be made by those ruffians, possibly in connection with the Chartists.' He innocently asked the Duke if the ministry should not also solicit the aid of some of the officers in the garrison in Paris to instruct it

> in what manner these experienced rioters commence their plans of disturbance that when they break out, all measures of precaution civil and military may be at once put in operation?
>
> It must be remember'd that on the continent riots are not of that irregular and ill-combined character they bear in this Country, but are organized with method, and carried into effect with discipline and persevering courage.

Any appreciation of Russell's timely concern for the safety of the country was swept aside by the Commander in Chief's professional and patriotic anger at the suggestion that the native forces of law and order were inadequate and that assistance should be sought from the ancient enemy he still suspected of harbouring military ambitions against Britain. It might be desirable to have assistance from the French police in identifying troublemakers, but:

If the Government does not feel confidence in those who would have to superintend the measures to be adopted for the preservation of the Metropolis at the period at which it may be expected that the Town will be the resort of foreigners of all descriptions during the Exhibition! I cannot but think that they will do well to bring over here French or other Foreign Officers in whom they will feel confidence!

All I can say is that as it appears that the Government begins to be sensible of the dangers during the period of the Exhibition, I feel no want of confidence in my own powers with the assistance of the Police and of the Officers on the Staff of the Army, to preserve the Publick peace and to provide for the general safety without requiring the assistance of the French Officers.

Russell hastened to assure the Duke in soothing phrases that he had made the suggestion only to be helpful, certainly not as an embarrassment, and the proposal of engaging French officers was promptly withdrawn.[27]

The Crystal Palace Exhibition may have prompted the fear that the dangers he had long foretold would finally be realized, but it also gave Wellington the chance to save the country by the practice of his military trade. He had lived with the reality or prospect of such a situation all his life and knew exactly what was required. A week after his sharp riposte to the Prime Minister he reported that preparations were well in hand to meet the challenge from 'mischievous Spirits, and *Hommes d'Action* as they are called, in Europe':

We are collecting here and in the neighbourhood as much of our disposable force as we can cover from the effects of the Weather!

I think that we ought to be prepared for a Campaign commencing on the 1st. of May and enduring 'till the end of August at least, possibly 'till the end of September! and we must provide for safety never losing sight of our Police force; nor of the customary privileges of the People.[28]

A week later the Duke completed a long memorandum on the military support for the police in the event of disorder. Buckingham Palace, the Houses of Parliament and the Crystal Palace were the most likely targets, but the government offices in Whitehall, particularly the Home Office, the Horse Guards and the police headquarters in Scotland Yard must also be secured. This could easily be done by linking the buildings and defending them in the first instance by the police. Plenty of troops would be available if required, but as usual Wellington intended to conceal them until they were needed. When they were brought into action he emphasized that it was 'bad policy to *hem in a Mob*, the force should be applied in *one direction and as many avenues for escape left open as possible.*'

Careful directions were laid down for protecting the buildings, including orders to shoot anyone who tried to climb over the fence of Buckingham Palace and a bayonet charge to clear the palace yard if it was actually invaded. In the case of the Crystal Palace itself, it was

> not at all impossible that from discontent or national Jealousy, riots may arise in the immediate neighbourhood of this fragile building, that is in the Park itself, and there will probably be frequently ten or twenty thousand people assembled between the building and the Serpentine River of all Classes, but including a large proportion of the lowish order, should any plausible cause for discontent take with the mob, and two or three evil disposed persons commence throwing stones at the building, such is the propensity to destructiveness among idle persons that very many would join in a general smash for amusement, if not prevented in time, others might join in the hopes of confusion and plunder.

Even the Duke was constrained to add that such an outburst was unlikely, though he thought it was better to be prepared. If there was a riot at the Crystal Palace it could be dealt with best by the cavalry.[29] But Peterloo was not re-enacted in Hyde Park in 1851. The exhibition went off without incident and became the source of much self-congratulation as orderly groups from all over the country took advantage of cheap railways to visit the capital and marvel at displays from around the globe.

At the opening ceremony on 1 May, the stooped, white-headed figure of the Duke, who was marking the completion of his eighty-second year, was conspicuous among the glittering assembly attending the Queen and Prince Albert under the central dome. The occasion was marked by a fine display of Victorian emotion with the ringing of church bells, prayers, speeches and singing by a 600-voice choir accompanied by a 200-piece orchestra and a gigantic organ. In the midst of all this festivity Wellington was undoubtedly alert to misadventure and danger, not so much from the 30,000 respectable guests within as from the half million variegated people outside.

He continued to be fearful until the exhibition closed in the middle of October as crowds surged past Apsley House and the great statue on the arch on their way to the Crystal Palace. In June he told the King of

Hanover, who had written to express his expectation of calamity during 'this foolish, absurd & unconstitutional Exhibition of Prince Albert's':

> There has been no disturbance of the publick Peace in the buildings, the Parks, or at all in the Town or Country. But there are many Foreigners, Poles Hungarians etc. in the Country who occasion a good deal of anxiety to those whose duty it is to consider of Measures for the preservation of the Publick Peace![30]

The foreigners about whom the Duke was so darkly suspicious were refugees from the defeated revolutions of 1848, particularly Hungarian nationalists who had hoped to achieve their country's independence from Austria. Wellington had been alerted to this danger by the persistent Thomas Paterson, who in May wrote to warn that the Hungarians had 'formed themselves into small detachments, and are dispersed in the provinces, Namely, Bradford, Leeds, Manchester and Liverpool the headquarters being still kept in London.' In the same letter he claimed that Feargus O'Connor, the Chartist leader, and the Irish democrats were also active.[31]

It would have taken a fine eye to discern in any of Paterson's communications of the past three years any information of value or even accuracy. But the Duke had been much pleased by this grass roots evidence for his own suspicions. Later in 1851 he went to the extraordinary length of providing Paterson with a testimonial when he wrote to say that he was going to petition the Queen for an appointment on the grounds that his eyesight was failing. Wellington assured him, and anyone else who read the letter addressed to this fine patriot who had worn out his eyes in the service of his country, that Paterson had 'frequently sent me Information which you had received of circumstances which had come to your knowledge in respect to the proceedings of Persons whose design was supposed to be to commit a breach of the Peace! which I considered useful!'[32]

When the Duke did go as a private visitor to the Glass Palace, as he called it, he was the principal exhibit. His presence ironically almost produced the disturbance he feared. He told his new friend Mrs Jones after one visit that he had never seen such a mob or received such a 'rubbing, scrubbing and mashing':

> There were 100,000 people in the Building. The Police advised me not to enter, and if they had not exerted themselves to take care of me, I should never have got out! They rushed upon me from all directions –

Men, Women and Children, all collecting into a crowd and
endeavouring to touch me!

He had gone in by the eastern entrance and sent his horses to the southern
one, whither they were followed by a multitude ready to greet him when
he emerged: 'I expected at every moment to be crushed, and I was saved
by the Police alive.'[33] His pleasure at this tumultuous reception was
difficult to conceal beneath unconvincing alarm.

The Whig government of which Wellington had been so prominent a
buttress since its formation did not long survive the closing of the Great
Exhibition. It had been in a precarious position for the past two years and
its proposal to meet 'papal aggression' – the restoration of Roman Catholic
dioceses which had disappeared at the time of the Reformation, announced
by the Pope in provocative terms in the autumn of 1850 – united both its
opponents and allies against it. The bill forbidding the assumption of
territorial titles by Catholic clergy on pain of stiff penalties introduced at
the beginning of the 1851 session was opposed by the Irish, the English
Catholics and the Peelites, now led by Gladstone, on the grounds of
religious freedom, and by the Protectionists as inadequate. But the Duke
stood staunchly by the admirable Protestantism of the ministry, even
though it meant taking issue with his old colleague, Lord Aberdeen. He
was willing to concede that the Pope was personally inoffensive but he
considered the language used to announce the restoration of titles
deliberately antagonistic to the Church of England. Permitting this
institutional papal organization would encourage agitation in Ireland as so
many other concessions, even Catholic emancipation he was now
prepared to admit, had done. Wellington solemnly advised the peers to
maintain the power and prerogatives of the crown and protect the
subjects, thereby guaranteeing the support and good wishes of all loyal
people in Ireland as well as England.[34]

Before the final, much altered bill made its acrimonious way through
both Houses of Parliament, only to remain a dead letter finally repealed by
Gladstone twenty years later, those opposed to it had managed to engineer
the ministry's resignation. The Protectionists protested that the 1851
budget did nothing for agriculture and, swallowing their objections to a
private member's bill giving the householders in the counties the franchise
on the same basis as those in the towns, secured the government's defeat by
staying away. When the cabinet promptly resigned, Wellington told
Prince Albert that he could not forgive the Protectionists' unscrupulous

opportunism. He thought that their coming into office and dissolving Parliament would lead to civil uproar: 'he had no feeling for Lord John Russell's Cabinet, measures, or principles, but he felt that the Crown and the country were only safe in these days by having the Liberals in office, else they would be driven to join the Radical agitation against the institutions of the country.'[35] Fortunately, from the Duke's point of view, Lord Stanley hesitated to take office without a majority in either House. The alternative was perfectly obvious, but the Queen and Prince Albert felt obliged to consult the oracle, who asked: '"Is your Majesty dissatisfied with your Ministers?" "No," replied the Queen. Said the Duke: "Then you had better keep them."'[36]

On the unheroic ground that no one else could form a government, Russell and his colleagues were summoned back and managed to last to the end of the Crystal Palace Exhibition. Shortly afterwards they suffered another crisis over the conduct of the Foreign Secretary. Palmerston was dissuaded from receiving the Hungarian nationalist hero Louis Kossuth only by the combined efforts of the Queen, the Prince and the rest of the cabinet, but when he made up for this by accepting addresses from a delegation of working men condemning the emperors of Austria and Russia, his great popularity alone saved him from dismissal. Not long afterwards he delivered himself into the hands of his enemies by expressing his approval of Louis Napoleon's *coup d'état* to the French ambassador in London while at the same time conveying to the British ambassador in Paris the instructions of the Queen and the cabinet to remain strictly neutral. Whatever the loss to his shaky ministry, Russell now felt that he had to remove Palmerston.

The irrepressible political veteran soon revenged himself on his former colleagues. Louis Napoleon's seizure of power raised anew the fear of France. At the beginning of the 1852 session the government revived the 1848 proposal, dropped later in that year, of embodying the militia. But rather than raising the regular militia, which would come directly under the crown, the legislation was restricted to the local militia. Appealing to alarmist sentiment in Parliament and the country, Palmerston argued for the regular militia and carried an amendment to that effect in the Commons by removing the word 'local.' Russell resigned and the Earl of Derby, as Stanley had recently become on the death of his father, put together an administration of inexperienced Protectionists which Palmerston refused to join. When Wellington was told the names of the ministers he is reputed to have said 'Who? Who?' only partly owing to his deafness. By that epithet the brief and unremarkable Derby government is known to history. But whatever his estimation of the abilities of the individuals or the expediency of the enterprise, the aristocratic names at least must have been familiar to the Duke.

Wisely deferring the issue of protection until after the general election, the ministry concentrated on those measures most likely gain it majorities in both Houses and establish its credentials for governing among the voters. The most significant of these, and the most gratifying to Wellington, was the one to revive the regular militia which could be used in any part of the kingdom and even outside if necessary. As the bill made its easy way through Parliament, the final realization of one of his principal objects for over a decade was the occasion of the Duke's last major statement in the House of Lords. Although what he really wanted was an increase in the regular army, he welcomed the militia as the first step in strengthening the country's defences. He told the House that the militiamen would free more of the army for service abroad, and while it would take years to make them efficient troops, he had no doubt that they would become so in time. In the Peninsular War he had found the militia regiments to be as disciplined and effective as any in the army. The new corps in time would become what their predecessors were, 'and if they ever do become what the former militia were, you may rely upon it they will perform all the services they may be required to perform.'[37]

Welcoming a step, however small, in the right direction was an appropriate end and vindication of Wellington's long career of defending and warning the country about domestic and foreign dangers. Two weeks later Parliament was dissolved and Derby appealed in vain to the country on the issue of protection.

There was no reason to suppose that the Duke of Wellington would not be in his place when the new Parliament assembled in November. Certainly he was feeble, but he had come back from the brink of death so often and still displayed such physical and mental vigour that he might have gone on at the same rate for another decade, as his mother had before him. 'Old as he was,' Lord Aberdeen told Princess Lieven later, 'everyone seemed to be as much surprized, as grieved by his death; and it was almost as if people thought that immortality belonged to the man, as well as to his actions.'[38]

When the final summons came, it was in the midst of life. The Duke was busy with his usual activities, his endless correspondence, the familiar complaints about the burdens he was forced to bear and the everlasting fears for his country. At Walmer Castle on 14 September 1852 he was wakened early by his valet but did not get up. An hour later Wellington sent for the apothecary. When he complained, as he already had to his son Charles, of indigestion, the apothecary was not seriously concerned and prescribed ammonia and other stimulants. But shortly afterwards he suffered a series of epileptic seizures from which he never regained consciousness. The apothecary and his son were called back, along with Dr McArthur, the Duke's near contemporary who had attended him on other occasions. Other doctors were summoned from London by telegraph, but did not arrive in time. Dr McArthur informed Queen Victoria's Physician in Ordinary that he had tried all the remedies that had been effective in the past – purgatives of mustard, calomel, extract of colocynth, tickling the throat with a feather and applying mustard poultices to the feet and legs – but this time to no avail. At twenty-five past three the Duke quietly expired.[39]

His favourite niece, Lady Westmorland (as Lady Burghersh had become on her husband's succession in 1841), arrived at Dover that afternoon on her way to Paris. Not seeing him at the railway station as they had arranged, she went to the hotel where she received a message that he was ill. Hurrying to the castle she found that he had died an hour before. 'I am deeply affected,' she wrote to her husband,

> and yet I feel it is not an event which we *ought* to mourn – for it has been a happy death to him without pain or suffering and in the *full* possession of all his faculties up to the last. But what a Loss! to the Country – to the Government – to *us* – and indeed to the world.[40]

As the news spread around the country ships lowered their flags to half-mast, muffled church bells were tolled, businesses half closed their shutters and military music was prohibited in garrisons. In churches and chapels ministers found ready inspiration in the text that a great prince had departed from Israel.[41] But after so long and eventful a life, so enviably full of glory and satisfaction if not conventional happiness, Wellington's swift and easy passing was fitting and enviable. In the words of Milton: 'Nothing is here for tears, nothing to wail/ Or knock the breast . . . nothing but well and fair,/ And what may quiet us in a death so noble.' Once people recovered from the immediate sensation, his death was almost anti-climatic, certainly less astonishing than yet another strong recovery would have been. The many lamentations about the loss of his services were stylized and not very persuasive. Most of those who commemorated him could not remember his achievements in the field while his ceaseless warnings about war and revolution, however admirable and well-intentioned, now seemed archaic and irrelevant in a country that had managed to undergo massive transformation since 1815 without any significant measure of disruption. In the complacent atmosphere that led the country to stumble into the Crimean War a year and a half later, the Duke was an exotic survivor from an heroic but alien age.

In his final pronouncement, Charles Greville declared him, 'In spite of some foibles and faults ... beyond all doubt, a very great man – the only great man of the present time – and comparable, in point of greatness, to the most eminent of those who have lived before him.' Perhaps because he had written so many premature obituaries or perhaps because, despite thirty years' critical observation, even he had at last fallen under the spell of Wellington's public reputation, Greville was unable to go beyond attributing his greatness to 'a perfect simplicity of character without a particle of vanity or conceit, but with a thorough and strenuous self-reliance, a severe truthfulness, never misled by fancy or exaggeration, and an ever-abiding sense of duty and obligation which made him the humblest of citizens and the most obedient of subjects.'[42] The Duke had at the last triumphed over 'the Gruncher'.

It was not to be expected that the national hero would be allowed to sink quietly into an honoured grave. Nor would he have expected it. Lord Derby, still Prime Minister until defeated by the new Parliament, immediately proposed a state funeral. The Queen readily agreed; but the participation of Parliament meant waiting two months until it met in November. In the meantime the embalmed body was kept at Walmer Castle.

During the three weeks preceding the funeral, craftsmen laboured night and day to produce a massive funeral car to a design approved by that arbiter of public taste, Prince Albert. The carriage may still be seen in the crypt of St Paul's Cathedral. In accordance with contemporary fashion, every appropriate surface was covered with symbols of Wellington's military victories. The sides of the car were blazoned with stylized trophies and the front with his arms; at the corners were pieces of artillery and cannon balls. The high bier was covered with a black velvet pall embroidered with the Duke's crest and crossed field marshal's batons. Over the relatively small coffin a canopy of silk and silver was suspended from four halberts. The whole hastily assembled and rickety structure was seventeen feet high, twenty-seven feet long, ten feet wide and weighed ten tons. Twelve dray horses, borrowed from a brewery, were caparisoned and plumed in black to pull it.

9 The funeral procession marshalling to leave the Horse Guards Parade – the military bands are in the foreground, St Paul's Cathedral is in the left background (lithograph by A. Maclure, Wellington Museum; reproduced by kind permission of the Victoria and Albert Museum)

While the car was being constructed, the local garrisons and inhabitants were permitted to view the coffin and the interior of Walmer Castle for two days. On 10 November the coffin was transported to London by hearse and railway. The guns at Walmer, Sandown and Deal saluted its departure and at every station along the line it was greeted by officials holding torches. In London the coffin lay in state for a week in the Chelsea Hospital. The hall was draped in black cloth trimmed with silver, the coffin, the silver trim in the drapes and the gold and silver decorations catching the light from gas jets and fifty-four huge candles in seven-foot holders.

On the first night the royal family and a few other privileged groups attended the lying-in-state. The next day was reserved for the aristocracy and others with tickets from the Lord Chamberlain. On this day 10,800 were admitted and thousands were turned away after waiting for hours in the rain.

No one seems to have anticipated great numbers when the public was allowed to view the spectacle on the following days. But long before the doors opened the first morning a dense and disorderly crowd was already blocking the streets and pushing against the hospital. As the pressure and panic increased the scene resembled Peterloo during the cavalry charge. The crowd steamed like a wet haystack; strong men perspired despite the cold; women fainted or were knocked down; and children were held overhead to save them from being crushed. Three people died, two from suffocation, and countless others were injured. The situation was eventually brought under control by the police and troops directed by the officer who had been in charge of police arrangements for the Crystal Palace Exhibition. Some 50,000 people managed to pass through the hall on the first day. The flow was more orderly on the last three days and only two more people died. By the time the doors finally closed about 235,000 people had paid their respects. The coffin was then moved to the Horse Guards whence the procession would begin the next day.

The funeral was in keeping with the preceding ceremonies. As a kind of lugubrious Roman triumph, it provided every opportunity for grandiose effect and sentimental excess. In paying tribute to the man they thought they knew so well, the Victorians were able to indulge their enjoyment of the celebration of death and mourning and honor themselves in hailing the individual who more than any other had been the very embodiment of work and duty.

Early on the morning of 18 November the coffin was installed on the funeral car inside a pavilion on the parade ground. At six o'clock the

10 The funeral car passing through the great arch bearing Wellington's statue and past the shuttered Apsley House on the left (lithography by T. Picke, from the original painting by Lewis Hague, Wellington Museum; reproduced by kind permission of the Victoria and Albert Museum)

troops began to assemble. At a quarter to eight minute guns were fired, the sides of the pavilion were raised, soldiers presented arms, drums rolled, arms were reversed and the procession started in the bright cold light that followed the heavy rain in the night. The whole assembly numbered about 10,000. As each band stepped into line it began to play the Dead March from Handel's 'Saul,' so that the tune could be heard at different stages from varying distances. The public buildings were draped in black and stands covered in black cloth were erected along the streets and in windows for the well-to-do who dressed in mourning. Others, decked in what bits of mourning they possessed, lined the route to a total of about a million and a half. Considering the numbers there were remarkably few mishaps: one man fell to his death from the roof of Drummond's Bank at Charing Cross; another was run over and killed by a cart as he was crossing the street to his seat; and a woman was badly trampled at the Old Bailey.

As the vast cortège made its way through St James's Park and past Buckingham Palace the Queen and her children watched it from the balcony (Prince Albert was in the procession) and then hurried across to St James's Palace to see it again. The procession went up Constitution Hill, through the great arch bearing the statue of the Duke, past the closed Apsley House and along the undulations of Piccadilly. Charles Greville, watching from Devonshire House, pronounced it, 'Rather a fine sight and all well done, except the Car, which was tawdry, cumbrous and vulgar.'[43] Going down St James's the carriage had to be restrained by men with ropes. Along Pall Mall the road gave way near the statue of the Duke of York, and the car had to be extricated by sixty constables. At Charing Cross eighty-three Chelsea pensioners, one for each year of the Duke's life, fell in behind their former commander. At Temple Bar, the canopy was mechanically lowered for the car to pass through and the procession was met by the Lord Mayor and other officials; taking precedence in the City, they led it along Fleet Street and up Ludgate Hill to the west door of St Paul's. There the troops divided to allow the car and mourners to approach the cathedral.

The cortège arrived just after noon, but there was a delay of an hour as the mechanism to swing the coffin off the car failed to work. The crowd of 20,000 people, who had been in the cathedral for some hours, continued to shiver as the cold winds blew through the door. Some of Wellington's friends must have reflected on how annoyed he would have been at the delay.

At length the coffin was carried in. All natural light had been blocked

11 The funeral procession in the nave of St Paul's Cathedral (from the *Illustrated London News*, 20 November 1982; reproduced by kind permission of the *Illustrated London News* Picture Library)

out and the cathredal was illuminated by 6000 gas jets and great candles around the bier. Two psalms in the service were sung to tunes by the Duke's father. As the coffin of the great army hero was lowered into the crypt to join the great naval hero Nelson, the much favoured Dead March was played for the last time by the organ and wind instruments. Lord Anglesey, who carried Wellington's English field marshal's baton, lurched forward on his wooden leg to touch the descending coffin and burst into tears. The service concluded with 'Sleepers Awake' and the congregation trooped out to trumpets at the west door and the guns of the Tower booming a last salute to its former Constable.[44]

It had been a fine public celebration of a national hero, which those who had witnessed would remember to the end of their days. Some of refined aesthetic sensitivities found the whole performance grotesque, bathetic and unworthy of the austere simplicity of the man whose life and work were being commemorated. There is no reason to think that any of it would have displeased the Duke. But he would not have shared the comforting belief that if the country would never look upon his like again it would not need to, for never again would it face dangers like those which he had helped it to survive. Just a few days before he died he had cheered J. W. Croker, who seemed likely to go before him, with what may stand as his final pronouncement: 'But at least, my dear Croker, it is some consolation to us who are so near the end of our career that we shall be spared seeing the consummation of the ruin that is gathering about us.'[45]

12 'A view in the park' – an engraving published on the day of his death of the Commander in Chief saluting the statue of Achilles erected to commemorate his conquests by the women of Britain in 1822 (coloured engraving by J. Harris from the original painting by Henry Daubrawa, published on 14 September 1852, Wellington Museum; reproduced by kind permission of the Victoria and Albert Museum)

NOTES

CHAPTER 1 CHARACTER AND CIRCUMSTANCE

1 Carola Oman, *The Gascoyne Heiress*, p. 106 (4 January 1834).
2 Mulgrave to Wellington, 19 October 1818; Wellington to Liverpool, 1 November 1818; Liverpool to Wellington, 9 November 1818. 2nd Duke of Wellington (ed.), *Supplementary Despatches, Correspondence, and Memoranda of Field Marshal Arthur, Duke of Wellington, K.G.*, vol. XII, pp. 776–7, 812–13 and 822.
3 'Apsley House,' *Quarterly Review*, March 1853, p. 447.
4 Philip Guedalla, *The Duke*, p. 449.
5 Lytton Strachey and Roger Fulford (eds), *The Greville Memoirs*, vol. IV, p. 10 (5 January 1838).
6 Wellington to Gurwood, 6 November 1838. Add. MSS. 38308 (Liverpool Papers).
7 Gurwood to Liverpool, 26 September 1842, *Ibid*.
8 Wellington to Rev. L. Sullivan, 23 March 1833. John Brooke and Julia Gardy (eds), *Wellington: Political Correspondence*, vol. I, p. 135.
9 Strachey and Fulford, *Greville Memoirs*, vol. I, p. 275 (19 March 1829).
10 Francis Bamford and the Duke of Wellington (eds), *The Journal of Mrs. Arbuthnot, 1820–1832*, vol. I, p. 169 (27 June 1822).
11 *Ibid.*, vol. II, pp. 5–6 (26 January 1826).
12 Richard Edgecumbe (ed.), *The Diary of Frances, Lady Shelley, 1787–1873*, vol. II, pp. 310–11.
13 Bamford and Wellington, *Journal of Mrs. Arbuthnot*, vol. I, pp. 300–1.

CHAPTER 2 THE GOLDEN AGE

1 Wellington to General Mann, Respecting the Inscription on a Brass Plate, 14–21 May 1823. 2nd Duke of Wellington (ed.), *Despatches, Correspondence, and Memoranda of Field Marshal Arthur, Duke of Wellington, K.G.* (hereafter cited as WND), vol. II, pp. 94–6.
2 Richard Edgecumbe (ed.), *The Diary of Frances, Lady Shelley, 1787–1873*, vol. II, p. 68 (10 October 1819).
3 Wellington to Lady Shelley, 14 September 1819. *Ibid.*, pp. 65–6.

4 Wellington to Major-General Sir J. Byng, 21 October 1819. WND, vol. I, pp. 80–2.
5 Philip Ziegler, *Addington*, p. 378.
6 Wellington to Sidmouth, 11 December 1819. WND, vol. I, pp. 89–90; Francis, Earl of Ellesmere, *Personal Reminiscences of the Duke of Wellington*, p. 32.
7 Edgecumbe, *Diary of Lady Shelley*, vol. II, p. 68 (10 October 1819).
8 Wellington to Lady Shelley, 26 February 1820. *Ibid.*, p. 101.
9 Carola Oman, *The Gascoyne Heiress*, p. 177 (6 September 1835).
10 Earl Stanhope, *Notes of Conversations with the Duke of Wellington, 1831–1851*, p. 92 (6 November 1836).
11 Wellington, Memorandum to the Earl of Liverpool Respecting the State of the Guards, June 1820. WND, vol. I, pp. 127–9; Francis Bamford and the Duke of Wellington (eds), *Journal of Mrs. Arbuthnot 1820–1832*, vol. I, p. 24 (17 June 1820).
12 Wellington to Liverpool, 30 July 1820. Add. MSS. 38196 (Liverpool Papers).
13 Parliamentary Debates, Second Series (hereafter cited as PD, 2s.), vol. IV, cols 108–11 (25 January 1821).
14 Countess Lieven to Metternich, 22 December 1820. Peter Quennell (ed.), *The Private Letters of Princess Lieven to Prince Metternich 1820–1826*, p. 98.
15 Stanhope, *Conversations*, pp. 44–5 (24 October 1833).
16 Wellington to Liverpool, 26 October 1821. WND, vol. I, pp. 192–6.
17 Bamford and Wellington, *Journal of Mrs. Arbuthnot*, vol. I, pp. 177 (29 August 1822).
18 Wellington to Mrs Arbuthnot, 10 August 1822. 7th Duke of Wellington (ed.), *Wellington and His Friends: Letters of the first Duke of Wellington*, p. 25.
19 Countess Lieven to Metternich, 21 August 1822. Quennell, *Private Letters of Princess Lieven*, pp. 198–9.
20 Wellington to Mrs Arbuthnot, 6 September 1822. Wellington, *Wellington and His Friends*, p. 29; Earl of Ellesmere, *Personal Reminiscences of the Duke of Wellington*, p. 171 (16 June 1841).
21 Wellington to Lord Wellesley, 21 February 1823. Add. MSS. 37415 (Wellesley Papers).
22 Wellington to Mrs Arbuthnot, 6 September 1822. Wellington, *Wellington and His Friends*, p. 29.
23 Wellington to King, 7 September 1822. WND, vol. I, pp. 274–6.
24 Countess Lieven to Metternich, 6 September 1822. Quennell, *Private Letters of Princess Lieven*, p. 203.
25 Wellington to Mrs Arbuthnot, 18 October 1822. Wellington, *Wellington and His Friends*, p. 34.
26 Liverpool to Arbuthnot, 1 November 1822. A. Aspinall (ed.), *The Correspondence of Charles Arbuthnot*, p. 35.
27 Wellington to Mrs Arbuthnot, 30 March and 6 April, 1823. Wellington, *Wellington and His Friends*, pp. 36–8; Bamford and Wellington, *Journal of Mrs. Arbuthnot*, vol. I, p. 209 (29 January 1823).
28 Rt. Hon. W.H. Fremantle to the Duke of Buckingham, 23 December 1823 and 22 May 1824. The Duke of Buckingham and Chandos, *Memoirs of the Court of George IV, 1820–1830*, vol. II, pp. 21 and 79.
29 Countess Lieven to Metternich, 4 October 1823. Quennel, *Private Letters of*

Princess Lieven, p. 292.

30 Bamford and Wellington, *Journal of Mrs. Arbuthnot*, vol. I, p. 339 (24 September 1824).

31 Countess Lieven to Metternich, 18 July 1823. Quennell, *Private Letters of Princess Lieven*, pp. 274–5.

32 Same to same, 17 June 1824. *Ibid.*, pp. 318–19.

33 Arbuthnot to Bathurst, 11 July 1824. Bathurst Papers, vol. 15.

34 Bamford and Wellington, *Journal of Mrs. Arbuthnot*, vol. I, pp. 258–9 (26 September 1823)

35 Wellington to Canning, 12 June 1824. WND, vol. II, p. 277.

36 Bamford and Wellington, *Journal of Mrs. Arbuthnot*, vol. I, p. 339 (24 September 1824).

37 Wellington to Mrs Arbuthnot, 9 October 1823. Wellington, *Wellington and His Friends*, p. 39.

38 Arbuthnot to Bathurst, 24 March 1824. Bathurst Papers, vol. 15; Bamford and Wellington, *Journal of Mrs. Arbuthnot*, vol. I, p. 300 (11 April 1824).

39 Wellington to Liverpool, 7 December; Liverpool to Wellington, 8 December 1824. WND, vol. II, pp. 364–6.

40 Wellington to Peel, 26 December; Peel to Wellington, 29 December; Wellington to Peel, 30 December 1824. *Ibid.*, pp. 377–8 and 383–6.

41 Bamford and Wellington, *Journal of Mrs. Arbuthnot*, vol. I, p. 134 (5 January 1822).

42 *Ibid.*, p. 318 (31 May 1824).

43 Wellington to Peel, 3 November 1824 and Memorandum. C.S. Parker, *Sir Robert Peel*, vol. I, pp. 348–9.

44 King to Peel, 19 November 1824. *Ibid*, p. 349.

45 Wellington to Peel, 23 November 1824. *Ibid.*, pp. 350–1.

46 Wellington, Memorandum to the Cabinet Recommending the Increase of Force Proposed by the Commander-in-Chief, 1 January 1825. WND, vol. II, pp. 390–4.

47 Bamford and Wellington, *Journal of Mrs. Arbuthnot*, vol. I, pp. 380–1 (5 March 1825).

48 Wellington, Memorandum on the Case of the Roman Catholics in Ireland. WND, vol. II, pp. 592–607.

49 Wellington to Lord Clancarty, 14 November 1825. *Ibid.*, p. 562–5.

50 Bamford and Wellington, *Journal of Mrs. Arbuthnot*, vol. I, p. 421.

51 Wellington to Wellesley, 13 October 1825. Add. MSS. 37415 (Wellesley Papers).

52 Wellington to Peel, 3 November; Peel to Wellington, 4 November 1825. Parker, *Peel*, vol. I, pp. 378–9.

53 Wellington to Wellesley, 6 February 1826. Add. MSS. 37415 (Wellesley Papers).

54 Wendy Hinde, *George Canning*, p. 405.

55 Wellington to Mrs Arbuthnot, 5 March and 4 April 1826. Wellington, *Wellington and His Friends*, pp. 56–8 and 62–3.

56 Same to same, 16 March 1826. *Ibid.*, p. 61.

57 Wellington to Liverpool, 23 June; Liverpool to Wellington, 24 June 1826. WND, vol. III, pp. 342–4.

58   C.D. Yonge, *The Life and Administration of Robert Banks, Second Earl of Liverpool, K.G.,* vol. II, p. 381.
59   Arbuthnot to Bathurst, 1 September 1826. *Report on the Manuscripts of Earl Bathurst,* pp. 584–5.
60   Yonge, *Liverpool,* vol. II, pp. 382–3; Arbuthnot to Bathurst, 1 September 1826. *Report on the Manuscripts of Earl Bathurst,* p. 614; Arbuthnot to Liverpool, 5 September 1826. Yonge, *Liverpool,* vol. II, pp. 393–5.
61   Wellington to Liverpool, 30 August; Liverpool to Wellington, 31 August; Liverpool to Arbuthnot, 8 September 1826. Yonge, *Liverpool,* vol. II, pp. 383–8 and 392–3.
62   Arbuthnot to Bathurst, 1 September 1826. *Report on the Manuscripts of Earl Bathurst,* p. 614.
63   Bamford and Wellington, *Journal of Mrs. Arbuthnot,* vol. II, p. 80–1 (16 February 1827).
64   Arbuthnot to Liverpool, 5 September 1826. Yonge, *Liverpool,* vol. II, pp. 393–5.
65   PD, 2s., vol. XVI, col. 348 (12 December 1826).
66   Wellington to Peel, 7 January 1827. WND, vol. III, p. 532–3.
67   Liverpool to Peel, 6 January 1827. Parker, *Peel,* vol. I, pp. 435–6.

CHAPTER 3 CHAOS AND ORDER

1   W.R. Brock, *Lord Liverpool and Liberal Toryism 1820–1827,* p. 283.
2   Canning to Peel, 23 February 1827. C.S. Parker, *Sir Robert Peel from his Private Papers,* vol. I, p. 450.
3   Louis J. Jennings (ed.), *The Correspondence and Diaries of John Wilson Croker,* vol. I, pp. 363–4 (18 February 1827).
4   Francis Bamford and the Duke of Wellington (eds), *Journal of Mrs. Arbuthnot 1820–1832,* vol. II, p. 89 (12 March 1827).
5   Buckingham to Wellington, 20 March; Wellington to Buckingham, 21 March 1827. 2nd Duke of Wellington, (ed.), *Despatches, Correspondence, and Memoranda of Field Marshal Arthur, Duke of Wellington, K. G.* (hereafter WND), vol. III, pp. 611–12; Bamford and Wellington, *Journal of Mrs. Arbuthnot,* vol. II, p. 95 (25 March 1827).
6   Bamford and Wellington, *Journal of Mrs. Arbuthnot,* vol. II, pp. 89–95 (12–25 March 1827).
7   S.R. Lushington to Sir William Knighton, 26 March 1827. A. Aspinall (ed.), *The Letters of George IV 1812–1830,* vol. III, pp. 207–10.
8   Bamford and Wellington, *Journal of Mrs. Arbuthnot,* vol. II, pp. 97–8 (30 March 1827); Wellington to Mrs Arbuthnot, 28 March 1827. 7th Duke of Wellington (ed.), *Wellington and His Friends: Letters of the first Duke of Wellington,* p. 72.
9   Bamford and Wellington, *Journal of Mrs. Arbuthnot,* vol. II, p. 102 (4 April 1827).
10   Canning to Wellington, 10 April; Wellington to Canning, 10 April; Canning to Wellington, 11 April; Wellington to Canning, 11 April 1827. WND, vol. III, pp. 628–9.
11   Wellington to King, 12 April; King to Wellington, 13 April 1827. *Ibid.,* pp. 630–1.
12   Londonderry to Wellington, 13 April 1827 and enclosure, Minute of Lord

Londonderry's Audience with His Majesty. *Ibid.*, pp. 631–5.

13 Wellington to Mrs Arbuthnot, 20 April 1827. Wellington, *Wellington and His Friends*, p. 74.

14 Lord Ashley to Mrs Arbuthnot, 20 April 1827. A. Aspinall (ed.), *The Formation of Canning's Ministry February to August 1827*, p. 40; *Journal of Mrs. Arbuthnot*, vol. II, pp. 110–11 (1 May 1827).

15 Bamford and Wellington, *Journal of Mrs. Arbuthnot*, vol. II, p. 109 (1 May 1827).

16 *Ibid.*, pp. 109–10 (1 May 1827).

17 Parliamentary Debates, Second Series (hereafter PD, 2s.), vol. XVII, cols 454–67 (2 May 1827); Memorandum on Quitting the Cabinet, 13 April 1827. WND, vol. III, pp. 636–42.

18 Bamford and Wellington, *Journal of Mrs. Arbuthnot*, vol. II, p. 110–13 (2 May 1827).

19 Taylor to Wellington, 20 May; Wellington to Taylor, 21 May 1827. WND, vol. IV, pp. 33–5.

20 King to Wellington, 21 May; Wellington to King, 22 May 1827. *Ibid.*, pp. 35–6.

21 Wellington to Lady Shelley, 25 May 1827. Richard Edgecumbe (ed.), *The Diary of Frances, Lady Shelley, 1787–1873*, vol. II, pp. 156–7.

22 The correspondence between Wellington and Huskisson is included in Wellington's speech in the House of Lords, 25 June 1827. PD, 2s., vol. XVII, cols 1384–90.

23 Arbuthnot to Bathurst, 15 July 1827. *Report on the Manuscripts of Earl Bathurst*, pp. 639–41.

24 Wellington to Lord Maryborough, 14 July 1827. WND, vol. IV, p 63; Bathurst to Countess Bathurst, 22 July 1827. *Report on The Manuscripts of Earl Bathurst*, pp. 641–3; Bamford and Wellington, *Journal of Mrs. Arbuthnot*, vol. II, pp. 131–3 (5 August 1827).

25 Taylor to Wellington, 21 July; Wellington to Maryborough, 26 July 1827. WND, vol. IV, pp. 64–5; Arbuthnot to Peel, 27 July 1827. Aspinall, *Formation of Canning's Ministry*, pp. 272–4.

26 Wellington to Bathurst, 1 August 1827. Wellington, *Wellington and His Friends*, p. 75.

27 Wellington to Mrs Arbuthnot, 9 August 1827. Wellington, *Wellington and His Friends*, p. 75.

28 King to Wellington, 15 August; Goderich to Wellington, 15 August; Wellington to King, 17 August 1827. WND, vol. IV, pp. 95–6; Bathurst to Peel, 19 August 1827. Parker, *Peel*, vol. II, p. 8.

29 Wellington to Westmorland, 17 August 1827. WND, vol. IV, pp. 97–8.

30 Bathurst to Wellington, 22 August; Wellington to Bathurst, 25 August 1827. *Ibid.*, pp. 104–6.

31 Bamford and Wellington, *Journal of Mrs. Arbuthnot*, vol. II, pp. 137–8 (21 August 1827).

32 *Ibid.*, pp. 138–9 (21 August 1827); Wellington to Arbuthnot, 21 August 1827. Wellington, *Wellington and His Friends*, pp. 76–7.

33 Huskisson to Viscount Granville, 31 August 1827. Add. MSS. 38750 (Huskisson Papers).

34 Wellington to Sir George Murray, 4 September 1827. WND, vol. IV, pp.

122–4. See also Wellington, Memorandum – Comparison Between Mr. Canning's Government and that of Lord Goderich, n.d. *Ibid.*, pp. 179–80.

35   Wellington to Eldon, 1 September 1827. *Ibid.*, pp. 121–2.

36   Wellington to Goderich, 1 December 1827. *Ibid.*, pp. 162–4.

37   Same to same, 1 December; Goderich to Wellington, 3 December 1827. *Ibid.*, pp. 162–5.

38   Wellington to Peel, 1 January 1828. Parker, *Peel*, vol. II, p. 26.

39   Wellington to Mrs Arbuthnot, 9 January 1828. Wellington, *Wellington and His Friends*, p. 80.

40   Jennings, *Correspondence and Diaries of Croker*, vol. I, p. 431 (17 September 1828).

41   Wellington to Peel, 9 January 1828. WND, vol. IV, pp. 183–4.

42   Wellington to Mrs Arbuthnot, 13 January 1828. Wellington, *Wellington and His Friends*, pp. 81–2; Bamford and Wellington, *Journal of Mrs. Arbuthnot*, vol, II, p. 158.

43   Wellington to Wellesley, 3 February 1828. Add. MSS. 37415 (Wellesley Papers).

44   Eldon to Lady F.J. Bankes, 30 January 1828. Horace Twiss, *The Public and Private Life of Lord Chancellor Eldon, With Selections from his Correspondence*, vol. III, pp. 29–30.

45   Bamford and Wellington, *Journal of Mrs. Arbuthnot*, vol. II, pp. 159–61 (29 January 1828); Wellington to Mrs Arbuthnot, 23 January; Wellington to Charles Arbuthnot, 26 January 1828; Wellington, *Wellington and His Friends*, pp. 82–3.

46   Wellington to Londonderry, 21 January 1828. Londonderry Papers D/Lo/C113.

47   Minute of the Cabinet, 25 January 1828. Aspinall, *Letters of George IV*, vol. III, p. 337.

48   Wellington to King, 25 January 1828. *Ibid.*, p. 376; Wellington to Hill, 1 February 1828. WND, vol. IV, p. 253.

49   Cumberland to Col. Cooke, 12 February 1828. *Ibid.*, pp. 262–3.

50   Lord Ellenborough, *A Political Diary 1828–1830*, vol. II, p. 3 (22 January 1828).

51   Bamford and Wellington, *Journal of Mrs. Arbuthnot*, vol. II, p. 161 (7 February 1828).

52   Creevey to Miss Ord, 20 March 1828. Sir Herbert Maxwell, *The Creevey Papers*, p. 498.

53   Croker to Lord Hertford, 24 January 1828. Jennings, *Correspondence and Diaries of Croker*, vol. I, p. 404.

54   Wellington to Peel, 27 January 1828. Add. MSS. 40307 (Peel Papers).

55   PD, 2s., vol. XVIII, cols 285–7 (11 February 1828).

56   *Ibid.*, cols 1497–1505 and 1583–4 (17 and 21 April 1828).

57   Wellington to King, 24 April 1828. Aspinall, *Letters of George IV*, vol. III, p. 401; Wellington to Duke of Montrose, 30 April 1828. WND, vol. IV, pp. 411–12.

58   PD, 2s., vol. XVIII, cols 1364–70 (31 March 1828).

59   Bamford and Wellington, *Journal of Mrs. Arbuthnot*, vol. II, p. 173 (21 March 1828).

60   Ellenborough, *Diary*, vol. I, p. 114 (23 May 1828).

61   Lytton Strachey and Roger Fulford (eds), *The Greville Memoirs*, vol. I, p. 209

(12 June 1828)

62 Ellenborough, *Diary*, vol. I, pp. 115–16 (23 May 1828); Huskisson to Wellington, 20 May 1828. WND, vol. IV, p. 449.

63 Ellenborough, *Diary*, vol. I, pp. 114–16 (23 May 1828); Memorandum Upon Lord Palmerston's Retirement, 20 May 1828. WND, vol. IV, pp. 453–5. This memorandum and the one on Huskisson's retirement were obviously completed about a week later as they refer to events up to 25 May.

64 Wellington to Ellenborough, 25 May 1828. WND, vol. IV, pp. 460–2.

65 Memorandum Upon Mr. Huskisson's Retirement from Office, 20 May 1828. *Ibid.*, pp. 451–3.

66 Wellington to Lord Cowley, 25 June 1829. *Ibid.*, p. 449; Strachey and Fulford, *Greville Memoirs*, vol. I, pp. 212–13 (18 June 1828).

67 Ellenborough, *Diary*, vol. I, p. 167 (17 July 1828); Mrs Arbuthnot to Lady Shelley, 21 July; Duke of Rutland to Lady Shelley, 25 September 1828. Edgecumbe, *Diary of Lady Shelley*, vol. II, pp. 176–7 and 183.

CHAPTER 4 A BATTLE LIKE WATERLOO

1 Sir Robert Peel, *Memoirs*, vol. I, pp. 127–8.

2 Parliamentary Debates, Second Series (hereafter PD, 2s.), vol. XIX, cols 1286–92 (10 June 1828).

3 Lytton Strachey and Roger Fulford (eds), *The Greville Memoirs*, vol. I, p. 212 (18 June 1828).

4 Lord Ellenborough, *A Political Diary 1828–1830*, vol. I, p. 143 (11 June 1828).

5 Bamford and Wellington, *Journal of Mrs. Arbuthnot*, vol. II, p. 198 (29 July 1828).

6 Ellenborough, *Diary*, vol. I, pp. 162–3 (15 July 1828).

7 Bamford and Wellington, *Journal of Mrs. Arbuthnot*, vol. II, pp. 198–200 (29 July 1828).

8 Wellington to King and Memorandum, 1 August; King to Wellington, 3 August 1828. 2nd Duke of Wellington (ed.), *Despatches, Correspondence and Memoranda of Field Marshal Arthur, Duke of Wellington, K.G.* (hereafter WND), vol. IV, pp. 564–70 and 573.

9 Wellington to Peel, 16 August 1828. Peel, *Memoirs*, vol. I, pp. 271–2.

10 Strachey and Fulford, *Greville Memoirs*, vol. I, p. 216 (16 August 1828).

11 Peel to Wellington, 24 August; Wellington to Peel, 26 August 1828. WND, vol. IV, pp. 662–3 and 666.

12 Anglesey to Lord Holland, 4 August 1828. The Marquess of Anglesey, *One Leg*, pp. 204–5.

13 Wellington to Bathurst, 24 November 1828. WND, vol. V, p. 280.

14 Wellington to Anglesey, 19 November; Anglesey to Wellington, 23 November 1828. *Ibid.*, pp. 270–4 and 278–80.

15 Wellington to Dr Curtis, 11 December 1828. *Ibid.*, vol. V, p. 326; Anglesey, *One Leg*, pp. 213–17.

16 Peel to Wellington, 12 January; Wellington to Peel, 17 January 1829. WND, vol. V, pp. 435–6 and 452.

17 Peel, Memorandum, 11 August 1828. Peel, *Memoirs*, vol. I, pp. 189–200.

18 Peel, *Memoirs*, vol. I, pp. 297–8.

19   Ellenborough, *Diary*, vol. I, p. 325 (28 January 1829).
20   Memorandum Upon the Roman Catholic Question – Points Intended to be Submitted to the King, 29 January 1829. WND, vol. V, pp. 435–6.
21   Ellenborough, *Diary*, vol. I, p. 336 (4 February 1829).
22   PD, 2s., vol. XX, cols 39–41 (5 February 1829).
23   Wellington to Duke of Rutland, 7 February; Rutland to Wellington, 8 February 1829. WND, vol. V, pp. 489–94.
24   Wellington to Duke of Cumberland, 2 February 1829. *Ibid.*, pp. 482–3.
25   Bamford and Wellington, *Journal of Mrs. Arbuthnot*, vol. II, pp. 244–6 (27 February 1829).
26   Peel, *Memoirs*, vol. I, pp. 343–7; Ellenborough, *Diary*, vol. I, pp. 376–7 (4 March 1829).
27   King to Wellington, 4 March; Wellington to King, 4 March; King to Wellington, 5 March 1829. WND, vol. V, p. 518; Bamford and Wellington, *Journal of Mrs. Arbuthnot*, vol. II, p. 248 (4 [should be 5] March 1829).
28   Bamford and Wellington, *Journal of Mrs. Arbuthnot*, vol. II, pp. 250–1 (8 and 10 March 1829).
29   *Ibid.*
30   *Ibid.*, pp. 254–5 (16 March 1829).
31   Winchelsea to Henry Nelson Coleridge, 16 March 1829, *Standard* newspaper, 16 March 1829. WND, vol. V, pp. 526–7.
32   Wellington to Winchelsea, 19 March; Memorandum, 20 March; Wellington to Winchelsea, 20 March 1829. *Ibid.*, pp. 553–5 and 537–8.
33   Winchelsea to Lord Falmouth, 20 March 1829. *Ibid.*, p. 539.
34   Lord Broughton, *Recollections of a Long Life*, vol. III, p. 313 (diary entry, 19 March 1829; obviously misdated).
35   Richard Edgecumbe (ed.), *The Diary of Frances, Lady Shelley, 1787–1873*, vol. II, pp. 73–4 (10 October 1819).
36   Dr Hume's Report to the Duchess of Wellington on the Duel with the Earl of Winchelsea, 21 March 1829. WND, vol. V, pp. 539–45.
37   Wellington to Duke of Buckingham, 21 April 1829. *Ibid.*, pp. 585–6.
38   Strachey and Fulford, *Greville Memoirs*, vol. I, pp. 275–7 and 279 (21 and 26 March 1829).
39   Bentham to Wellington, 22 and 23 March 1829. WND, vol. V, pp. 546–7 and 554–5.
40   Bamford and Wellington, *Journal of Mrs. Arbuthnot*, vol. II, pp. 261–2 (29 and 31 March 1829).
41   PD, 2s., vol. XXI, cols 41–58 (2 April 1829).
42   *Ibid.*, cols 407–10 (6 April 1829).
43   Bamford and Wellington, *Journal of Mrs. Arbuthnot*, vol. II, pp. 264–6 (7 April 1829).
44   Wellington to King, 9 April 1829. WND, vol. V, pp. 577–8; Ellenborough, *Diary*, vol. II, pp. 9 and 11 (9 and 11 April 1829).
45   Wellington to Lord Clancarty, 16 July 1829. WND, vol. VI, pp. 18–19.
46   Wellington to Duke of Northumberland, 4 August 1829. *Ibid.*, pp. 70–1.
47   Ellenborough, *Diary*, vol. II, pp. 15–21 (15–18 April 1829).
48   Bamford and Wellington, *Journal of Mrs. Arbuthnot*, vol. II, p. 278 (1 June 1829).
49   *Ibid.*, p. 321 (16 December 1829).

50   Wellington to Charles Arbuthnot, 14 October 1829. WND, vol. VI, pp. 222–5.
51   PD, 2s., vol. XXII, cols 34–41 (4 February 1830).
52   *Ibid.*, vol. XXIII, cols 530–3 (18 March 1830).
53   *Ibid.*, vol. XXV, cols 990–2 (6 July 1830).
54   Memorandum Upon the Beer Bill, 18 August 1831. WND, vol. VII, pp. 499–500.
55   PD, 2s., vol. XXV, cols 707–9 (29 June 1830).
56   Strachey and Fulford, *Greville Memoirs*, vol. II, p. 15 (26 July 1830).
57   *Ibid.*, p. 3 (18 July 1830).
58   Memorandum of a Letter from the Duke of Wellington to Sir Robert Peel, n.d. (but obviously written before George IV's death). WND, vol. VII, pp. 106–8.
59   Norman Gash, 'English reform and French revolution in the general election of 1830'.
60   The best account of the election and the events leading to the passage of the 1832 Reform Bill is Michael Brock, *The Great Reform Act*.
61   Strachey and Fulford, *Greville Memoirs*, vol. II, pp. 40–1 and 44 (31 August and 9 September 1830).
62   Philip Ziegler, *Melbourne: A Biography of William Lamb, 2nd Viscount Melbourne*, pp. 115–16.
63   Huskisson to Graham, 26 August 1830. J.T. Ward, *Sir James Graham*, p. 89.
64   Bamford and Wellington, *Journal of Mrs. Arbuthnot*, vol. II, pp. 385–7 (26 September 1830).
65   Ellenborough, *Diary*, vol. II, p. 370 (28 September 1830).
66   Strachey and Fulford, *Greville Memoirs*, vol. II, p. 47 (18 September 1830).
67   Wharncliffe to Wellington, 21 September 1830. Wharncliffe Papers.
68   Wellington to Lord Clive, 30 September 1830. WND, vol. VII, p. 281.
69   PD, 2s., vol. XXV, cols 1290–1 (20 July 1830).
70   Wellington to Duke of Northumberland, 10 October 1830. WND, vol. VII, p. 295.
71   PD, 3s., vol. I, cols 44–53 (2 November 1830).
72   Muriel E. Chamberlain, *Lord Aberdeen: A Political Biography*, p. 252.
73   Strachey and Fulford, *Greville Memoirs*, vol. II, p. 52 (8 November 1830).
74   PD, 3s., vol. I, col. 198 (4 November 1830).
75   *Ibid.*, cols 250–3 (8 November 1830); Ellenborough, *Diary*, vol. II, pp. 418–22 (7 November 1830).
76   Strachey and Fulford, *Greville Memoirs*, vol. II, p. 56 (10 November 1830).
77   Memorandum – Precautions to be Taken to Defend Apsley House in Case of Attack, 9 November 1830. WND, vol. VII, pp. 354–5; Ellenborough, *Diary*, vol. II, p. 427 (9 November 1830).
78   Wellington to Peel, 9 November 1830. Add. MSS. 40309 (Peel Papers).
79   Strachey and Fulford, *Greville Memoirs*, vol. II, p. 55 (10 November 1830); Ellenborough, *Diary*, vol. II, pp. 427–8 (10 November 1830).
80   Bamford and Wellington, *Journal of Mrs. Arbuthnot*, vol. II, p. 401 (15 November 1830).
81   *Ibid.*, pp. 401–2 (20 November 1830); Ellenborough, *Diary*, vol. II, p. 438 (19 November 1830).

82 Bamford and Wellington, *Journal of Mrs. Arbuthnot*, vol. II, p. 402 (20 November 1830); Ellenborough, *Diary*, Vol. II, p. 438 (19 November 1830).
83 Wellington to Mrs Arbuthnot, 26 and 28 December 1830. Wellington, *Wellington and His Friends*, pp. 91–2.
84 Wellington to Sir J. Malcolm, 5 July 1831. WND, vol. VII, p. 460.

CHAPTER 5 MAN'S SECOND FALL

1 Francis Bamford and the Duke of Wellington (eds), *The Journal of Mrs. Arbuthnot, 1820–1832*, vol. II, p. 407 (22 December 1830).
2 Croker to Lord Hertford, 18 November 1830. Louis J. Jennings (ed.), *The Correspondence and Diaries of John Wilson Croker*, vol. II, pp. 77–8.
3 Same to same, 8 December 1830. *Ibid.*, pp. 80–1.
4 Wellington to Duke of Buckingham, 21 November 1830. The Duke of Buckingham and Chandos, *Memoirs of the Courts and Cabinets of William IV and Victoria*, vol. I, p. 144.
5 Wellington to Mrs Arbuthnot, 26 December 1830. 7th Duke of Wellington, *Wellington and His Friends: Letters of the first Duke of Wellington*, pp. 91–2.
6 Wellington to Duke of Buckingham, 4 December 1830. 2nd Duke of Wellington (ed.), *Despatches, Correspondence, and Memoranda of Field Marshal Arthur, Duke of Wellington, K.G.,* (hereafter WND), vol. VII, p. 373.
7 Wellington to Earl of Malmsbury, 6 December 1830. *Ibid.*, pp. 373–4.
8 Jennings, *Correspondence and Diaries of Croker*, vol. II, p. 104 (26 January 1831).
9 Lord Broughton, *Recollections of a Long Life*, vol. IV, pp. 87–8 (1 March 1831).
10 A. Aspinall (ed.), *Three Early Nineteenth Century Diaries*, p. 62 (Ellenborough, 3 March 1831).
11 Wellington to Duke of Buckingham, 14 March 1831. WND, vol. VII, pp. 409–10.
12 Wellington to Rev. G.R. Gleig, 11 April 1831. WND, vol. VIII, pp. 20–2.
13 Wellington to Peel, 4 March 1831. Add. MSS. 40309 (Peel Papers).
14 Wellington to Duke of Buckingham, 14 March 1831. WND, vol. VII, pp. 409–10.
15 T.B. Macauley to Rev. Francis Ellis, 30 March 1831. G.O. Trevelyan, *The Life and Letters of Lord Macauley*, vol. I, pp. 201–3.
16 Wellington to Duke of Buckingham, 24 March 1831. Buckingham, *Memoirs of the Courts and Cabinets of William IV and Victoria*, vol. I, pp. 260–1.
17 Wellington to Falmouth, 3 April 1831. WND, vol. VII, pp. 424–6.
18 Wellington to Earl of Westmorland, 5 April 1831. *Ibid.*, pp. 427–8.
19 Wellington to Duke of Buckingham, 21 May 1831. *Ibid.*, p. 440.
20 Wellington to Lord Wharncliffe, 23 April 1831. *Ibid.*, p. 432.
21 Wellington to Mrs Arbuthnot, 24 April 1831. Wellington, *Wellington and His Friends*, p. 94.
22 Same to same, 5 May 1831. *Ibid.*, p. 96.
23 Same to same, 27 April 1831. *Ibid.*, p. 94.
24 Same to same, 28 and 29 April 1831. *Ibid.*, pp. 94–5.
25 Same to same, 1 May 1831. *Ibid.*, pp. 95–6.
26 Wellington to M. Fitzgerald, 21 May 1831. WND, vol. VII, pp. 439–40.

27 Wellington to Cowley, 15 July 1831. *Ibid.*, pp. 469–70.
28 Aspinall, *Three Diaries*, pp. 131–2 (Ellenborough, 21 September 1831).
29 Parliamentary Debates, Third Series (hereafter PD, 3s.), vol. VII, cols 1186–1205 (4 October 1831).
30 Wellington to William Ballantyne, 6 October 1831. WND, vol. VII, p. 557.
31 Wellington to M. Fitzgerald, 13 October 1831. *Ibid.*, pp. 561–2.
32 Wellington to Mrs Arbuthnot, 12 October 1831 (two letters). Wellington, *Wellington and His Friends*, pp. 98–9.
33 Same to same, 10 November 1831. *Ibid.*, p. 100; Wellington to Mr Jenkinson, 8 November 1831. WND, vol. VIII, p. 42.
34 Wellington to Lord Fitzroy Somerset, November 1831. WND, vol. VIII, pp. 23–6.
35 Wellington to King, 5 November and enclosure, Memorandum on the Constitutional Forces of the Country, and upon the Forming and Arming of Political Unions; King to Wellington, 9 November 1831. *Ibid.*, pp. 30–4.
36 Earl Grey to Wellington, 10 November; Wellington to Grey, 20 November 1831. *Ibid.*, pp. 56–7 and 73.
37 Wellington to Wharncliffe, 19 November 1831. *Ibid.*, pp. 69–71.
38 Wellington to Duke of Rutland, 7 December 1831. *Ibid.*, p. 120.
39 Wellington to Bishop of Exeter, 6 January 1832. *Ibid.*, p. 147.
40 Croker to Lord Hertford, 21 February 1832. Jennings, *Correspondence and Diaries of Croker*, vol. II, pp. 150–1.
41 Buckingham to Wellington, 1 January; Wellington to Buckingham, 2 January 1832. WND, vol. VIII, pp. 142–5.
42 Wellington to Aberdeen, 18 February 1832. *Ibid.*, pp. 226–7.
43 Wellington to Wharncliffe, 3 February 1832. *Ibid.*, pp. 205–9.
44 PD, 3s., vol. XI, cols 869–70 (26 March 1832).
45 *Ibid.*, vol. XII, cols 159–75 (10 April 1832).
46 Wellington to Bathurst, 27 April 1832. WND, vol. VIII, p. 286.
47 Jennings, *Correspondence and Diaries of Croker*, vol. II, pp. 154–6 (10 May 1832).
48 Lyndhurst to Wellington, 10 May; Wellington to Lyndhurst, 10 May 1832. WND, vol. VIII, p. 303; Jennings, *Correspondence and Diaries of Croker*, vol. II, pp. 157–8 (12 May 1832); Aspinall, *Three Diaries*, p. 248 (Ellenborough, 11 May 1832).
49 Arbuthnot to Wellington, 12 May 1832. WND, vol. VIII, p. 308.
50 Jennings, *Correspondence and Diaries of Croker*, vol. II, pp. 161–2 (12 and 13 May 1832); Bathurst to Wellington, 10 May 1832. WND, vol. VIII, pp. 304–5.
51 Aspinall, *Three Diaries*, p. 250 (Ellenborough, 12 May 1832).
52 Speaker to Wellington, 14 May 1832. WND, vol. VIII, p. 315; Lytton Strachey and Roger Fulford (eds), *The Greville Memoirs*, vol. II, p. 298 (17 May 1832).
53 Hardinge to Wellington, 14 May; Wellington to Hardinge, 14 May 1832. WND, vol. VIII, pp. 317–18; Strachey and Fulford, *Greville Memoirs*, vol. II, pp. 298–9 (17 May 1832); Jennings, *Correspondence and Diaries of Croker*, vol. II, pp 166–7 (14 May 1832).
54 Wellington to Sir Herbert Taylor, 17 May 1832. WND, vol. VIII, pp. 332–3.
55 Buckingham to Wellington, 15 May; Wellington to Buckingham, 15 May 1832. *Ibid.*, pp. 322–3.
56 Wellington to Rev. G.R. Gleig, 21 May 1832. *Ibid.*, p. 340.

CHAPTER 6 THE DARK DEFILE

1 Arbuthnot to his son Charles, 15 March 1833; to Mrs Arbuthnot, 9 July 1833; A. Aspinall (ed.), *The Correspondence of Charles Arbuthnot*, pp. 167-8 and 171.
2 Louis J. Jennings (ed.), *Correspondence and Diaries of John Wilson Croker*, vol. II, p. 207 (15 March 1833).
3 Wellington to Mrs Arbuthnot, 14 December 1833. 7th Duke of Wellington (ed.), *Wellington and His Friends: Letters of the first Duke of Wellington*, pp. 109-11.
4 Eldon to Lord Stowell, 19 June 1832. Horace Twiss, *The Public and Private Life of Lord Chancellor Eldon*, vol. III, pp. 180-1; 2nd Duke of Wellington (ed.), *Despatches, Correspondence, and Memoranda of Field Marshal Arthur, Duke of Wellington, K. G.* (hereafter WND), vol. VIII, pp. 359-60.
5 Lytton Strachey and Roger Fulford (eds), *The Greville Memoirs*, vol. II, pp. 372-3 (19 May 1833).
6 Wellington to Mr - - -, 4 December 1832. WND, vol. VIII, pp. 472-3.
7 Wellington to Rev. G.R. Gleig, 6 June 1832. *Ibid.*, p. 357.
8 Wellington to J.W. Croker, 6 March 1833. Jennings, *Correspondence and Diaries of Croker*, vol. II, pp. 205-6.
9 Strachey and Fulford, *Greville Memoirs*, vol. II, pp. 362-3 (27 February 1833).
10 Wellington to Lord Londonderry, 7 March 1833. John Brooke and Julia Gardy (eds), *Wellington: Political Correspondence*, vol. I, pp. 111-12.
11 Wellington to Rev. G.R. Gleig, 26 February 1833. *Ibid.*, p. 93.
12 Londonderry to Buckingham, 25 March 1833. Duke of Buckingham and Chandos, *Memoirs of the Courts and Cabinets of William and Victoria*, vol. II, p. 37.
13 Wellington to Mrs Arbuthnot, 22 July 1833. Wellington, *Wellington and His Friends*, pp. 106-7.
14 Same to same, 26 July 1833. *Ibid.*, p. 107.
15 Rosslyn to Mrs Arbuthnot, 5 August 1833. Aspinall, *Correspondence of Charles Arbuthnot*, pp. 174-5.
16 Carola Oman, *The Gascoyne Heiress*, p. 90 (25 October 1833).
17 Herries to Wellington, 7 January 1833. Brooke and Gandy, *Wellington: Political Correspondence*, vol. I, pp. 16-18.
18 Wellington to Peel, 23 July 1833. *Ibid.*, p. 265.
19 Arbuthnot to his son Charles, 20 August 1833. Aspinall, *Correspondence of Charles Arbuthnot*, pp. 175-6.
20 Parliamentary Debates, Third Series (hereafter PD, 3s.), vol. XVIII, cols 1180-94 (25 June 1833).
21 *Ibid.*, vol. XX, cols 245-7 (1 August 1833).
22 Wellington to Duke of Cumberland, 1 January 1834. Brooke and Gandy, *Wellington: Political Correspondence*, vol. I, p. 407.
23 Wellington to Buckingham, 31 January 1834. *Ibid.*, pp. 442-3.
24 Wellington to Londonderry, 17 June 1834. *Ibid.*, pp. 561-2.
25 Same to same, 19 June 1834. *Ibid.*, p. 569.
26 George Pellew, *The Life and Correspondence of the Rt. Hon. Henry Addington, First Viscount Sidmouth*, vol. III, pp. 436-7.
27 Wellington to Bathurst, 28 November 1833. Brooke and Gandy, *Wellington: Political Correspondence*, vol. I, pp. 361-3.
28 Hayward Cox to Wellington, n.d.; Wellington to Cox (18 January 1834). C.S.

Parker, *Sir Robert Peel from his Private Papers*, vol. II, pp. 229–31.

29 Arbuthnot to Lord Aberdeen, 2 May 1834. *Ibid.*, p. 232.

30 Aberdeen to Peel, 5 May 1834; Note (of a conversation with Lord Aberdeen on 9 May 1834) by Sir Robert Peel, 10 May 1834. *Ibid.*, pp. 233–5 and 236–9.

31 Arbuthnot to Peel, 12 May 1834. *Ibid.*, pp. 240–2.

32 Strachey and Fulford, *Greville Memoirs*, vol. III, pp. 46–7 (15 June 1834).

33 Wellington to Croker, 3 June; Croker to his wife, 9 June 1834. Jennings, *Correspondence and Diaries of Croker*, vol. II, pp. 224–5.

34 Croker to his wife, 9–11 June 1834. *Ibid.*, pp. 225–8; Oman, *Gascoyne Heiress*, pp. 116–23 (10–13 June 1834).

35 Oman, *Gascoyne Heiress*, p. 127 (29 June 1834).

36 PD, 3s., vol. XXIV, cols 1319–23 (9 July 1834); Strachey and Fulford, *Greville Memoirs*, vol. III, p. 53 (10 July 1834).

37 Wellington to King, 12 July 1834. Brooke and Gandy, *Wellington: Political Correspondence*, vol. I, pp. 602–4.

38 PD, 3s., cols 832–40 (1 August 1834).

39 *Ibid.*, cols 40–4 (17 July 1834).

40 *Ibid.*, cols 268–70 (21 July 1834).

41 Oman, *Gascoyne Heiress*, pp. 132–3 (2 August 1834).

42 Strachey and Fulford, *Greville Memoirs*, vol. III, p. 66 (5 August 1834).

43 Christine Terhune Herrick (ed.), *The Letters of the Duke of Wellington to Miss J. 1834–1851*.

44 Wellington to Aberdeen, 23 August 1834. Wellington, *Wellington: Political Correspondence*, vol. I, pp. 639–41.

45 King to Wellington, 14 November; Sir Herbert Taylor to Wellington, 14 November 1834. *Ibid.*, pp. 738–9.

46 Wellington to Peel, 15 November 1834 (two letters). Sir Robert Peel, *Memoirs*, vol. II, pp. 18–23.

47 Strachey and Fulford, *Greville Memoirs*, vol. III, p. 96–102 (17 November 1834).

48 *Ibid.*, p. 103 (19 November 1834).

49 Creevey to Miss Ord, 22 November 1834. Sir Herbert Maxwell, *The Creevey Papers*, pp. 640–1.

50 Wellington to Peel, 22 November 1834. Peel, *Memoirs*, vol. II, p. 28.

51 Same to same, 30 November 1834. *Ibid.*, pp. 28–30.

52 Wellington to Lord Francis Egerton, 29 November 1834. Wellington Papers.

53 Wellington to Lord Melville, 22 November 1834. Wellington Papers.

54 Wellington to Peel, 30 November 1834. Peel, *Memoirs*, vol. II, pp. 28–30.

55 Strachey and Fulford, *Greville Memoirs*, vol. III, pp. 108–12 (27 and 28 November 1834).

56 Wellington to Lord Londonderry, 1 December 1834. Londonderry Papers D/Lo/C113.

57 Strachey and Fulford, *Greville Memoirs*, vol. III, pp. 120–1 (10 December 1834).

58 Wellington to Londonderry, 20 December 1834. Londonderry Papers D/Lo/C113.

59 Wellington to Sir Charles Brook Vere, 5 December 1834. Wellington Papers.

60 Strachey and Fulford, *Greville Memoirs*, vol. III, pp. 160–2 (20 and 21 February 1835).

61 Arbuthnot to his son Charles, 17 March 1835. Aspinall, *Correspondence of Charles*

Arbuthnot, p. 191.
62 PD, 3s., vol. XXVI, cols 82–7 (24 February 1835).
63 Strachey and Fulford, *Greville Memoirs*, vol. III, p. 169 (25 February 1835).
64 *Ibid.*, pp. 171–3 (14 and 15 March 1835).
65 PD, 3s., vol. XXVI, cols 1006–8 (16 March 1835).
66 Oman, *Gascoyne Heiress*, p. 156 (8 March 1835).
67 *Ibid.*, pp. 159–60 (29 March 1835).
68 Paper sent in circulation to the Cabinet, 25 March 1835. Parker, *Peel*, vol. II, p. 293.
69 Wellington to Peel, 25 March 1835. *Ibid.*, pp. 294–5.
70 Oman, *Gascoyne Heiress*, p. 161 (29 March 1835).
71 *Ibid.*, pp. 163–4 (7 April 1835).

CHAPTER 7 HOLDING THE LINE

1 Carola Oman, *The Gascoyne Heiress*, p. 164 (13 May 1835).
2 Memorandum from the Duke of Buckingham to Wellington, 15 May 1835. Wellington Papers.
3 Memorandum from Wellington to Lyndhurst, 8 May 1835. Wellington Papers.
4 Peel to Wellington, 24 April. C.S. Parker, *Sir Robert Peel from his Private Papers*, vol. II, p. 313; Wellington to Peel, 25 April 1835. Add. MSS. 40310 (Peel Papers).
5 Oman, *Gascoyne Heiress*, p. 167 (10 June 1835).
6 Memorandum on Commission appointed to inquire into State of Corporations, 23 May 1835 and Memorandum on the Corporation Bill as published in the *Standard* of 6 June 1835, 8 June 1835. Wellington Papers.
7 See George Kitson Clark, *Peel and the Conservative Party: A Study in Party Politics 1832–1841*, pp. 255–95 for Peel's attitude towards the bill; the conduct of the House of Lords; and the summary of correspondence between him and his informants in the Lords, particularly Lord Fitzgerald.
8 Lytton Strachey and Roger Fulford (eds), *The Greville Memoirs*, vol. III, p. 230 (4 August 1835).
9 Parliamentary Debates, Third Series (hereafter PD, 3s.), vol. XXX, cols 356–62 (12 August 1835).
10 Sir Theodore Martin, *A Life of Lord Lyndhurst*, p. 341.
11 Sir Herbert Taylor to Wellington, 3 September 1835. Wellington Papers.
12 Strachey and Fulford, *Greville Memoirs*, vol. III, p. 251 (6 September 1835).
13 Oman, *Gascoyne Heiress*, p. 177 (8 September 1835).
14 *Ibid.*, p. 175 (6 September 1835).
15 Wellington to Goulburn, 8 December 1835. Goulburn Papers.
16 Wellington to Aberdeen, 19 January 1836. Wellington Papers.
17 Wellington to Peel, 11 February 1836. Parker, *Peel*, vol. II, p. 324.
18 Peel to Wellington, 12 March 1836. Wellington Papers.
19 PD, 3s., vol. XXXIII, cols 727–9 (9 May 1836).
20 *Ibid.*, vol. XXXIV, cols 948–55 (27 June 1836).
21 *Ibid.*, vol. XXXV, cols 441–3 (22 July 1836).

22 Wellington to Roden, 19 February 1837. Wellington Papers.
23 Wellington to Peel, 22 February 1837. Wellington Papers.
24 Wellington to Bishop of Exeter, 28 January 1837. Wellington Papers.
25 PD, 3s., vol. XXXVIII, cols 550–6 and 598–9 (5 May 1837).
26 Philip Ziegler, *King William IV*, p. 289.
27 PD, 3s., vol. XXXVIII, cols 1550–1 (22 June 1837).
28 Wellington to unknown correspondent, 26 July 1837. 7th Duke of Wellington (ed.), *A Selection from the Private Correspondence of the First Duke of Wellington*, p. 204.
29 Arbuthnot to his son Charles, 28 June 1837. A. Aspinall (ed.), *Correspondence of Charles Arbuthnot*, p. 196.
30 Wellington to Lady Burghersh, 23 June 1837. Lady Rose Weigall (ed.), *Correspondence of Lady Burghersh with the Duke of Wellington*, pp. 98–9.
31 Wellington to unknown correspondent, 26 July 1837. Wellington, *Private Correspondence of Wellington*, p. 204.
32 Oman, *Gascoyne Heiress*, pp. 247–8 (9 July 1837).
33 Robert Blake, *The Conservative Party from Peel to Churchill*, pp. 44–9.
34 Oman, *Gascoyne Heiress*, p. 256 (23 August 1837).
35 Wellington to Lady Burghersh, 31 August; Lady Burghersh to Wellington, 9 September 1837. Wellington Papers.
36 Wellington, Memoranda on conversations with King Leopold on 7 and 9 September. Written on 9 and 21 September 1837. Wellington Papers.
37 Wellington to Wilton, 31 October 1837. Wellington Papers.
38 Strachey and Fulford, *Greville Memoirs*, vol. IV, pp. 6–7 (4 January 1838).
39 PD, 3s., vol. XXXIX, cols 1308–12 (21 December 1837).
40 Strachey and Fulford, *Greville Memoirs*, vol. IV, pp. 2, 6 and 10 (2 and 5 January 1838).
41 PD, 3s., vol. XL, cols 3–4 (16 January 1838).
42 Strachey and Fulford, *Greville Memoirs*, vol. IV, p. 16 (28 January 1838).
43 PD, 3s., vol. XXXIX, cols 1380–82 (21 December 1837).
44 Oman, *Gascoyne Heiress*, p. 273 (19 February 1838).
45 Wellington to Peel, 27 February; Peel to Wellington, 28 February 1838. Parker, *Peel*, vol. II, pp. 364–5.
46 PD, 3s., vol. XLIV, cols 710–15 (27 July 1838).
47 Strachey and Fulford, *Greville Memoirs*, vol. IV, p. 52 (7 May 1838).
48 *Ibid.*, pp. 66–72 (16–29 June 1838); Oman, *Gascoyne Heiress*, pp. 285–9 (22 June – 3 July 1838).
49 Wellington to J.W. Croker, 9 May 1838. Add. MSS. 38078 (Croker Papers).
50 Same to same, 2 July 1838. Louis J. Jennings (ed.), *Correspondence and Diaries of John Wilson Croker*, vol. II, p. 330.
51 Strachey and Fulford, *Greville Memoirs*, vol. IV, p. 56 (11 May 1838).
52 *Ibid.*, pp. 75–6 (14 July 1838).
53 PD, 3s., vol. XLIV, cols 1032–4 and 1096–1101 (7 and 9 August 1838).
54 Wellington to Lady Wilton, 8 November 1838. 7th Duke of Wellington (ed.), *Wellington and His Friends: Letters of the First Duke of Wellington*, p. 118.
55 Gurwood to Lord Liverpool, 24 January 1838. Add. MSS. 38303 (Liverpool Papers).
56 Earl Stanhope, *Notes of Conversations with the Duke of Wellington, 1831–1851*, p.

135 (February and 4 March 1839).
57 PD, 3s., vol. XLV, cols 565-71 and 592-7 (18 February 1839); vol. XLVI, cols 604-5 (14 March 1839).
58 *Ibid.*, vol. XLV, cols 1156-8 (4 March 1839).
59 Wellington to Peel, 23 and 28 March; Peel to Wellington, 25 March 1839. Parker, *Peel*, vol. II, pp. 384-6.
60 Strachey and Fulford, *Greville Memoirs*, vol. IV, pp. 200-1 (15 August 1838); Parker, *Peel*, vol. II, pp. 388-98; Elizabeth Longford, *Victoria R.I.*, pp. 108-13; Philip Ziegler, *Melbourne*, pp. 291-6.
61 PD, 3s., vol. XLVII, cols 1186-8 (31 May 1838).
62 Strachey and Fulford, *Greville Memoirs*, vol. IV, p. 175 (1 June 1838).
63 PD, 3s., vol. XLIX, cols 1215-27 (5 August 1838).
64 *Ibid.*, cols. 373-5 (16 July 1839).
65 *Ibid.*, cols. 450-3 (18 July 1839).
66 *Ibid.*, cols. 586-94 (22 July 1838).
67 Wellington to Aberdeen, 20 July; Aberdeen to Wellington, 21 July; Wellington to Aberdeen, 21 July 1839. Wellington Papers.
68 Wellington to Rev. Joshua Wood, 26 July 1839. Wellington Papers.
69 Wellington to Oswald Milne and others, 20 August 1839. Wellington Papers.
70 Wellington to Lord Francis Egerton, 23 August 1839. Wellington Papers.
71 PD, 3s., vol. L, cols 547-55 (23 August 1839).
72 Wellington to Londonderry, 20 August 1839. Wellington Papers.
73 Wellington to Lord Francis Egerton, 26 August 1839. Wellington Papers.
74 Wellington to Mr Monteith, 4 April 1840. Wellington Papers.
75 Stanhope, *Conversations*, p. 195 (13 November 1839).

CHAPTER 8 INTIMATIONS OF MORTALITY

1 Wellington to Lady Wilton, 1 September 1839. 7th Duke of Wellington (ed.), *Wellington and His Friends: Letters of the First Duke of Wellington*, pp. 120-2; Lytton Strachey and Roger Fulford (eds), *The Greville Memoirs*, vol. IV, pp. 207-8 (4 September 1839).
2 Earl Stanhope, *Notes of Conversations with the Duke of Wellington, 1831-1851*, pp. 186-7 and 196-206 (16 October and 23 November 1839).
3 Strachey and Fulford, *Greville Memoirs*, vol. IV, p. 218 (23 November 1838); Lord Broughton, *Recollections of a Long Life*, vol. V, p. 235 (21 November 1839).
4 Wellington to Peel, 6, 18 and 23 December; Peel to Arbuthnot, 20 December 1839. C.S. Parker, *Sir Robert Peel from his Private Papers*, vol. II, pp. 413-27.
5 Strachey and Fulford, *Greville Memoirs*, vol. IV, p. 189 (19 July 1839).
6 Gurwood to Liverpool, 30 January 1840. Add. MSS. 38303 (Liverpool Papers).
7 Wellington to Lady Wilton, 4 February 1840. Wellington, *Wellington and His Friends*, p. 129.
8 Lord Cowley to Charles Arbuthnot, 11 February 1840. A. Aspinall (ed.), *The Correspondence of Charles Arbuthnot*, p. 217.
9 Wellington to Lady Wilton, 18 August 1840. Wellington, *Wellington and His Friends*, pp. 139-40 (24 January 1840).
10 Parliamentary Debates, Third Series (hereafter PD, 3s.), vol. LI, cols 544-6

(24 January 1840).

11 Wellington to Mr Elves and Mr Tomkins, 1 February 1840. Wellington Papers.

12 PD, 3s., vol. LI, cols 1210–14 (4 February 1840).

13 Strachey and Fulford, *Greville Memoirs*, vol. IV, pp. 241–5 (15–19 February 1840); Stanhope, *Conversations*, pp. 214–16 (February 1840).

14 Stanhope, *Conversations*, pp. 236–7 (27 April 1840).

15 PD, 3s., vol. LIII, cols 1164–71 and 1178–9 (27 April 1840).

16 Arbuthnot to Graham, 13 June 1840. Parker, *Peel*, vol. II, p.443.

17 Same to same, 10 June 1840. *Ibid.*, pp. 440–2.

18 PD, 3s., vol. LV, cols 239–45 (30 June 1840).

19 Stanhope, *Conversations*, p. 241 (30 June 1840).

20 Aberdeen to Arbuthnot, 14 July 1840. Aspinall, *Correspondence of Charles Arbuthnot*, pp. 220–1.

21 Stanhope, *Conversations*, pp. 241–2 (15 and 20 July 1840).

22 Peel to Arbuthnot, 9 November; Arbuthnot to Peel, 19 November 1840. Parker, *Peel*, vol. II, pp. 448–51.

23 Louis J. Jennings (ed.), *Correspondence and Diaries of John Wilson Croker*, vol. II, p. 401 (30 January 1841).

24 Stanhope, *Conversations*, pp. 262–3 (5 February 1841); Strachey and Fulford, *Greville Memoirs*, vol. IV, p. 353 (9 February 1841); Lord Melbourne to Queen, 5 February 1841. A.C. Benson and Viscount Esher, *The Letters of Queen Victoria: A Selection from Her Majesty's Correspondence between the Years 1837 and 1861*, vol. I, p. 259.

25 Wellington to Gleig, 28 February 1841. Wellington Papers.

26 Wellington to Mr R. Stephens, n.d., but replying to Stephens's letter of 24 February 1841. Wellington Papers.

27 Strachey and Fulford, *Greville Memoirs*, vol. IV, p. 427 (24 November 1841).

28 *Ibid.*, p. 368 (19 March 1841); Sir James Graham to Charles Arbuthnot, 12 March 1841. Aspinall, *Corrrespondence of Charles Arbuthnot*, pp. 226–7.

29 PD, 3s., vol. LVII, cols 9–11 and 183–4 (7 and 11 May 1841).

30 *Ibid.*, vol. LIX, cols 72–81 (24 August 1841).

31 Arbuthnot to Peel, 12 May 1841. Parker, *Peel*, vol. II, pp. 460–1.

32 Wellington to Peel, 17 May. Parker, *Peel*, vol. II, pp. 461–2; Peel to Wellington, 18 May 1841. Wellington Papers.

33 Wellington to Wellesley, 26 August 1841. Add. MSS. 37415 (Wellesley Papers).

34 Wellington to Lady Wilton, 8 September 1841. Wellington, *Wellington and His Friends*, pp. 170–1.

35 Wellington to Lady Burghersh, 30 November 1841. Wellington Papers.

36 Gurwood to Liverpool, 30 September 1841. Add. MSS. 38303 (Liverpool Papers).

37 Wellington to Lady Wilton, 29 October 1841. Wellington, *Wellington and His Friends*, p. 173; Strachey and Fulford, *Greville Memoirs*, vol. IV, pp. 430–1 (3 December 1841).

38 Wellington to Aberdeen, 9 January 1842. Wellington Papers.

39 Strachey and Fulford, *Greville Memoirs*, vol. V, pp. 157–8 (9 February 1844).

40 Wellington to Lady Wilton, 14 March 1842. Wellington, *Wellington and His*

Friends, pp. 181–2.

41 Memorandum on the Corn Laws, January 1842. Wellington Papers.
42 PD, 3s., vol. LXII, cols 781–9 (19 April 1842).
43 Peel to Arbuthnot, 5 April; Arbuthnot to Peel, 9 and 10 April and 29 July 1842. Parker, *Peel*, vol. II, pp. 535–6.
44 Peel to Wellington, 10 August; Wellington to Peel, 10 August 1842. Wellington Papers. Peel to Wellington, 11 August 1842. Add. MSS. 40459 (Peel Papers).
45 Wellington, Memorandum, 12 August 1842; Wellington to Peel, 17 August 1842. Add. MSS. 40459 (Peel Papers).

CHAPTER 9 THE DEFENCE OF THE REALM

1 Wellington to Mrs Caroline Landall, 17 September 1847. Wellington Papers. The best account of Wellington at the Horse Guards is G.R. Gleig, *The Life of Arthur Duke of Wellington*, pp. 336–9, based on information from General Sir George Brown.
2 Lytton Strachey and Roger Fulford (eds), *The Greville Memoirs*, vol. V, p. 25 (5 June 1842).
3 Earl of Ellesmere, *Personal Reminiscences of the Duke of Wellington*, p. 177 (11 June 1843).
4 Wellington to Lady Wilton, 11 November 1842. 7th Duke of Wellington, *Wellington and His Friends: Letters of the first Duke of Wellington*, p. 184.
5 Same to same, 2 December 1844; 23 and 28 January 1845. *Ibid.*, pp. 196–9.
6 Lord Hatherton, diary entry, 8 October 1843. Iris Butler, *The Eldest Brother: The Marquess Wellesley, The Duke of Wellington's Eldest Brother*, p. 576.
7 Col. John Gurwood to Lord Liverpool, 8 October 1842. Add. MSS. 38308 (Liverpool Papers).
8 Parliamentary Debates, Third Series (hereafter PD, 3s.), vol. LXXIV, cols 340–6 (29 April 1842) and cols 778–80 (7 May 1842).
9 Wellington to Sir James Graham, 12, 19, 21 and 22 August 1842 and Memorandum on Disturbed Districts, 15 August 1842. Wellington Papers.
10 Wellington to Ellenborough, 3 September 1842. Wellington Papers.
11 Strachey and Fulford, *Greville Memoirs*, vol. V, pp. 77 and 83 (7 February and 19 March 1843).
12 Wellington to Graham, 10 June 1843. C.S. Parker, *Life and Letters of Sir James Graham, 1792–1861*, vol. I, p. 361.
13 Wellington to Stanley, 3 June 1843. Wellington Papers.
14 Graham to Peel, 18 June 1843. Parker, *Graham*, vol. I, p. 361.
15 Wellington to Graham, 3 September 1843. *Ibid.*, pp. 367–8.
16 Graham to Peel, 16 September; Peel to Graham, 18 September 1843. C.S. Parker, *Sir Robert Peel from his Private Papers*, vol. III, pp. 63–4.
17 Graham to Wellington, 2 October; Graham to Peel, 3 October; Wellington to Graham, 5 October; Graham to Wellington, 9 October; Wellington to Graham, n.d.; Wellington to Graham, 11 October 1844. Parker, *Graham*, vol. I, pp. 408–16 and 418–20.
18 Strachey and Fulford, *Greville Memoirs*, vol. V, pp. 185 and 190 (5 July and 14

September 1844).

19 Wellington to Henry Goulburn, 12 August 1843. Wellington Papers.
20 Stanley to Peel, 27 July 1844. Parker, *Peel*, vol. III, pp. 154–6.
21 Wellington to Peel, 28 July 1844. Wellington Papers (partly printed in Parker, *Peel*, vol. III, pp. 156–7); Peel to Wellington, 29 July 1844. Parker, *Peel*, vol. III, pp. 156–7.
22 PD, 3s., vol. LXXX, cols 1160–74 (2 June 1845); vol. LXXI, cols 567–75 (16 June 1845).
23 Wellington to Peel, 15 and 17 August 1844. Add. MSS. 40461 (Peel Papers).
24 Same to same, 7 August 1845. Parker, *Peel*, vol. III, pp. 201–6.
25 Peel to Wellington, 8 and 9 August 1845. *Ibid.*, pp. 206–16; Wellington to Peel, 12 August 1845. Wellington Papers.
26 Wellington to Sir George Murray, 13 October 1845. Add. MSS. 40461 (Peel Papers).
27 Peel to Arbuthnot, 14 August 1845. Parker, *Peel*, vol. III, pp. 218–19.
28 Peel to Wellington, 15 October 1845. Wellington Papers; Graham to Peel, 17 October 1845. Parker, *Peel*, vol. III, p. 224.
29 Wellington to Peel, 17 October 1845. Wellington Papers (partly printed in Parker, *Peel*, vol. III, p. 225).
30 Wellington to Lord Alvanley, 28 November 1845. Wellington Papers.
31 The best account of the political events of the repeal of the corn laws is Norman Gash, *Sir Robert Peel: The Life of Sir Robert Peel after 1830*, pp. 526–615.
32 Wellington to Peel and Memorandum, 30 November 1845. Sir Robert Peel, *Memoirs*, vol. II, pp. 198–201.
33 Queen to Wellington, 12 December 1845; Wellington to Queen, 12 December 1845. A.C. Benson and Viscount Esher (eds), *The Letters of Queen Victoria: A selection from Her Majesty's Correspondence between the years 1837 and 1861*, vol. II, pp. 55–6.
34 Peel to Queen, 21 December 1845. *Ibid.*, pp. 62–3; Arbuthnot to Peel, 26 December; Peel to Arbuthnot, 28 December 1845. Parker, *Peel*, vol. III, pp. 290–91.
35 Strachey and Fulford, *Greville Memoirs*, vol. V, pp. 282–3 (13 January 1846); Memorandum by Prince Albert, 25 December 1845. Benson and Esher, *Letters of Queen Victoria*, vol. II, pp. 65–7.
36 Redesdale to Wellington, 14 December; Wellington to Redesdale, 21 and 29 December 1845. Wellington Papers.
37 Wellington to Beaufort, 22 December 1845. Wellington Papers.
38 Rutland to Wellington (copy to Peel), 12 January 1846. Add. MSS. 40461 (Peel Papers).
39 Croker to Wellington, 4 January; Wellington to Croker, 6 January 1846. Louis J. Jennings (ed.), *Correspondence and Diaries of John Wilson Croker*, vol. III, pp. 51–5.
40 Wellington to Ellenborough, 2 January 1846. Wellington Papers.
41 PD, 3s., vol. LXXXIII, cols 166–76 (26 January 1846).
42 Wellington to Lady Wilton, 27 January 1846. Wellington, *Wellington and His Friends*, p. 203.
43 Same to same, 9 February 1846. *Ibid.*, pp. 203–4.
44 Stanley to Wellington, 10 February 1846. Wellington Papers.

45 PD, 3s., vol. LXXXVI, cols 1401–5 (28 May 1846).
46 Strachey and Fulford, *Greville Memoirs*, vol. V, pp. 329–30 (28 May 1846).
47 Lady Westmorland to her husband, 23 July 1846. Lady Rose Weigall (ed.), *Lady Burghersh with the Duke of Wellington*, pp. 177; J.W. Croker to J.G. Lockhart, 19 August 1846. Jennings, *Correspondence and Diaries of Croker*, vol. III, p. 76.
48 Wellington to Stanley, 9 December 1846. Wellington Papers.
49 Same to same, 29 October 1847. Wellington Papers.
50 Russell to Queen, 1 July 1846. Royal Archives RA C25/16.
51 Lord Grey to Lord John Russell, 18 November 1848. Public Record Office (hereafter PRO) 30 22/7D (Russell Papers).
52 Wellington to Lord John Russell, 12 August 1846. PRO 30 22/5A; Wellington memorandum, 8 February 1847. PRO 30 22/6B (Russell Papers).
53 Strachey and Fulford, *Greville Memoirs*, vol. V, pp. 439–40 (10 and 18 April 1847).
54 Wellington to General Burgoyne, 9 January 1847. Richard Edgecumbe (ed.), *The Diary of Frances, Lady Shelley, 1787–1873*, vol. II, pp. 272–8.
55 Wellington to Lady Shelley, 23, 27, 28 and 30 January and 1 February 1848. *Ibid.*, vol. II, pp. 281–9.
56 Wellington to King of Hanover, 16 March 1848. Wellington Papers.
57 Wellington to Earl of Glengall, 27 March 1848. Wellington Papers.
58 Wellington to Lt. General Sir Edward Blakeney and Memorandum on Measures of Precaution in Case of Disturbances in Dublin, 2 March 1848. Wellington Papers.
59 J.C. Hobhouse, diary entry, 8 April 1848. Lord Broughton, *Recollections of a Long Life*, vol. VI, p. 216.
60 Strachey and Fulford, *Greville Memoirs*, vol. VI, p. 51 (9 April 1848).
61 Wellington to Lady Wilton, 10 April 1848. Wellington, *Wellington and His Friends*, pp. 210–11.
62 Queen to Wellington, 11 April 1848. Wellington Papers.
63 David Garraway to Wellington, 10 April 1848 (but completed a few days later). Wellington Papers.

CHAPTER 10 APOTHEOSIS

1 John Physick, *The Wellington Monument*, pp. 1–9.
2 Wellington to Croker, 18 May 1846. Louis J. Jennings (ed.), *Correspondence and Diaries of John Wilson Croker*, vol. III, p. 120.
3 Same to same, 31 October 1846. *Ibid.*, p. 120–1.
4 Wellington to Angela Burdett-Coutts, 26 November 1846. 7th Duke of Wellington (ed.), *Wellington and His Friends: Letters of the First Duke of Wellington*, pp. 236–7.
5 Same to same, 8 December 1846. *Ibid.*, p. 238.
6 Wellington to Croker, 14 June 1847. Jennings, *Correspondence and Diaries of Croker*, vol. III, p. 126.
7 Bentinck to Croker, 30 June 1847. *Ibid.*, p. 127.
8 Russell to Queen, 9 July 1847. Royal Archives RA D16/74.

9   Bentinck to Croker, 10 July 1847. Jennings, *Correspondence and Diaries of Croker*, vol. III, p. 128.

10 Queen to Wellington, 12 July 1847. Royal Archives RA B10/120; Wellington to Queen, 12 July 1847. A.C. Benson and Viscount Esher (eds), *Letters of Queen Victoria: A Selection from Her Majesty's Correspondence between the Years 1837 and 1861*, vol. II, pp. 123-4.

11 Queen to Wellington, 1 December 1846; Wellington to Queen, 2 December 1846. *Ibid.*, pp. 112-13.

12 Lytton Strachey and Roger Fulford (eds), *The Greville Memoirs*, vol. V, pp. 460-1 (13 July 1847).

13 Wellington to Angela Burdett-Coutts, 8 February 1847. Wellington, *Wellington and His Friends*, pp. 242-3.

14 Same to same, 6 August 1848. *Ibid.*, pp. 263-4.

15 Wellington to Anglesey, 17 June 1848. Wellington Papers.

16 Russell to Wellington, 7 December 1848. Sir Spencer Walpole, *The Life of Lord John Russell*, vol. II, p. 30; Wellington to Russell, 8 December 1848. G.P. Gooch (ed.), *The Later Correspondence of Lord John Russell 1840–1878*, vol. I, p. 266; Russell to Wellington, 16 December 1848. Walpole, *Life of Lord John Russell*, vol. II, p. 31.

17 Prince Albert, Memorandum, 3 and 4 April 1850 and letter to Wellington, 6 April 1850. Sir Theodore Martin, *The Life of His Royal Highness the Prince Consort*, vol. II, pp. 210–16.

18 Parliamentary Debates, Third Series (hereafter PD, 3s.), vol. CXII, col. 865 (4 July 1850).

19 Wellington to Lady Salisbury, 19 August 1850. Lady Burgclere (ed.), *A Great Man's Friendship: Letters of the Duke of Wellington to Mary, Marchioness of Salisbury, 1850–1852*, pp. 73–4.

20 Strachey and Fulford, *Greville Memoirs*, vol. VI, p. 254 (25 August 1850).

21 Wellington to Lady Salibsury, 21 August 1850. Burgclere, *A Great Man's Friendship*, pp. 74–5.

22 Marquess of Anglesey, *One Leg: The Life and Letters of Henry William Paget, First Marquess of Anglesey, K.G., 1768–1854*, p. 332.

23 Wellington to Lady Salisbury, 18 October 1850. Burgclere, *A Great Man's Friendship*, pp. 137–8.

24 Wellington to Mrs Richard Wellesley, 15 October 1850. Wellington Papers.

25 Strachey and Fulford, *Greville Memoirs*, vol. VI, pp. 297–8 (25 July 1851).

26 Paterson to Wellington, 28 March 1851. Wellington Papers.

27 Russell to Wellington, 2 April; Wellington to Russell, 2 April; Russell to Wellington, 2 April 1851. Wellington Papers.

28 Wellington to Russell, 9 April 1851. Wellington Papers.

29 Wellington, Memorandum on the local circumstances of Westminster and the Parks, with a view to Military Support to the Civil Power in case of Riot or disturbance of the Peace, 16 April 1851. Wellington Papers.

30 King of Hanover to Wellington, 11 April; Wellington to King of Hanover, 12 June 1851. Wellington Papers.

31 Paterson to Wellington, 15 May 1851. Wellington Papers.

32 Wellington to Paterson, 25 October 1851. Wellington Papers.

33 Wellington to Mrs Jones, 7 October 1851. *My Dear Mrs. Jones: The Letters of the*

Duke of Wellington to Mrs. Jones of Pantglas, pp. 11–12.
34 PD, 3s., vol. CXVII, cols 1113–16 (21 July 1851).
35 Memorandum by Prince Albert, 23 February 1851. Benson and Esher, *Letters of Queen Victoria,* vol. I, pp. 293–6.
36 John Cam Hobhouse, diary entry, 3 March 1851. Lord Broughton, *Recollections of a Long Life,* vol. VI, p. 275.
37 PD, 3s., vol. CXXII, cols 728–31 (15 June 1852).
38 Aberdeen to Princess Lieven, 14 October 1852. E. Jones Parry (ed.), *The Correspondence of Lord Aberdeen and Princess Lieven 1832–1854,* pp. 636–7.
39 Dr McArthur to Sir James Clark, 20 September 1852. Royal Archives RA M53/188.
40 Lady Westmorland to her husband, 14 September 1852. Lady Rose Weigall (ed.), *Correspondence of Lady Burghersh with the Duke of Wellington,* pp. 202–4.
41 *Annual Register,* 1852, Chronicle, p. 144.
42 Strachey and Fulford, *Greville Memoirs,* vol. VI, pp. 360–4 (18 September 1852).
43 *Ibid.,* p. 370 (21 November 1852).
44 A good, illustrated description of the funeral procession and the car is Michael Greehalgh, 'The funeral of the Duke of Wellington,' *Apollo,* September 1973; *Annual Register,* 1852, Chronicle, pp. 188–95 and 482–96.
45 Croker to Lord Palmerston, 25 April 1856. Jennings, *Correspondence and Diaries of Croker,* vol. III, p. 361.

BIBLIOGRAPHY

MANUSCRIPT SOURCES

Wellington Papers (Apsley House Collection, now in the University of
  Southampton Library)
Royal Archives (Windsor Castle)
Goulburn Papers (Surrey Record Office)
Londonderry Papers (Durham Record Office)
Russell Papers (Public Record Office)
Wharncliffe Papers (Sheffield City Library)
British Library:
  Bathurst Papers
  Croker Papers
  Huskisson Papers
  Liverpool Papers
  Peel Papers
  Wellesley Papers

PUBLISHED SOURCES

Anglesey, Marquess of, *One Leg: The Life and Letters of Henry William Paget, First Marquess of Anglesey, K.G. 1768–1854*, London Reprint Society, [1961] 1963.
Annual Register 1818–1852.
Apollo: The Magazine of the Arts, September 1973 (Apsley House); July 1975 (Stratfield Saye).
'Apsley House,' *Quarterly Review*, March 1853.
Aspinall, A., ed., *The Correspondence of Charles Arbuthnot*, London, Royal Historical Society, 1941 (Camden Society, Third Series, vol. LXV).
Aspinall, A., ed., *The Formation of Canning's Ministry February to August 1827*, London, Royal Historical Society, 1937 (Camden Society, Third Series, vol. LIX).
Aspinall, A., ed., *The Letters of George IV 1812–1830*, 3 vols, Cambridge, Cambridge University Press, 1938.
Aspinall, A., ed., *Three Early Nineteenth Century Diaries* [Sir Denis LeMarchant, Edward John Littleton and Lord Ellenborough, November 1830–June 1834],

London, Williams & Norgate, 1952.

Bamford, Francis and the Duke of Wellington, eds., *The Journal of Mrs. Arbuthnot 1820–1832*, 2 vols, London, Macmillan, 1950.

Bell, Herbert C.F., *Lord Palmerston*, 2 vols, London, Hodder & Stoughton, 1922.

Benson, A.C. and Viscount Esher, eds, *The Letters of Queen Victoria: A Selection from Her Majesty's Correspondence between the Years 1837 and 1861*, 3 vols, London, John Murray, 1908.

Blake, Robert, *The Conservative Party from Peel to Churchill*, New York, St Martin's Press, 1970.

Bourne, Kenneth, *The Foreign Policy of Victorian England 1830–1902*, Oxford, Clarendon Press, 1970.

Bourne, Kenneth, *Palmerston: The Early Years 1784–1841*, New York, Macmillan, 1982.

Brock, Michael, *The Great Reform Act*, London, Hutchinson University Library, 1973.

Brock, W.R., *Lord Liverpool and Liberal Toryism 1820–1827*, Cambridge, Cambridge University Press, 1941.

Brooke, John and Julia Gandy, eds, *Wellington: Political Correspondence*, vol. I: 1833–November 1834, London, HMSO, 1975.

Broughton, Lord, *Recollections of A Long Life*, 6 vols, ed. Lady Dorchester, London, John Murray, 1909–11.

Buckingham and Chandos, Duke of, *Memoirs of the Court of George IV 1820–1830*, 2 vols, London, Hurst & Blackett, 1859.

Buckingham and Chandos, Duke of, *Memoirs of the Courts and Cabinets of William IV and Victoria*, 2 vols, London, Hurst & Blackett, 1861.

Burgclere, Lady, ed., *A Great Man's Friendship: Letters of the Duke of Wellington to Mary, Marchioness of Salisbury, 1850–1852*, London, John Murray, 1927.

Butler, Iris, *The Eldest Brother: The Marquess Wellesley, The Duke of Wellington's Eldest Brother*, London, Hodder & Stoughton, 1973.

Butler, J.R.M., *The Passing of the Great Reform Bill*, London, Longmans & Co., 1914.

Butler, Lord, ed., *The Conservatives: A History from their Origins to 1965*, London, Allen & Unwin, 1977.

Chadwick, Owen, *The Victorian Church*, vol. I, London, Adam & Charles Black, 1966.

Chamberlain, Muriel E., *Lord Aberdeen: A Political Biography*, London, Longman, 1983.

Clark, George Kitson, *Peel and the Conservative Party: A Study in Party Politics 1832–1841*, 2nd edn, New York, Archon Books, [1929] 1964.

Cookson, J.E., *Lord Liverpool's Administration: The Critical Years 1815–1822*, Edinburgh, Scottish Academic Press, 1975.

Edgecumbe, Richard, ed., *The Diary of Frances Lady Shelley, 1787–1873*, 2 vols, London, John Murray, 1912–13.

Ellenborough, Lord, *A Political Diary 1828–1830*, ed. Lord Colchester, London, Richard Bentley, 1881.

Ellesmere, Francis, first Earl of, *Personal Reminiscences of the Duke of Wellington*, ed. Countess of Stafford, London, John Murray, 1903.

Feiling, Keith Graham, *The Second Tory Party 1714–1832*, London, Macmillan, [1938] 1951.

Finlayson, Geoffrey B.A.M., *England in the Eighteen Thirties: Decade of Reform*, London, Edward Arnold, 1969.

Flick, Carlos, 'The fall of Wellington's government,' *Journal of Modern History*, vol. 37 (1965), pp. 62–71.

Gash, Norman, *Aristocracy and People: Britain 1815–1865*, London, Edward Arnold, 1979.

Gash, Norman, 'English reform and French revolution in the general election of 1830,' in *Essays Presented to Sir Lewis Namier*, ed. Richard Pares and A.J.P. Taylor, London, Macmillan, 1956.

Gash, Norman, *Mr. Secretary Peel: The Life of Sir Robert Peel to 1830*, London, Longmans, 1961.

Gash, Norman, *Reaction and Reconstruction in English Politics 1832–1852*, Oxford, Clarendon Press, 1965.

Gash, Norman, *Sir Robert Peel: The Life of Sir Robert Peel after 1830*, London, Longmans, 1972.

Gleig, Rev. G.R., *Personal Reminiscences of the First Duke of Wellington*, Edinburgh, William Blackwell & Sons, 1904.

Gleig, Rev. G.R., *The Life of Arthur Duke of Wellington*, London, J.M. Dent, [1864] 1909.

Gooch, G.P., ed., *The Later Correspondence of Lord John Russell 1840–1878*, 2 vols, London, Longmans, Green, 1925.

Guedalla, Philip, *The Duke*, London, Hodder & Stoughton, [1931] 1949.

Halévy, Elie, *A History of the English People in the Nineteenth Century*, 6 vols, trans. E.I. Watkins, New York, Barnes & Noble, [1913–1948] 1961.

Harrison, J.F.C., *The Early Victorians 1832–1851*, London, Weidenfeld & Nicolson, 1971.

Healey, Edna, *Lady Unknown: The Life of Angela Burdett-Coutts*, London, Sidgwick & Jackson, 1978.

Hearnshaw, F.J.C., ed., *The Political Principles of Some Notable Prime Ministers of the Nineteenth Century*, London, Macmillan, 1926.

Henriques, Ursula, *Religious Toleration in England 1787–1833*, London, Routledge & Kegan Paul, 1961.

Herrick, Christine Terhune, ed., *The Letters of the Duke of Wellington to Miss J. 1834–1851*, London, T. Fisher Unwin, [1889] 1924.

Hinde, Wendy, *George Canning*, London, Collins, 1973.

Hyde, H. Montgomery, *The Strange Death of Lord Castlereagh,* London, Heinemann, 1959.

Jennings, Louis J., ed., *The Correspondence and Diaries of John Wilson Croker*, 3 vols, London, John Murray, 1884.

Johnston, H.J.M., *British Emigration Policy 1815–1830: 'Shovelling Out Paupers'*, Oxford, Clarendon Press, 1972.

Jones, W.D., *'Prosperity' Robinson: The Life of Viscount Goderich 1782–1859*, London, Macmillan, 1967.

Knighton, Lady, *Memoirs of Sir William Knighton*, Philadelphia, Carey, Lea & Blanchard, 1838.

LeStrange, Guy, ed. and trans., *Correspondence of Princess Lieven and Earl Grey*, 3 vols, London, Richard Bentley, 1890.

Lever, Sir Tresham, ed., *The Letters of Lady Palmerston*, London, John Murray, 1957.

Longford, Elizabeth, *Victoria R.I.*, London, Weidenfeld & Nicolson, 1964.

Longford, Elizabeth, *Wellington: Pillar of State*, London, Weidenfeld & Nicolson, 1972.

McCord, Norman, *The Anti-Corn Law League 1838–1846*, London, Allen & Unwin, [1958] 1968.

McGee, Michael C., 'The fall of Wellington: a case study of the relationship between theory, practice and rhetoric in history,' *Quarterly Journal of Speech*, vol. 63 (February 1977), pp. 28–42.

Machin, G.I.T., *Politics and the Churches in Great Britain 1832–1868*, Oxford, Clarendon Press, 1977.

Machin, G.I.T., 'The Duke of Wellington and Catholic emancipation,' *Journal of Ecclesiastical History*, vol. 14 (1963), pp. 190–209.

Macintyre, Angus, *The Liberator: Daniel O'Connell and the Irish Party 1830–1847*, London, Hamish Hamilton, 1965.

Martin, Sir Theodore, *A Life of Lord Lyndhurst*, London, John Murray, 1883.

Martin, Sir Theodore, *The Life of His Royal Highness The Prince Consort*, 5 vols, New York, Appleton, 1877–80.

Maxwell, Sir Herbert, *The Creevey Papers*, New York, E.P. Dutton, 1904.

Maxwell, Sir Herbert, *The Life of Wellington: The Restoration of the Martial Power of Great Britain*, 2 vols, London, Sampson Low, Marston & Co., 1899.

Melville, Lewis, ed., *The Huskisson Papers*, London, Constable, 1931.

Melville, Lewis, ed., *The Wellesley Papers: The Life and Correspondence of Richard Colley Wellesley, 1760–1842*, 2 vols, London, Herbert Jenkins, 1914.

Moore, D.C., 'Concession or cure: the sociological premises of the first reform act,' *The Historical Journal*, vol. IX (1966), pp. 39–59.

Moore, D.C., 'The other face of reform,' *Victorian Studies*, September 1961.

My Dear Mrs. Jones: The Letters of the Duke of Wellington to Mrs. Jones of Pantglas, London, Rosdale Press, 1954.

New, Chester, *Lord Durham: A Biography of John George Lambton First Earl of Durham*, Oxford, Oxford University Press, 1929.

Oman, Carola, *The Gascoyne Heiress: The Life and Diaries of Frances Mary Gascoyne-Cecil 1802–39*, London, Hodder & Stoughton, 1968.

Parker, Charles Stuart, *Life and Letters of Sir James Graham, 1792–1861*, 2 vols, London, John Murray, 1907.

Parker, Charles Stuart, *Sir Robert Peel from his Private Papers*, 3 vols, 2nd edn, London, John Murray, 1899.

Parliamentary Debates, Second and Third Series.

Parry, E. Jones, ed., *The Correspondence of Lord Aberdeen and Princess Lieven 1832–1854*, 2 vols, London, Royal Historical Society, 1938–9 (Camden Society, Third Series, vol. LX).

Patterson, Clara Burdette, *Angela Burdett-Coutts and the Victorians*, London, John Murray, 1953.

Peel, Sir Robert, *Memoirs*, 2 vols, New York, Kraus Reprint, [1956] 1969.

Pellew, George, *The Life and Correspondence of the Rt. Hon. Henry Addington, First Viscount Sidmouth*, 3 vols, London, John Murray, 1847.

Physick, John, *The Wellington Monument*, London, HMSO, 1970.

Quennell, Peter, ed., *The Private Letters of Princess Lieven to Prince Metternich 1820–1826*, New York, E.P. Dutton, 1938.

Raikes, Thomas, *A Portion of the Journal Kept by Thomas Raikes, Esq. from 1831 to 1847*, 2 vols, London, Longman, Brown, Longmans and Roberts, 1858.

Raikes, Thomas, *Private Correspondence of Thomas Raikes with the Duke of Wellington and Other Distinguished Contemporaries*, ed. Harriet Raikes, London, Richard Bentley, 1861.

Report on the Manuscripts of Earl Bathurst, Preserved at Cirencester Park, London, Historical Manuscripts Commission, 1923.

Ridley, Jasper, *Lord Palmerston*, London, Constable, 1970.

Russell, Rollo, ed., *Early Correspondence of Lord John Russell, 1805–40*, 2 vols, London, T. Fisher Unwin, 1913.

Silver, Allan, 'Social and ideological bases of British elite reactions to domestic crisis in 1829–1832,' *Politics and Society*, February 1971, pp. 179–201.

Stanhope, Earl, *Notes of Conversations with the Duke of Wellington, 1831–1851*, London, Oxford University Press, [1886] 1947.

Stapleton, A.G., *The Political Life of the Rt. Hon. George Canning*, 3 vols, 2nd edn, London, Longman, Rees, Orme, Brown & Green, 1831.

Stewart, Robert, *The Foundations of the Conservative Party 1830–1867*, London, Longman, 1978.

Strachey, Lytton and Roger Fulford, eds, *The Greville Memoirs 1814–1860*, 8 vols, London, Macmillan, 1938.

Thompson, F.M.L., *English Landed Society in the Nineteenth Century*, London, Routledge & Kegan Paul, 1963.

Timbs, John, *Wellingtoniana: Anecdotes, Maxims, and Characteristics, of the Duke of Wellington*, London, Ingraham, Cooke, 1852.

Trevelyan, G.M., *Lord Grey of the Reform Bill*, London, Longmans, Green, 1920.

Trevelyan, G.O., *The Life and Letters of Lord Macaulay*, 2 vols, London, Longmans, Green, 1876.

Turberville, A.S., 'Aristocracy and revolution: the British peerage, 1789–1832,' *History*, March 1942, pp. 240–63.

Turberville, A.S., *The House of Lords in the Age of Reform 1784–1837*, London, Faber & Faber, 1958.

Twiss, Horace, *The Public and Private Life of Lord Chancellor Eldon, With Selections from his Correspondence*, 3 vols, John Murray, 1844.

Van Thal, Herbert, ed., *The Prime Ministers*, 2 vols, London, Allen & Unwin, 1974.

Walpole, Sir Spencer, *A History of England from the Conclusion of the Great War in 1815*, 6 vols, London, Longmans, Green, 1890.

Walpole, Sir Spencer, *The Life of Lord John Russell*, 2 vols, London, Longmans, Green, 1889.

Ward, J.T., *Chartism*, London, Batsford, 1973.

Ward, J.T., *Popular Movements c. 1830–1850*, London, Macmillan, 1970.

Ward, J.T., *Sir James Graham*, New York, St Martin's Press, 1967.

Weigall, Lady Rose, ed., *Correspondence of Lady Burghersh with the Duke of Wellington*, London, John Murray, 1903.

Wellesley, Muriel, *The Man Wellington Through the Eyes of Those Who Knew Him*, London, Constable, 1937.

Wellesley, Muriel, *Wellington in Civil Life Through the Eyes of Those Who Knew Him*, London, Constable, 1939.

Wellington, 2nd Duke of, ed., *Despatches, Correspondence, and Memoranda of Field*

Marshal Arthur, Duke of Wellington, K.G., 8 vols, London, John Murray, 1867–80.

Wellington, 2nd Duke of, ed., *Supplementary Despatches, Correspondence, and Memoranda of Field Marshal Arthur, Duke of Wellington, K.G.*, 15 vols, London, John Murray, 1858–72.

Wellington, 7th Duke of, ed., *A Selection from the Private Correspondence of the First Duke of Wellington*, London, Roxburghe Club, 1952.

Wellington, 7th Duke of, ed., *The Conversations of the First Duke of Wellington with George William Chad*, Cambridge, The Saint Nicholas Press, 1956.

Wellington, 7th Duke of, ed., *Wellington and His Friends: Letters of the First Duke of Wellington to The Rt. Hon. Charles and Mrs. Arbuthnot, the Earl and Countess of Wilton, Princess Lieven, and Miss Burdett-Coutts*, London, Macmillan, 1965.

Willis, G.M., *Ernest Augustus Duke of Cumberland and King of Hanover*, London, Arthur Barker, 1964.

Woodward, Sir Llewellyn, *The Age of Reform 1815–1870*, 2nd edn, Oxford, Clarendon Press, [1938] 1962.

Yonge, C.D., *The Life and Administration of Robert Banks, Second Earl of Liverpool*, 3 vols, London, Macmillan, 1868.

Ziegler, Philip, *Addington: A Life of Henry Addington, First Viscount Sidmouth*, New York, John Day, 1965.

Ziegler, Philip, *King William IV*, London, Collins, 1971.

Ziegler, Philip, *Melbourne: A Biography of William Lamb, 2nd Viscount Melbourne*, London, Collins, 1976.

INDEX

W = Wellington
E = Earl
M = Marquis
D = Duke

B = Baron
V = Viscount
K = King
Q = Queen